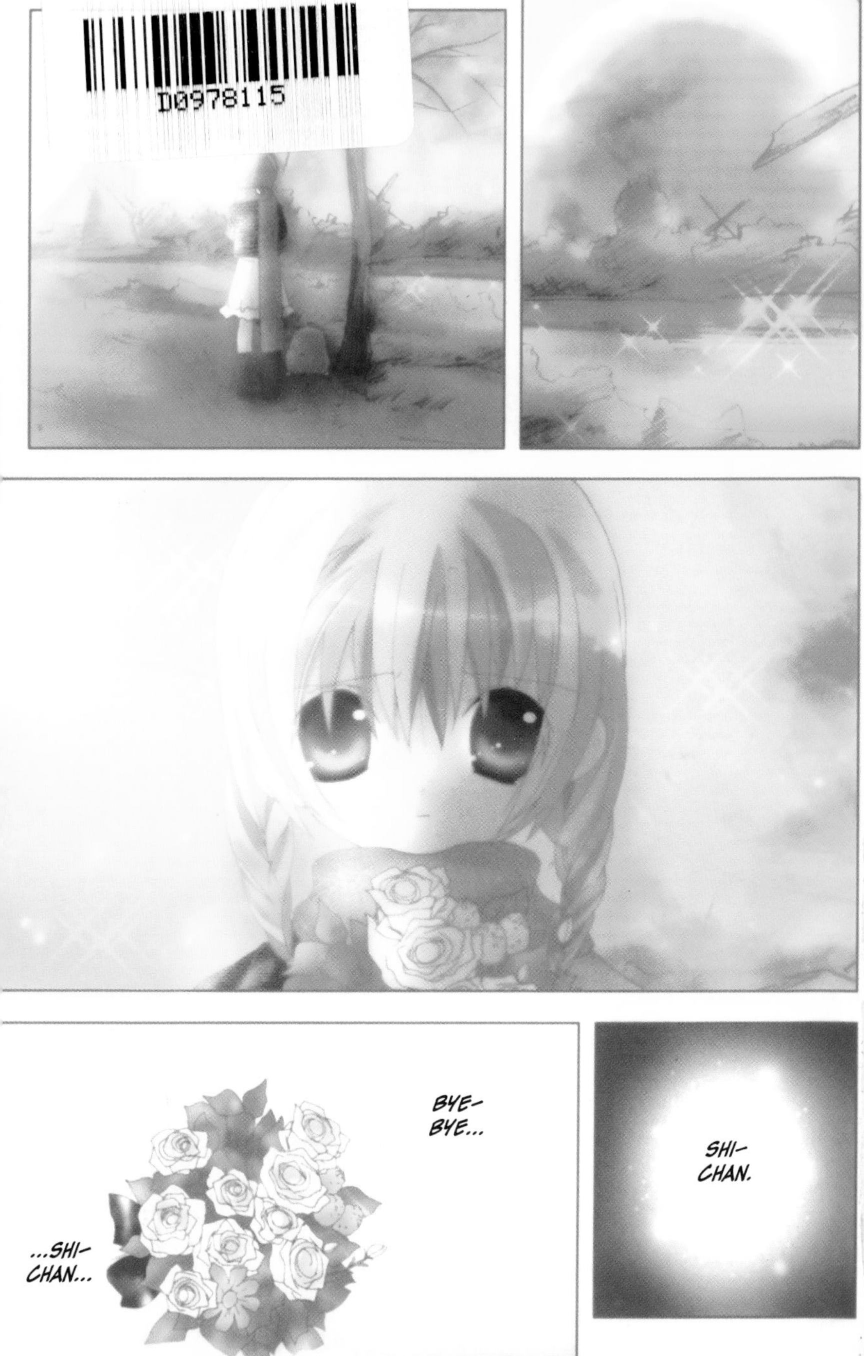
SHI-
CHAN.
BYE-
BYE...
...SHI-
CHAN...

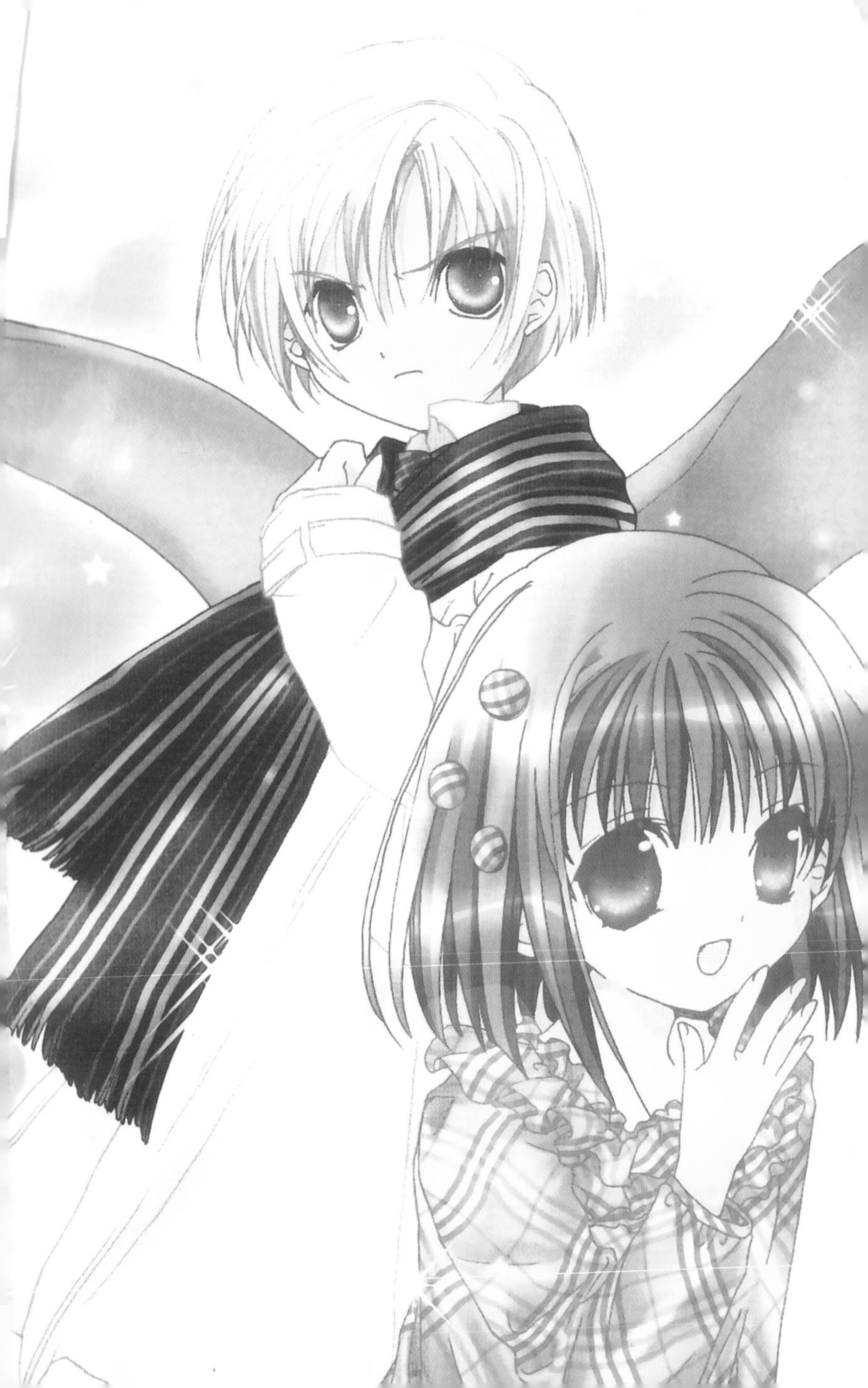

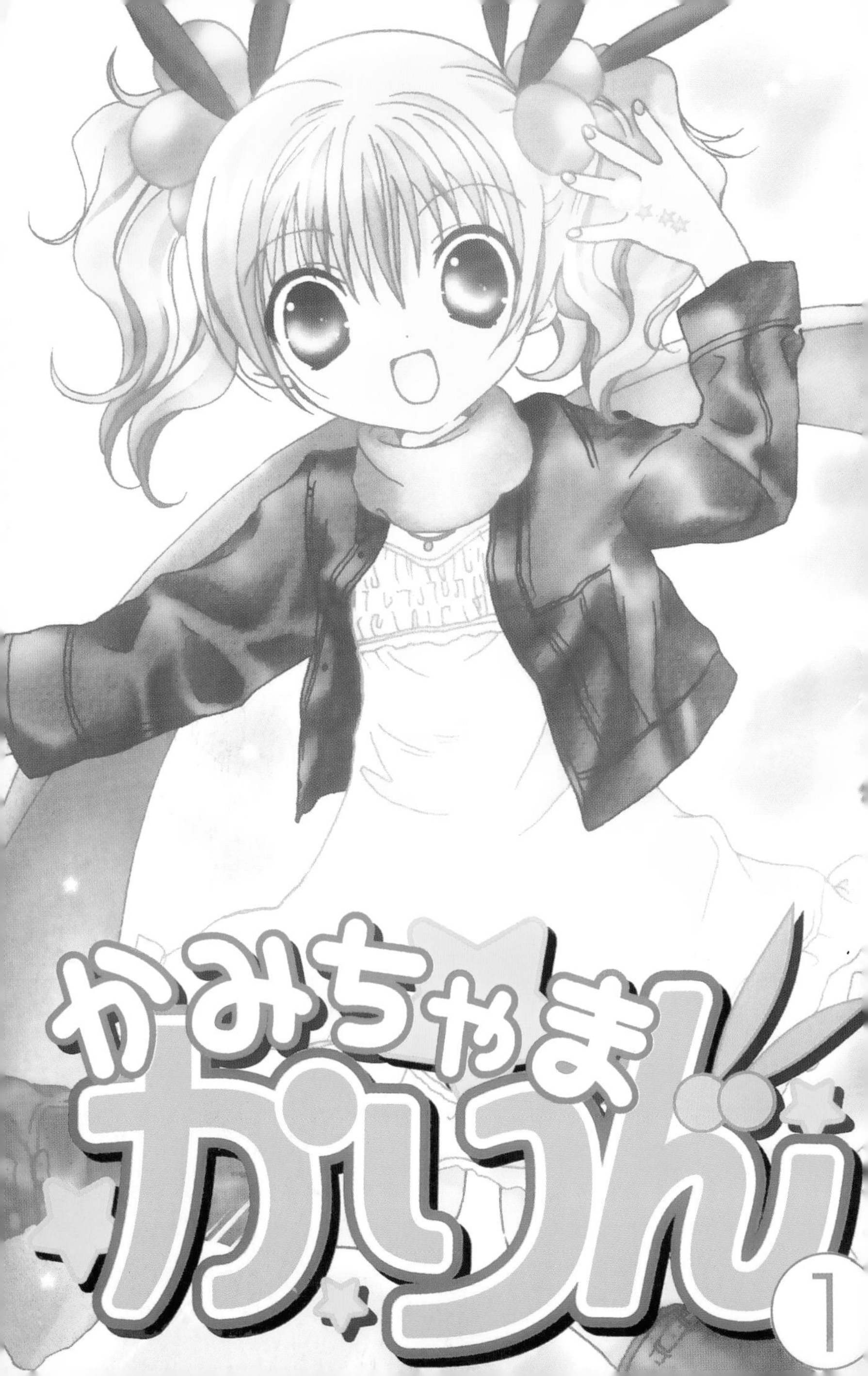
かみちゃま
かりん
1

kamichama karin

Volume 1

Created by
Koge-Donbo

TOKYOPOP

HAMBURG // LONDON // LOS ANGELES // TOKYO

Kamichama Karin Vol. 1
created by Koge-Donbo

Translation - Nan Rymer
English Adaptation - Lianne Sentar
Retouch and Lettering - James Lee
Production Artist - Chris Anderson and Irene Woori Choi
Cover Design - Thea Willis

Editor - Carol Fox
Digital Imaging Manager - Chris Buford
Production Managers - Jennifer Miller and Mutsumi Miyazaki
Managing Editor - Jill Freshney
VP of Production - Ron Klamert
Publisher and E.I.C. - Mike Kiley
President and C.O.O. - John Parker
C.E.O. - Stuart Levy

A  Manga

TOKYOPOP Inc.
5900 Wilshire Blvd. Suite 2000
Los Angeles, CA 90036

E-mail: info@TOKYOPOP.com
Come visit us online at www.TOKYOPOP.com

ISBN: 1-59532-847-5

First TOKYOPOP printing: September 2005

10 9 8 7 6 5 4 3 2 1

Printed in the USA

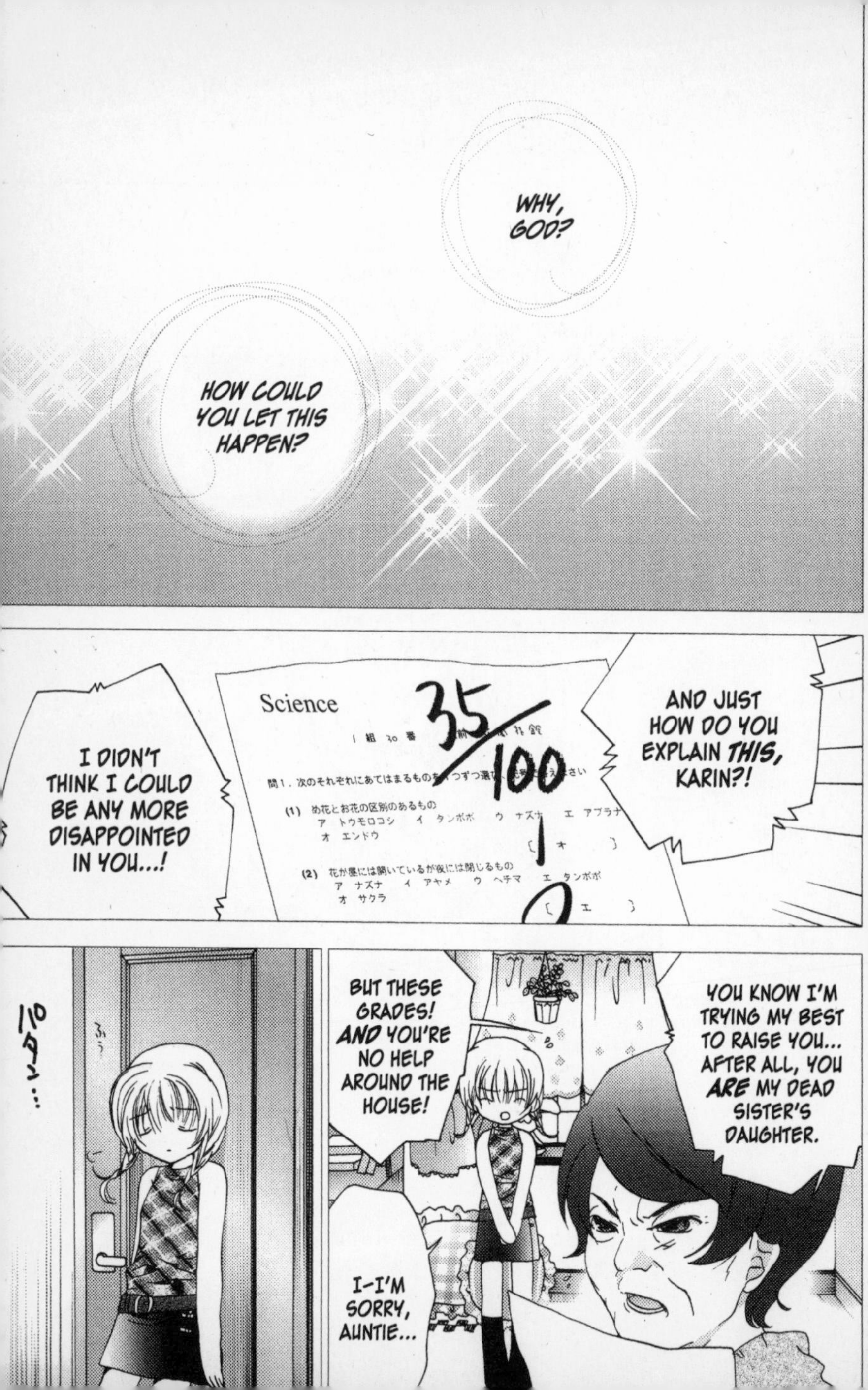
WHY, GOD?
HOW COULD YOU LET THIS HAPPEN?
AND JUST HOW DO YOU EXPLAIN *THIS*, KARIN?!
Science
35/100
(1) め花とお花の区別のあるもの
ア トウモロコシ イ タンポポ ウ ナズナ エ アブラナ
オ エンドウ
〔 オ 〕
(2) 花が昼には開いているが夜には閉じるもの
ア ナズナ イ アヤメ ウ ヘチマ エ タンポポ
オ サクラ
〔 エ 〕
I DIDN'T THINK I COULD BE ANY MORE DISAPPOINTED IN YOU...!
YOU KNOW I'M TRYING MY BEST TO RAISE YOU... AFTER ALL, YOU *ARE* MY DEAD SISTER'S DAUGHTER.
BUT THESE GRADES! *AND* YOU'RE NO HELP AROUND THE HOUSE!
I-I'M SORRY, AUNTIE...
パタン…
ふぅ

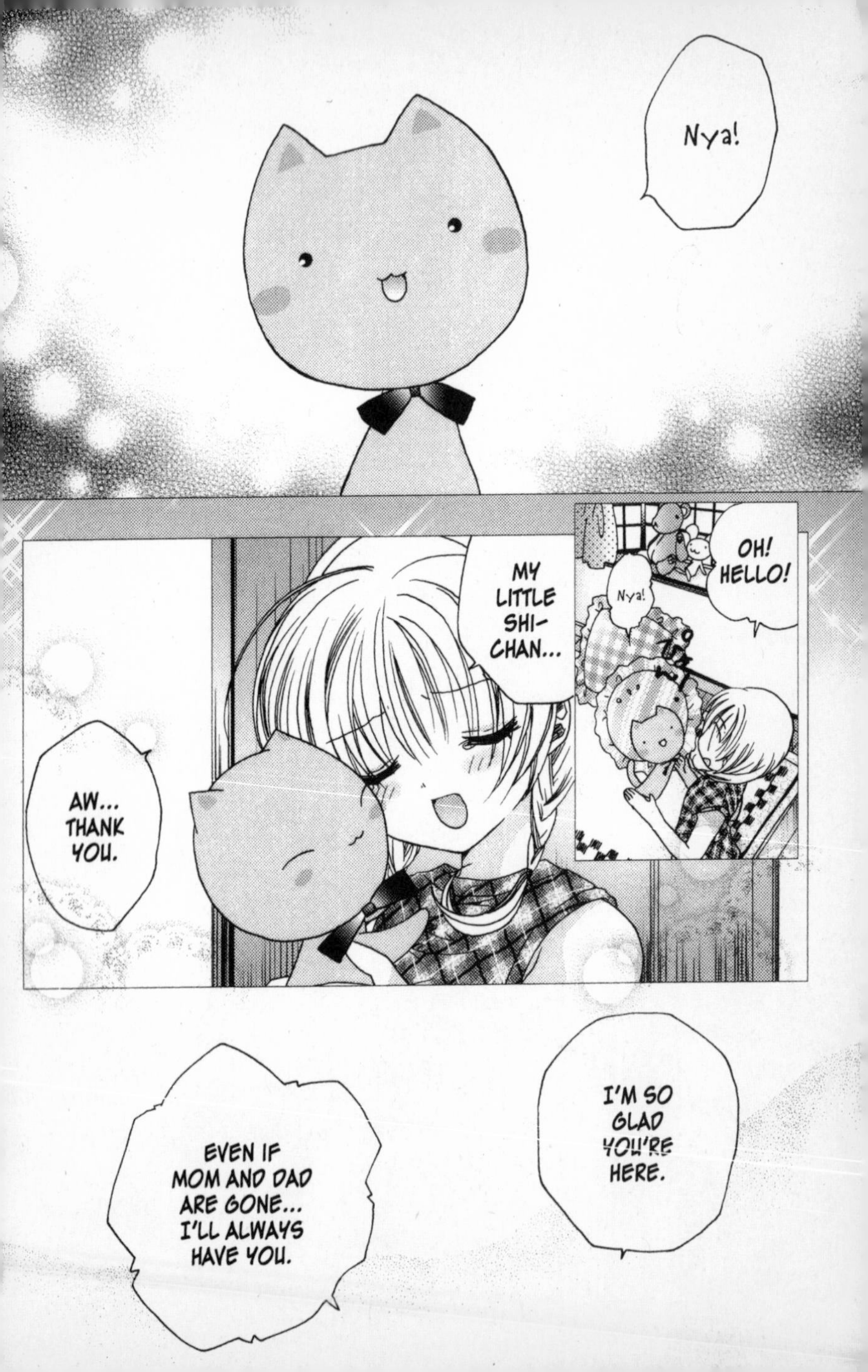
Nya!
OH! HELLO!
Nya!
MY LITTLE SHI-CHAN...
AW... THANK YOU.
I'M SO GLAD YOU'RE HERE.
EVEN IF MOM AND DAD ARE GONE... I'LL ALWAYS HAVE YOU.

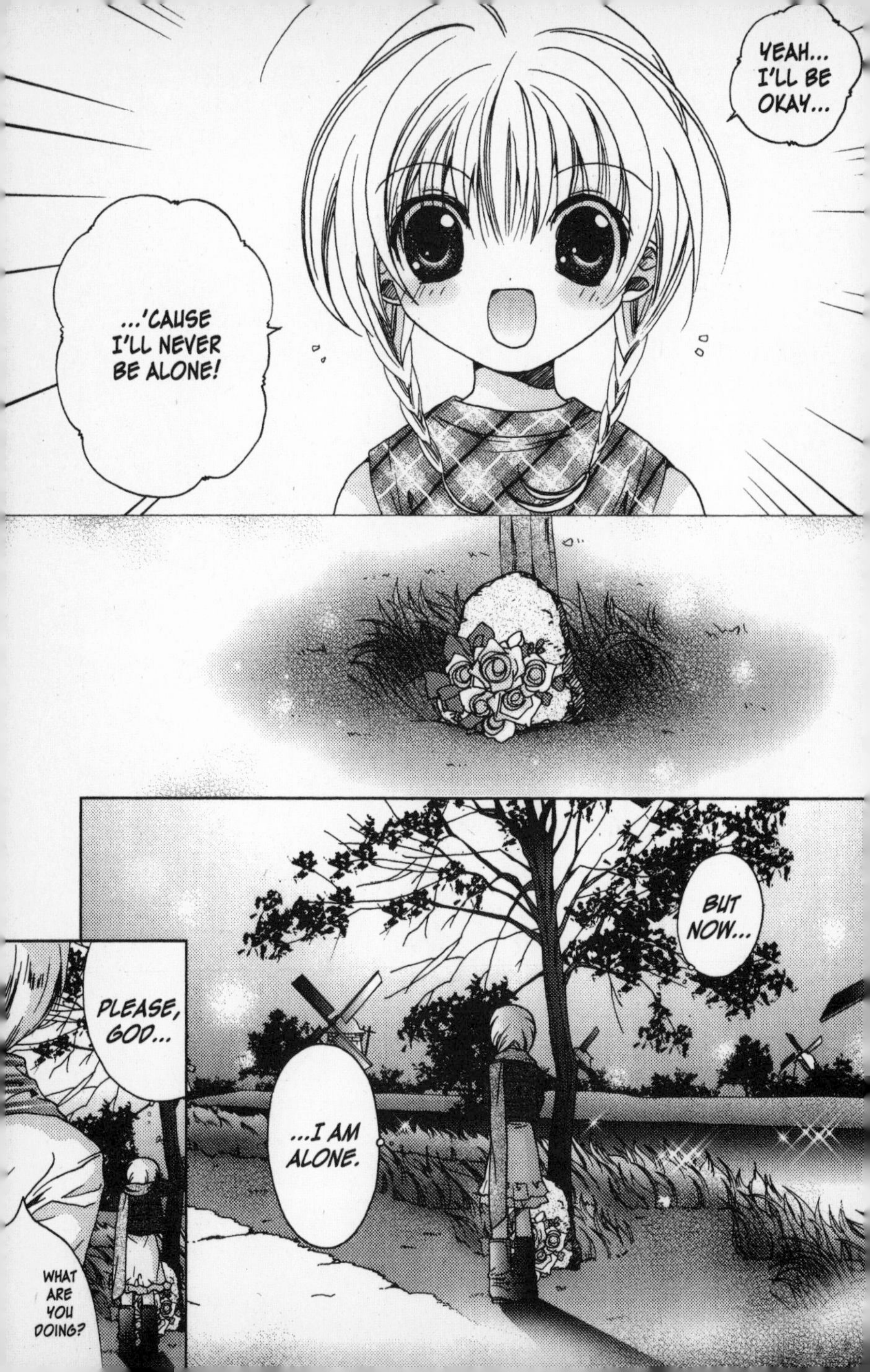
YEAH... I'LL BE OKAY...
...'CAUSE I'LL NEVER BE ALONE!
BUT NOW...
...I AM ALONE.
PLEASE, GOD...
WHAT ARE YOU DOING?

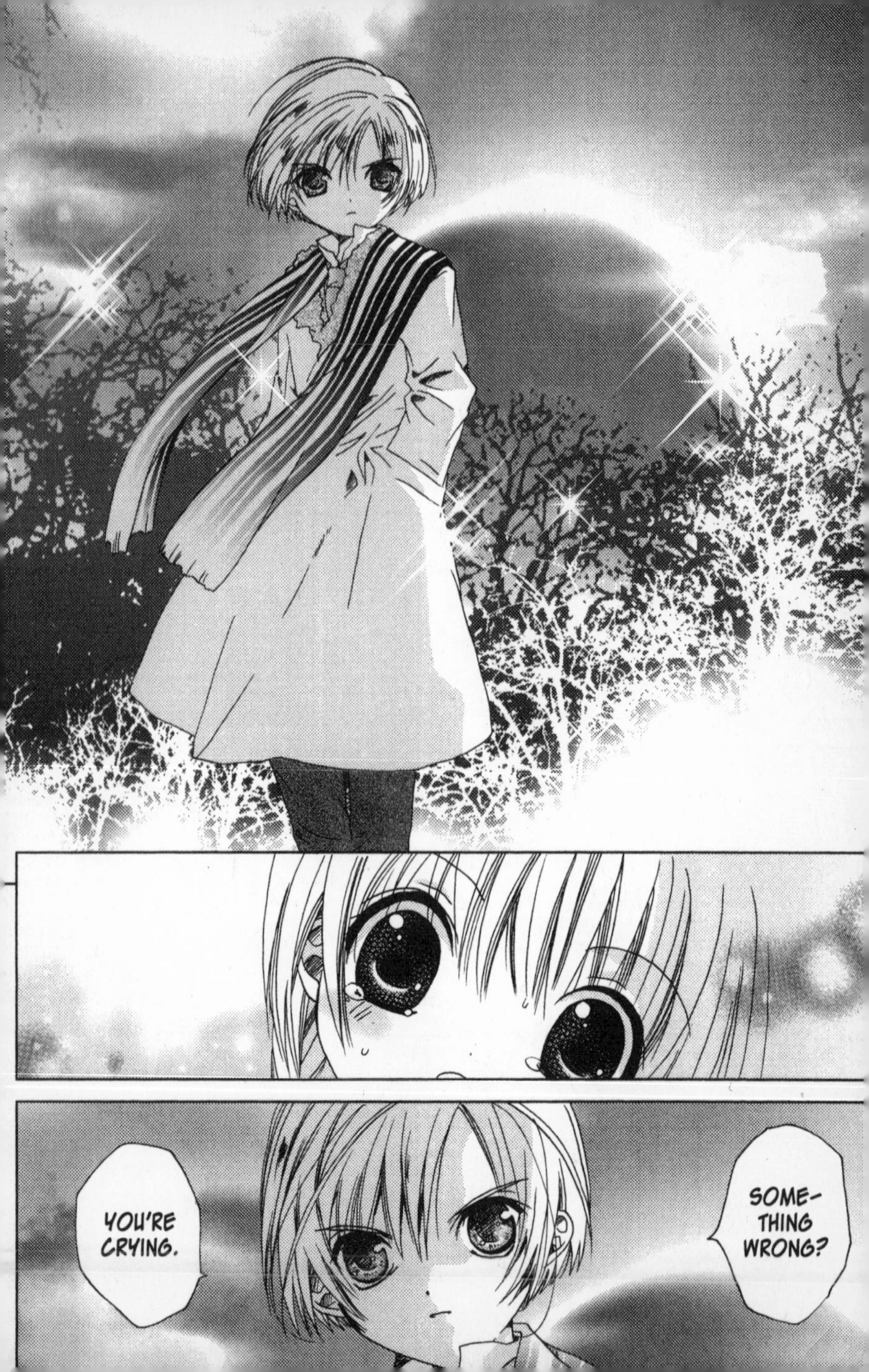
SOME-
THING
WRONG?
YOU'RE
CRYING.

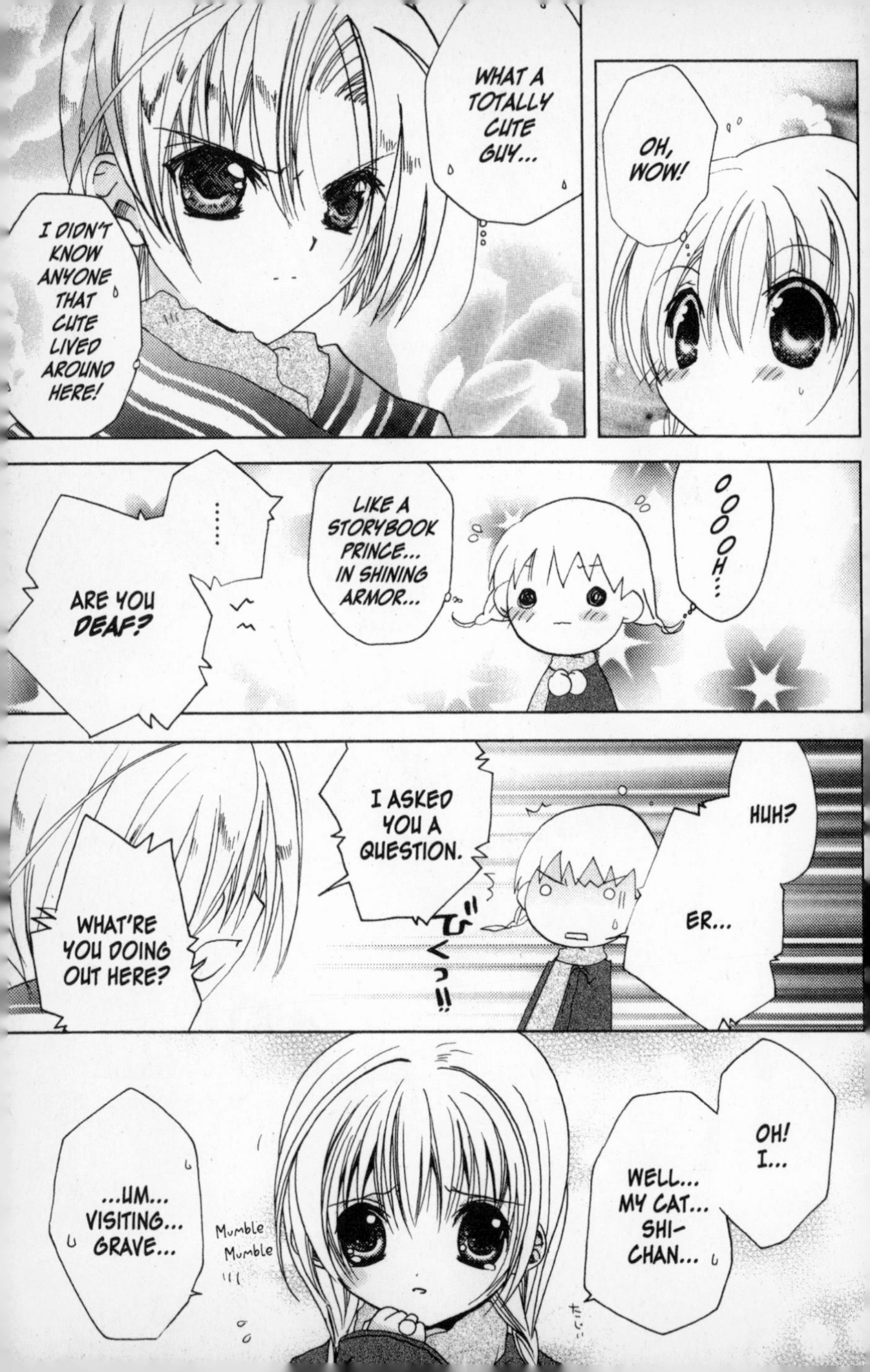
OH, WOW!
WHAT A TOTALLY CUTE GUY...
I DIDN'T KNOW ANYONE THAT CUTE LIVED AROUND HERE!
OOOOH...
LIKE A STORYBOOK PRINCE... IN SHINING ARMOR...
......
ARE YOU DEAF?
HUH?
ER...
I ASKED YOU A QUESTION.
びくっ!!
WHAT'RE YOU DOING OUT HERE?
OH! I...
WELL... MY CAT... SHI-CHAN...
...UM... VISITING... GRAVE...
Mumble Mumble

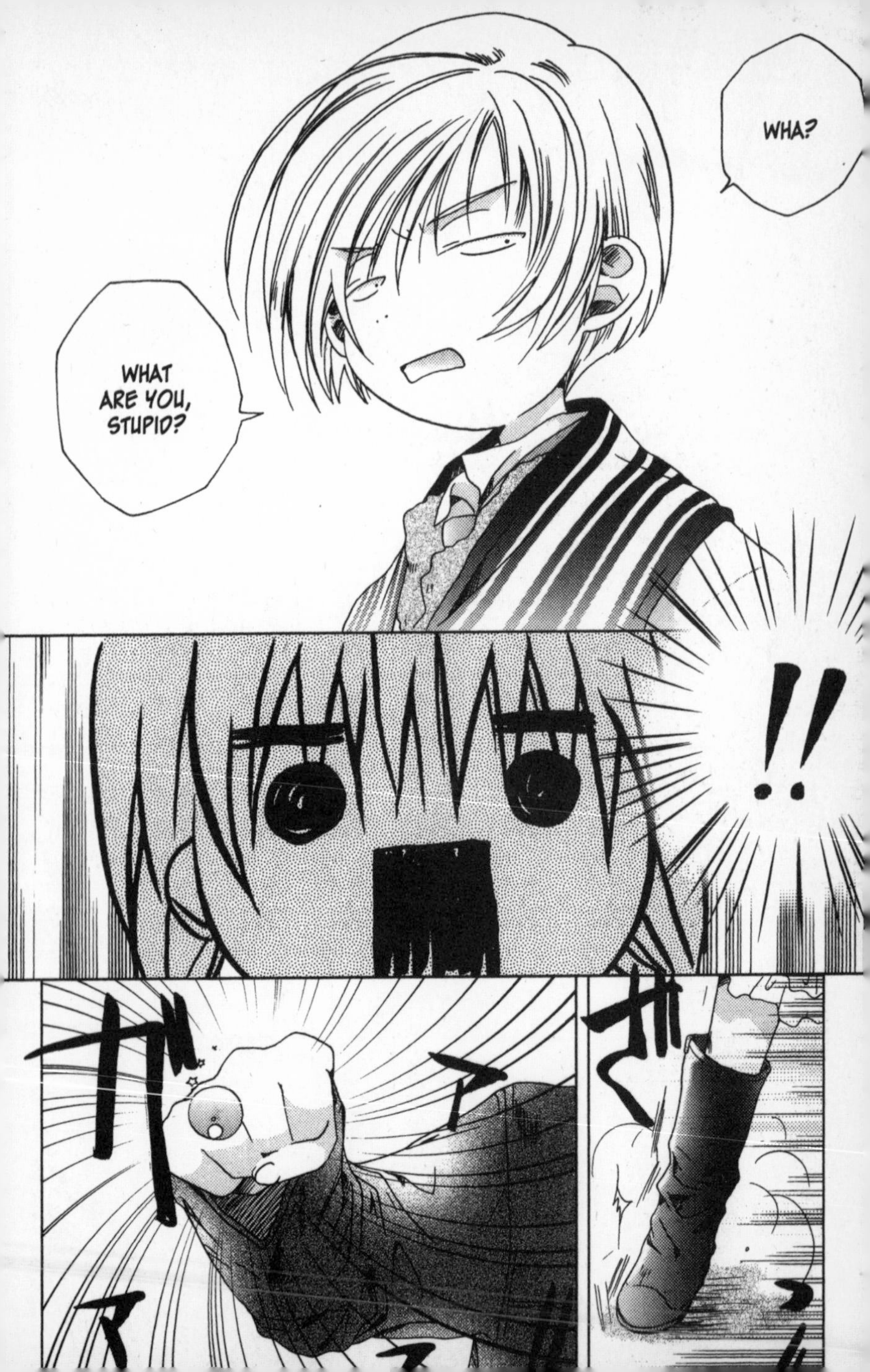
WHA?
WHAT ARE YOU, STUPID?
!!

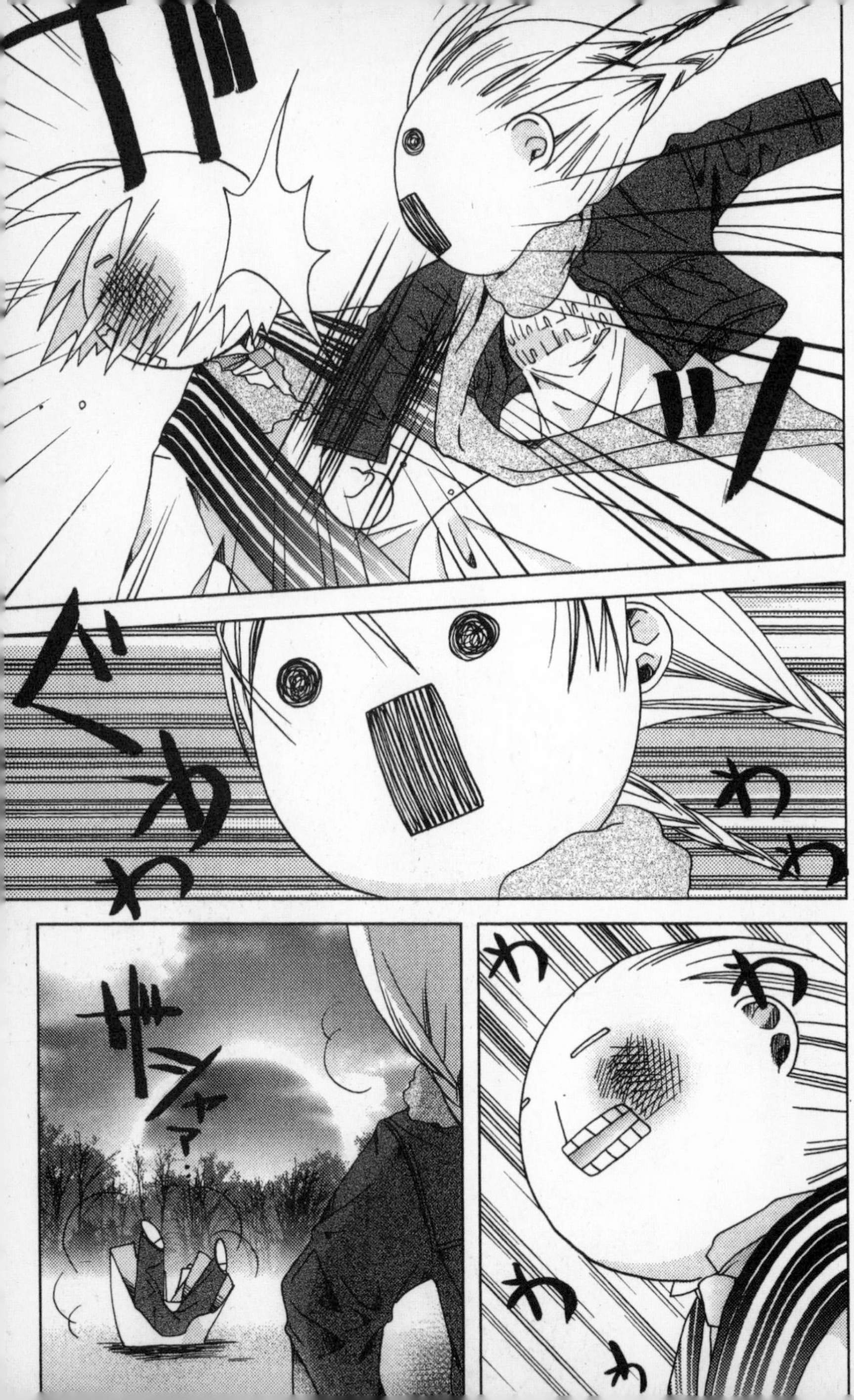
わわ
ぐわわ
わわわ
ザァァ…

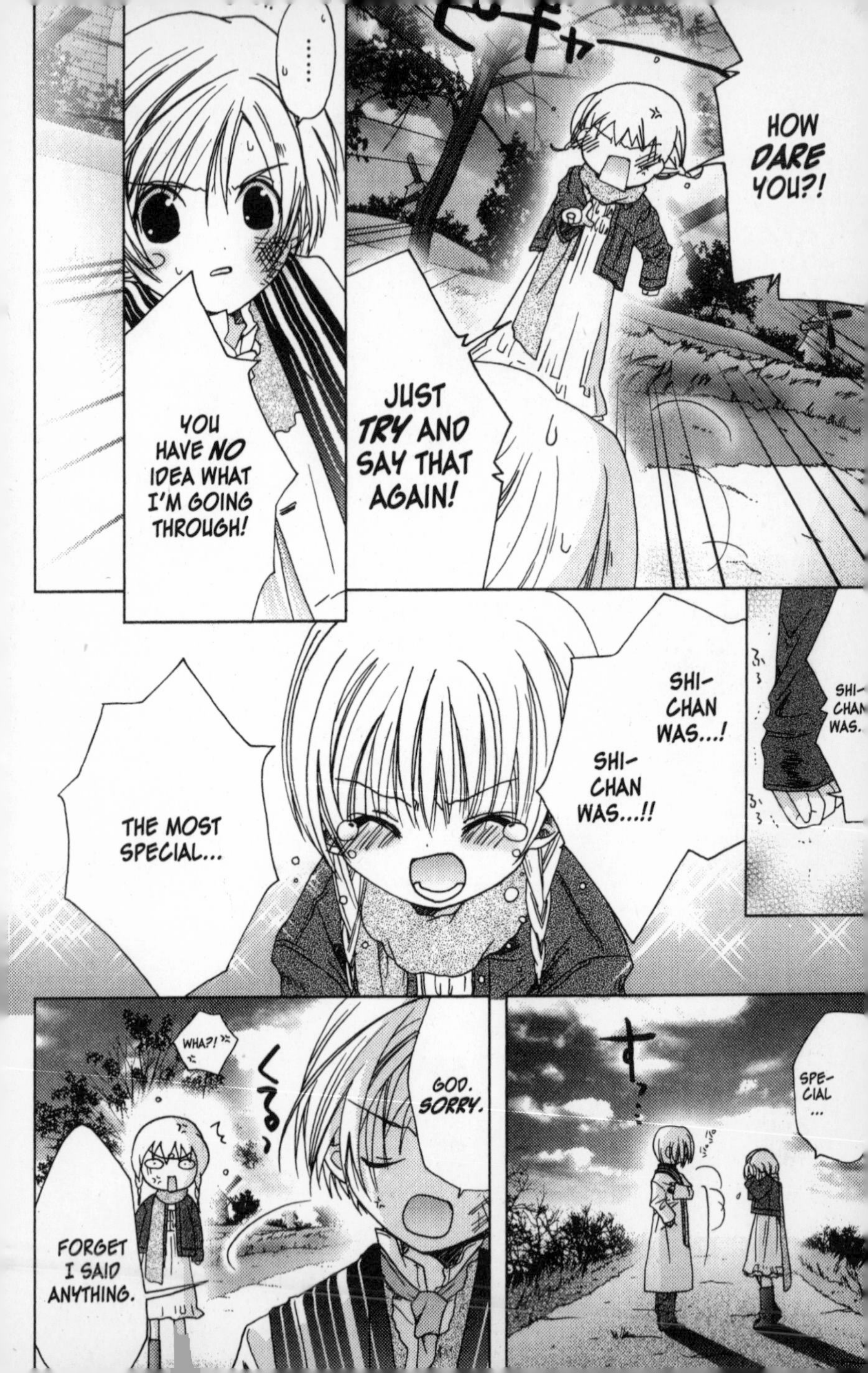
HOW DARE YOU?!
JUST TRY AND SAY THAT AGAIN!
......
YOU HAVE NO IDEA WHAT I'M GOING THROUGH!
SHI-CHAN WAS.
SHI-CHAN WAS...!
SHI-CHAN WAS...!!
THE MOST SPECIAL...
SPE-CIAL ...
GOD. SORRY.
WHA?!
FORGET I SAID ANYTHING.

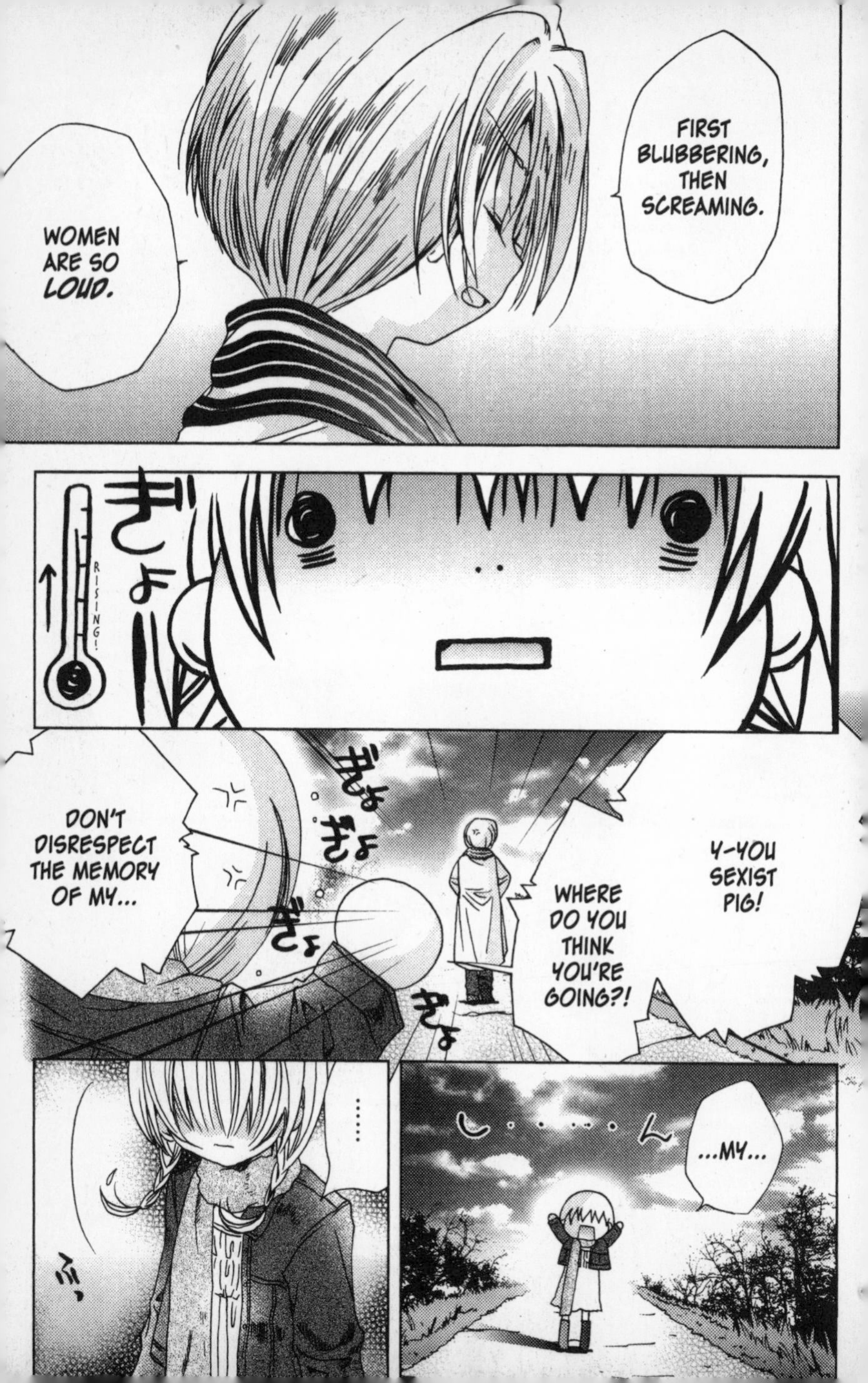
FIRST BLUBBERING, THEN SCREAMING.
WOMEN ARE SO LOUD.
ぎょ!!
RISING!
Y-YOU SEXIST PIG!
WHERE DO YOU THINK YOU'RE GOING?!
DON'T DISRESPECT THE MEMORY OF MY...
...MY...
し・・・・・ん
......
ふっ

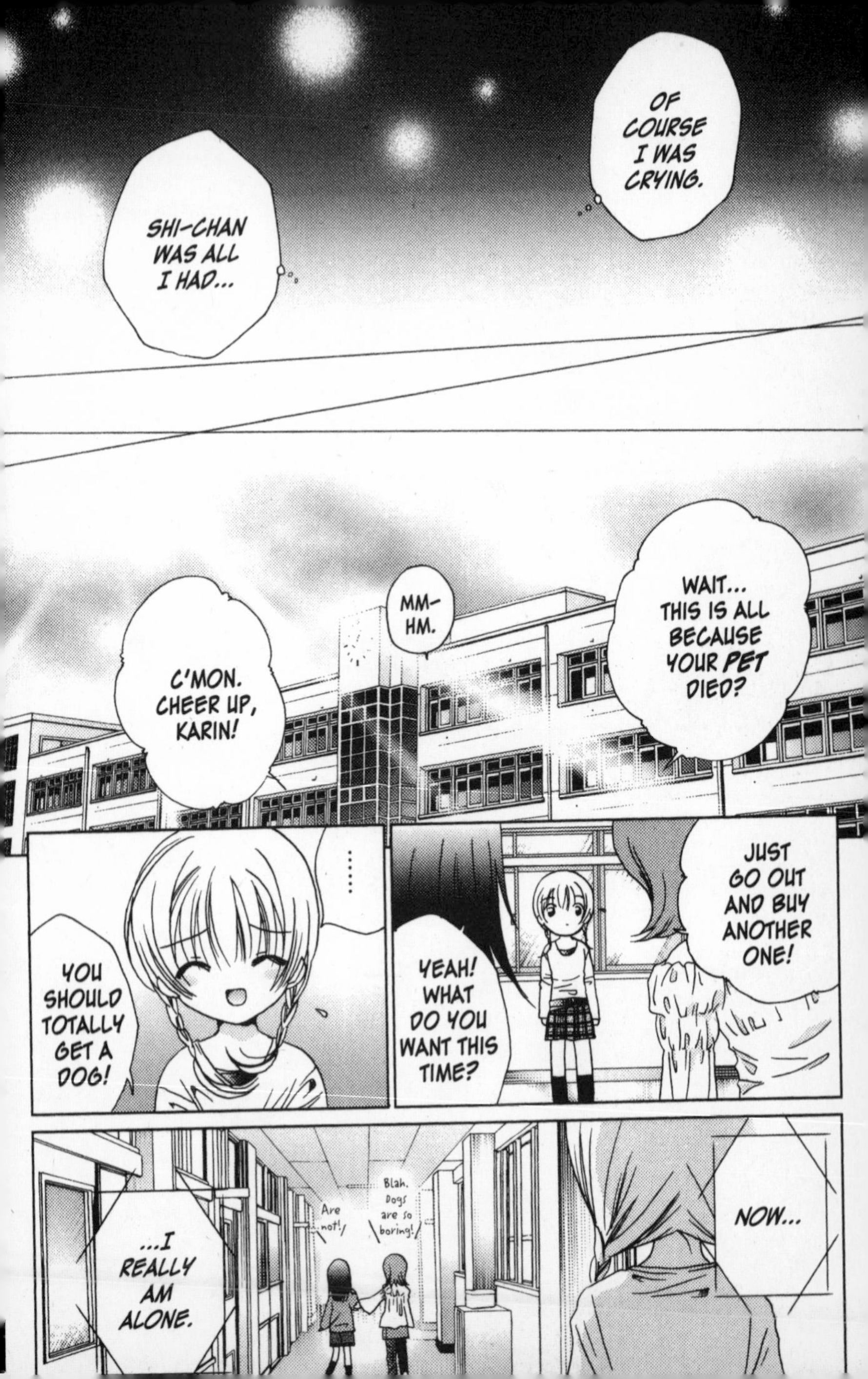
OF COURSE I WAS CRYING.
SHI-CHAN WAS ALL I HAD...
WAIT... THIS IS ALL BECAUSE YOUR *PET* DIED?
MM-HM.
C'MON. CHEER UP, KARIN!
JUST GO OUT AND BUY ANOTHER ONE!
YEAH! WHAT DO YOU WANT THIS TIME?
......
YOU SHOULD TOTALLY GET A DOG!
NOW...
Blah. Dogs are so boring!
Are not!
...I REALLY AM ALONE.

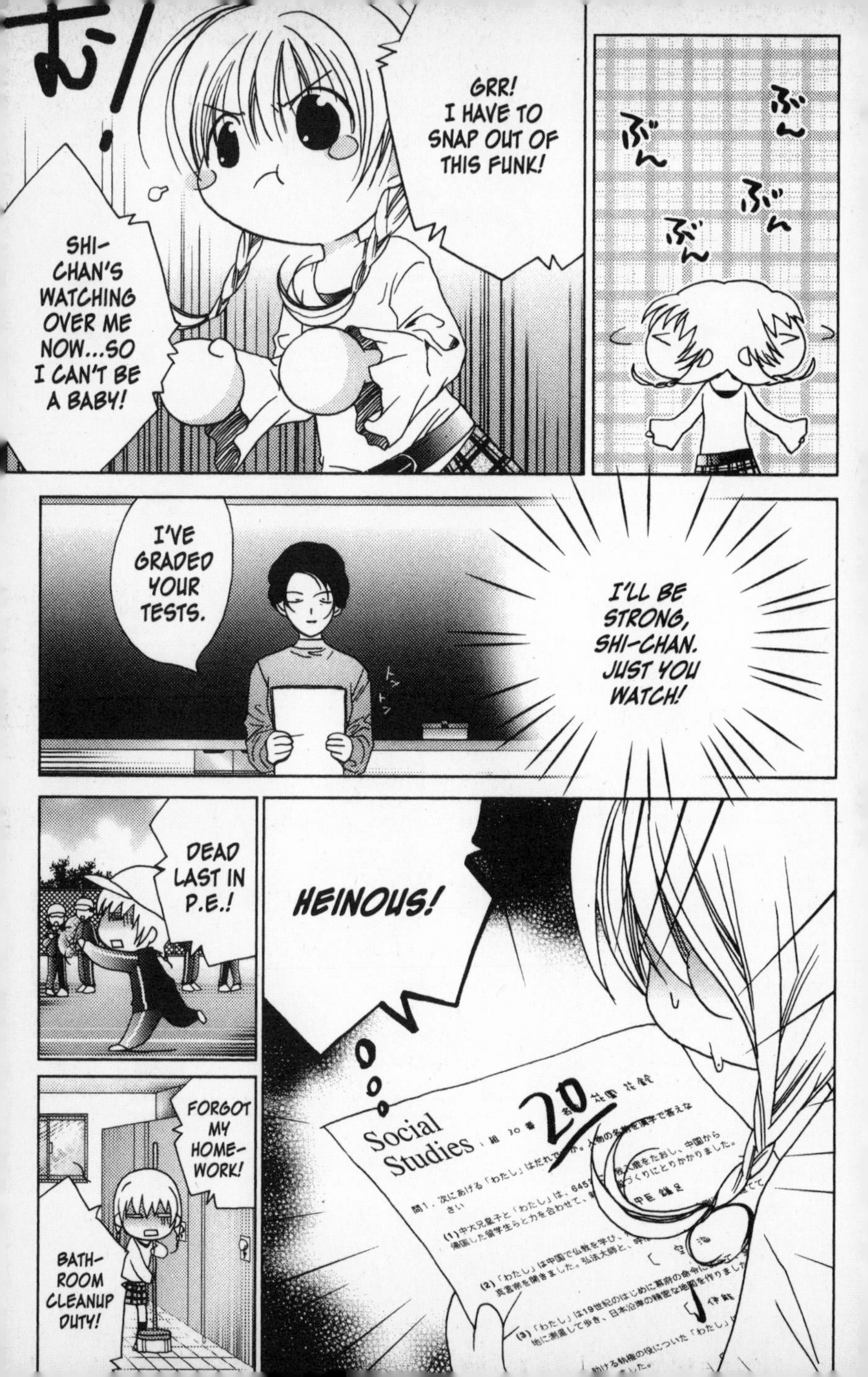
ぶん ぶん
ぶん ぶん
む！
GRR! I HAVE TO SNAP OUT OF THIS FUNK!
SHI-CHAN'S WATCHING OVER ME NOW...SO I CAN'T BE A BABY!
I'LL BE STRONG, SHI-CHAN. JUST YOU WATCH!
I'VE GRADED YOUR TESTS.
HEINOUS!
Social Studies
20
DEAD LAST IN P.E.!
FORGOT MY HOME-WORK!
BATH-ROOM CLEANUP DUTY!

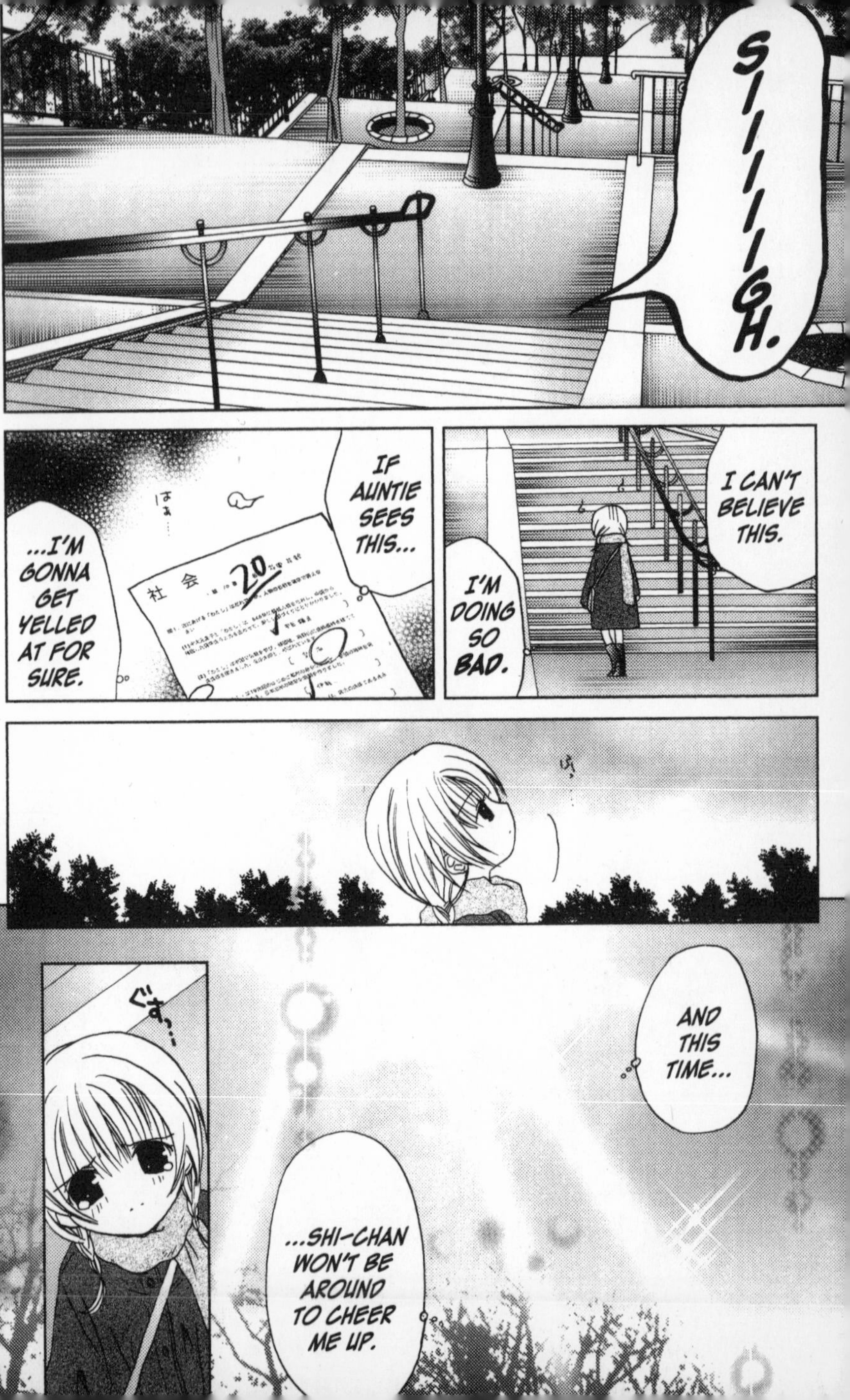
SIIIIIGH.
I CAN'T BELIEVE THIS.
I'M DOING SO BAD.
IF AUNTIE SEES THIS...
はぁ…
...I'M GONNA GET YELLED AT FOR SURE.
社会
20
AND THIS TIME...
...SHI-CHAN WON'T BE AROUND TO CHEER ME UP.

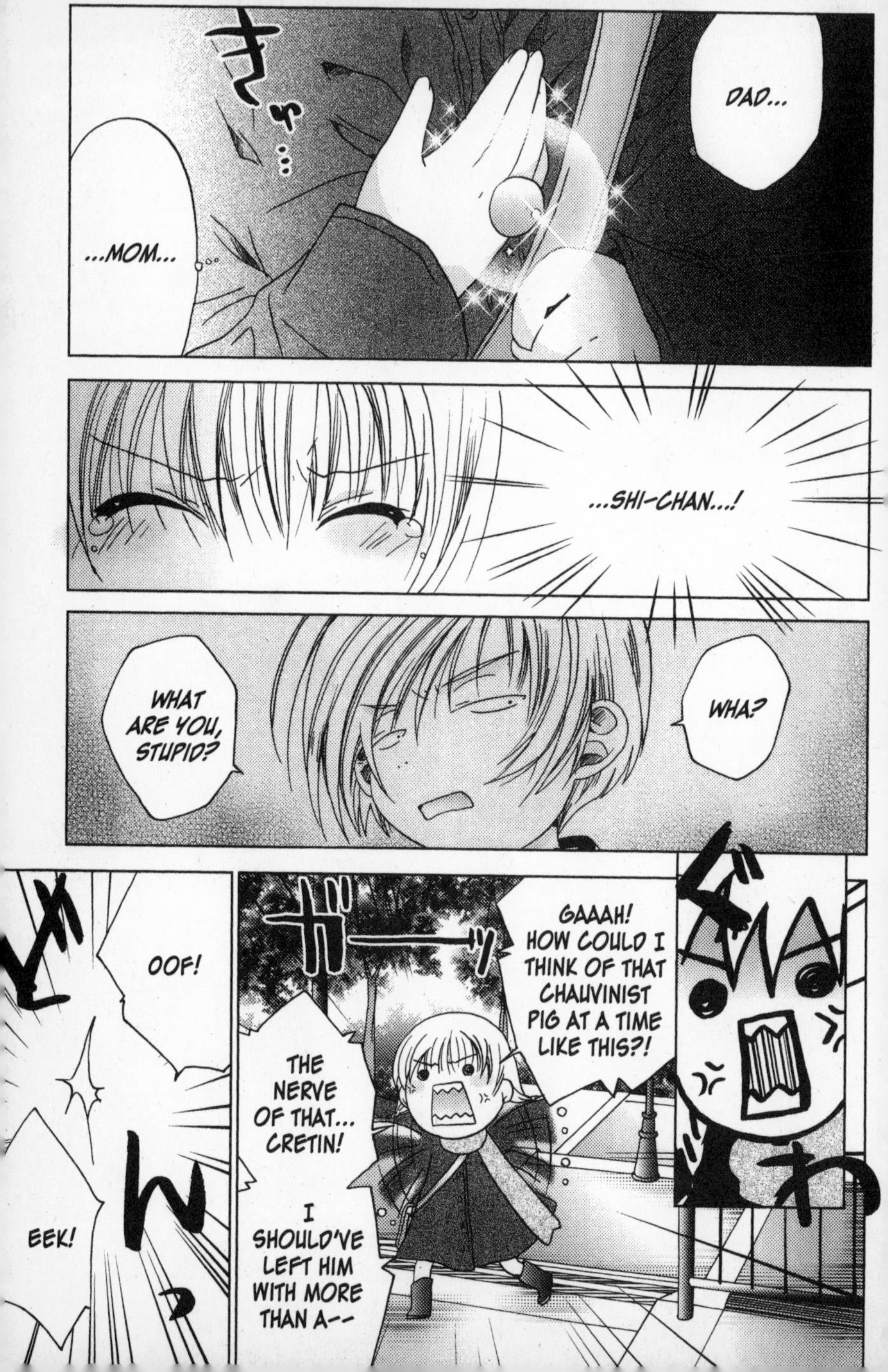
DAD...
...MOM...
...SHI-CHAN...!
WHA?
WHAT ARE YOU, STUPID?
GAAAH! HOW COULD I THINK OF THAT CHAUVINIST PIG AT A TIME LIKE THIS?!
THE NERVE OF THAT... CRETIN!
I SHOULD'VE LEFT HIM WITH MORE THAN A--
OOF!
EEK!

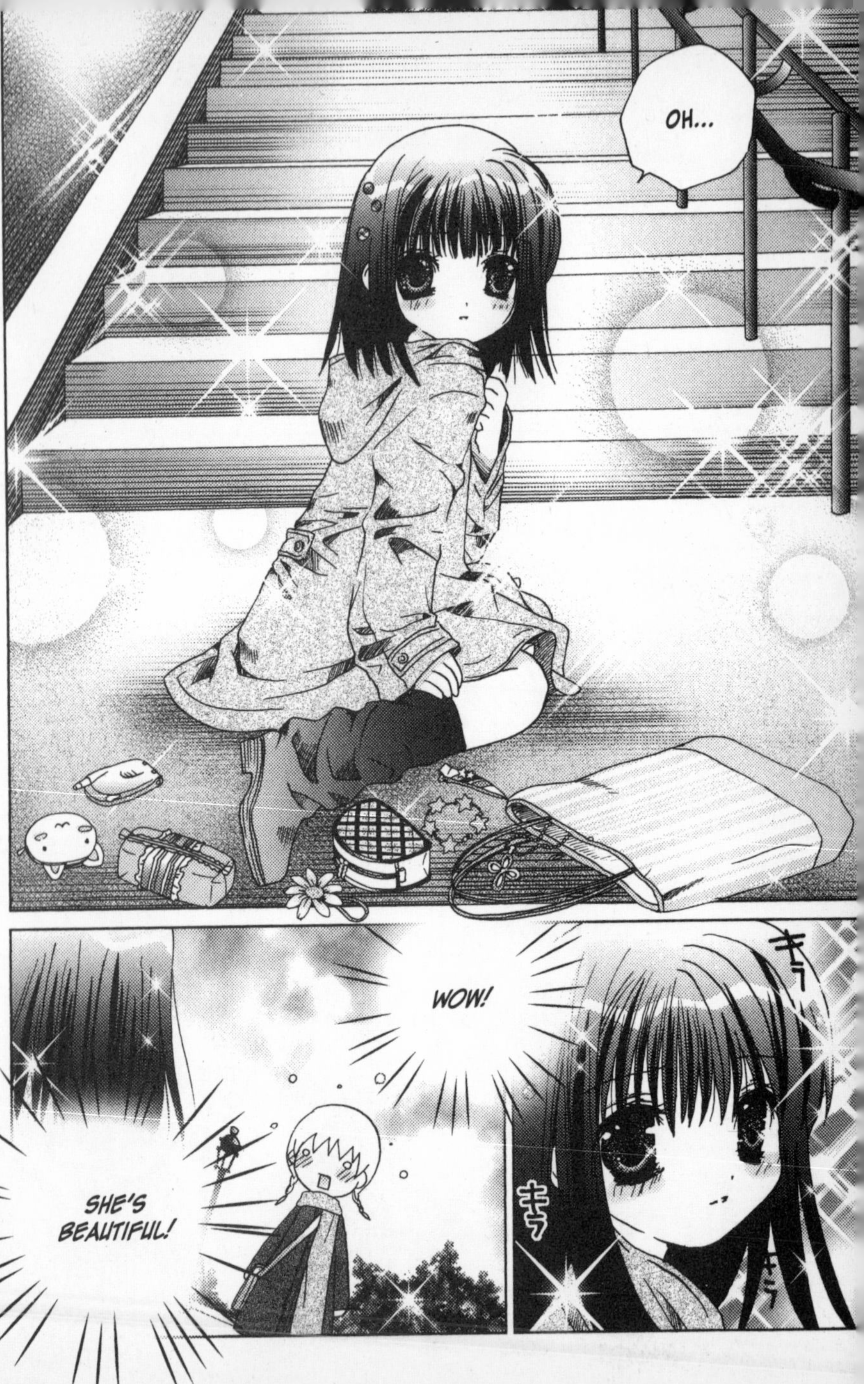
OH...
キラ
キラ
キラ
WOW!
SHE'S BEAUTIFUL!

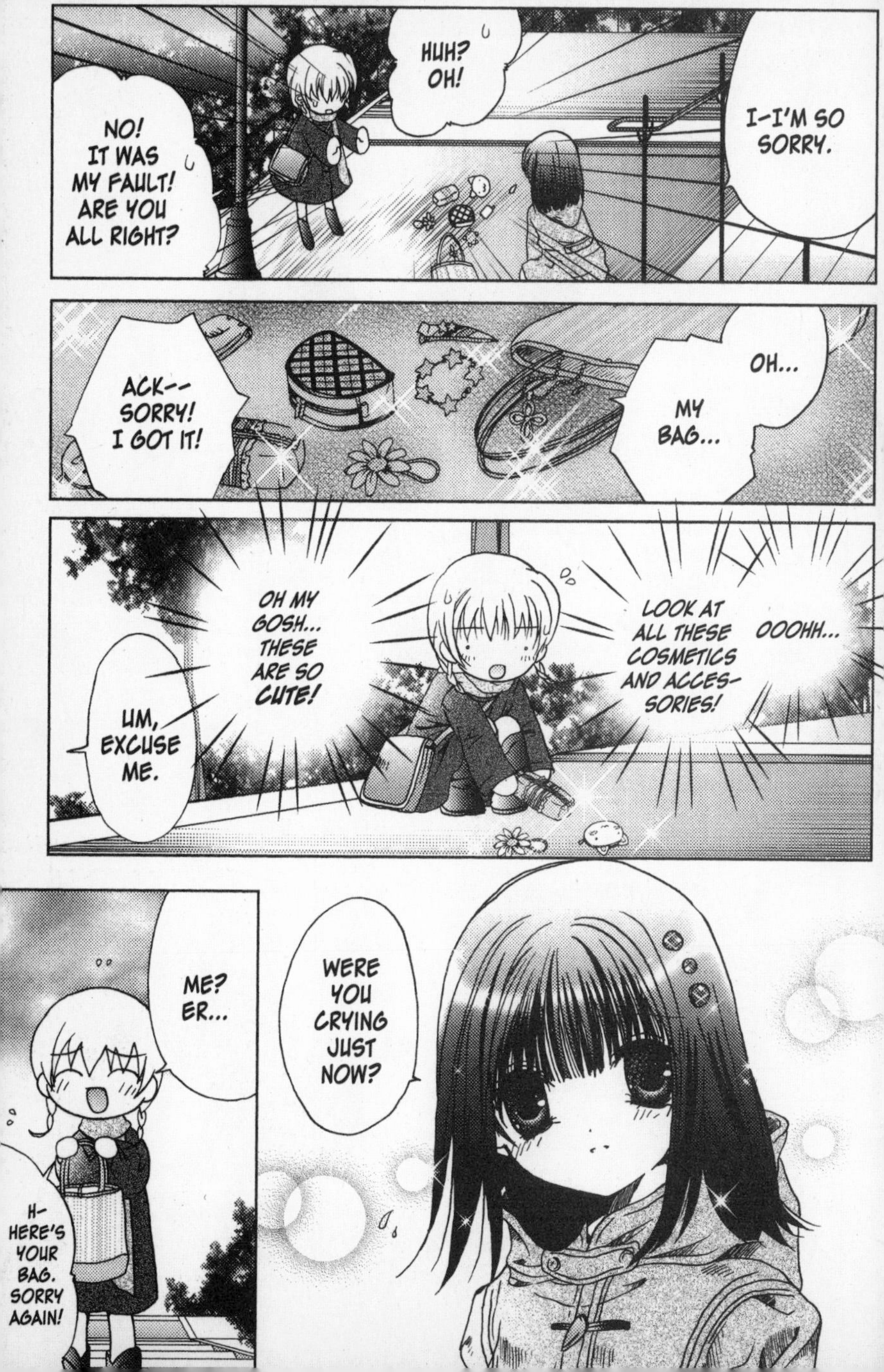
I-I'M SO SORRY.
HUH? OH!
NO! IT WAS MY FAULT! ARE YOU ALL RIGHT?
OH...
MY BAG...
ACK-- SORRY! I GOT IT!
OOOHH...
LOOK AT ALL THESE COSMETICS AND ACCES-SORIES!
OH MY GOSH... THESE ARE SO CUTE!
UM, EXCUSE ME.
WERE YOU CRYING JUST NOW?
ME? ER...
H-HERE'S YOUR BAG. SORRY AGAIN!

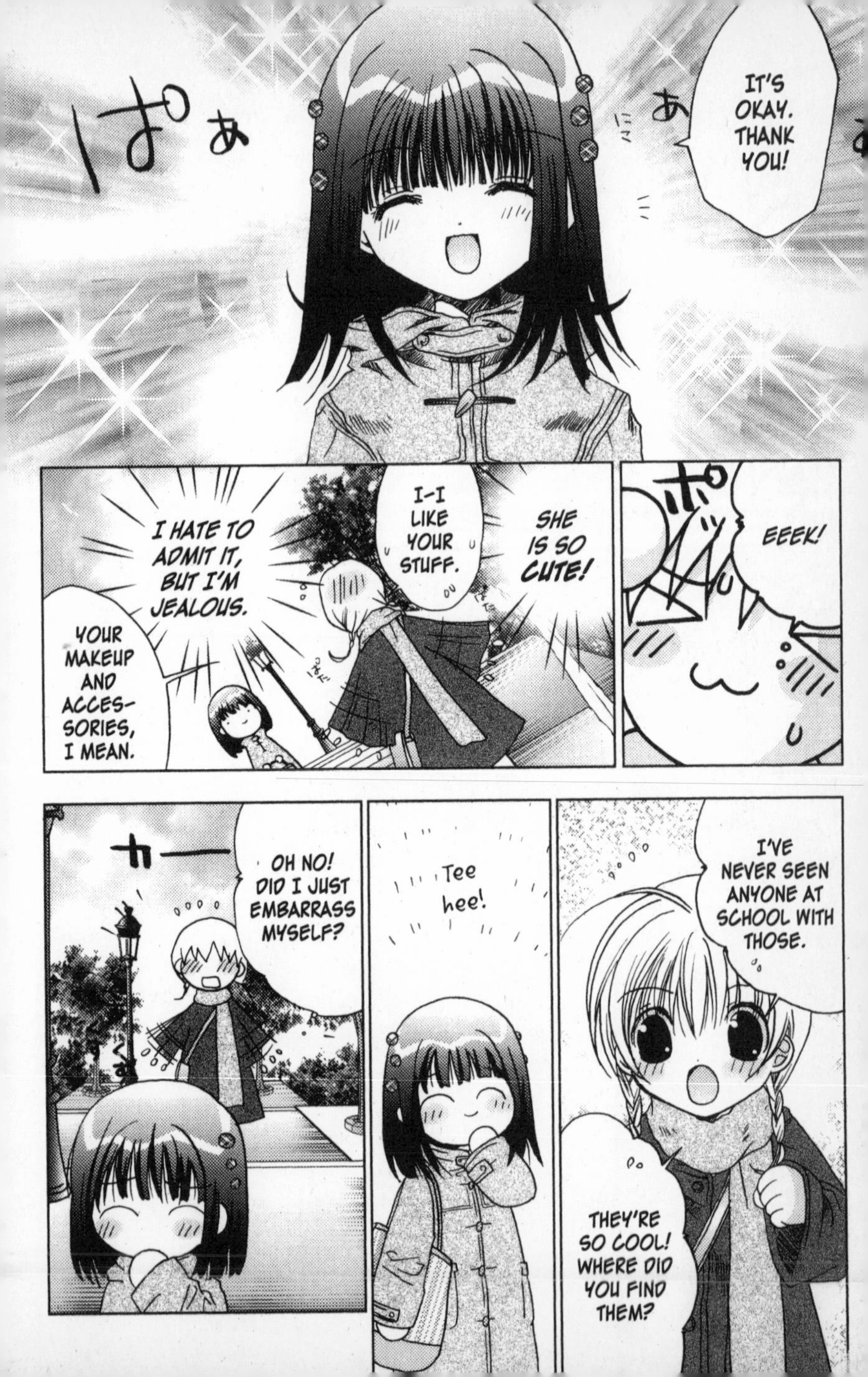
ぱぁ
あ
IT'S OKAY. THANK YOU!
ポッ
EEEK!
I-I LIKE YOUR STUFF.
SHE IS SO CUTE!
I HATE TO ADMIT IT, BUT I'M JEALOUS.
YOUR MAKEUP AND ACCES-SORIES, I MEAN.
I'VE NEVER SEEN ANYONE AT SCHOOL WITH THOSE.
THEY'RE SO COOL! WHERE DID YOU FIND THEM?
Tee hee!
カー
OH NO! DID I JUST EMBARRASS MYSELF?

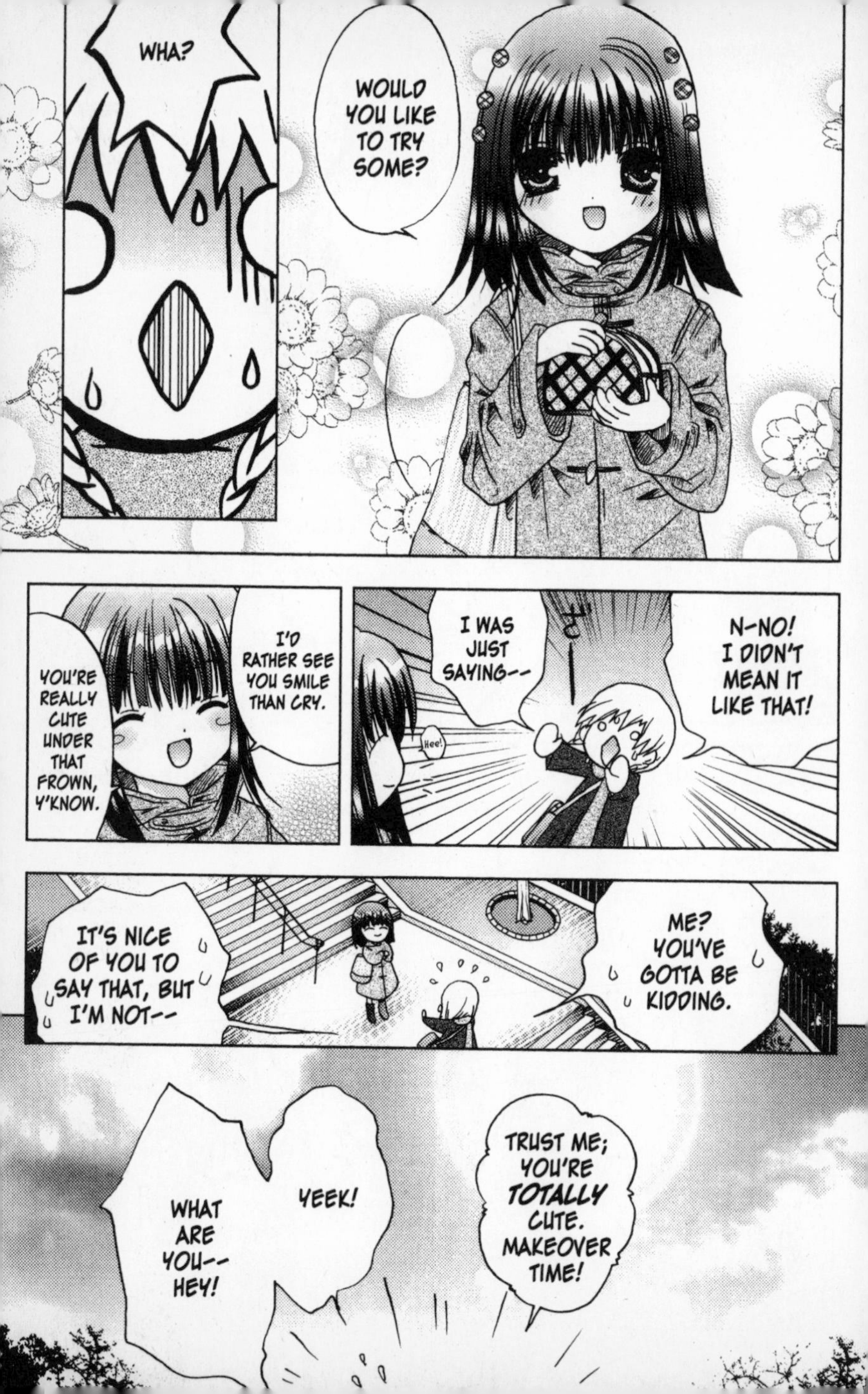
WOULD YOU LIKE TO TRY SOME?
WHA?
N-NO! I DIDN'T MEAN IT LIKE THAT!
I WAS JUST SAYING--
Hee!
I'D RATHER SEE YOU SMILE THAN CRY.
YOU'RE REALLY CUTE UNDER THAT FROWN, Y'KNOW.
ME? YOU'VE GOTTA BE KIDDING.
IT'S NICE OF YOU TO SAY THAT, BUT I'M NOT--
TRUST ME; YOU'RE *TOTALLY* CUTE. MAKEOVER TIME!
YEEK!
WHAT ARE YOU--HEY!

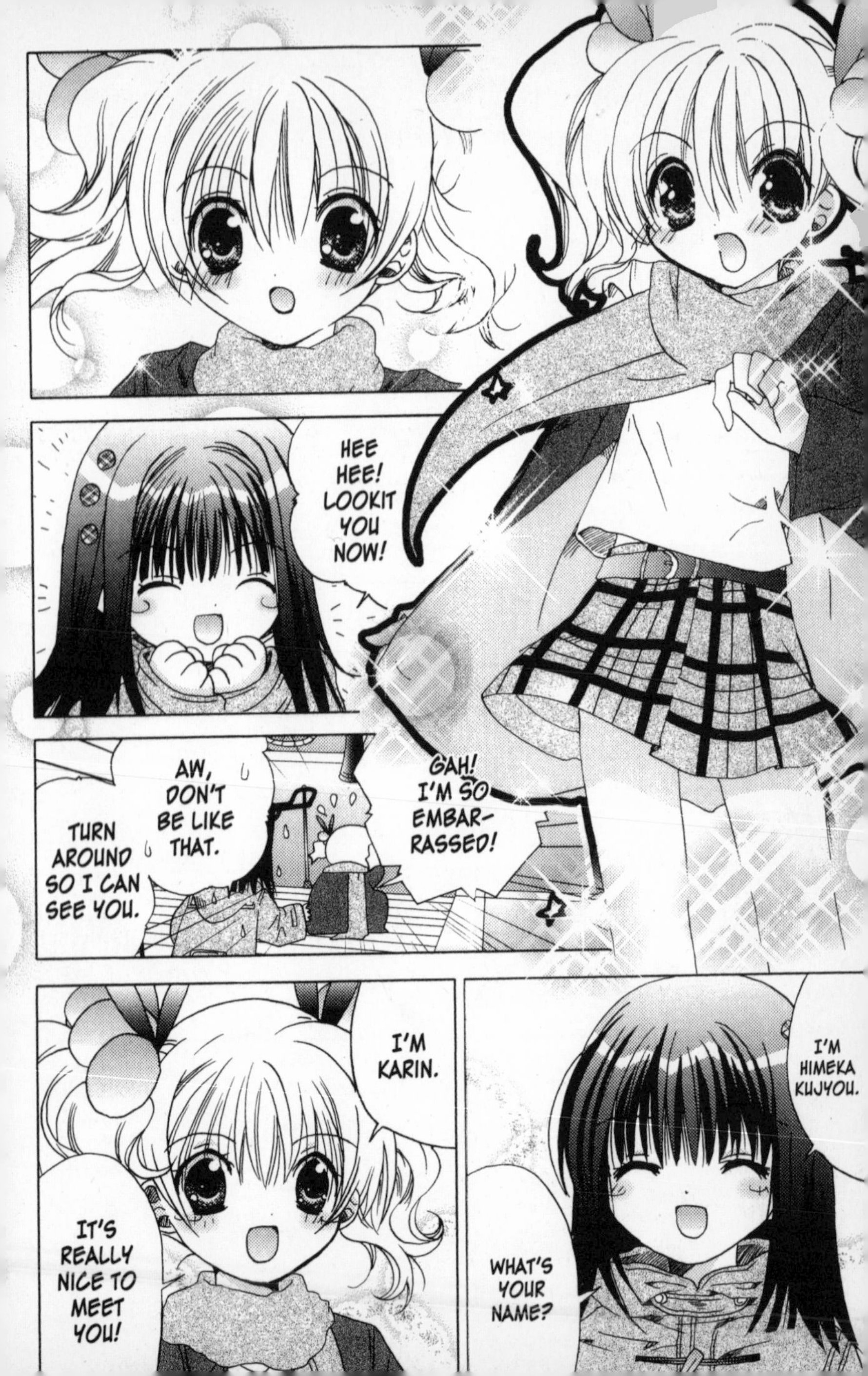
HEE HEE! LOOKIT YOU NOW!
GAH! I'M SO EMBAR-RASSED!
AW, DON'T BE LIKE THAT.
TURN AROUND SO I CAN SEE YOU.
I'M HIMEKA KUJYOU.
WHAT'S YOUR NAME?
I'M KARIN.
IT'S REALLY NICE TO MEET YOU!

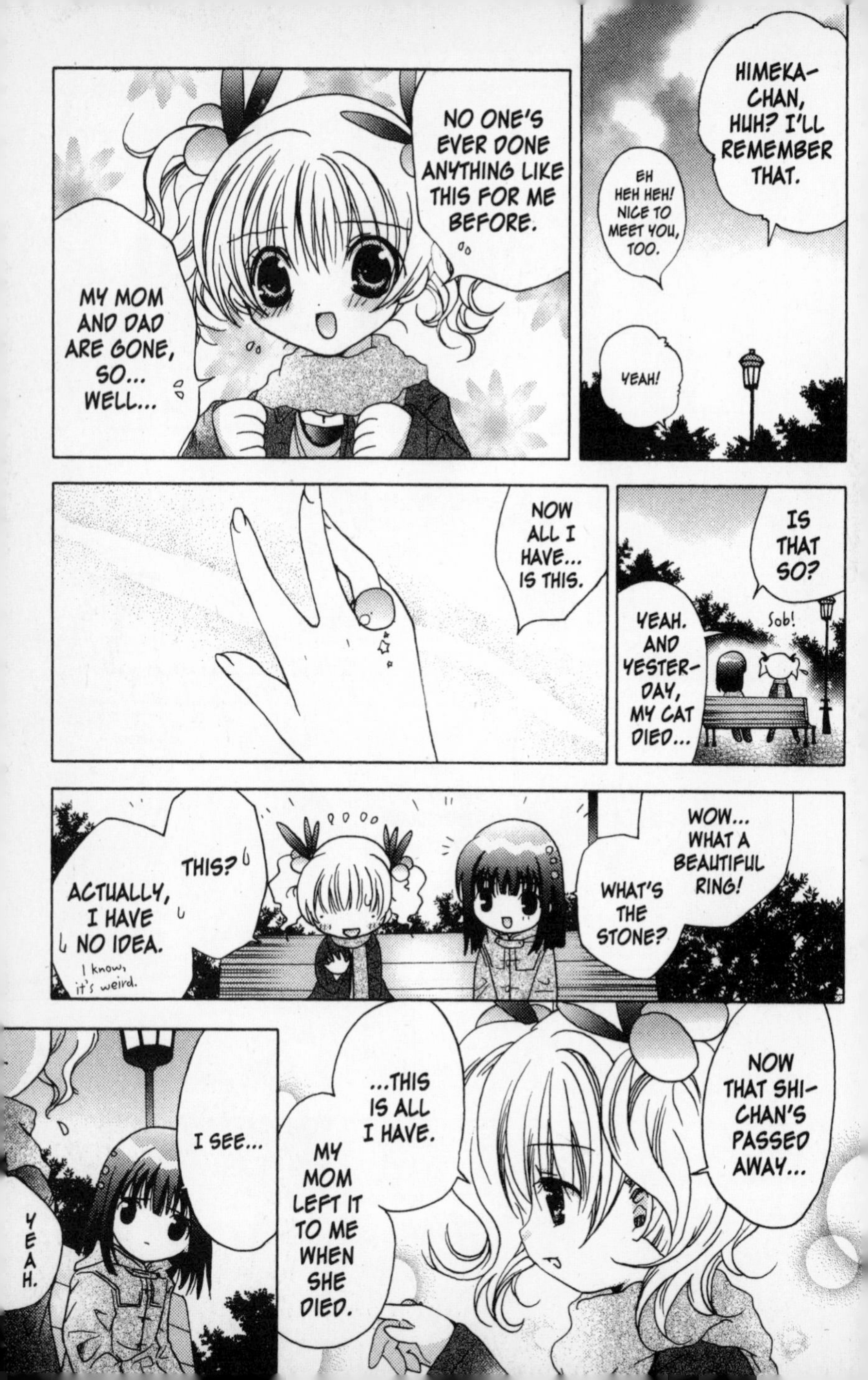
HIMEKA-CHAN, HUH? I'LL REMEMBER THAT.
EH HEH HEH! NICE TO MEET YOU, TOO.
YEAH!
NO ONE'S EVER DONE ANYTHING LIKE THIS FOR ME BEFORE.
MY MOM AND DAD ARE GONE, SO... WELL...
IS THAT SO?
YEAH. AND YESTER-DAY, MY CAT DIED...
Sob!
NOW ALL I HAVE... IS THIS.
WOW... WHAT A BEAUTIFUL RING!
WHAT'S THE STONE?
THIS?
ACTUALLY, I HAVE NO IDEA.
I know, it's weird.
NOW THAT SHI-CHAN'S PASSED AWAY...
...THIS IS ALL I HAVE.
MY MOM LEFT IT TO ME WHEN SHE DIED.
I SEE...
YEAH.

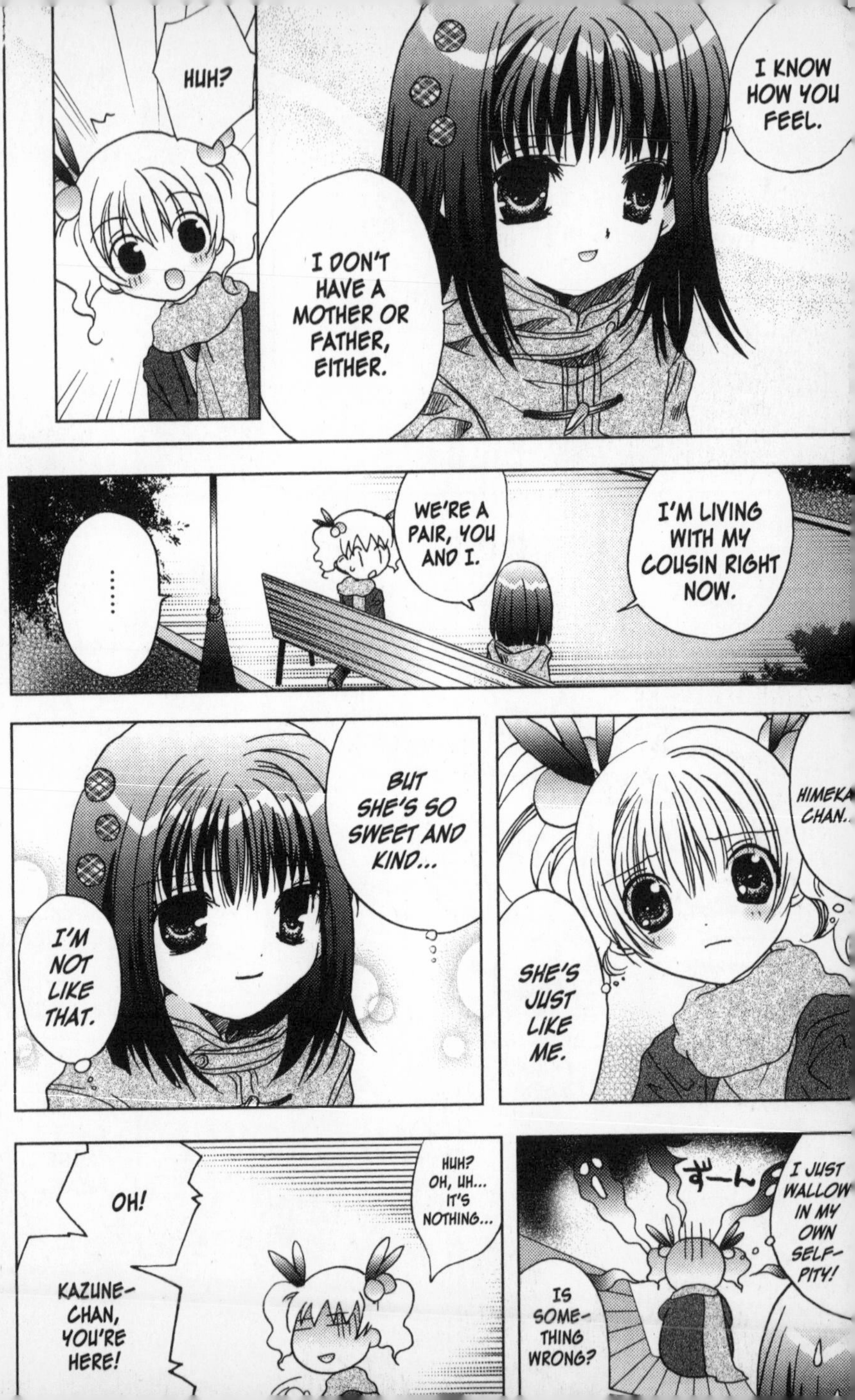
I KNOW HOW YOU FEEL.
I DON'T HAVE A MOTHER OR FATHER, EITHER.
HUH?
I'M LIVING WITH MY COUSIN RIGHT NOW.
WE'RE A PAIR, YOU AND I.
......
HIMEKA CHAN..
SHE'S JUST LIKE ME.
BUT SHE'S SO SWEET AND KIND...
I'M NOT LIKE THAT.
I JUST WALLOW IN MY OWN SELF-PITY!
ずーん
IS SOMETHING WRONG?
HUH? OH, UH... IT'S NOTHING...
OH!
KAZUNE-CHAN, YOU'RE HERE!

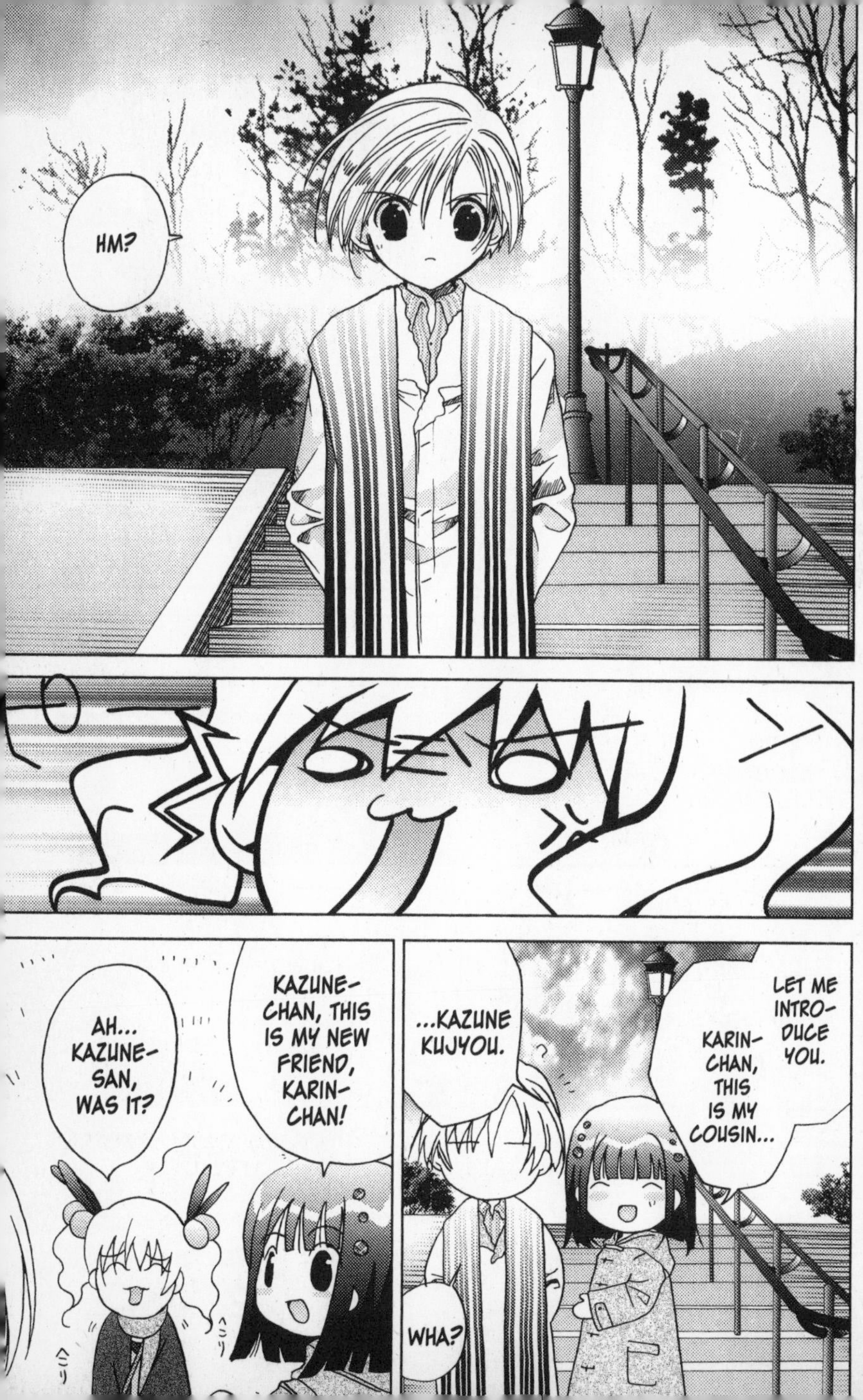
HM?
LET ME INTRODUCE YOU.
KARIN-CHAN, THIS IS MY COUSIN...
...KAZUNE KUJYOU.
WHA?
KAZUNE-CHAN, THIS IS MY NEW FRIEND, KARIN-CHAN!
AH... KAZUNE-SAN, WAS IT?

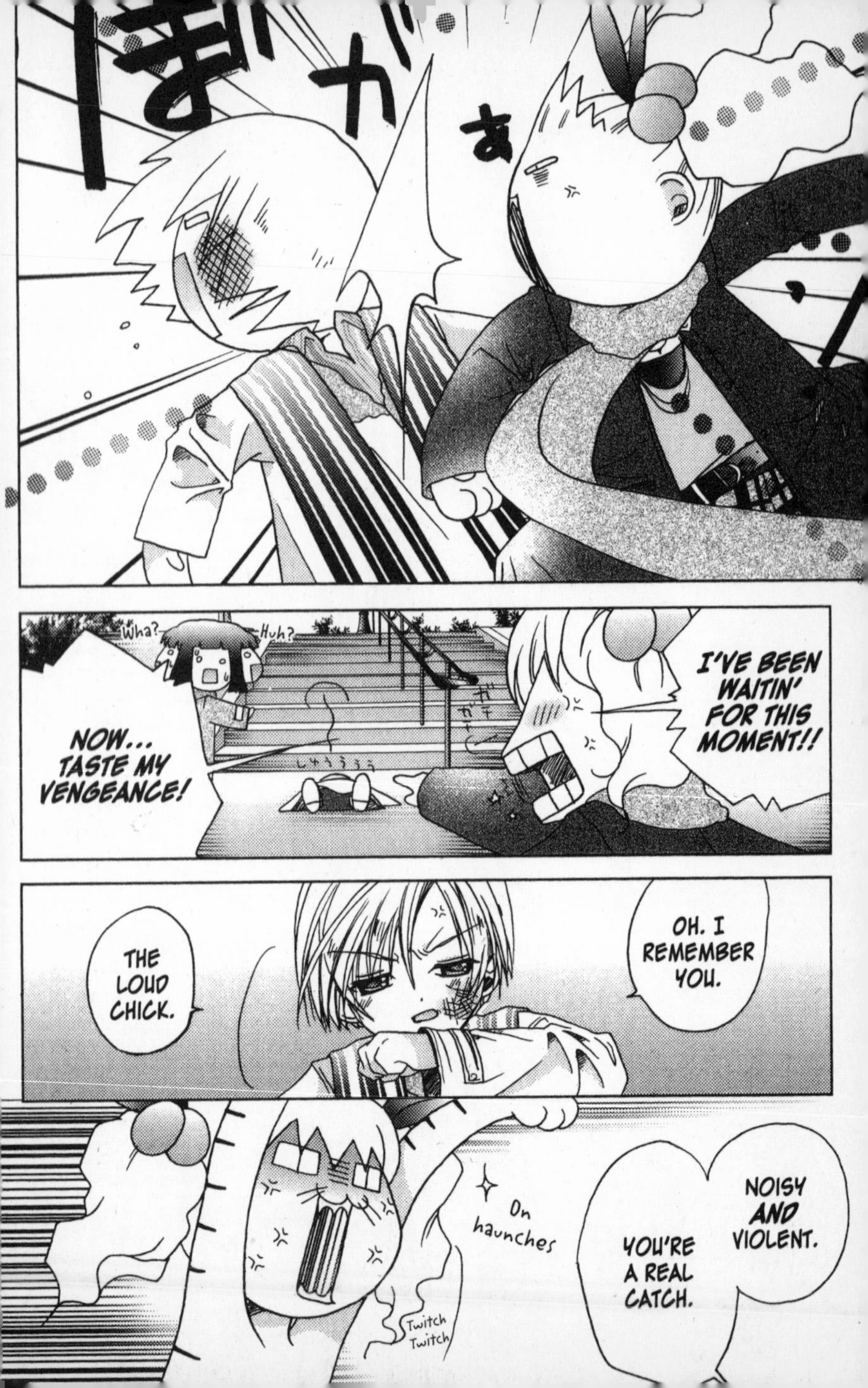
I'VE BEEN WAITIN' FOR THIS MOMENT!!
Huh?
Wha?
NOW... TASTE MY VENGEANCE!
OH. I REMEMBER YOU.
THE LOUD CHICK.
NOISY AND VIOLENT.
YOU'RE A REAL CATCH.
On haunches
Twitch Twitch

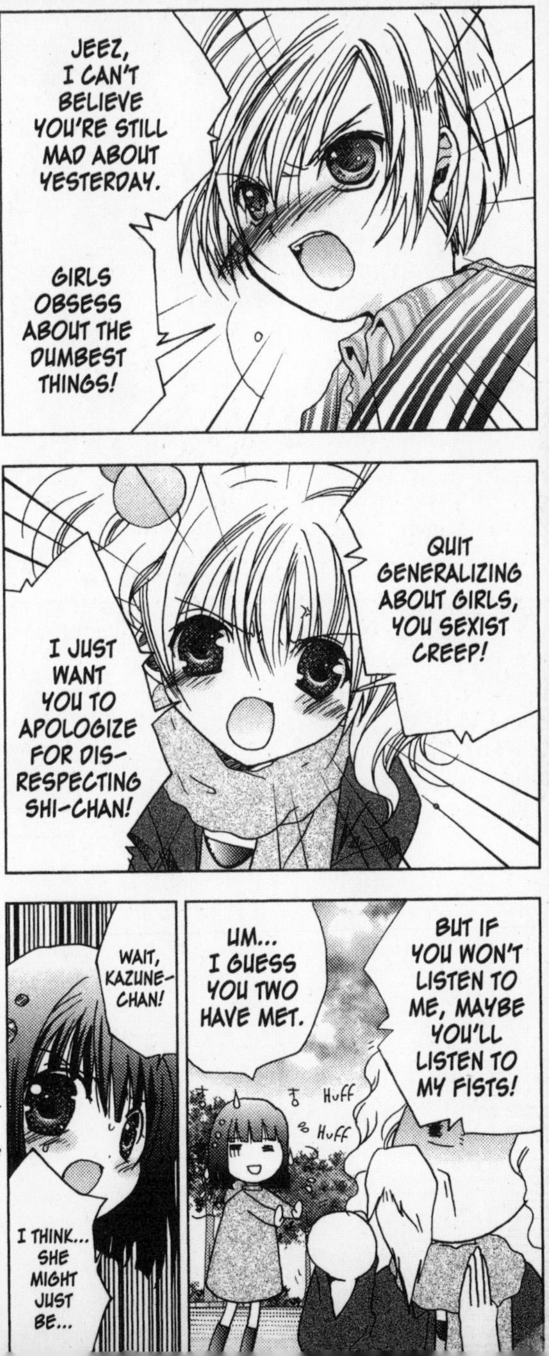
JEEZ, I CAN'T BELIEVE YOU'RE STILL MAD ABOUT YESTERDAY.
GIRLS OBSESS ABOUT THE DUMBEST THINGS!
QUIT GENERALIZING ABOUT GIRLS, YOU SEXIST CREEP!
I JUST WANT YOU TO APOLOGIZE FOR DIS-RESPECTING SHI-CHAN!
BUT IF YOU WON'T LISTEN TO ME, MAYBE YOU'LL LISTEN TO MY FISTS!
UM... I GUESS YOU TWO HAVE MET.
Huff
Huff
WAIT, KAZUNE-CHAN!
I THINK... SHE MIGHT JUST BE...

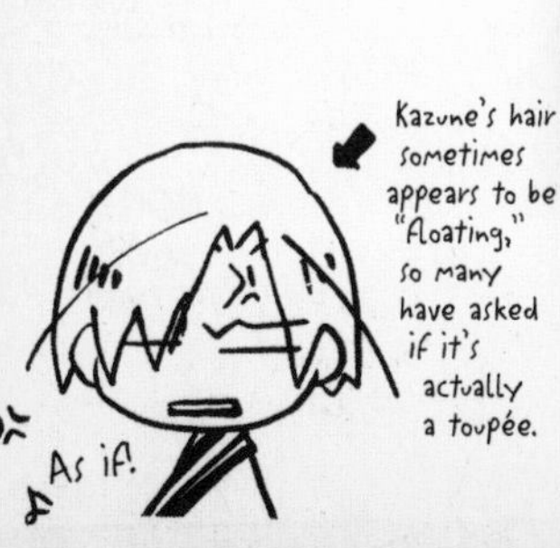
Kazune's hair sometimes appears to be "floating," so many have asked if it's actually a toupée.
As if!

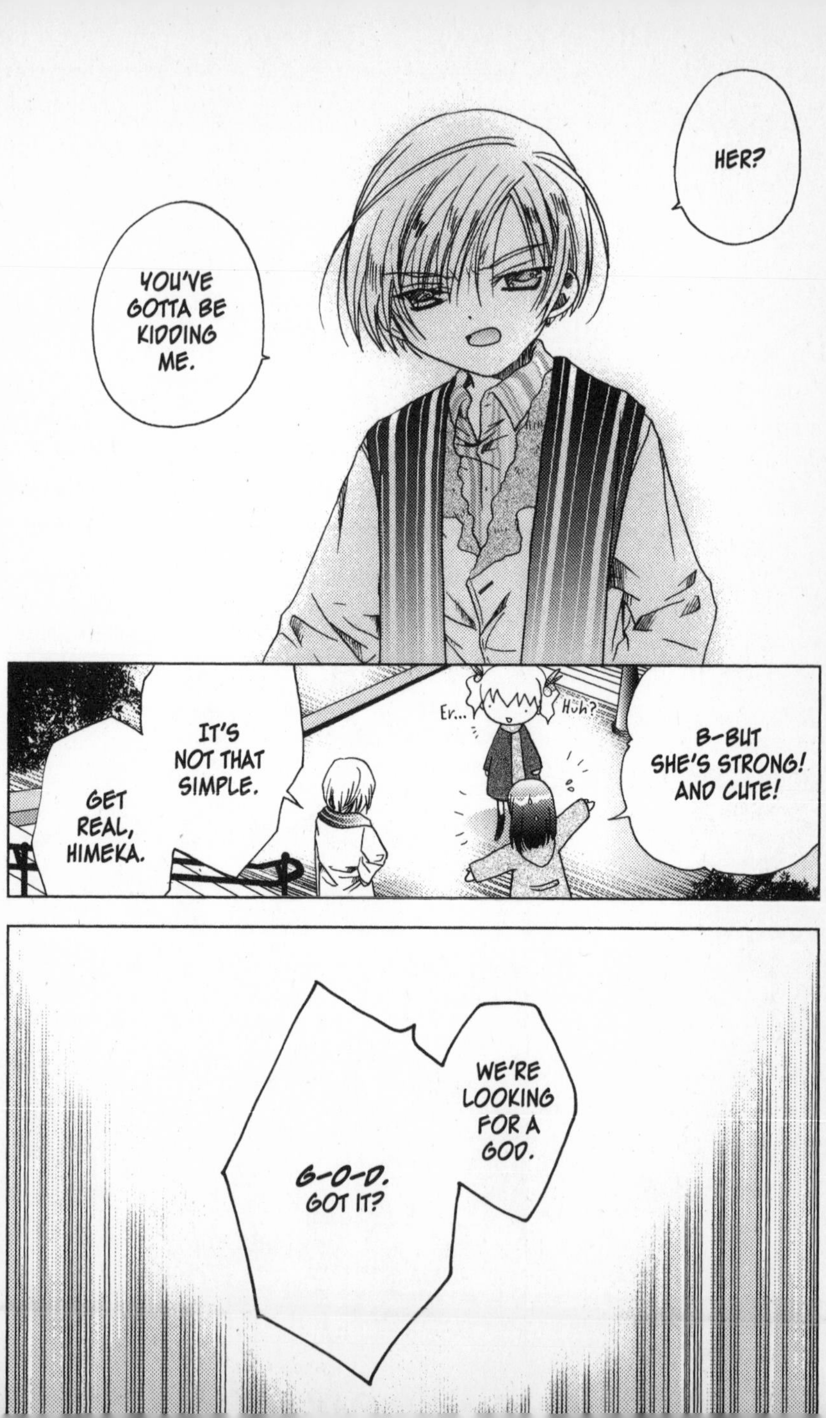
HER?
YOU'VE GOTTA BE KIDDING ME.
B-BUT SHE'S STRONG! AND CUTE!
Huh?
Er...
IT'S NOT THAT SIMPLE.
GET REAL, HIMEKA.
WE'RE LOOKING FOR A GOD.
G-O-D. GOT IT?

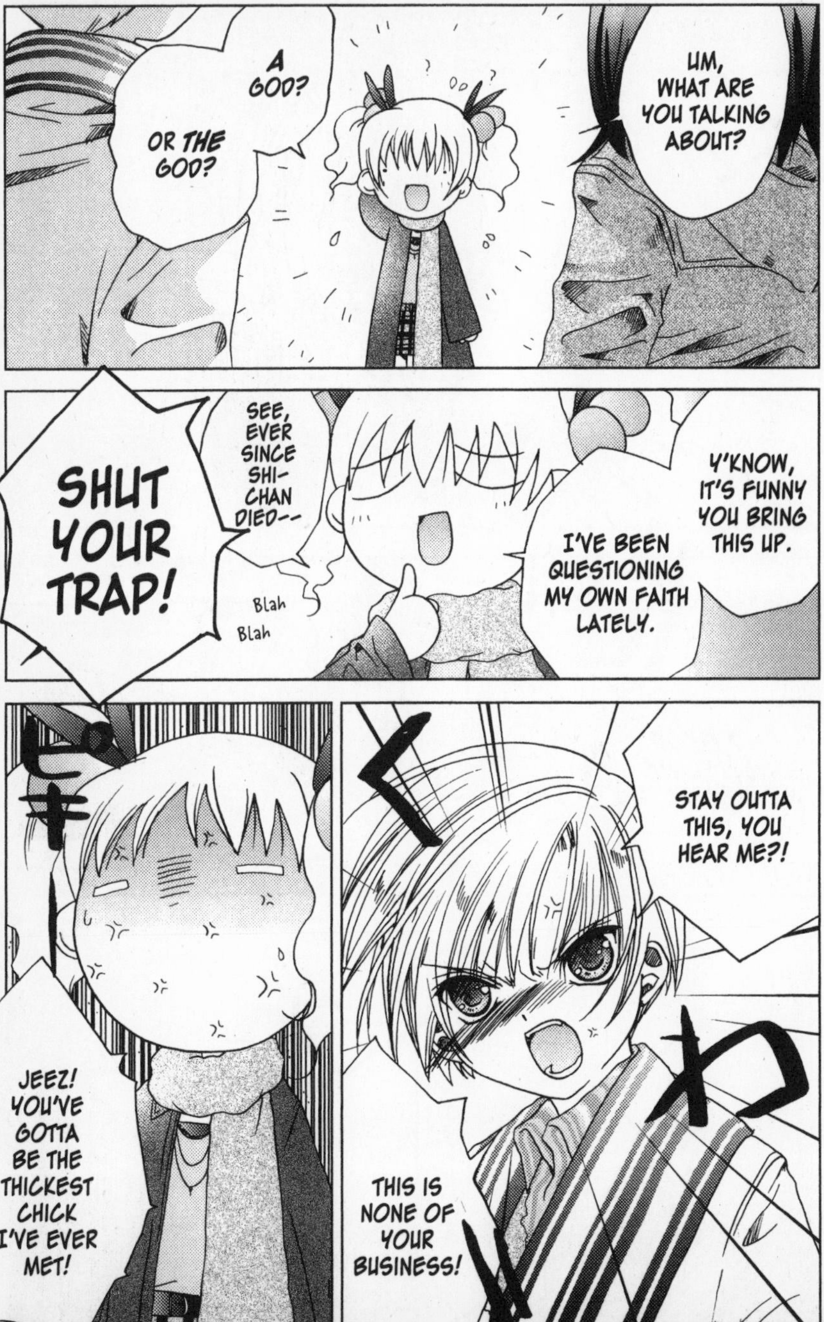
UM, WHAT ARE YOU TALKING ABOUT?
A GOD?
OR THE GOD?
Y'KNOW, IT'S FUNNY YOU BRING THIS UP.
I'VE BEEN QUESTIONING MY OWN FAITH LATELY.
SEE, EVER SINCE SHI-CHAN DIED--
Blah
Blah
SHUT YOUR TRAP!
STAY OUTTA THIS, YOU HEAR ME?!
THIS IS NONE OF YOUR BUSINESS!
JEEZ! YOU'VE GOTTA BE THE THICKEST CHICK I'VE EVER MET!

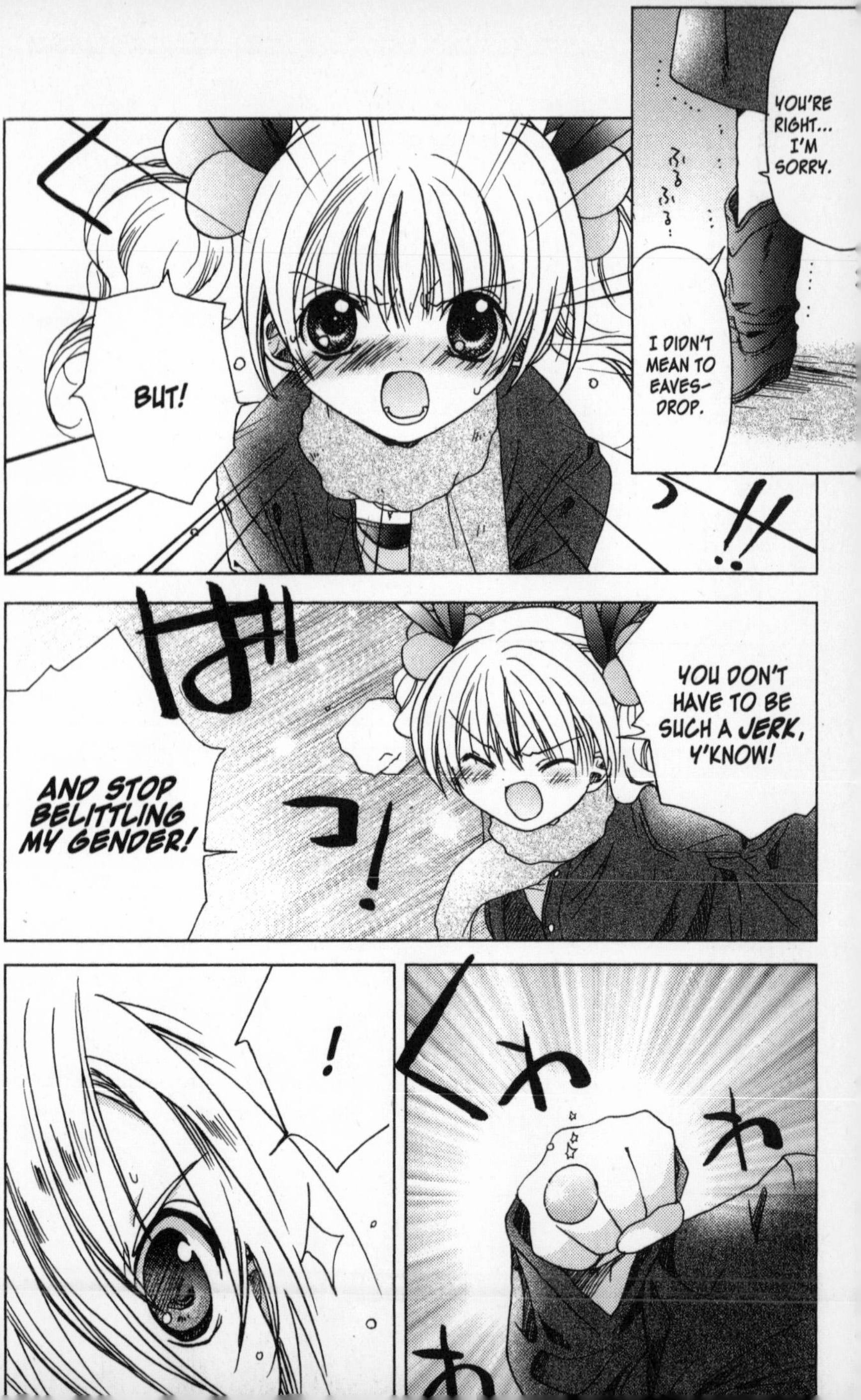
YOU'RE RIGHT... I'M SORRY.
I DIDN'T MEAN TO EAVES-DROP.
BUT!
!!
YOU DON'T HAVE TO BE SUCH A JERK, Y'KNOW!
AND STOP BELITTLING MY GENDER!
!

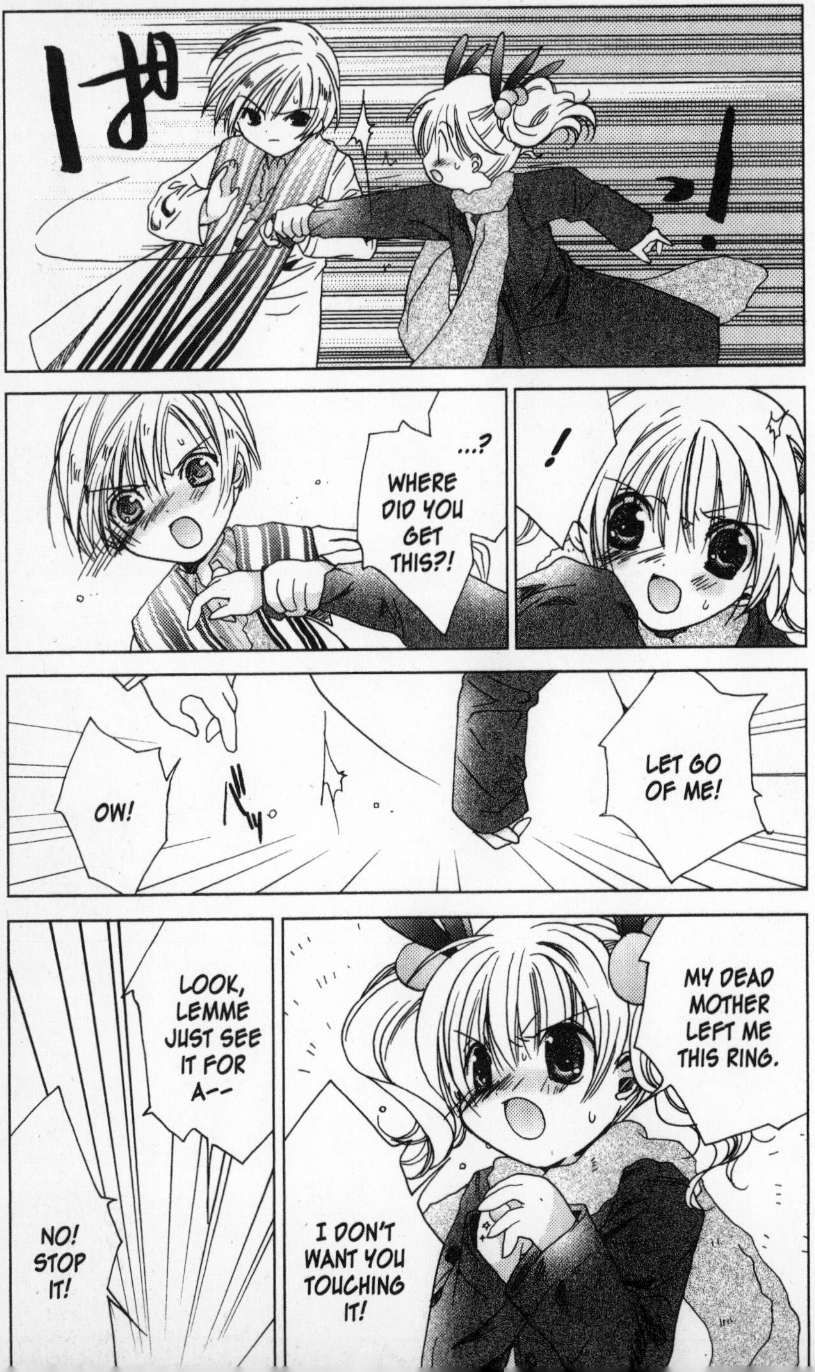
ぱっ!
!
...?
WHERE DID YOU GET THIS?!
LET GO OF ME!
OW!
MY DEAD MOTHER LEFT ME THIS RING.
I DON'T WANT YOU TOUCHING IT!
LOOK, LEMME JUST SEE IT FOR A--
NO! STOP IT!

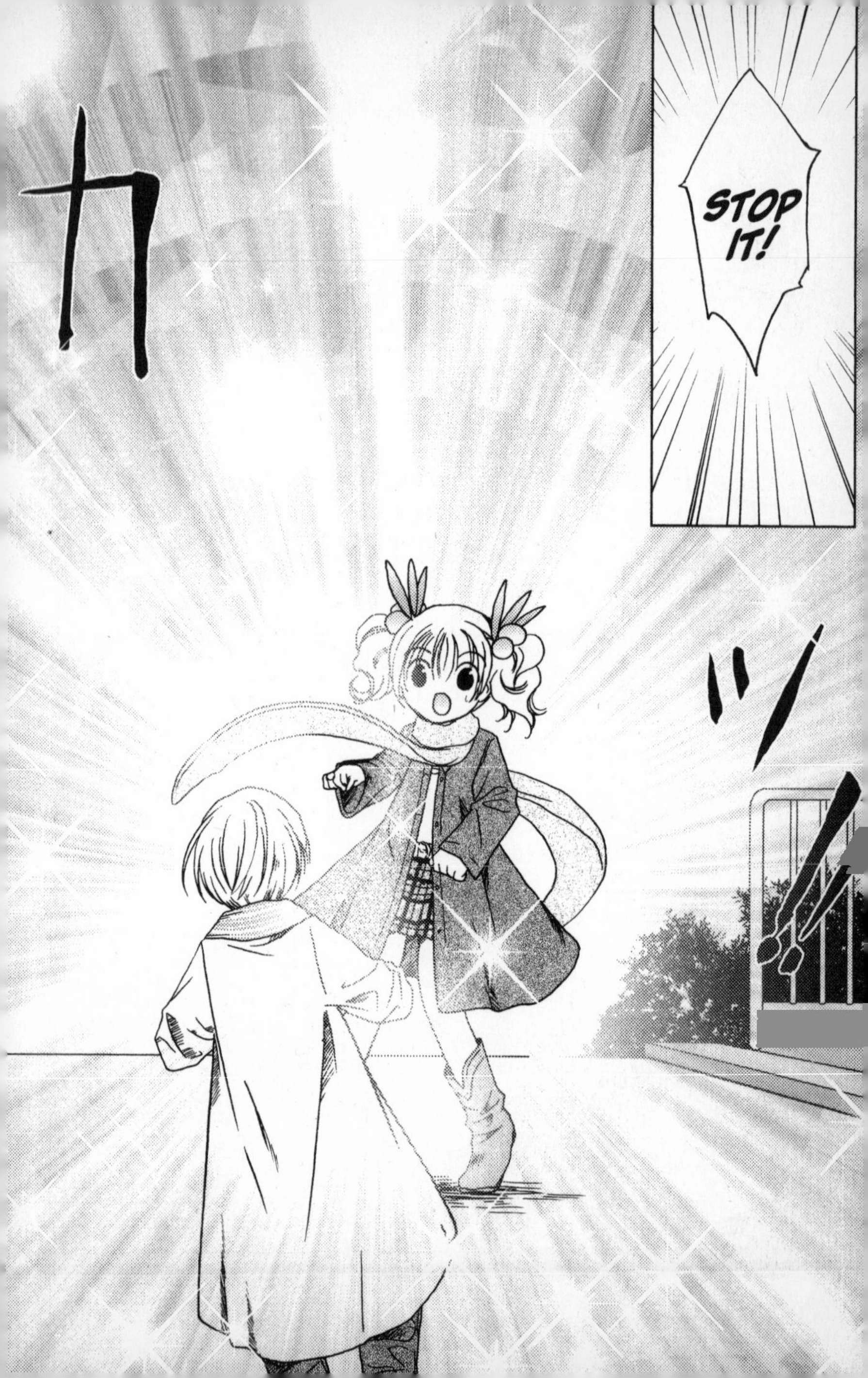
STOP IT!
カッ

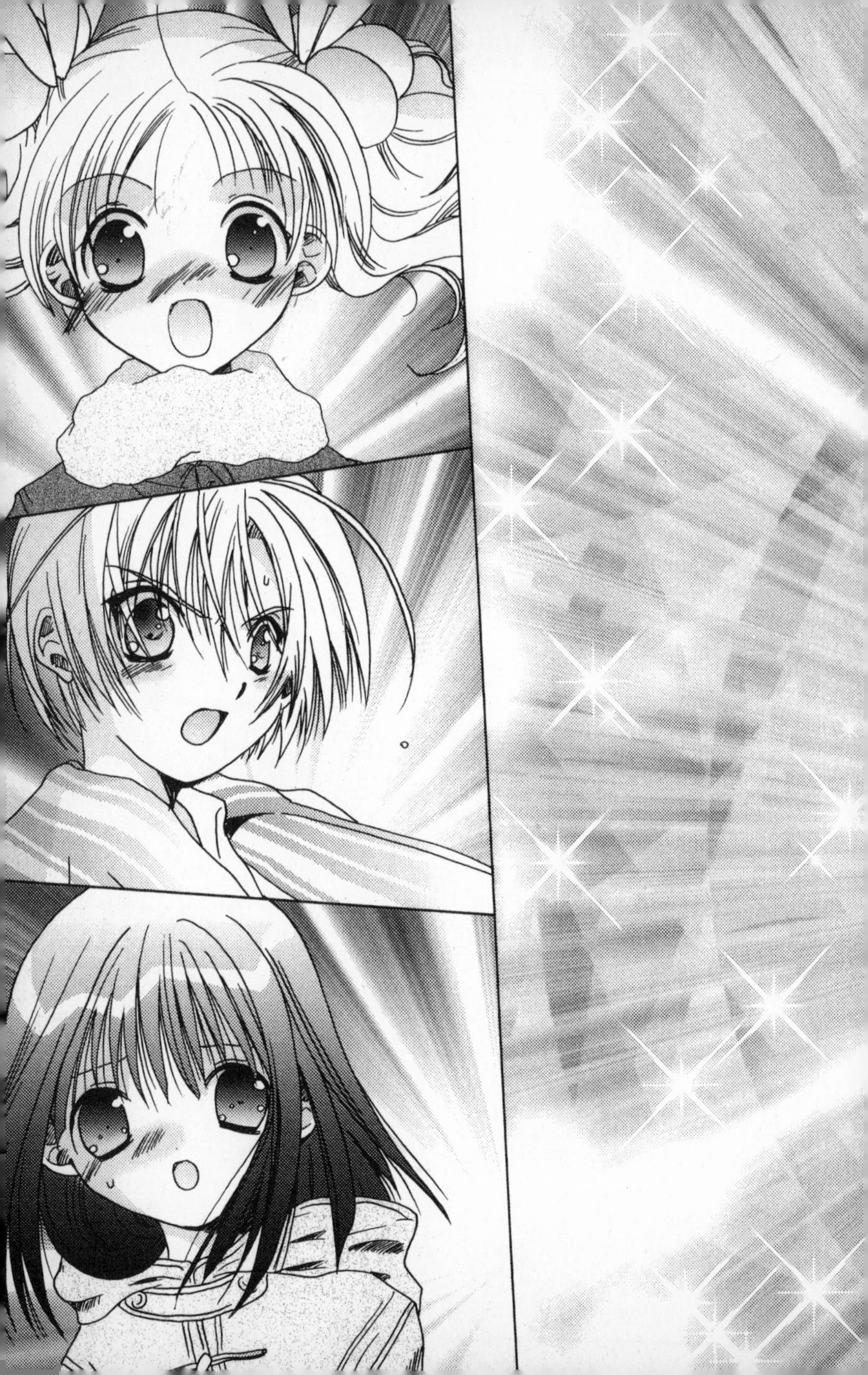

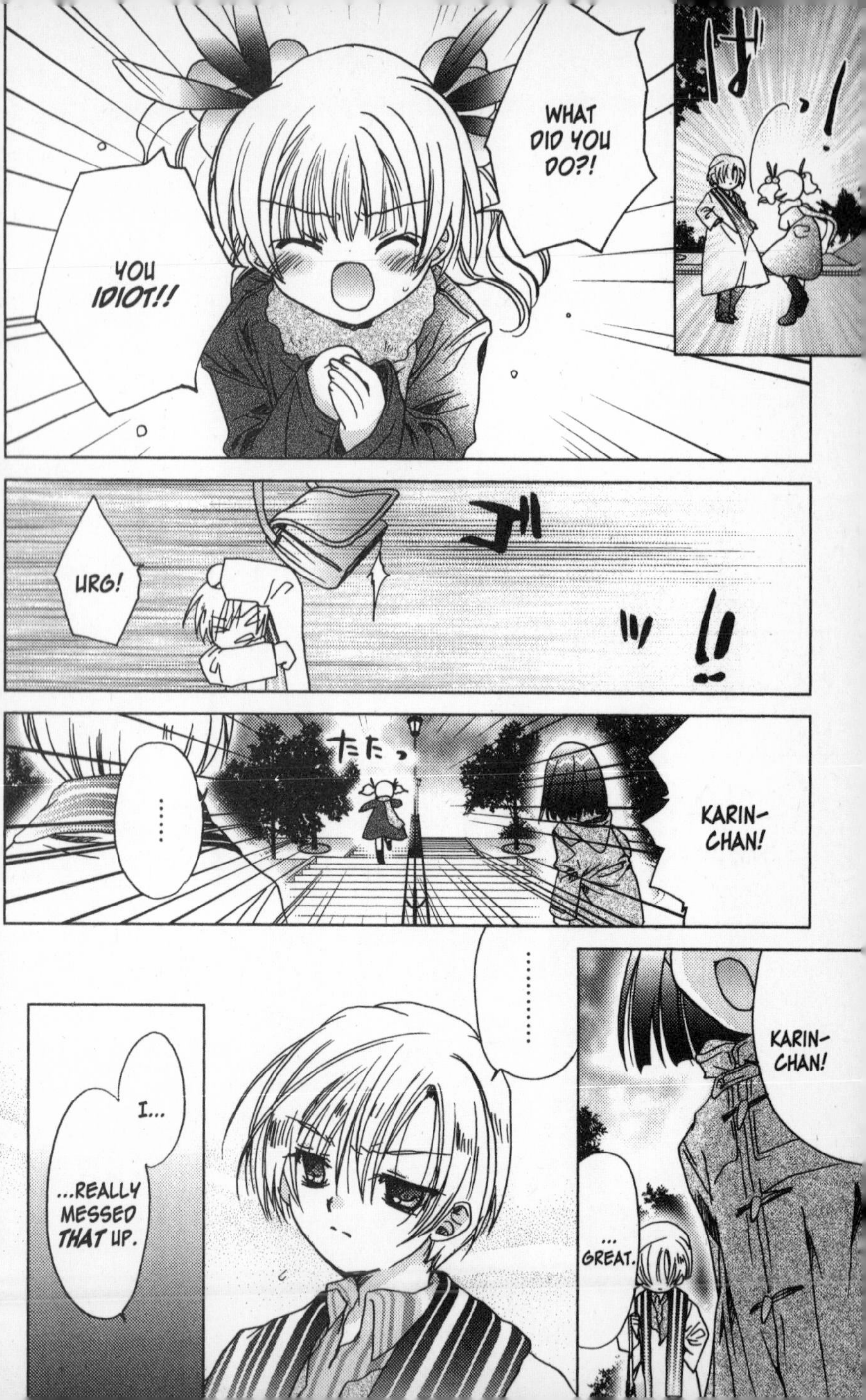
ぱっ!
WHAT DID YOU DO?!
YOU IDIOT!!
ゴッ!!
URG!
KARIN-CHAN!
たたっ
......
KARIN-CHAN!
... GREAT.
......
I...
...REALLY MESSED *THAT* UP.

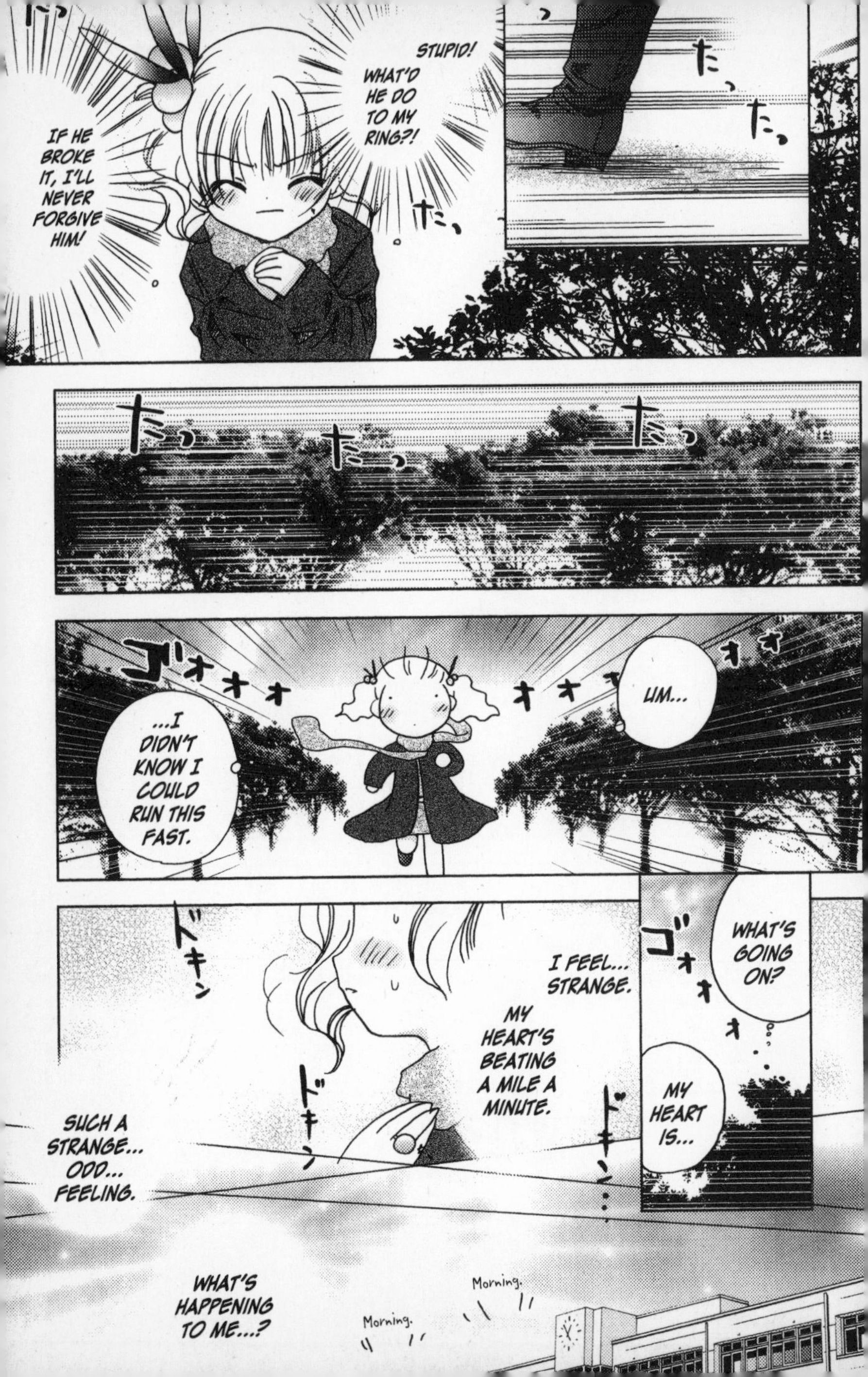
たっ たっ
STUPID!
WHAT'D HE DO TO MY RING?!
IF HE BROKE IT, I'LL NEVER FORGIVE HIM!
たっ
たっ たっ たっ
UM...
...I DIDN'T KNOW I COULD RUN THIS FAST.
WHAT'S GOING ON?
MY HEART IS...
I FEEL... STRANGE.
MY HEART'S BEATING A MILE A MINUTE.
ドキン
SUCH A STRANGE... ODD... FEELING.
Morning.
Morning.
WHAT'S HAPPENING TO ME...?

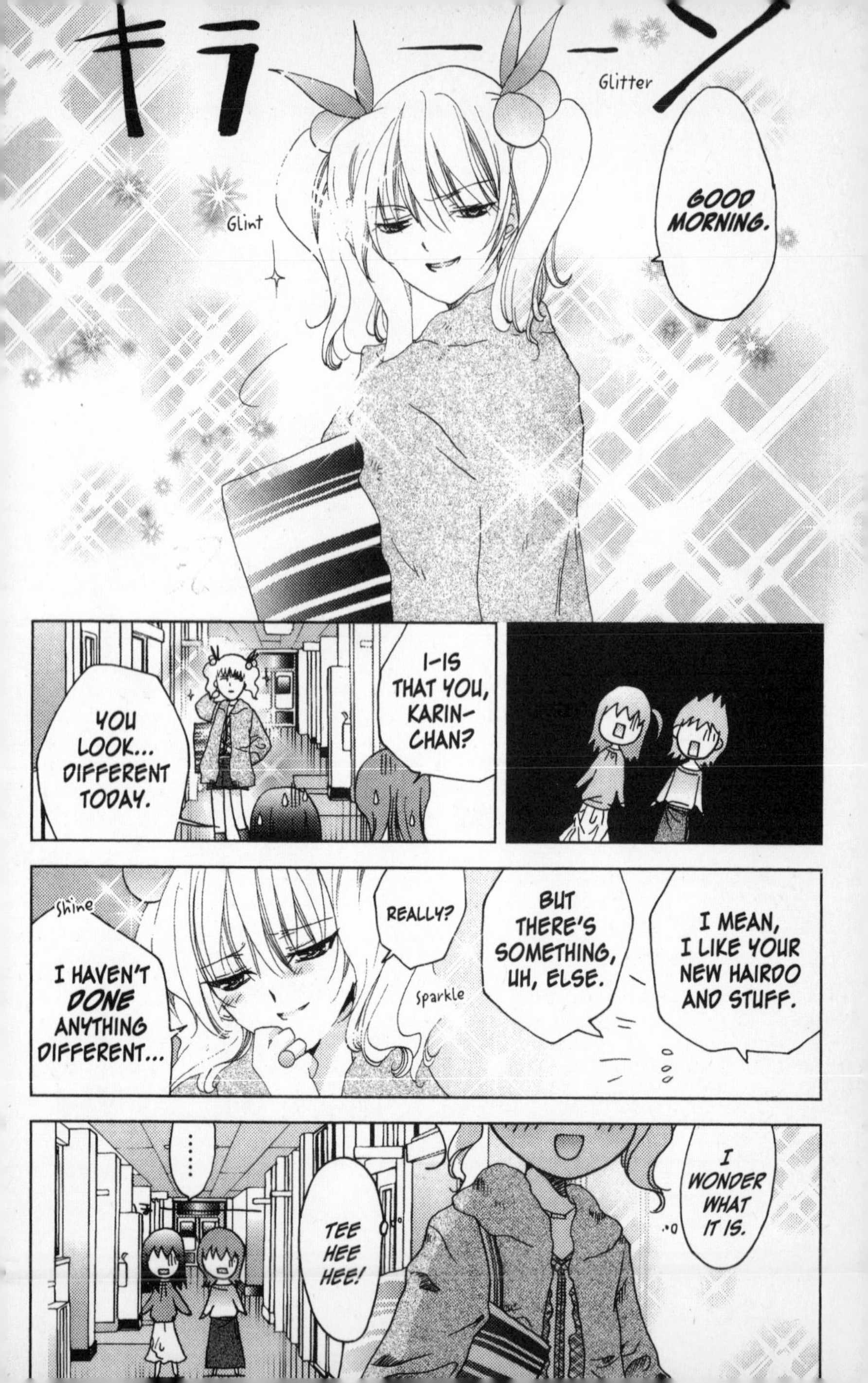
キラーーーン
Glitter
GOOD MORNING.
Glint
I-IS THAT YOU, KARIN-CHAN?
YOU LOOK... DIFFERENT TODAY.
I MEAN, I LIKE YOUR NEW HAIRDO AND STUFF.
BUT THERE'S SOMETHING, UH, ELSE.
REALLY?
Sparkle
Shine
I HAVEN'T DONE ANYTHING DIFFERENT...
I WONDER WHAT IT IS.
TEE HEE HEE!
......

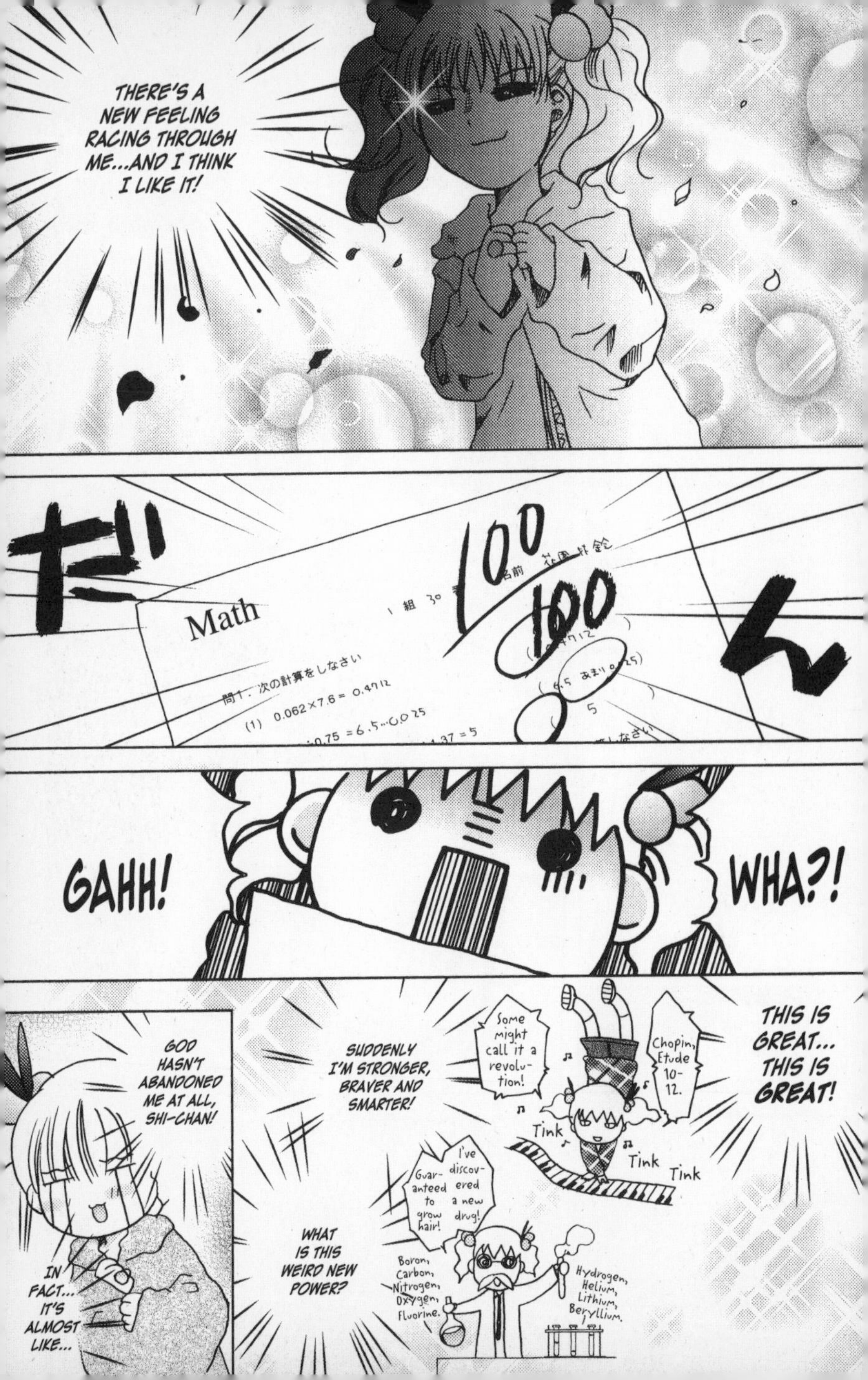
THERE'S A NEW FEELING RACING THROUGH ME...AND I THINK I LIKE IT!
だん
Math
1組
100
名前
問1. 次の計算をしなさい
(1) 0.062×7.6 = 0.4712
WHA?!
GAHH!
THIS IS GREAT... THIS IS GREAT!
Chopin, Etude 10-12.
Some might call it a revolution!
Tink
Tink
Tink
SUDDENLY I'M STRONGER, BRAVER AND SMARTER!
I've discovered a new drug!
Guaranteed to grow hair!
Hydrogen, Helium, Lithium, Beryllium.
Boron, Carbon, Nitrogen, Oxygen, Fluorine.
WHAT IS THIS WEIRD NEW POWER?
GOD HASN'T ABANDONED ME AT ALL, SHI-CHAN!
IN FACT... IT'S ALMOST LIKE...

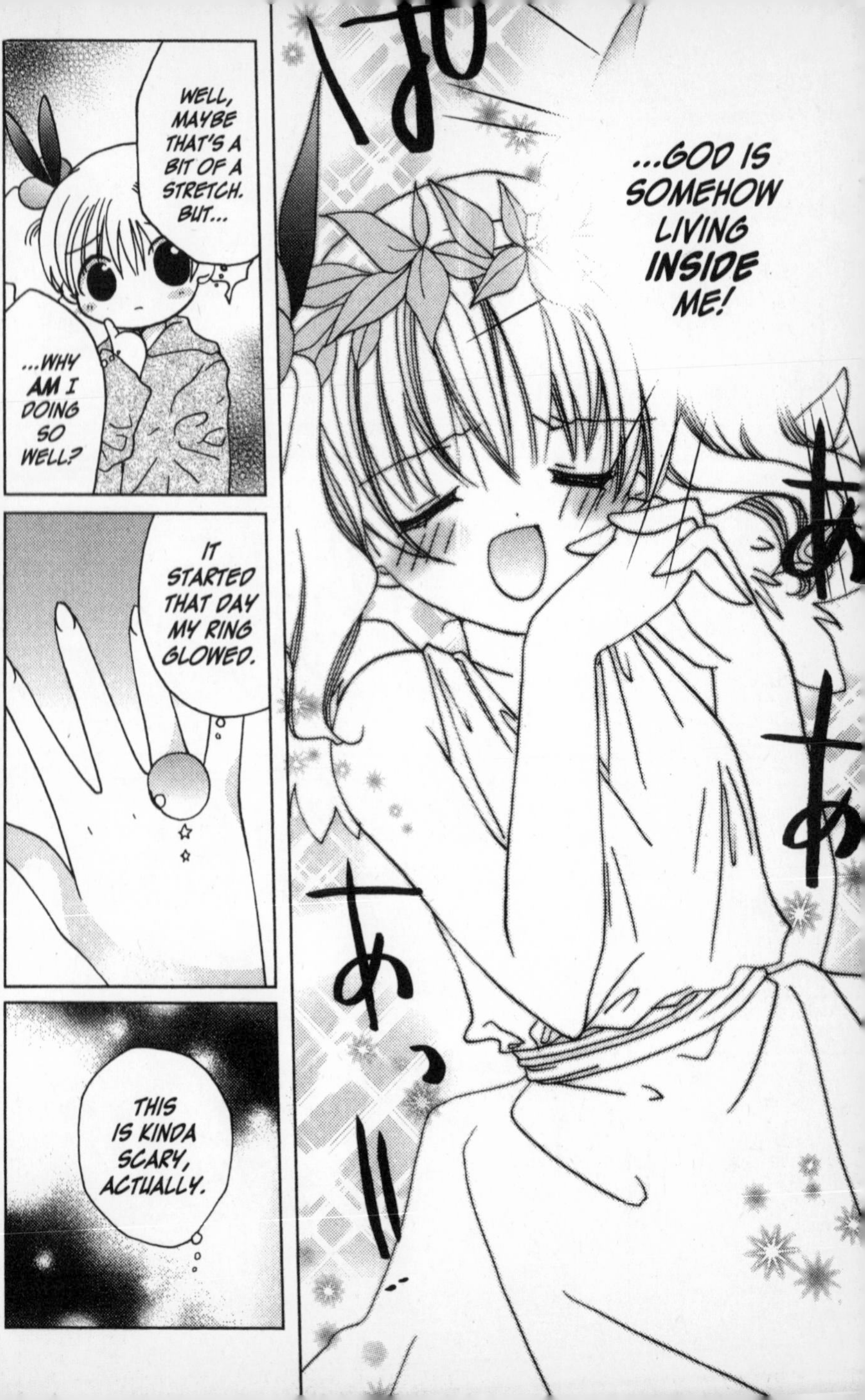
...GOD IS SOMEHOW LIVING INSIDE ME!
ぱあああっ
WELL, MAYBE THAT'S A BIT OF A STRETCH. BUT...
...WHY AM I DOING SO WELL?
IT STARTED THAT DAY MY RING GLOWED.
THIS IS KINDA SCARY, ACTUALLY.

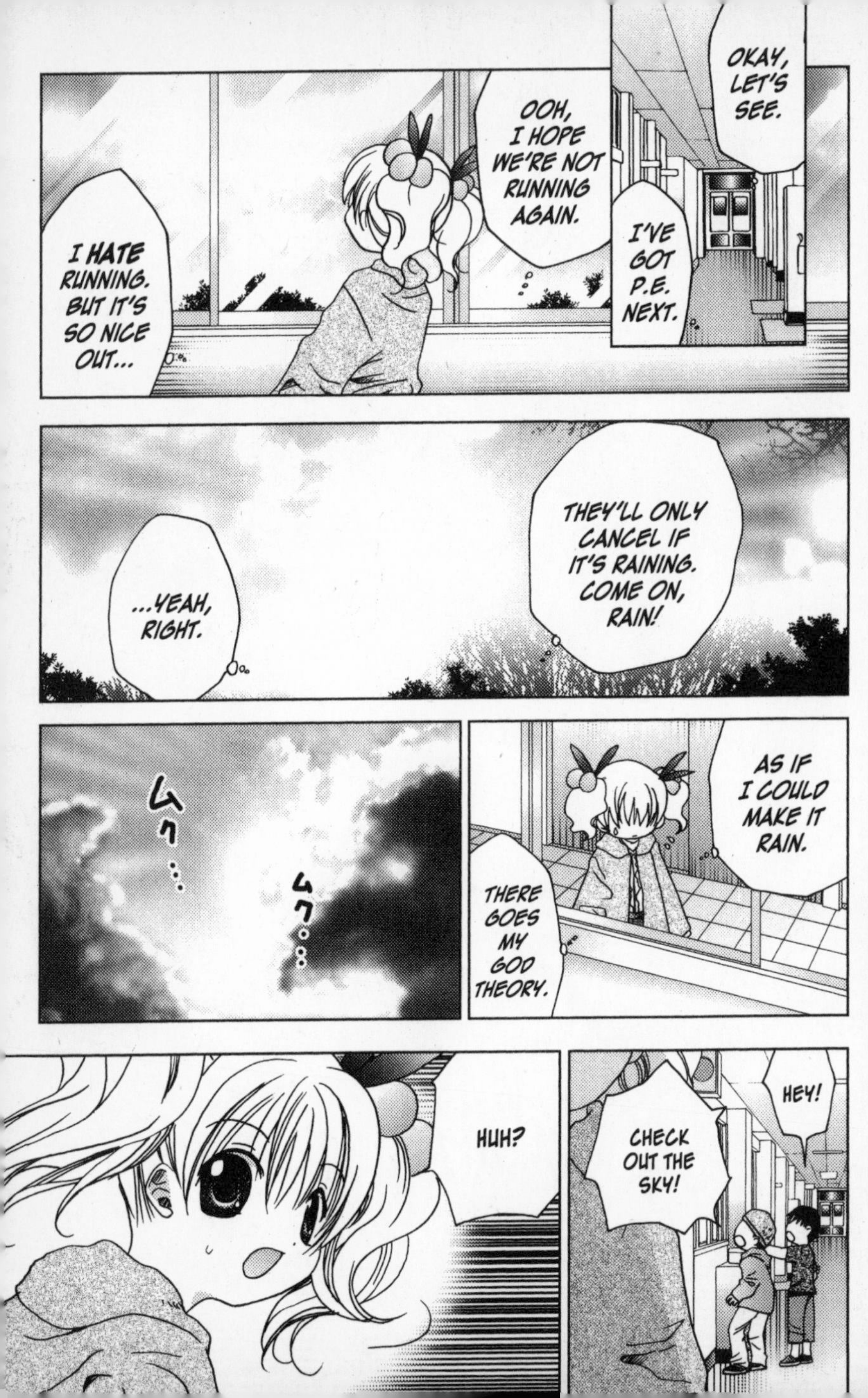
OKAY, LET'S SEE.
I'VE GOT P.E. NEXT.
OOH, I HOPE WE'RE NOT RUNNING AGAIN.
I HATE RUNNING. BUT IT'S SO NICE OUT...
THEY'LL ONLY CANCEL IF IT'S RAINING. COME ON, RAIN!
...YEAH, RIGHT.
AS IF I COULD MAKE IT RAIN.
THERE GOES MY GOD THEORY.
ムク…
ムク…
HEY!
CHECK OUT THE SKY!
HUH?

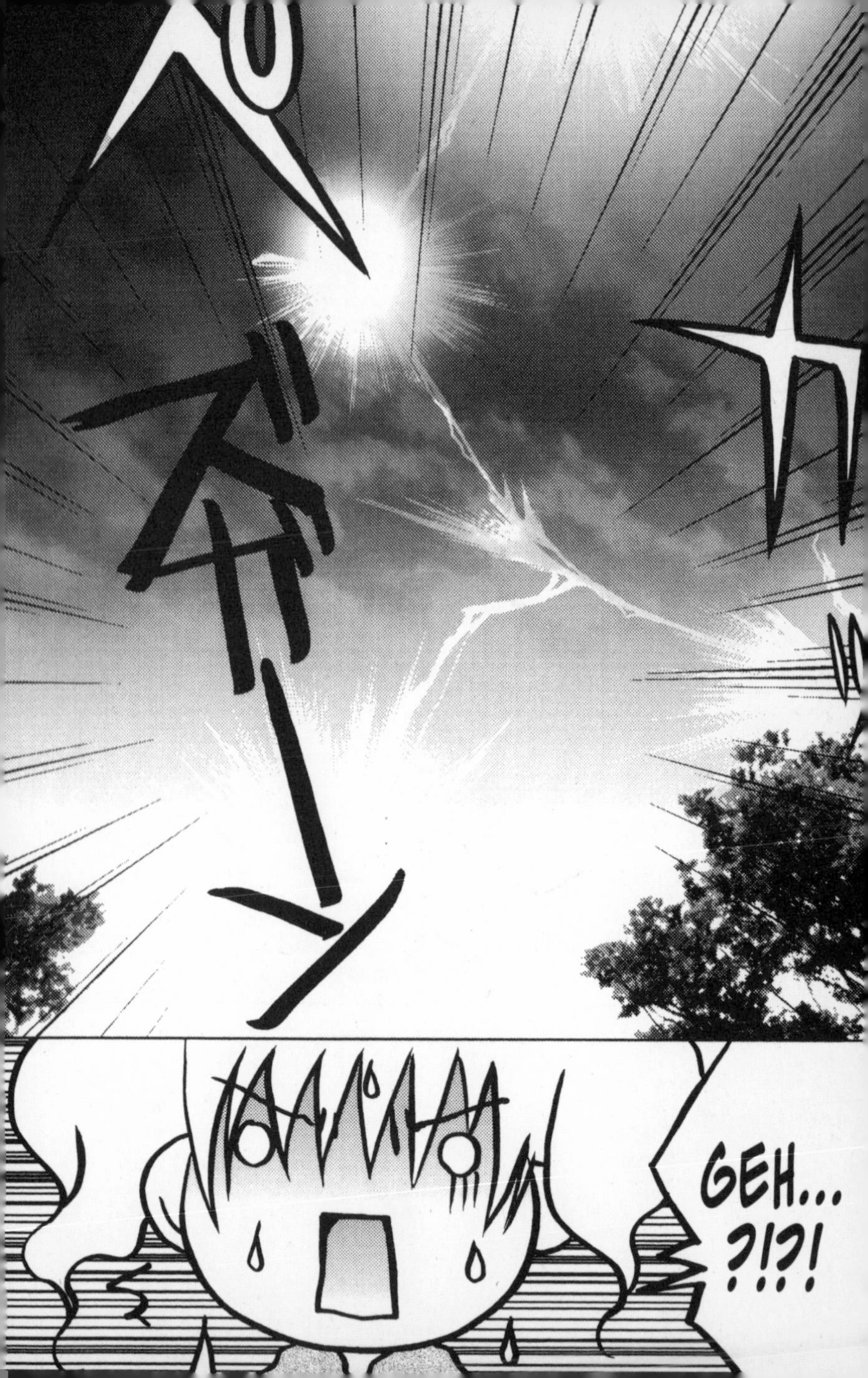
ズガーン
GEH...
?!?!

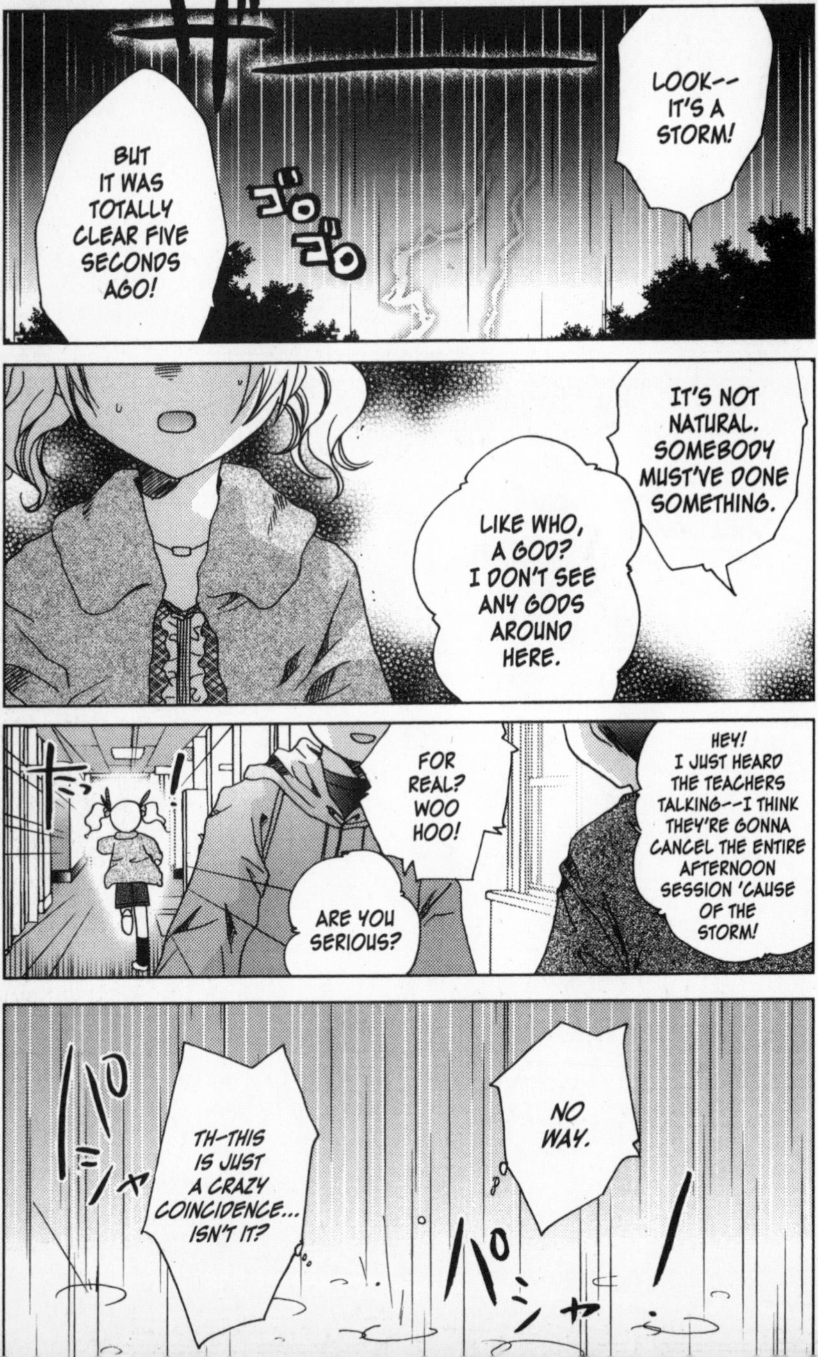
LOOK-- IT'S A STORM!
BUT IT WAS TOTALLY CLEAR FIVE SECONDS AGO!
IT'S NOT NATURAL. SOMEBODY MUST'VE DONE SOMETHING.
LIKE WHO, A GOD? I DON'T SEE ANY GODS AROUND HERE.
HEY! I JUST HEARD THE TEACHERS TALKING--I THINK THEY'RE GONNA CANCEL THE ENTIRE AFTERNOON SESSION 'CAUSE OF THE STORM!
FOR REAL? WOO HOO!
ARE YOU SERIOUS?
NO WAY.
TH-THIS IS JUST A CRAZY COINCIDENCE... ISN'T IT?

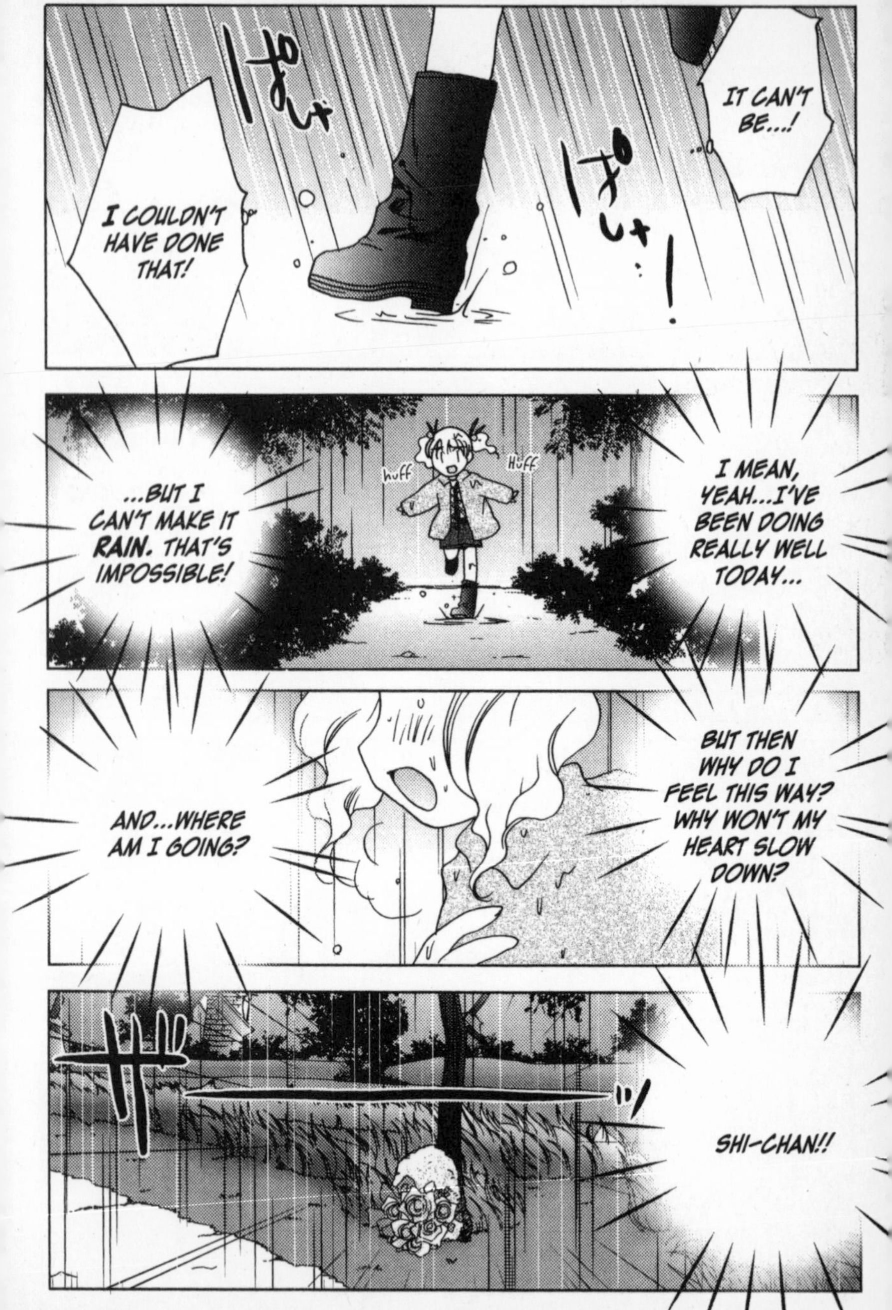
IT CAN'T BE...!
ぱしゃ!
ぱしゃ
I COULDN'T HAVE DONE THAT!
HUFF
huff
I MEAN, YEAH...I'VE BEEN DOING REALLY WELL TODAY...
...BUT I CAN'T MAKE IT RAIN. THAT'S IMPOSSIBLE!
BUT THEN WHY DO I FEEL THIS WAY? WHY WON'T MY HEART SLOW DOWN?
AND...WHERE AM I GOING?
SHI-CHAN!!
ザッ

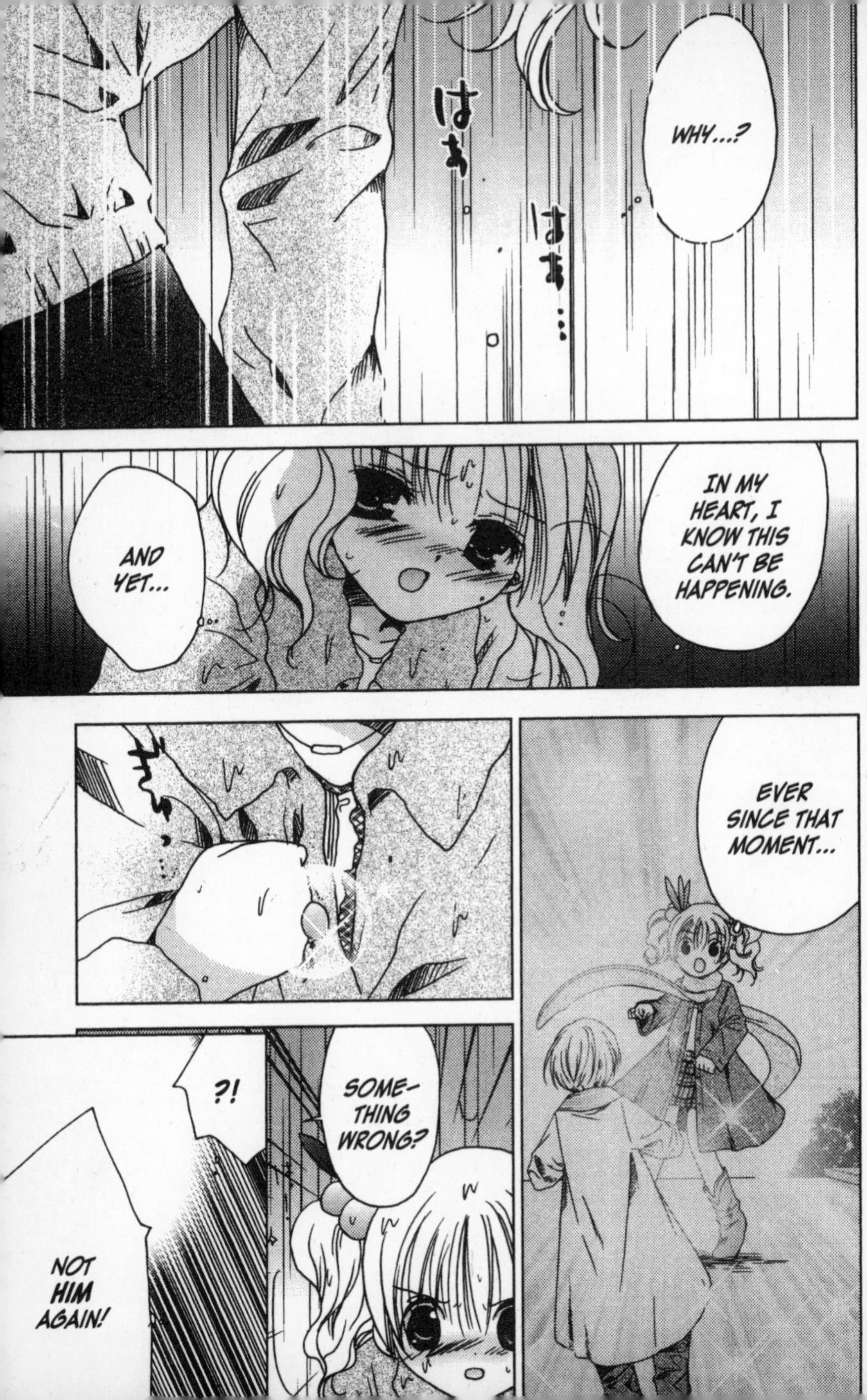
WHY...?
はぁ
はぁ…
IN MY HEART, I KNOW THIS CAN'T BE HAPPENING.
AND YET...
EVER SINCE THAT MOMENT...
SOME-THING WRONG?
?!
NOT HIM AGAIN!

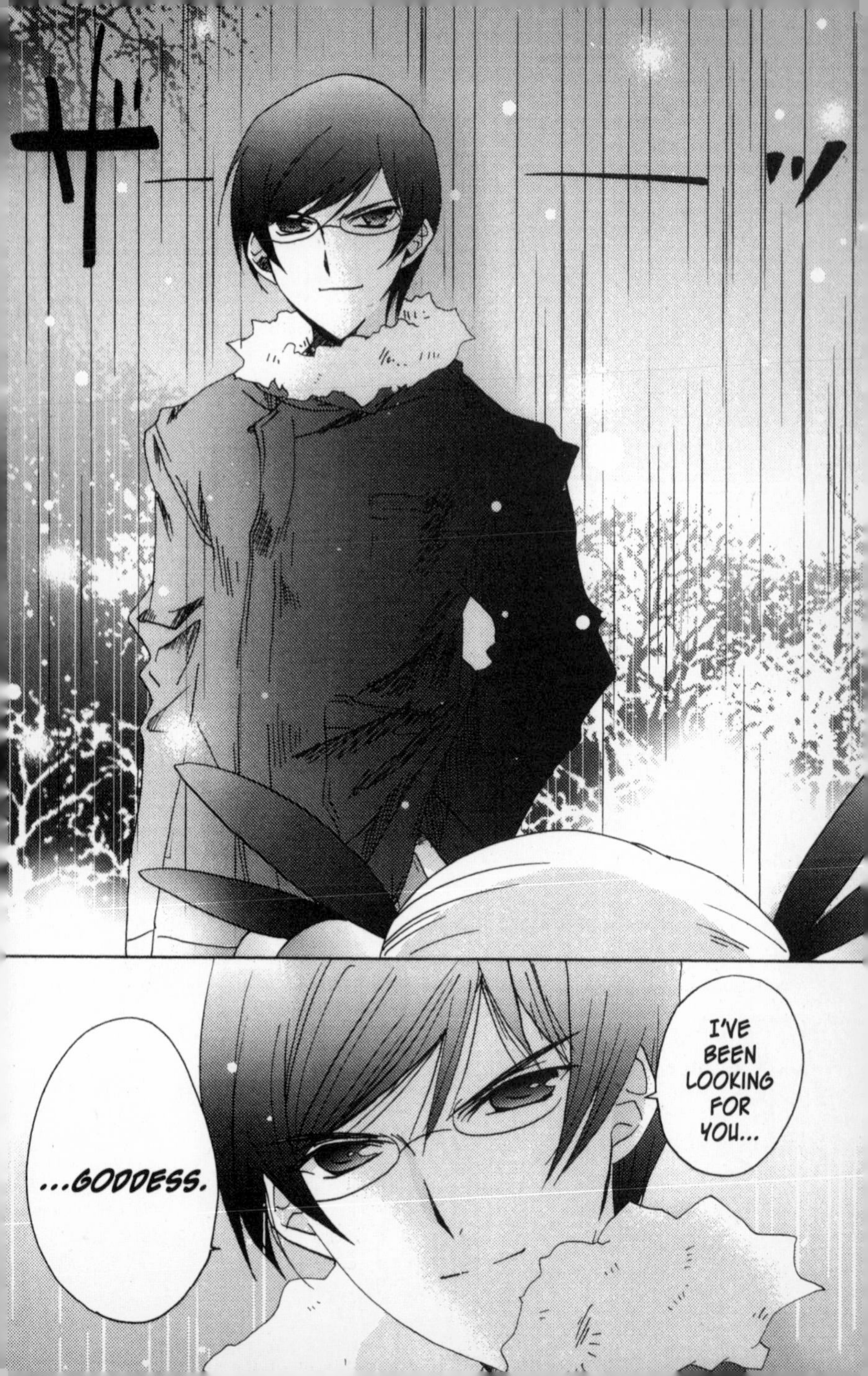
ザーッ
I'VE BEEN LOOKING FOR YOU...
...GODDESS.

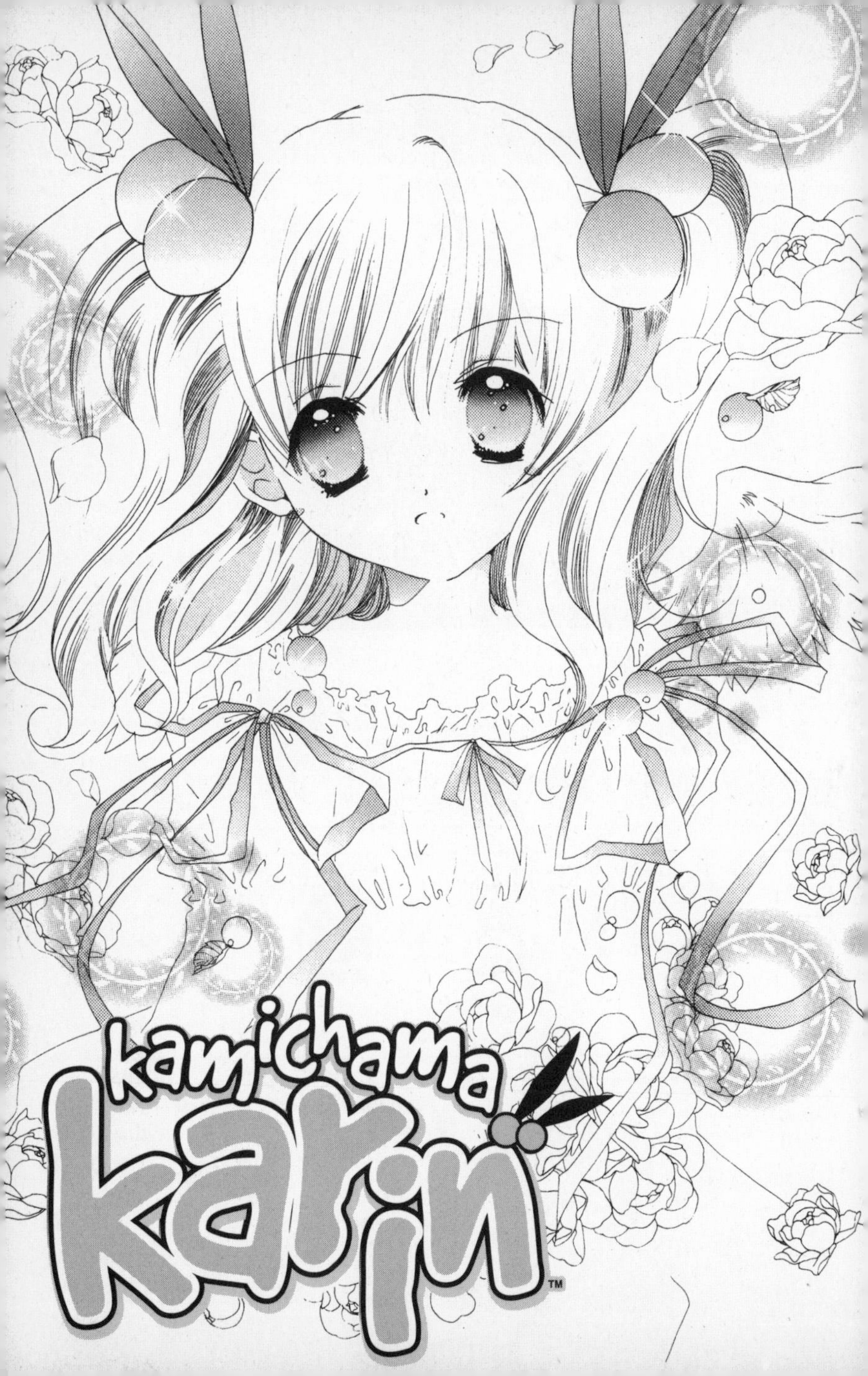
kamichama
karin™

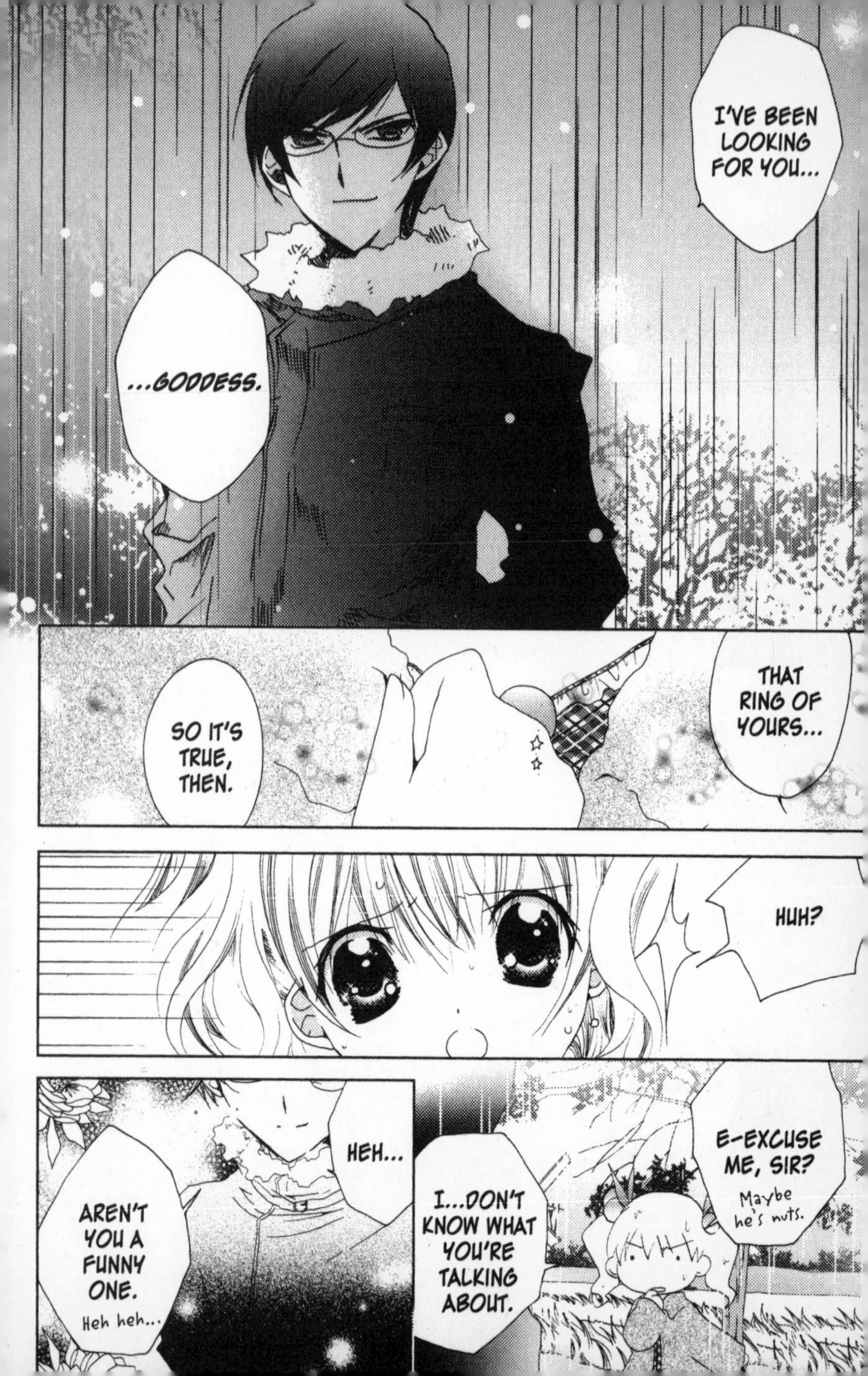
I'VE BEEN LOOKING FOR YOU...
...GODDESS.
THAT RING OF YOURS...
SO IT'S TRUE, THEN.
HUH?
E-EXCUSE ME, SIR?
Maybe he's nuts.
I...DON'T KNOW WHAT YOU'RE TALKING ABOUT.
HEH...
AREN'T YOU A FUNNY ONE.
Heh heh...

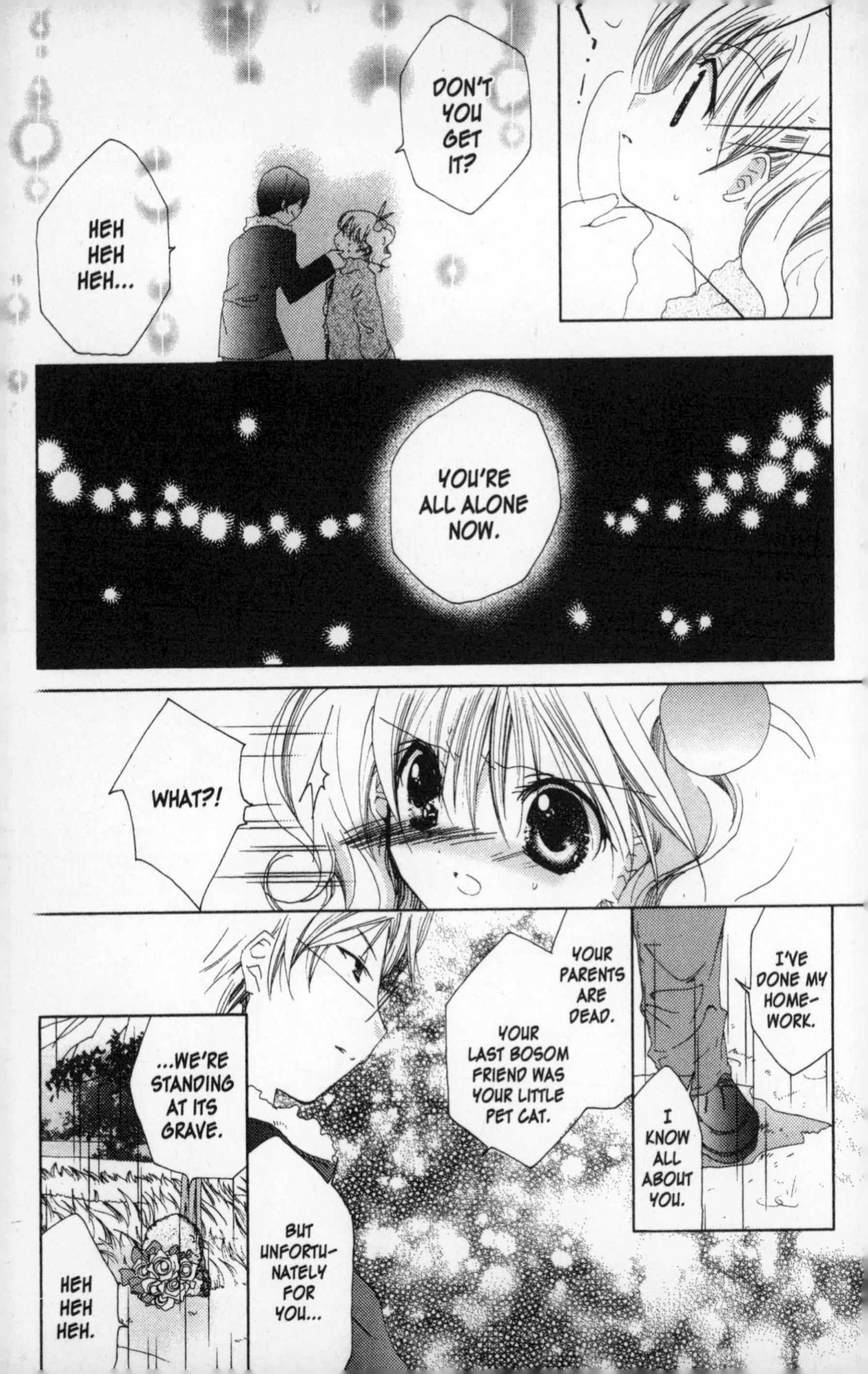
DON'T YOU GET IT?
HEH HEH HEH...
YOU'RE ALL ALONE NOW.
WHAT?!
I'VE DONE MY HOME-WORK.
I KNOW ALL ABOUT YOU.
YOUR PARENTS ARE DEAD.
YOUR LAST BOSOM FRIEND WAS YOUR LITTLE PET CAT.
BUT UNFORTU-NATELY FOR YOU...
...WE'RE STANDING AT ITS GRAVE.
HEH HEH HEH.

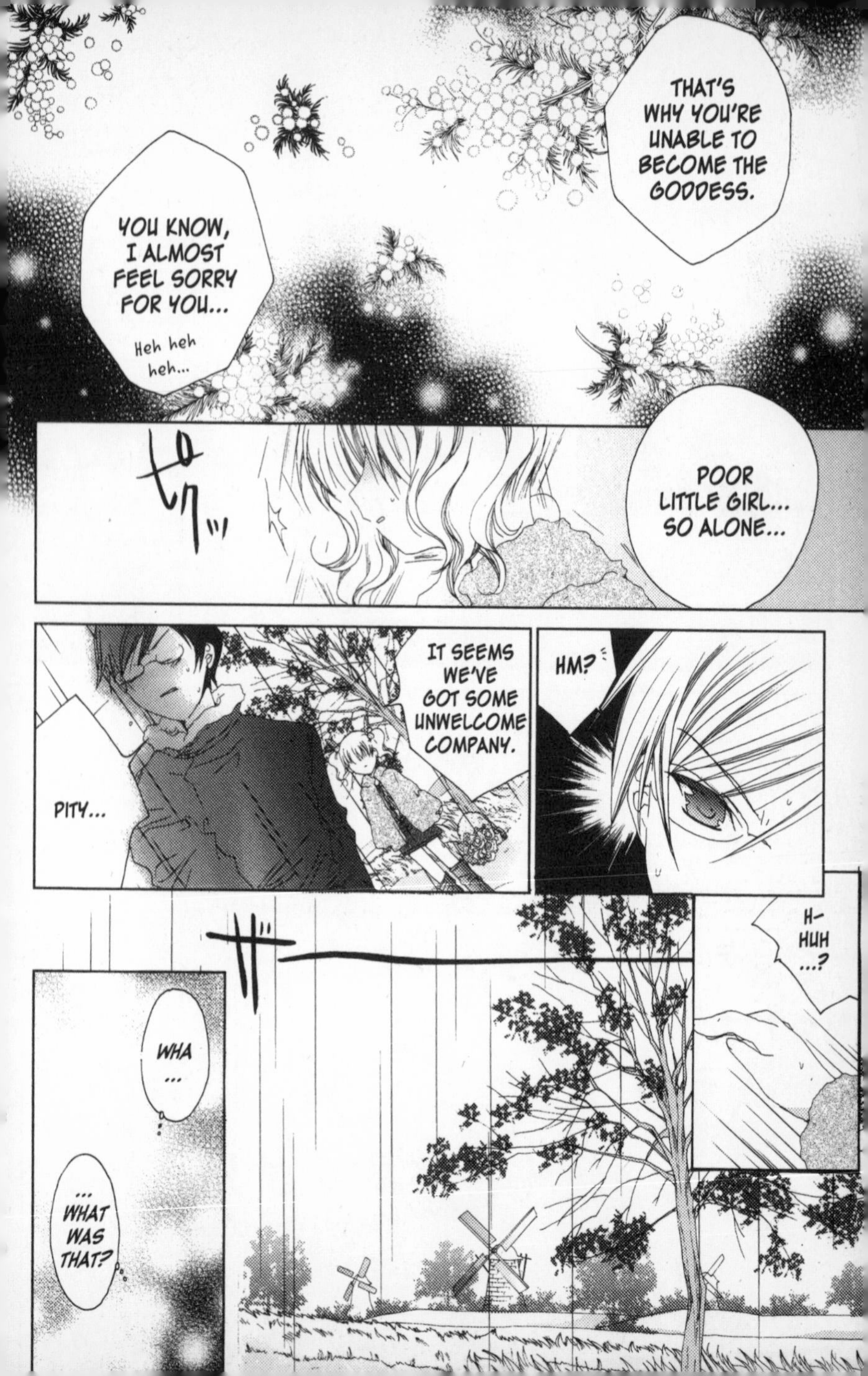
THAT'S WHY YOU'RE UNABLE TO BECOME THE GODDESS.
YOU KNOW, I ALMOST FEEL SORRY FOR YOU...
Heh heh heh...
POOR LITTLE GIRL... SO ALONE...
ピクッ
HM?
IT SEEMS WE'VE GOT SOME UNWELCOME COMPANY.
PITY...
H-HUH ...?
ザー
WHA ...
... WHAT WAS THAT?

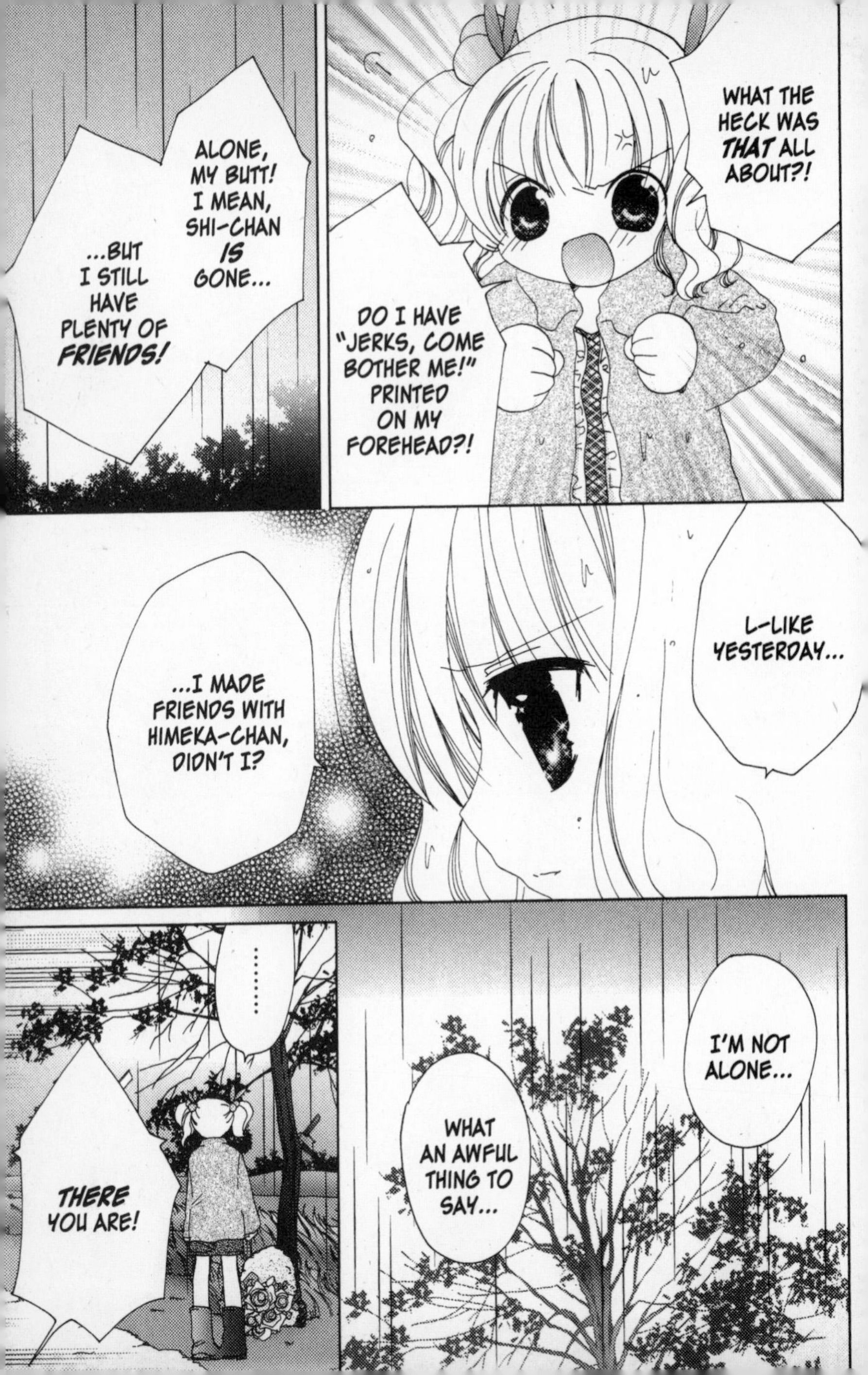
WHAT THE HECK WAS *THAT* ALL ABOUT?!
DO I HAVE "JERKS, COME BOTHER ME!" PRINTED ON MY FOREHEAD?!
ALONE, MY BUTT! I MEAN, SHI-CHAN *IS* GONE...
...BUT I STILL HAVE PLENTY OF *FRIENDS!*
L-LIKE YESTERDAY...
...I MADE FRIENDS WITH HIMEKA-CHAN, DIDN'T I?
I'M NOT ALONE...
WHAT AN AWFUL THING TO SAY...
......
THERE YOU ARE!

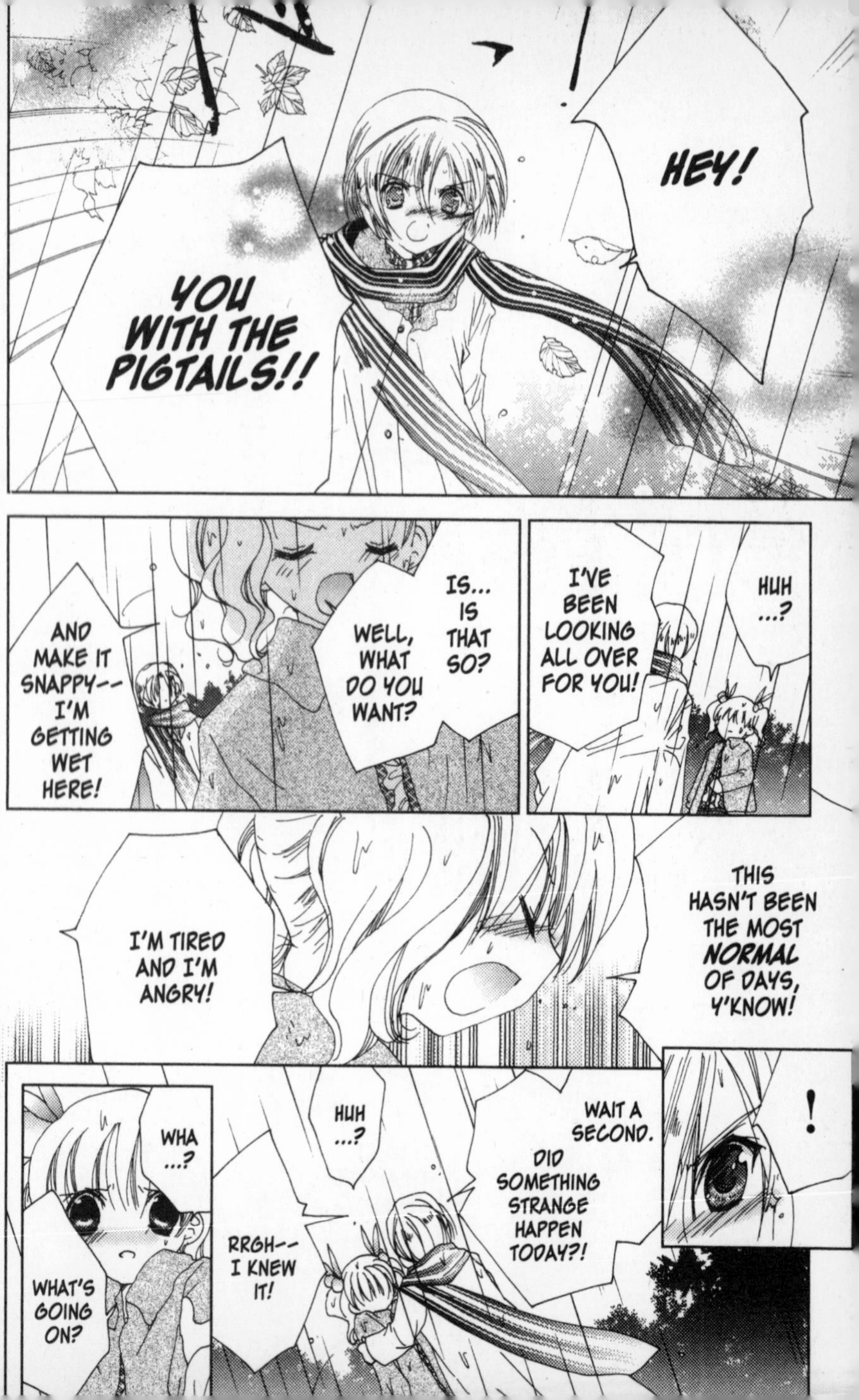
HEY!
YOU WITH THE PIGTAILS!!
HUH ...?
I'VE BEEN LOOKING ALL OVER FOR YOU!
IS... IS THAT SO?
WELL, WHAT DO YOU WANT?
AND MAKE IT SNAPPY-- I'M GETTING WET HERE!
THIS HASN'T BEEN THE MOST NORMAL OF DAYS, Y'KNOW!
I'M TIRED AND I'M ANGRY!
!
WAIT A SECOND.
DID SOMETHING STRANGE HAPPEN TODAY?!
HUH ...?
RRGH-- I KNEW IT!
WHA ...?
WHAT'S GOING ON?

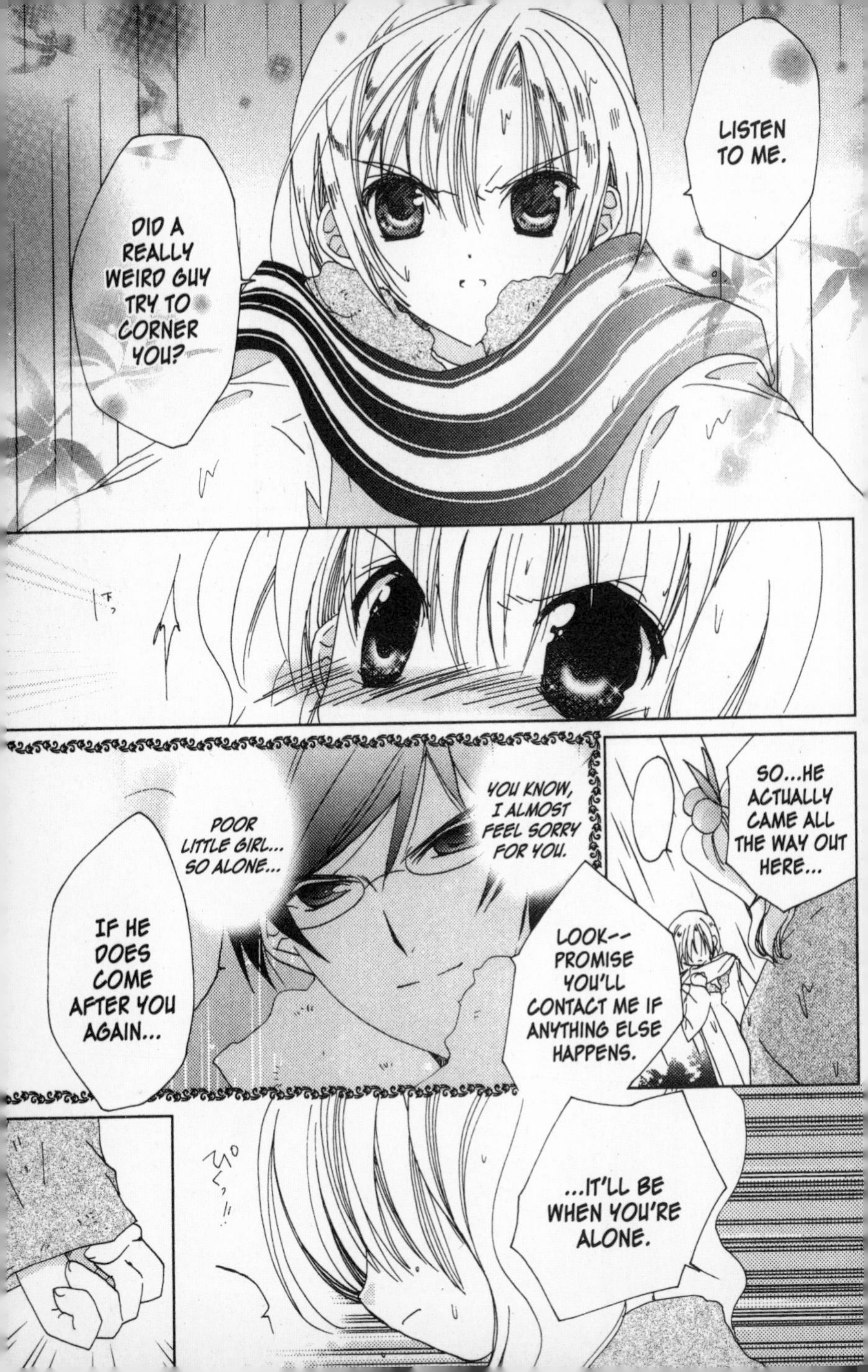
LISTEN TO ME.
DID A REALLY WEIRD GUY TRY TO CORNER YOU?
SO...HE ACTUALLY CAME ALL THE WAY OUT HERE...
LOOK--PROMISE YOU'LL CONTACT ME IF ANYTHING ELSE HAPPENS.
YOU KNOW, I ALMOST FEEL SORRY FOR YOU.
POOR LITTLE GIRL... SO ALONE...
IF HE DOES COME AFTER YOU AGAIN...
...IT'LL BE WHEN YOU'RE ALONE.

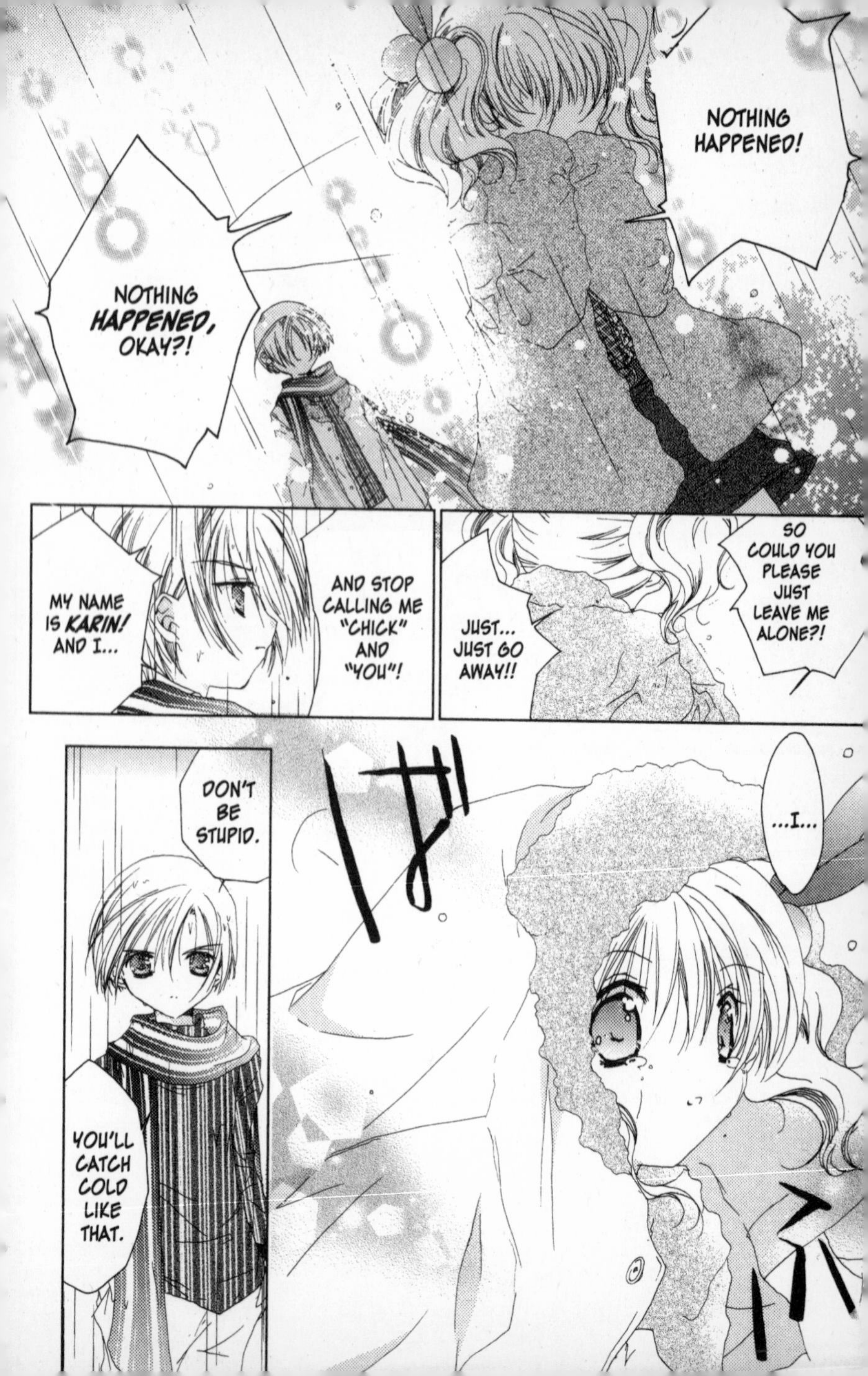
NOTHING HAPPENED!
NOTHING HAPPENED, OKAY?!
SO COULD YOU PLEASE JUST LEAVE ME ALONE?!
JUST... JUST GO AWAY!!
AND STOP CALLING ME "CHICK" AND "YOU"!
MY NAME IS KARIN! AND I...
...I...
DON'T BE STUPID.
YOU'LL CATCH COLD LIKE THAT.

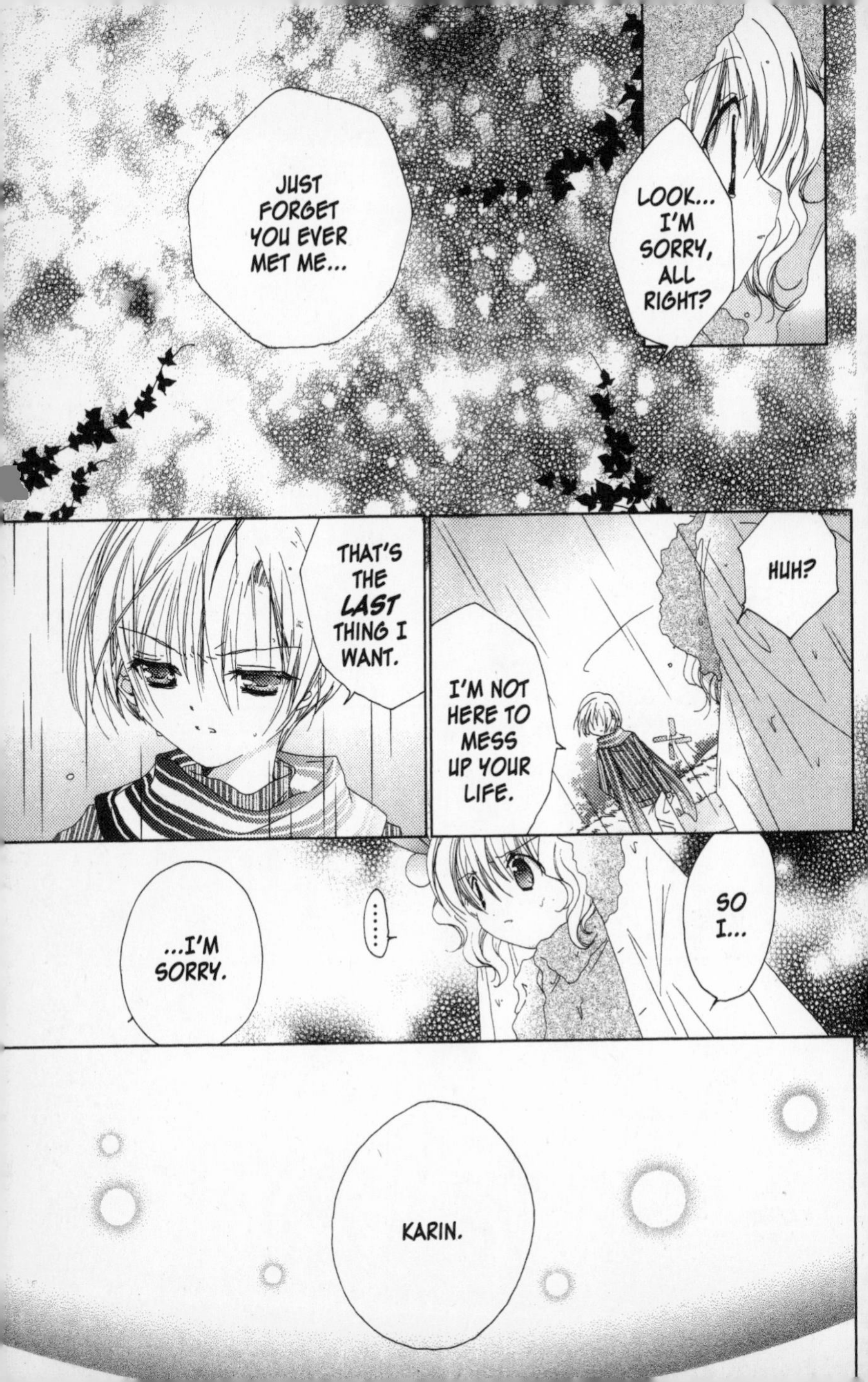
LOOK... I'M SORRY, ALL RIGHT?
JUST FORGET YOU EVER MET ME...
HUH?
I'M NOT HERE TO MESS UP YOUR LIFE.
THAT'S THE *LAST* THING I WANT.
SO I...
......
...I'M SORRY.
KARIN.

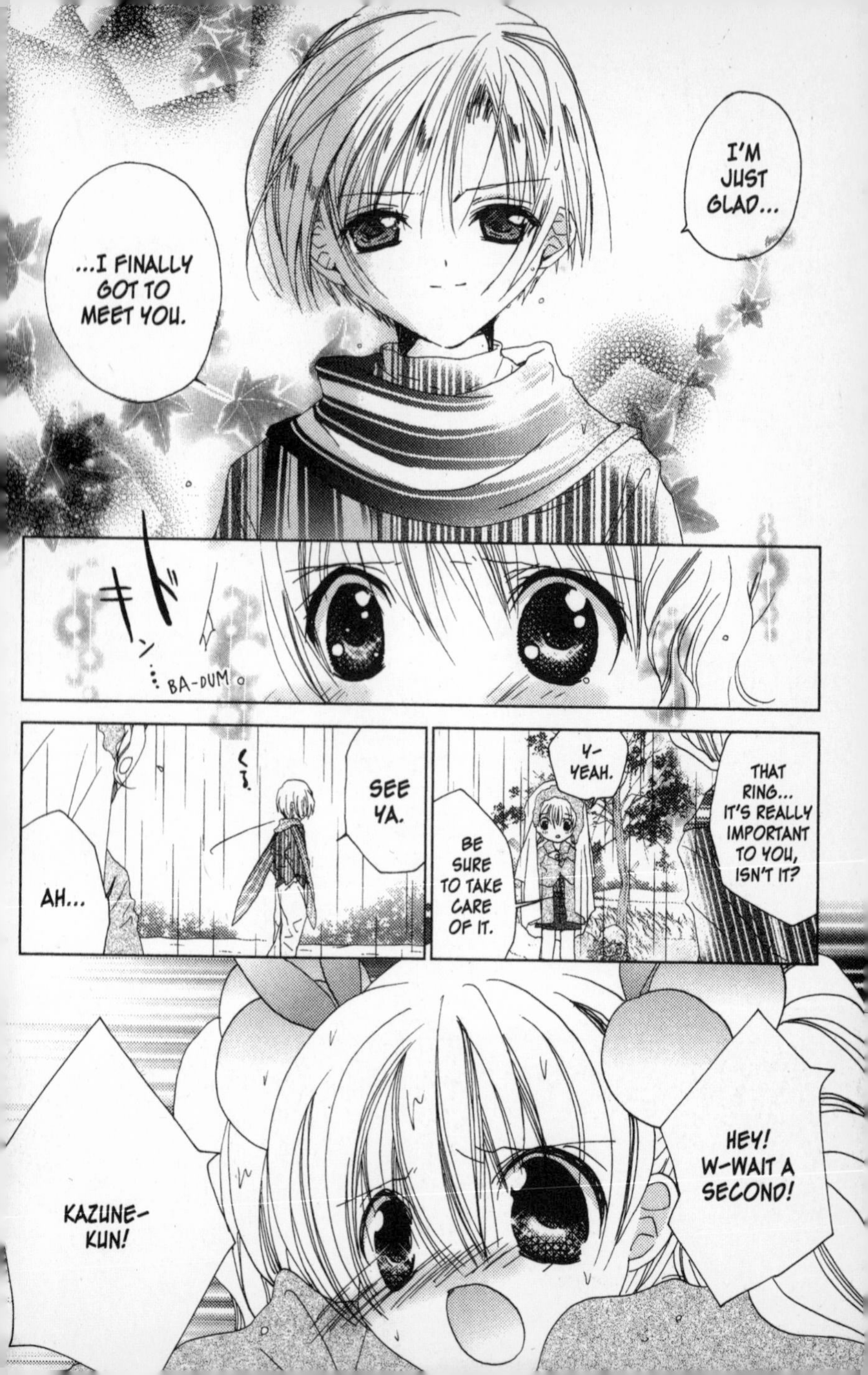
I'M JUST GLAD...
...I FINALLY GOT TO MEET YOU.
BA-DUM
THAT RING... IT'S REALLY IMPORTANT TO YOU, ISN'T IT?
Y-YEAH.
BE SURE TO TAKE CARE OF IT.
SEE YA.
AH...
HEY! W-WAIT A SECOND!
KAZUNE-KUN!

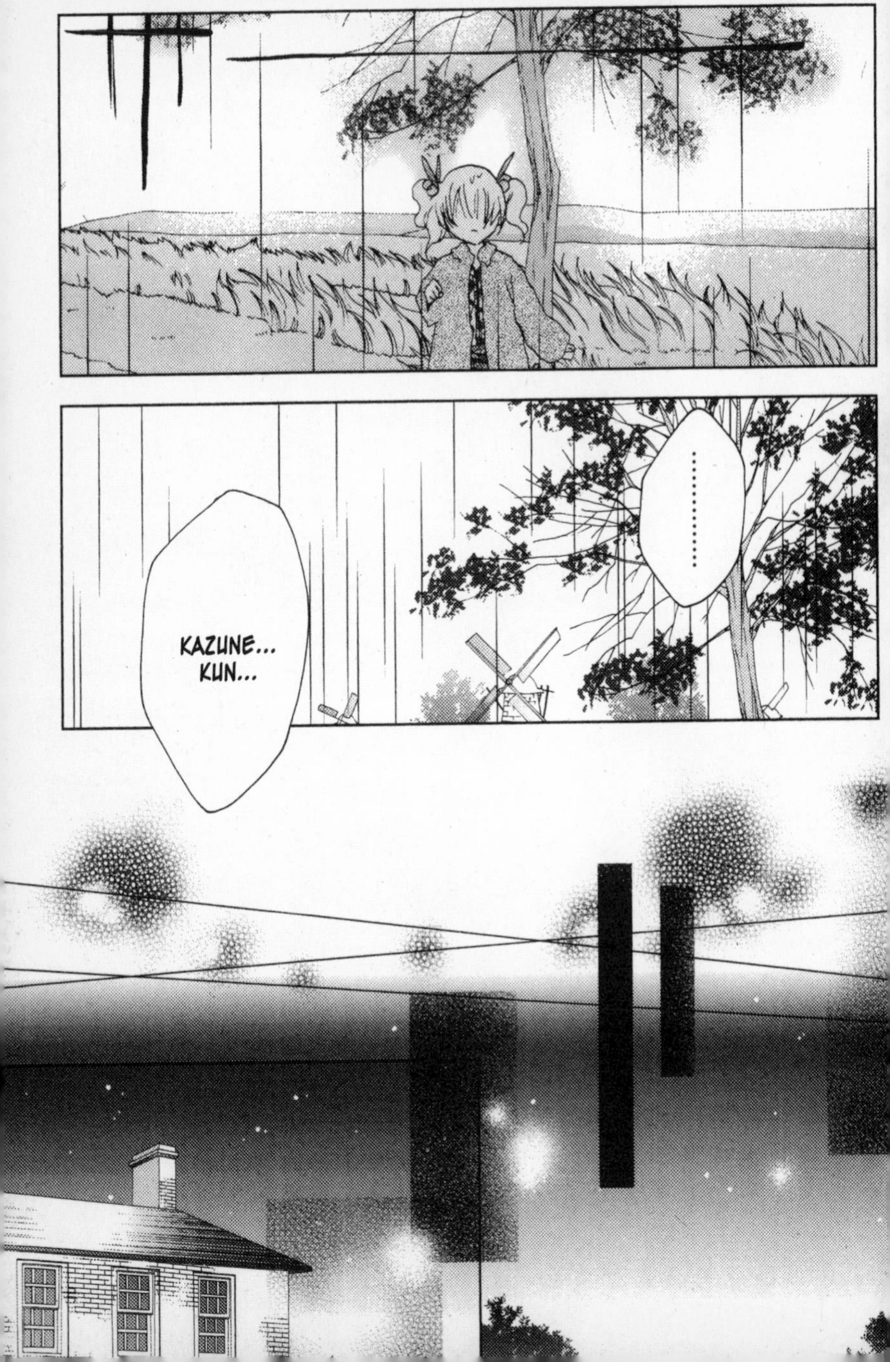
......
KAZUNE... KUN...

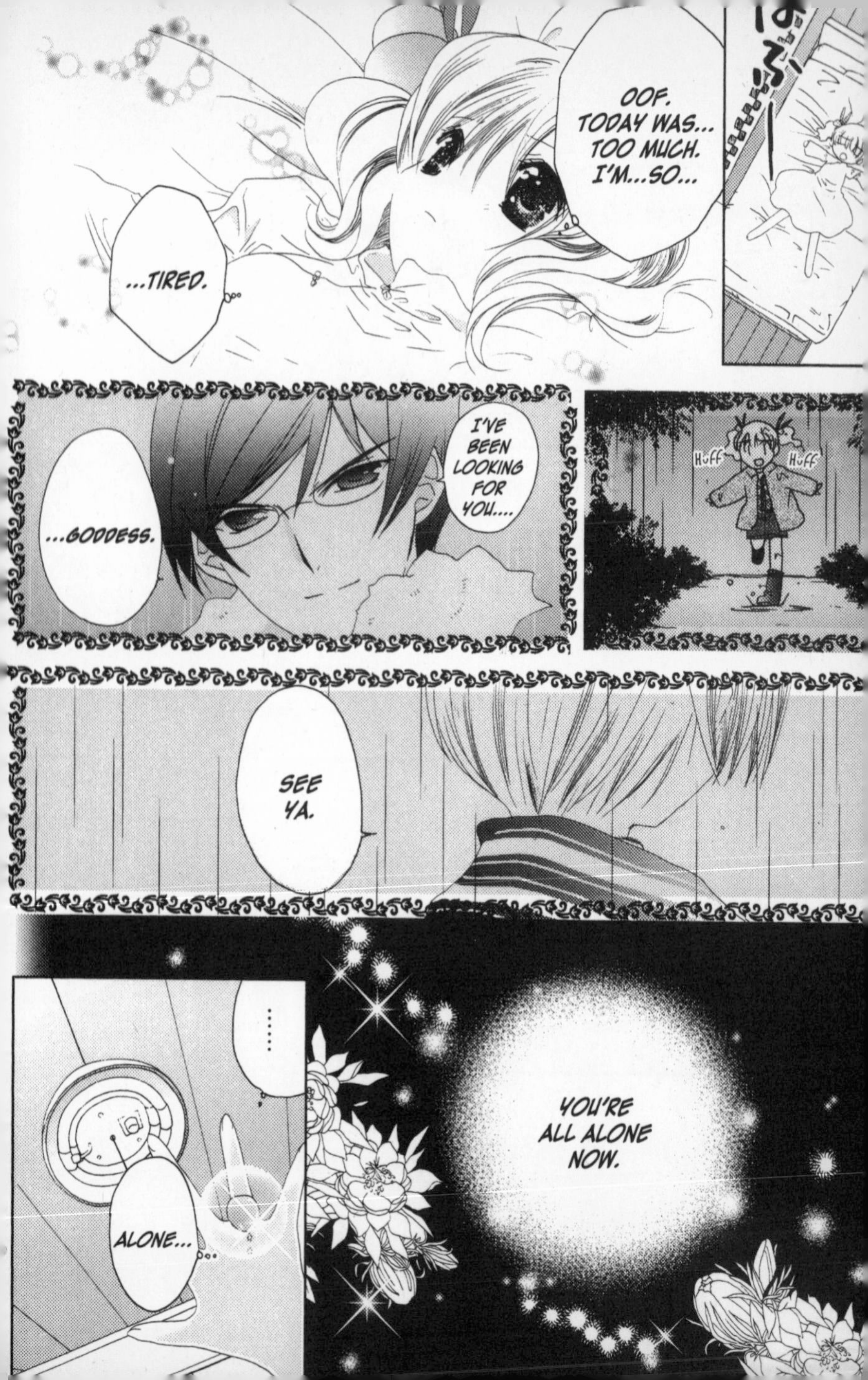
OOF. TODAY WAS... TOO MUCH. I'M...SO...
...TIRED.
Huff Huff
I'VE BEEN LOOKING FOR YOU....
...GODDESS.
SEE YA.
YOU'RE ALL ALONE NOW.
......
ALONE...

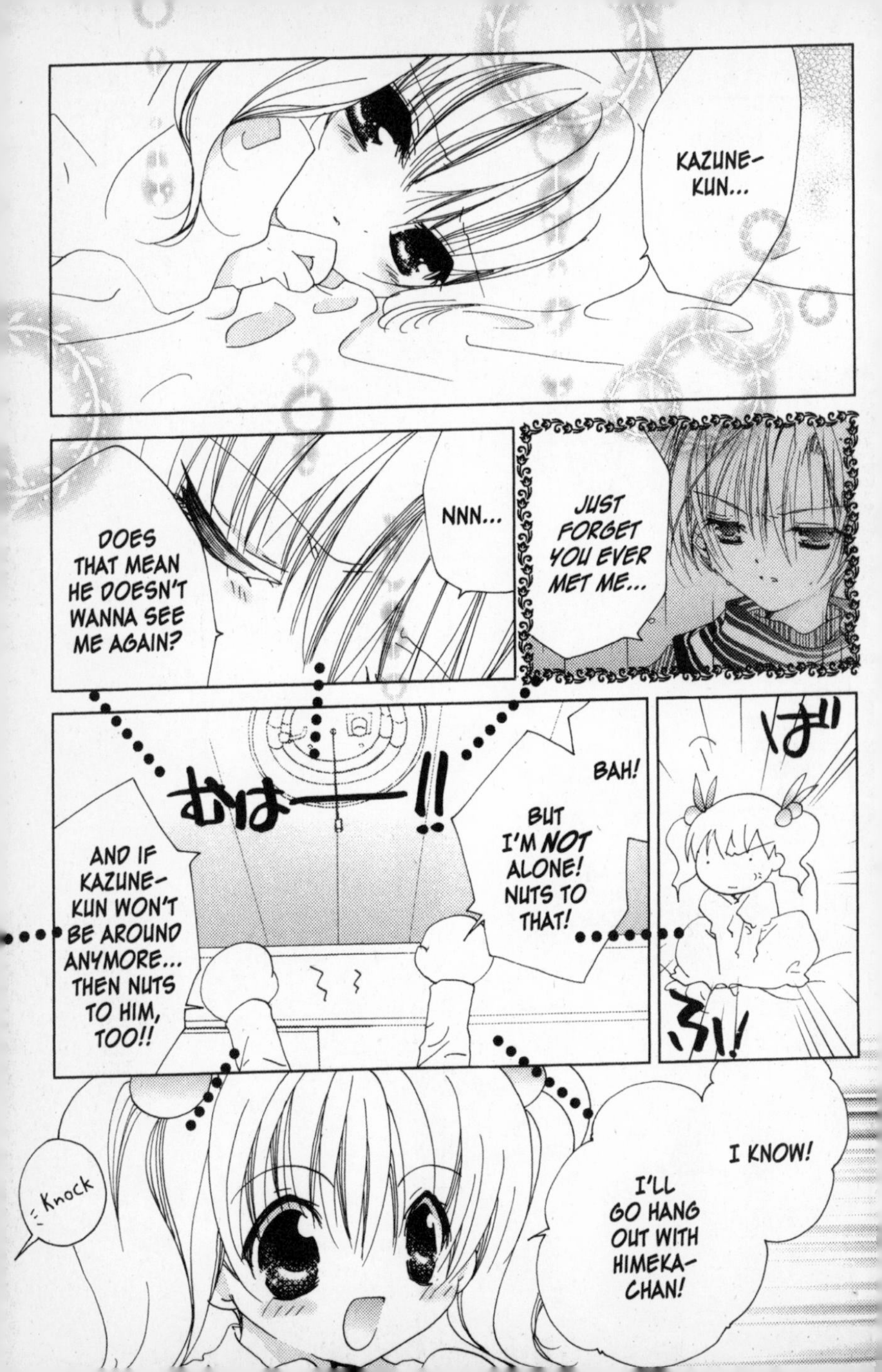
KAZUNE-KUN...
JUST FORGET YOU EVER MET ME...
NNN...
DOES THAT MEAN HE DOESN'T WANNA SEE ME AGAIN?
ぱ
ふ!
BAH!
BUT I'M ***NOT*** ALONE! NUTS TO THAT!
むはー!!
AND IF KAZUNE-KUN WON'T BE AROUND ANYMORE... THEN NUTS TO HIM, TOO!!
I KNOW!
I'LL GO HANG OUT WITH HIMEKA-CHAN!
Knock

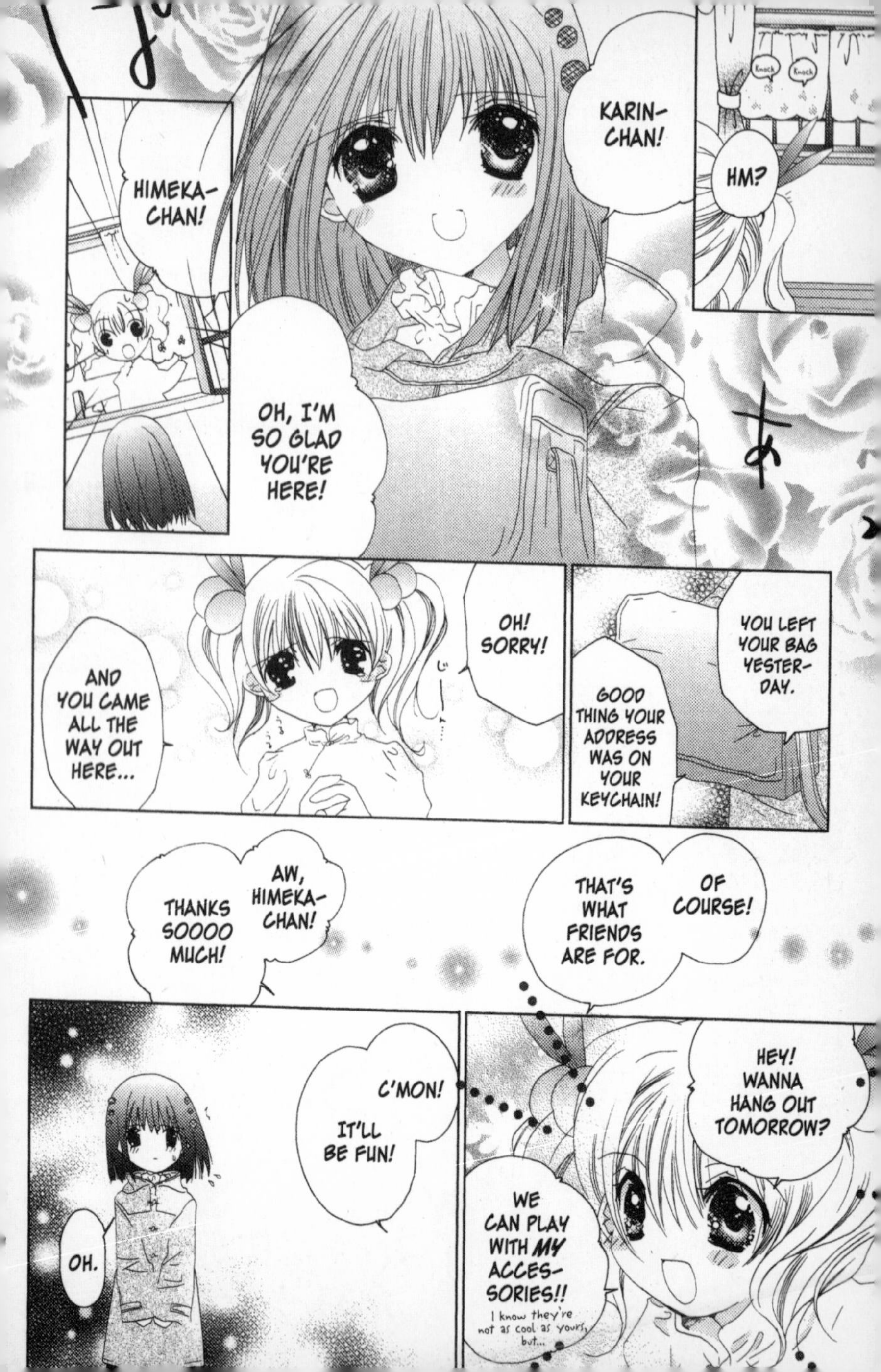
Knock
Knock
HM?
KARIN-CHAN!
HIMEKA-CHAN!
OH, I'M SO GLAD YOU'RE HERE!
YOU LEFT YOUR BAG YESTERDAY.
GOOD THING YOUR ADDRESS WAS ON YOUR KEYCHAIN!
OH! SORRY!
AND YOU CAME ALL THE WAY OUT HERE...
OF COURSE!
THAT'S WHAT FRIENDS ARE FOR.
AW, HIMEKA-CHAN!
THANKS SOOOO MUCH!
HEY! WANNA HANG OUT TOMORROW?
WE CAN PLAY WITH *MY* ACCES-SORIES!!
I know they're not as cool as yours, but...
C'MON!
IT'LL BE FUN!
OH.

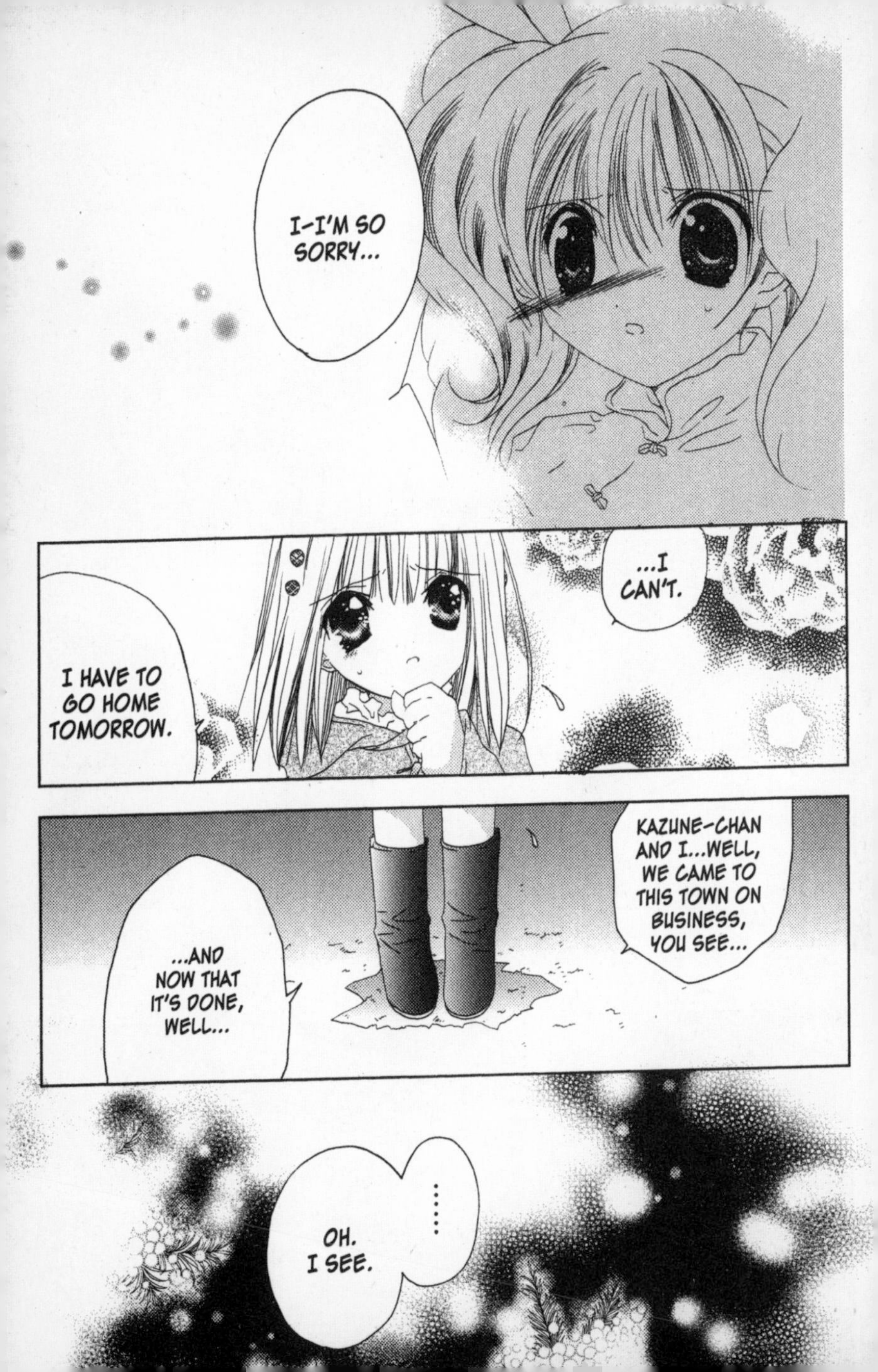
I-I'M SO SORRY...
...I CAN'T.
I HAVE TO GO HOME TOMORROW.
KAZUNE-CHAN AND I...WELL, WE CAME TO THIS TOWN ON BUSINESS, YOU SEE...
...AND NOW THAT IT'S DONE, WELL...
......
OH. I SEE.

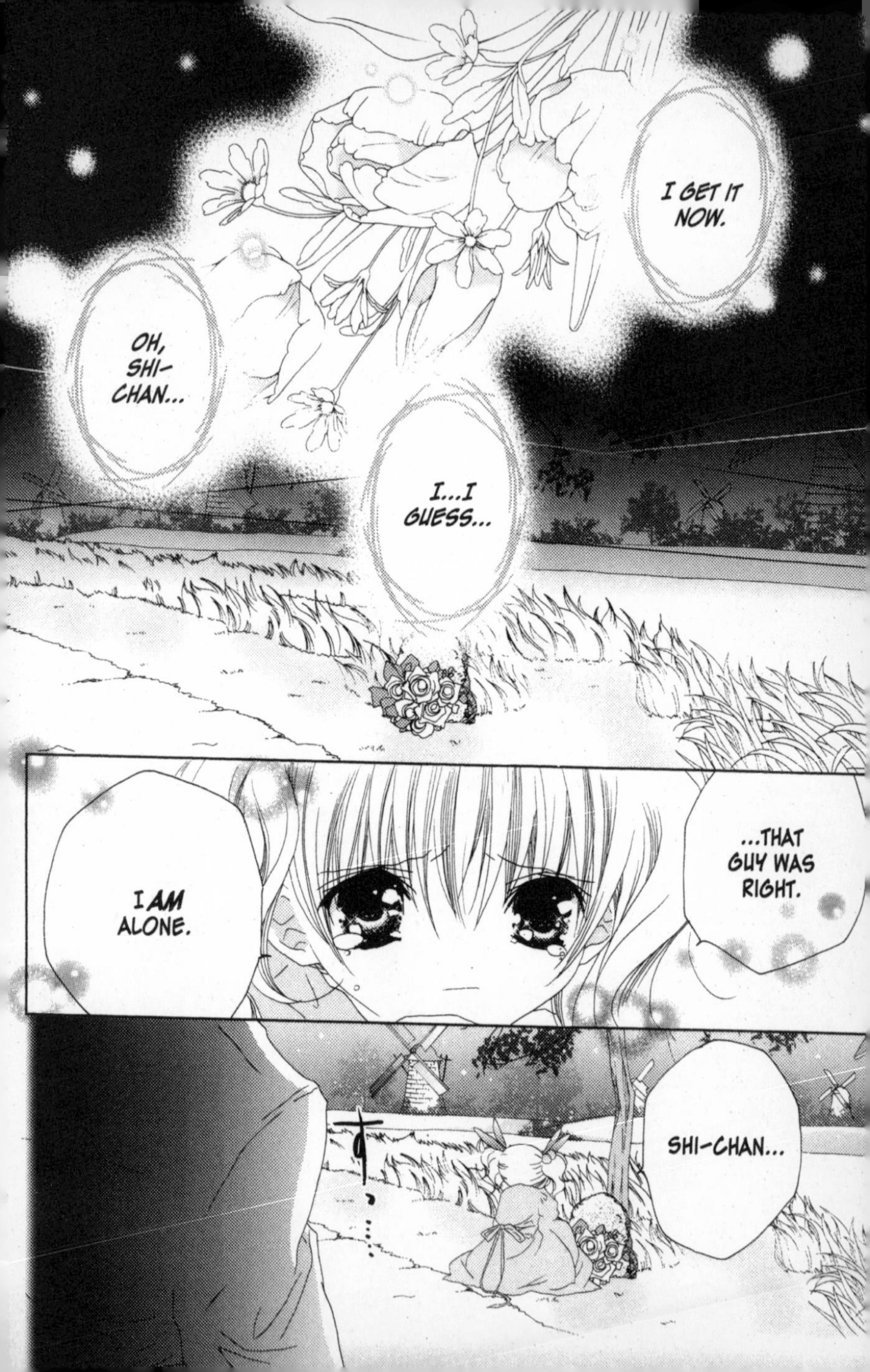
I GET IT NOW.
OH, SHI-CHAN...
I...I GUESS...
...THAT GUY WAS RIGHT.
I AM ALONE.
SHI-CHAN...

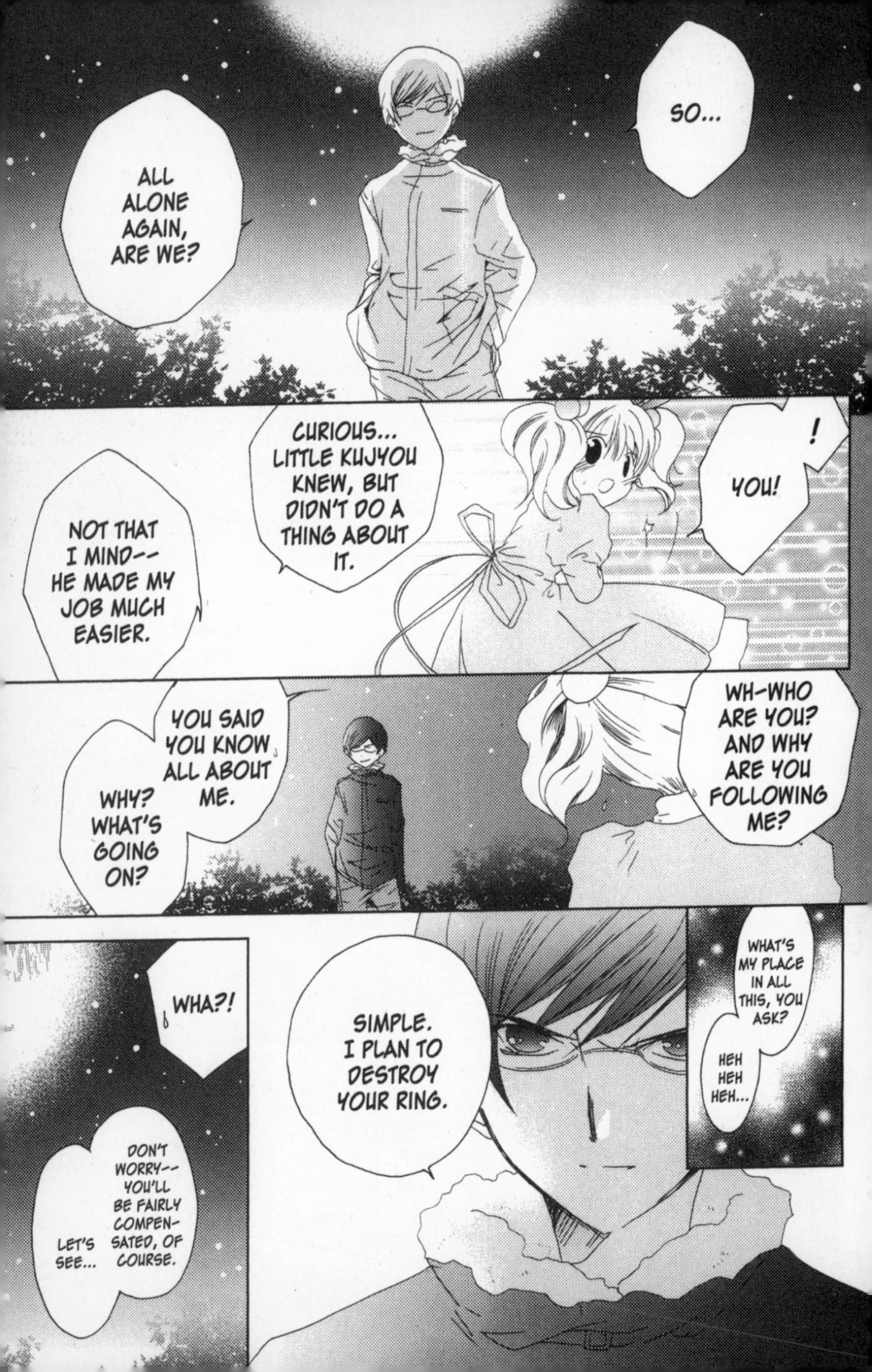
SO...
ALL ALONE AGAIN, ARE WE?
!
YOU!
CURIOUS... LITTLE KUJYOU KNEW, BUT DIDN'T DO A THING ABOUT IT.
NOT THAT I MIND-- HE MADE MY JOB MUCH EASIER.
WH-WHO ARE YOU? AND WHY ARE YOU FOLLOWING ME?
YOU SAID YOU KNOW ALL ABOUT ME.
WHY? WHAT'S GOING ON?
WHAT'S MY PLACE IN ALL THIS, YOU ASK?
HEH HEH HEH...
SIMPLE. I PLAN TO DESTROY YOUR RING.
WHA?!
DON'T WORRY-- YOU'LL BE FAIRLY COMPEN-SATED, OF COURSE.
LET'S SEE...

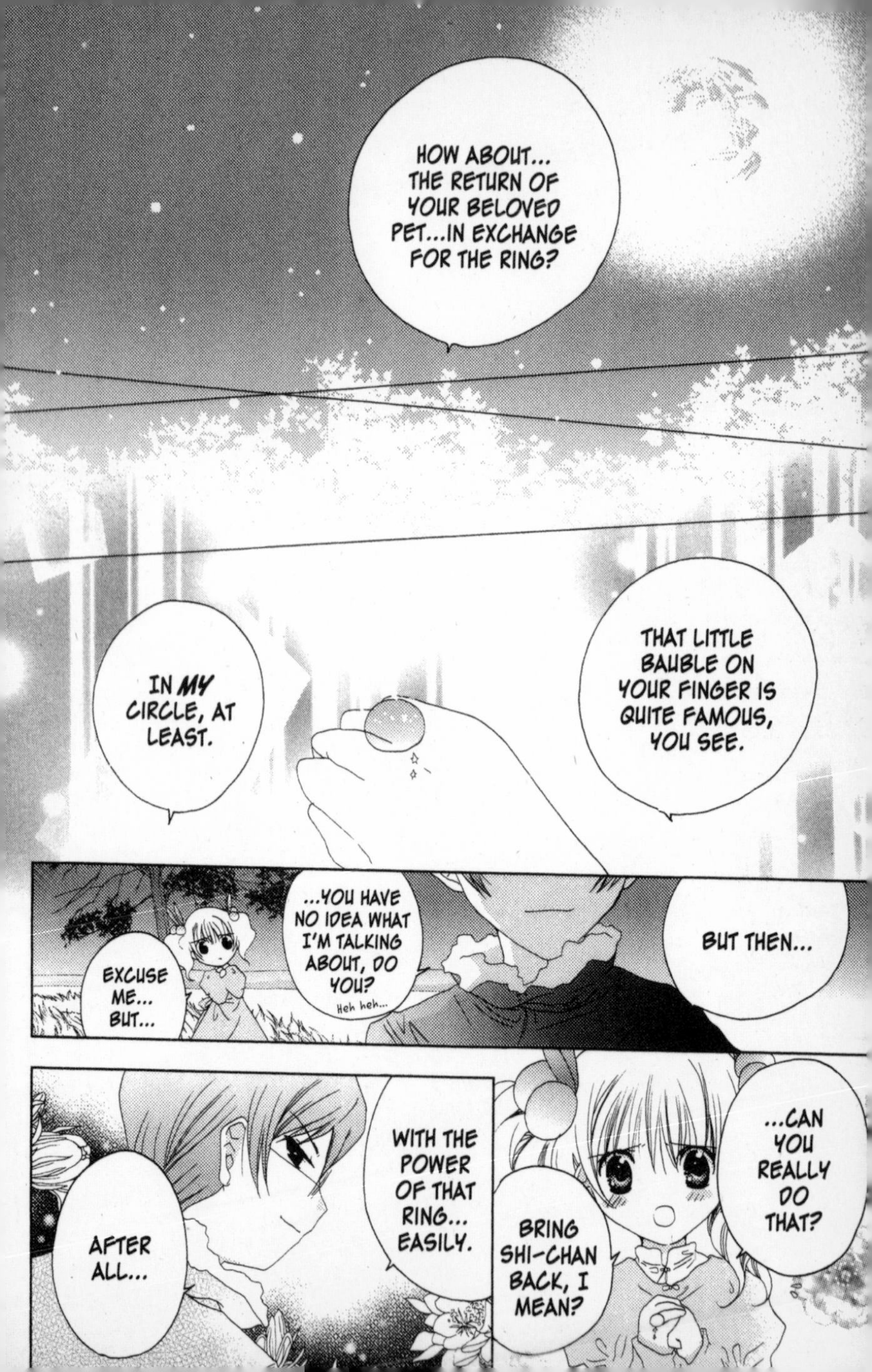
HOW ABOUT... THE RETURN OF YOUR BELOVED PET...IN EXCHANGE FOR THE RING?
THAT LITTLE BAUBLE ON YOUR FINGER IS QUITE FAMOUS, YOU SEE.
IN MY CIRCLE, AT LEAST.
BUT THEN...
...YOU HAVE NO IDEA WHAT I'M TALKING ABOUT, DO YOU?
Heh heh...
EXCUSE ME... BUT...
...CAN YOU REALLY DO THAT?
BRING SHI-CHAN BACK, I MEAN?
WITH THE POWER OF THAT RING... EASILY.
AFTER ALL...

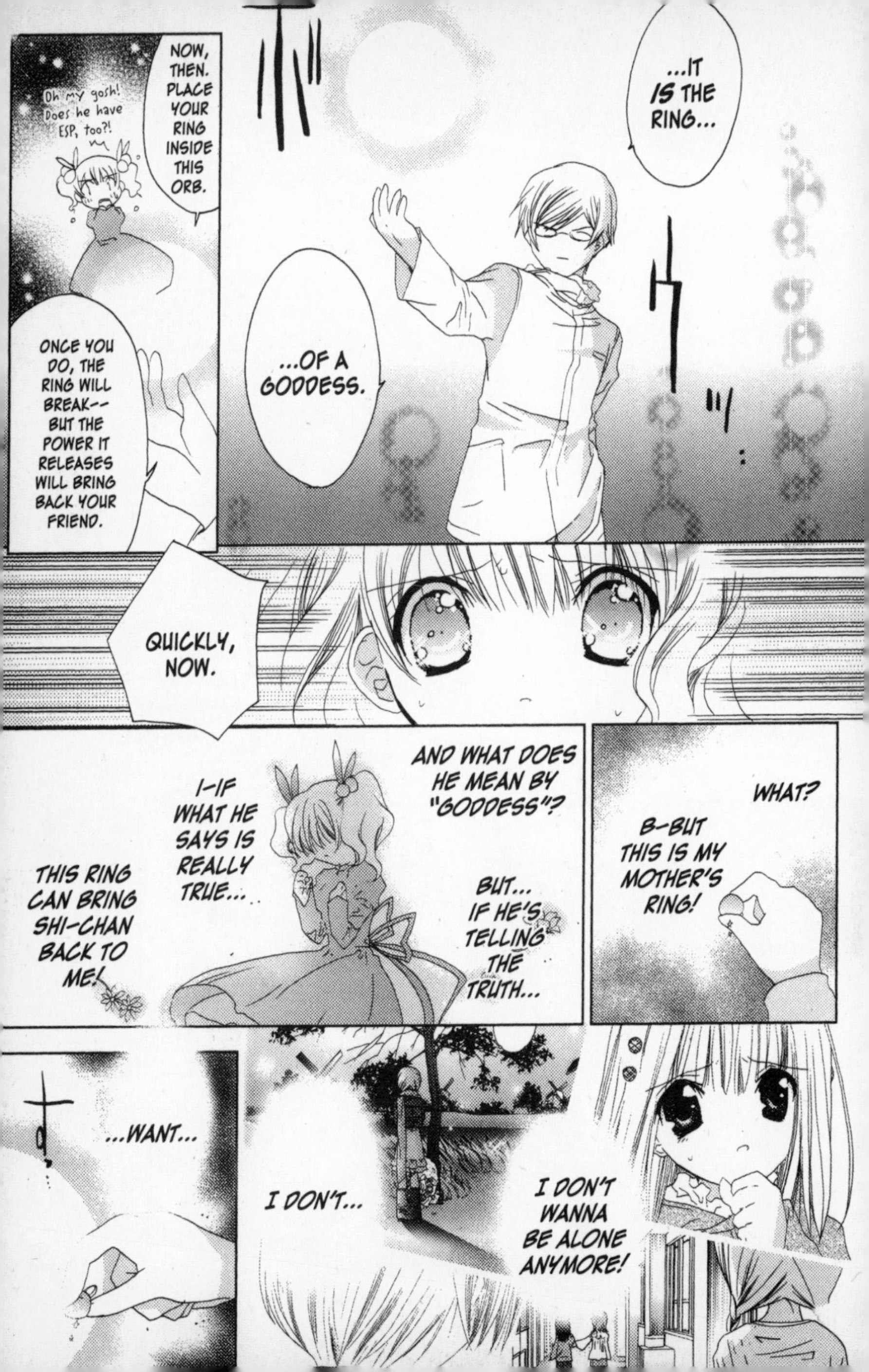
...IT IS THE RING...
...OF A GODDESS.
NOW, THEN. PLACE YOUR RING INSIDE THIS ORB.
Oh my gosh! Does he have ESP, too?!
ONCE YOU DO, THE RING WILL BREAK-- BUT THE POWER IT RELEASES WILL BRING BACK YOUR FRIEND.
QUICKLY, NOW.
WHAT?
B-BUT THIS IS MY MOTHER'S RING!
AND WHAT DOES HE MEAN BY "GODDESS"?
BUT... IF HE'S TELLING THE TRUTH...
I-IF WHAT HE SAYS IS REALLY TRUE...
THIS RING CAN BRING SHI-CHAN BACK TO ME!
I DON'T WANNA BE ALONE ANYMORE!
I DON'T...
...WANT...

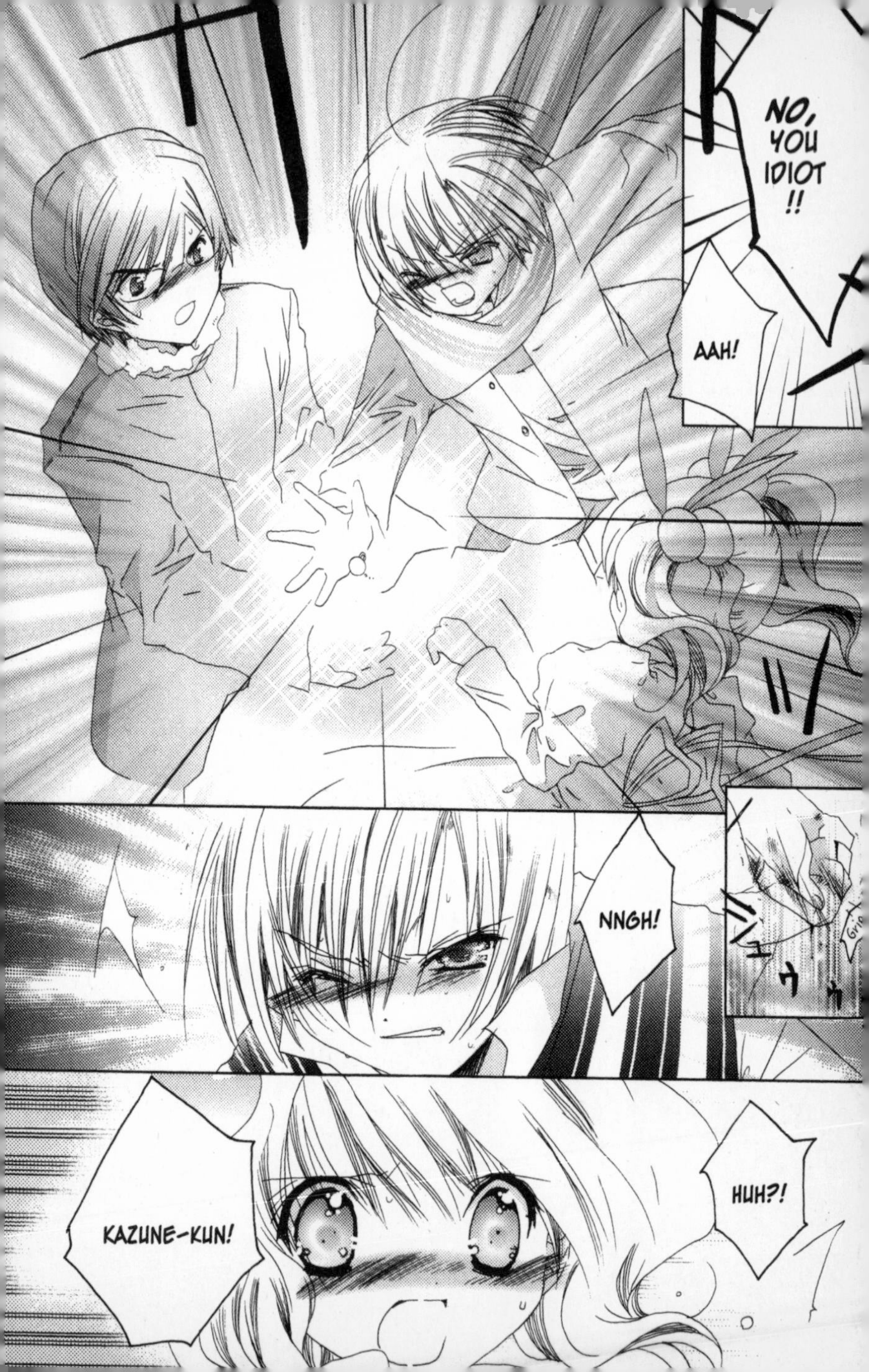
NO, YOU IDIOT!!
AAH!
Grip
NNGH!
HUH?!
KAZUNE-KUN!

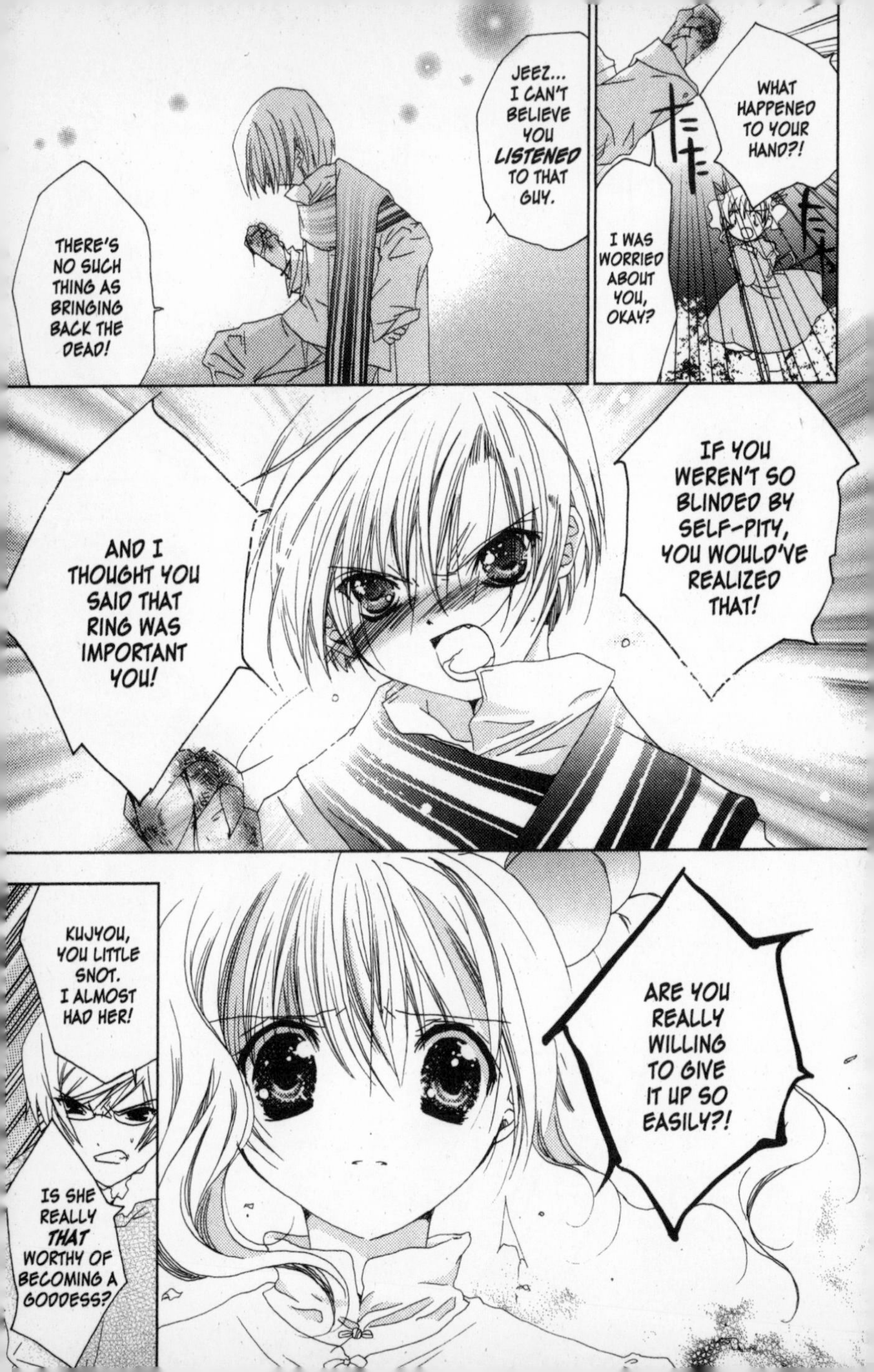
WHAT HAPPENED TO YOUR HAND?!
I WAS WORRIED ABOUT YOU, OKAY?
JEEZ... I CAN'T BELIEVE YOU *LISTENED* TO THAT GUY.
THERE'S NO SUCH THING AS BRINGING BACK THE DEAD!
IF YOU WEREN'T SO BLINDED BY SELF-PITY, YOU WOULD'VE REALIZED THAT!
AND I THOUGHT YOU SAID THAT RING WAS IMPORTANT YOU!
ARE YOU REALLY WILLING TO GIVE IT UP SO EASILY?!
KUJYOU, YOU LITTLE SNOT. I ALMOST HAD HER!
IS SHE REALLY *THAT* WORTHY OF BECOMING A GODDESS?

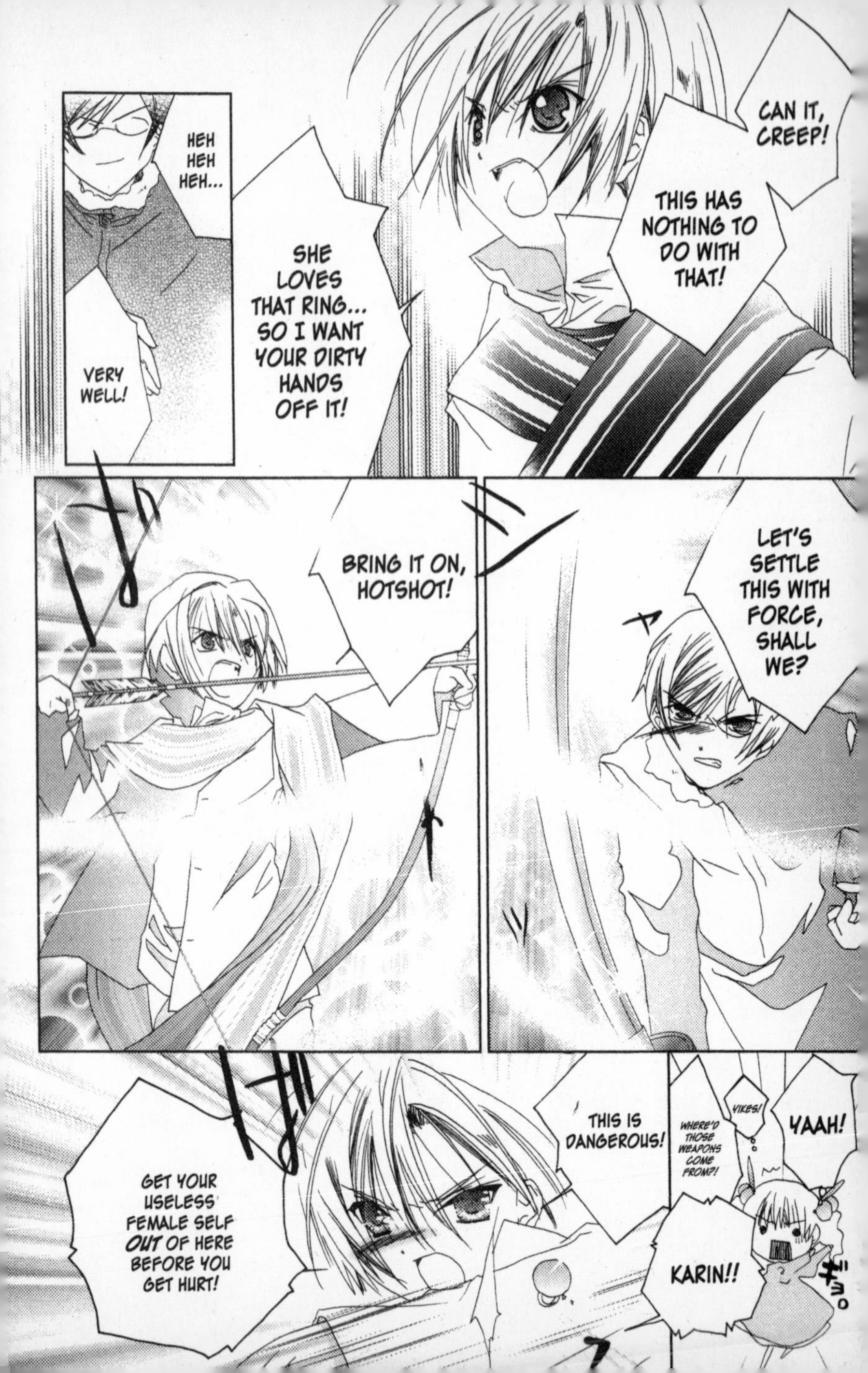
CAN IT, CREEP!
THIS HAS NOTHING TO DO WITH THAT!
SHE LOVES THAT RING... SO I WANT YOUR DIRTY HANDS OFF IT!
HEH HEH HEH...
VERY WELL!
LET'S SETTLE THIS WITH FORCE, SHALL WE?
BRING IT ON, HOTSHOT!
YAAH!
YIKES!
WHERE'D THOSE WEAPONS COME FROM?!
THIS IS DANGEROUS!
KARIN!!
GET YOUR USELESS FEMALE SELF OUT OF HERE BEFORE YOU GET HURT!

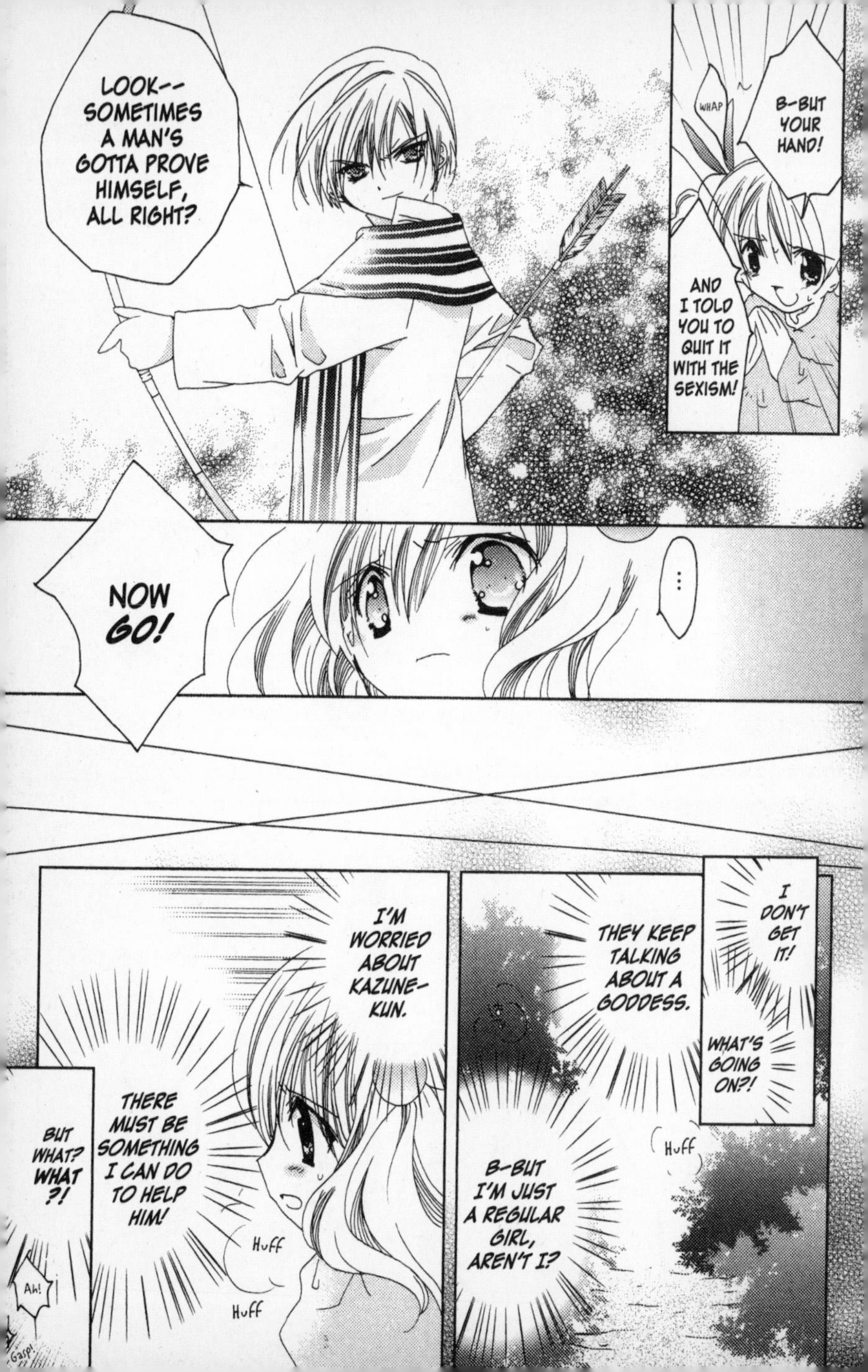
WHAP
B-BUT YOUR HAND!
AND I TOLD YOU TO QUIT IT WITH THE SEXISM!
LOOK-- SOMETIMES A MAN'S GOTTA PROVE HIMSELF, ALL RIGHT?
NOW GO!
...
I DON'T GET IT!
WHAT'S GOING ON?!
THEY KEEP TALKING ABOUT A GODDESS.
Huff
B-BUT I'M JUST A REGULAR GIRL, AREN'T I?
I'M WORRIED ABOUT KAZUNE-KUN.
THERE MUST BE SOMETHING I CAN DO TO HELP HIM!
Huff
Huff
BUT WHAT? WHAT?!
Ah!
Gasp!

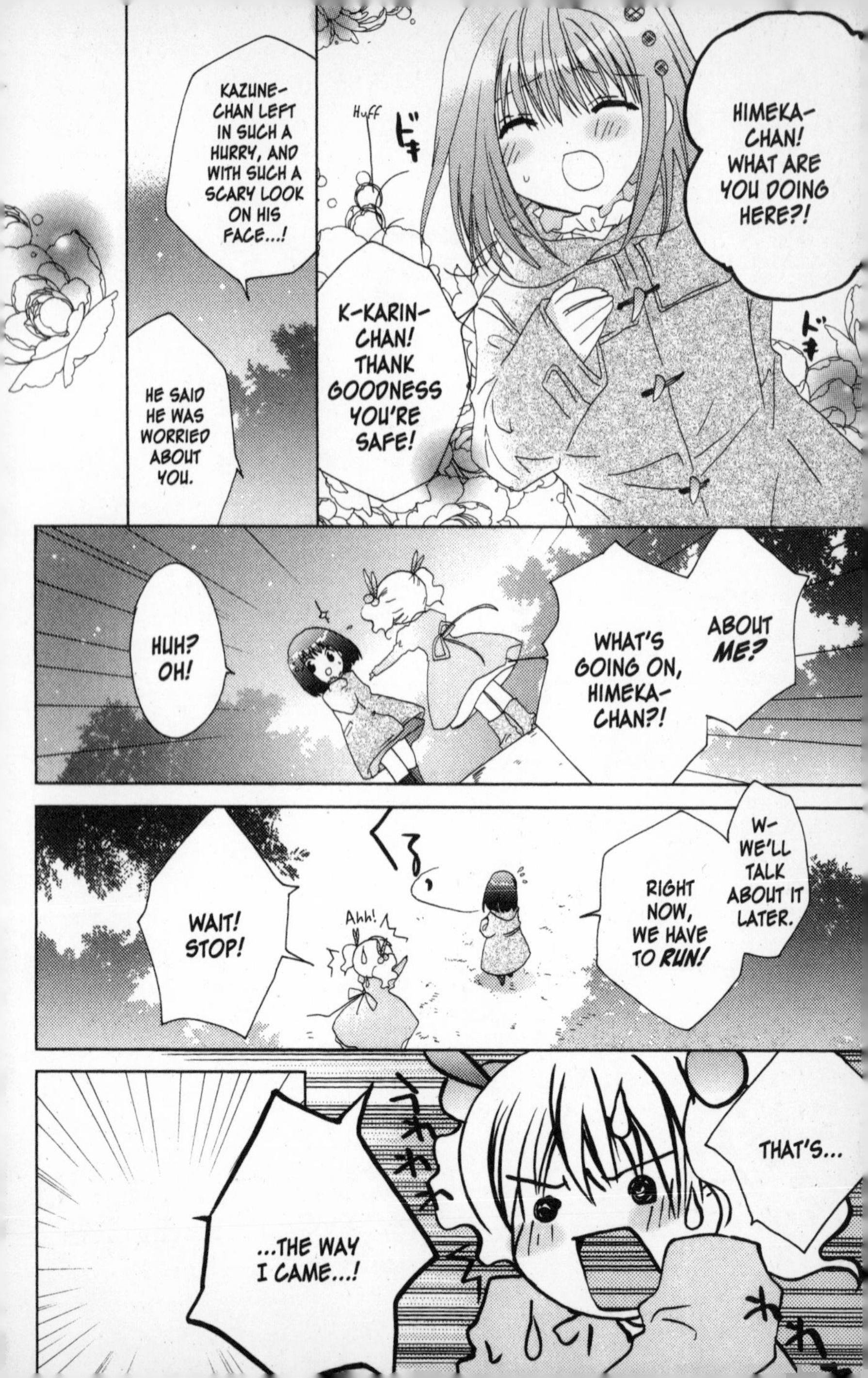
HIMEKA-CHAN! WHAT ARE YOU DOING HERE?!
Huff
K-KARIN-CHAN! THANK GOODNESS YOU'RE SAFE!
KAZUNE-CHAN LEFT IN SUCH A HURRY, AND WITH SUCH A SCARY LOOK ON HIS FACE...!
HE SAID HE WAS WORRIED ABOUT YOU.
ABOUT *ME?*
WHAT'S GOING ON, HIMEKA-CHAN?!
HUH? OH!
W-WE'LL TALK ABOUT IT LATER.
RIGHT NOW, WE HAVE TO *RUN!*
Ahh!
WAIT! STOP!
THAT'S...
...THE WAY I CAME...!

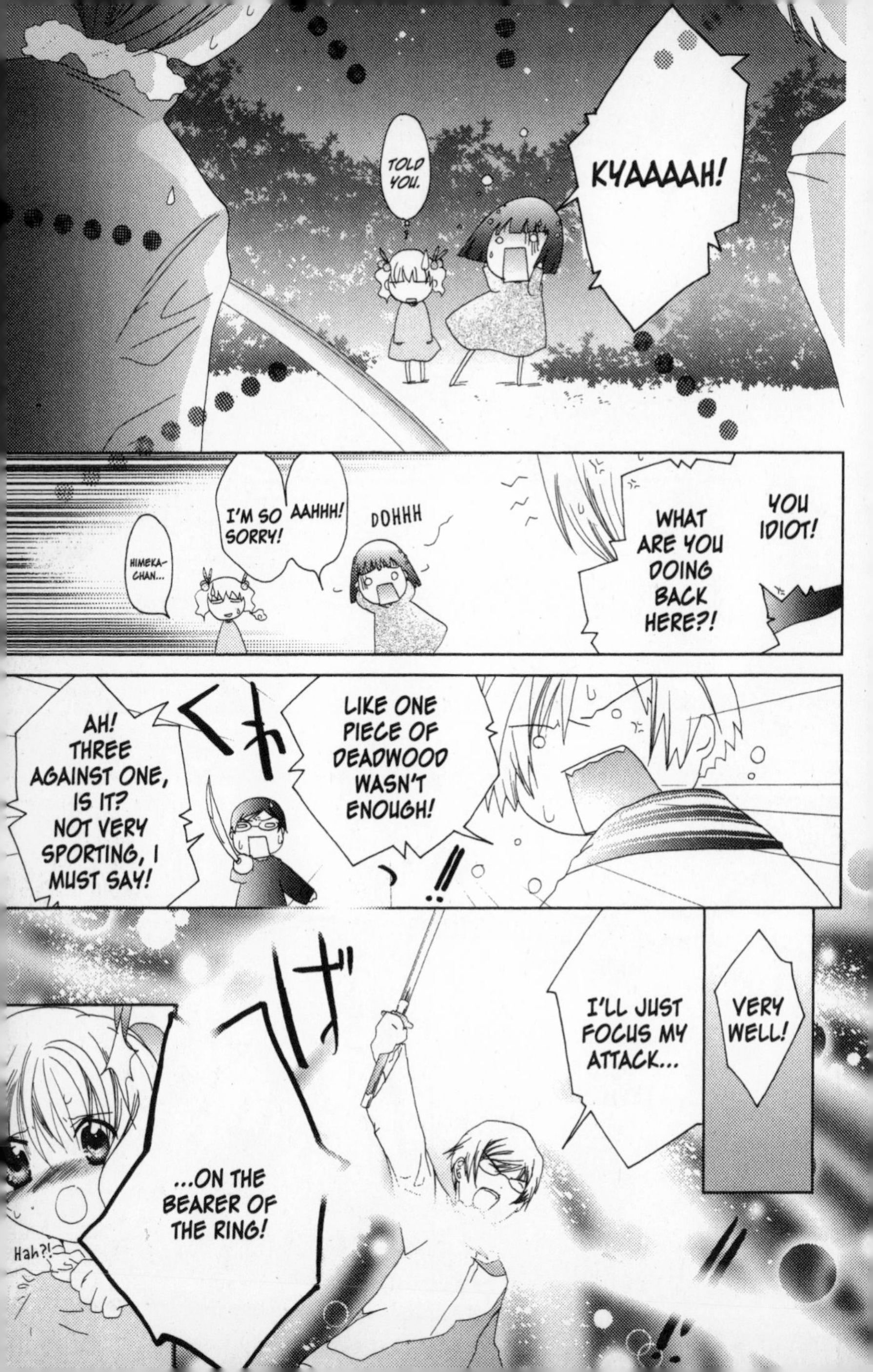
KYAAAAH!
TOLD YOU.
YOU IDIOT!
WHAT ARE YOU DOING BACK HERE?!
DOHHH
AAHHH!
I'M SO SORRY!
HIMEKA-CHAN...
LIKE ONE PIECE OF DEADWOOD WASN'T ENOUGH!
AH! THREE AGAINST ONE, IS IT? NOT VERY SPORTING, I MUST SAY!
VERY WELL!
I'LL JUST FOCUS MY ATTACK...
...ON THE BEARER OF THE RING!
Hah?!

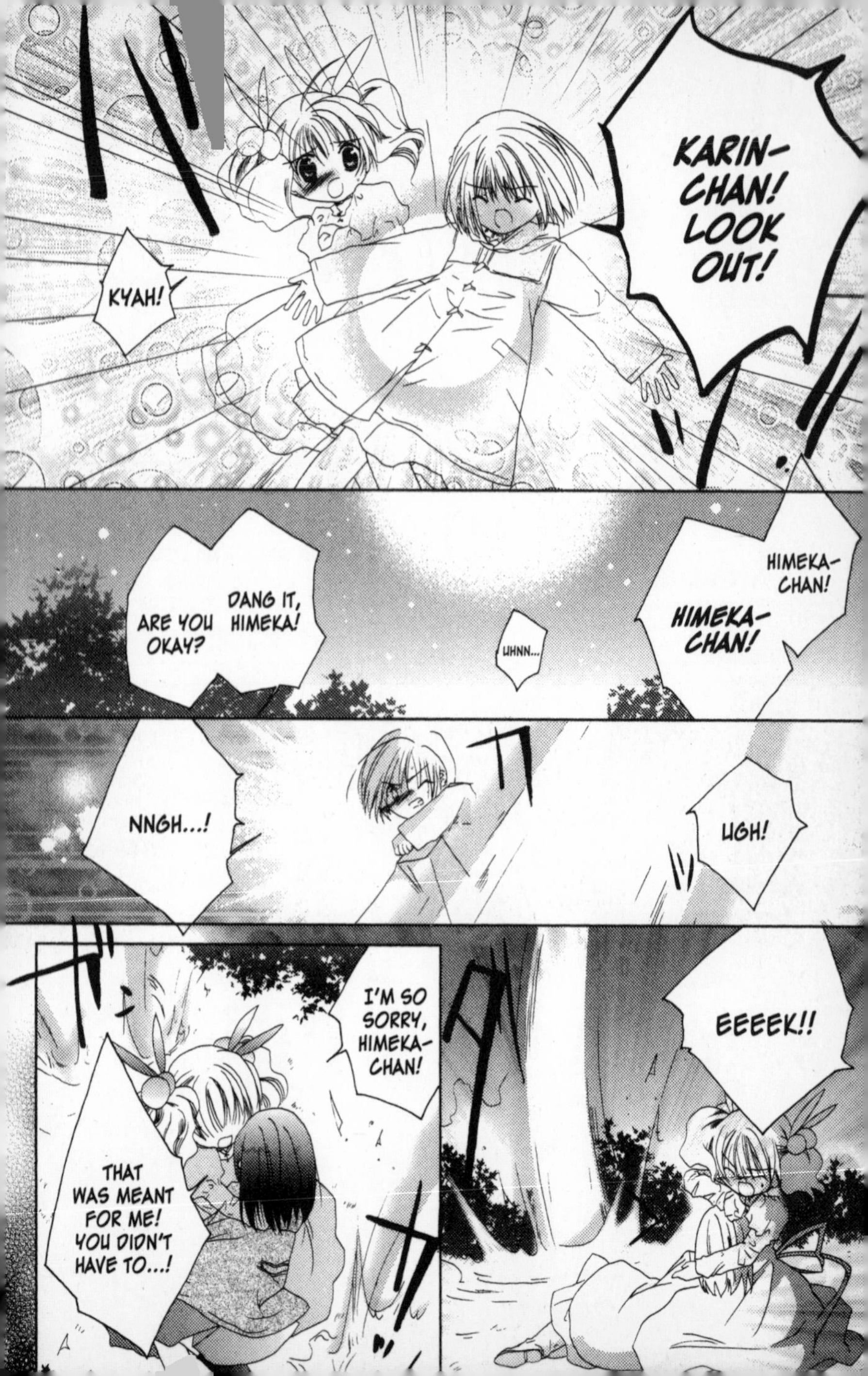
KARIN-CHAN! LOOK OUT!
KYAH!
HIMEKA-CHAN!
HIMEKA-CHAN!
UHNN...
DANG IT, HIMEKA!
ARE YOU OKAY?
UGH!
NNGH...!
EEEEK!!
I'M SO SORRY, HIMEKA-CHAN!
THAT WAS MEANT FOR ME! YOU DIDN'T HAVE TO...!

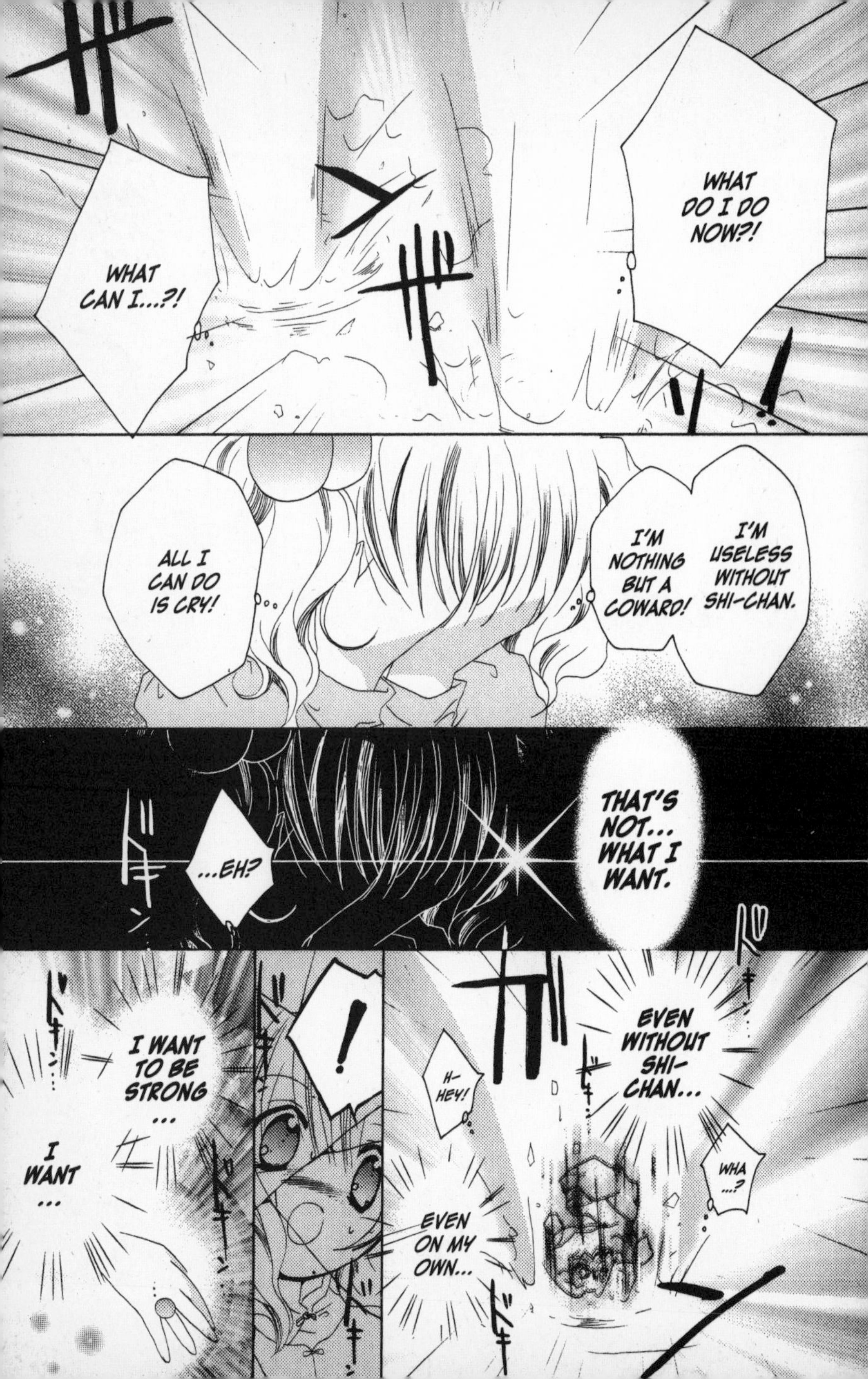
WHAT DO I DO NOW?!
WHAT CAN I...?!
I'M USELESS WITHOUT SHI-CHAN.
I'M NOTHING BUT A COWARD!
ALL I CAN DO IS CRY!
THAT'S NOT... WHAT I WANT.
...EH?
EVEN WITHOUT SHI-CHAN...
H-HEY!
WHA...?
EVEN ON MY OWN...
!
I WANT TO BE STRONG...
I WANT...

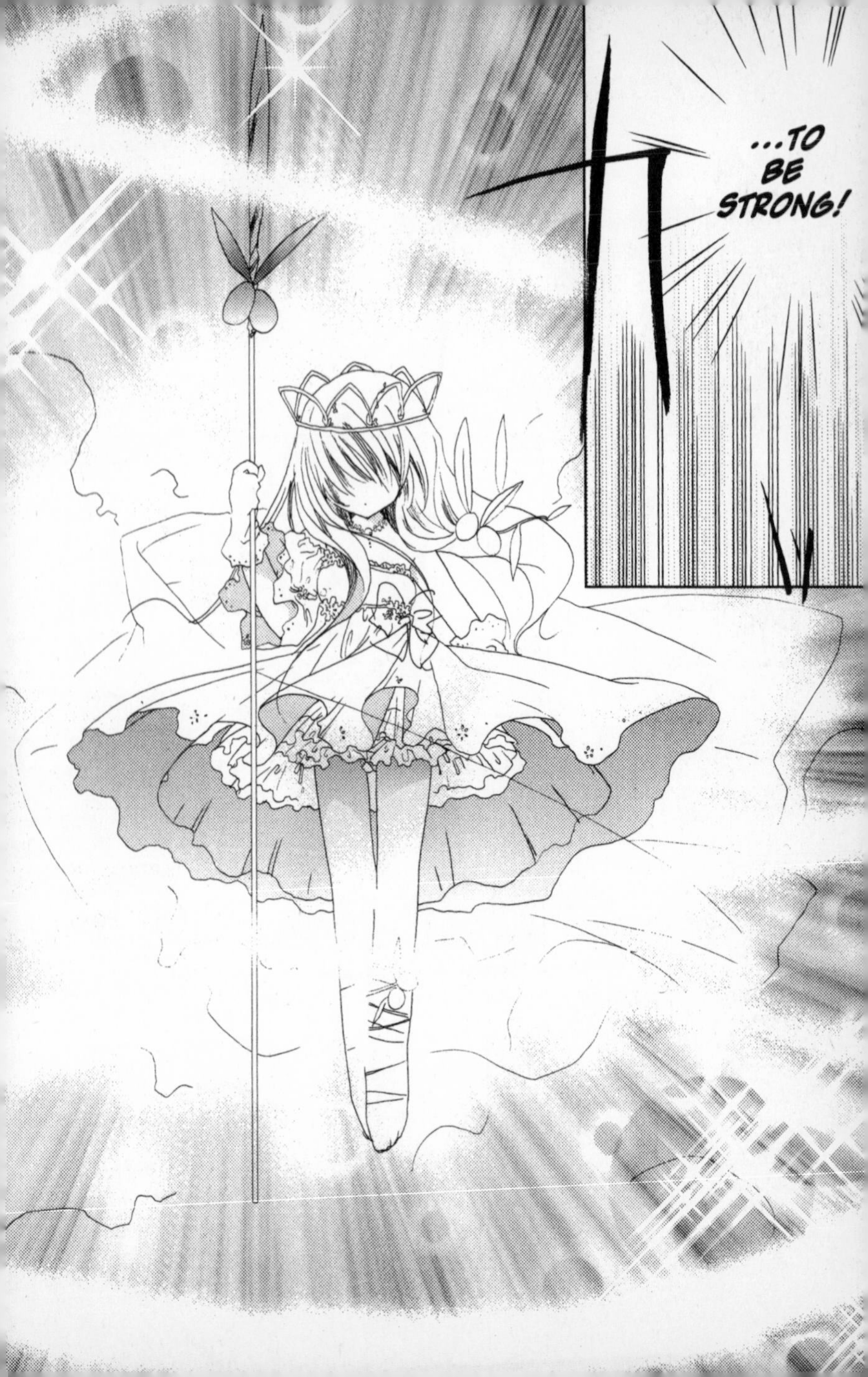
...TO BE STRONG!

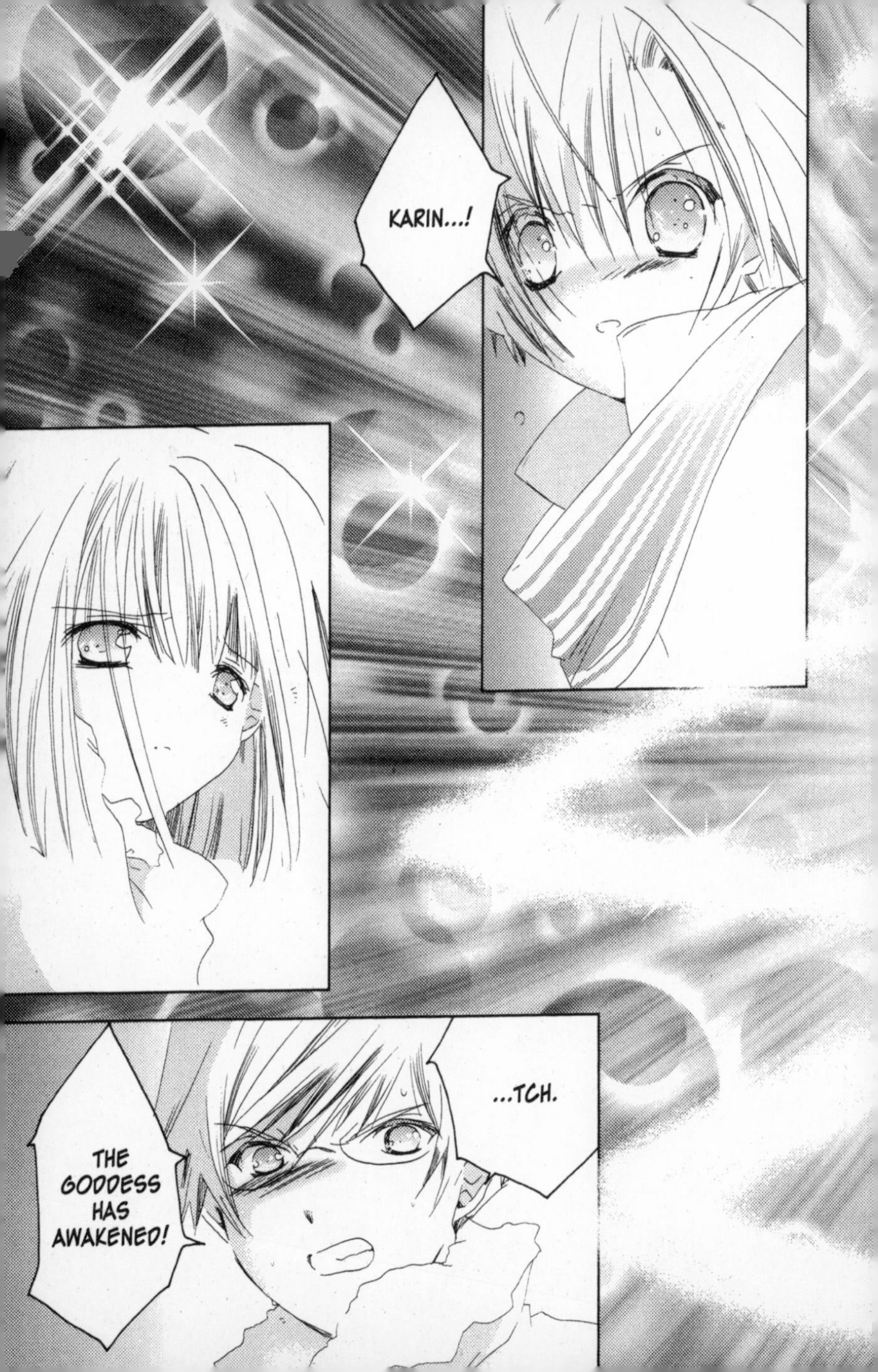
KARIN...!
...TCH.
THE GODDESS HAS AWAKENED!

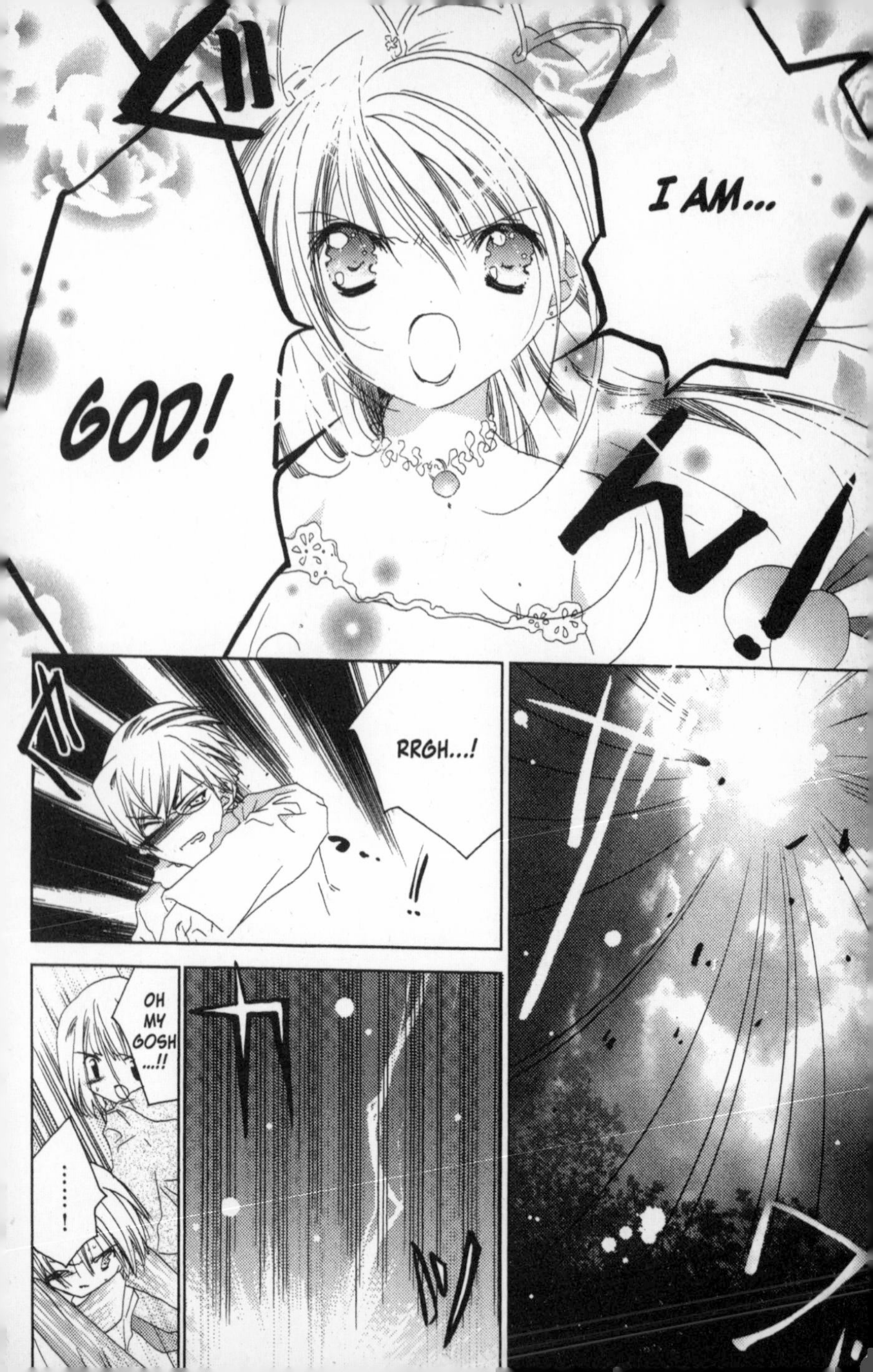
I AM...
GOD!
RRGH...!
OH MY GOSH ...!!
......!

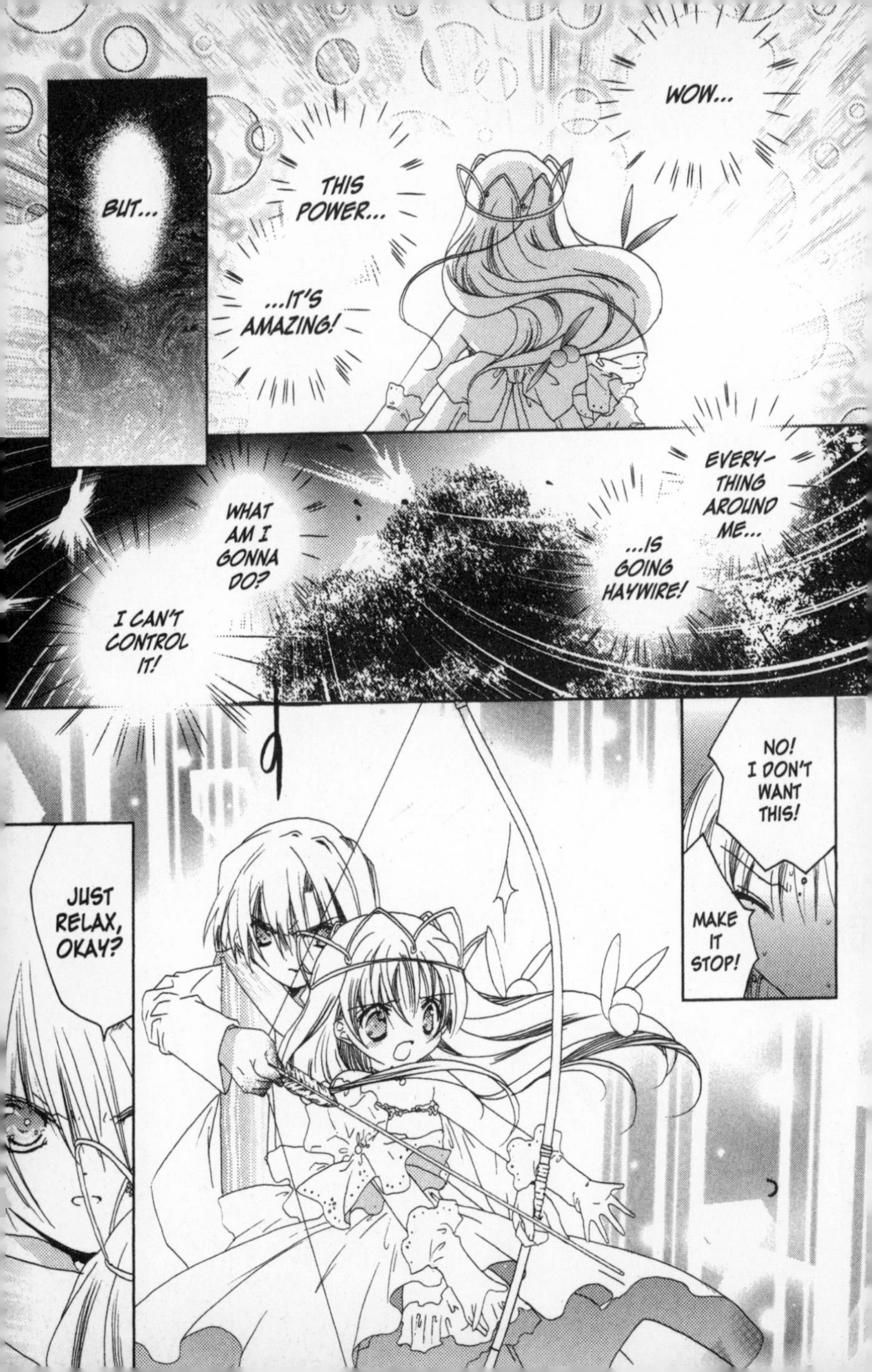
WOW...
THIS POWER...
...IT'S AMAZING!
BUT...
EVERY-THING AROUND ME...
...IS GOING HAYWIRE!
WHAT AM I GONNA DO?
I CAN'T CONTROL IT!
NO! I DON'T WANT THIS!
MAKE IT STOP!
JUST RELAX, OKAY?

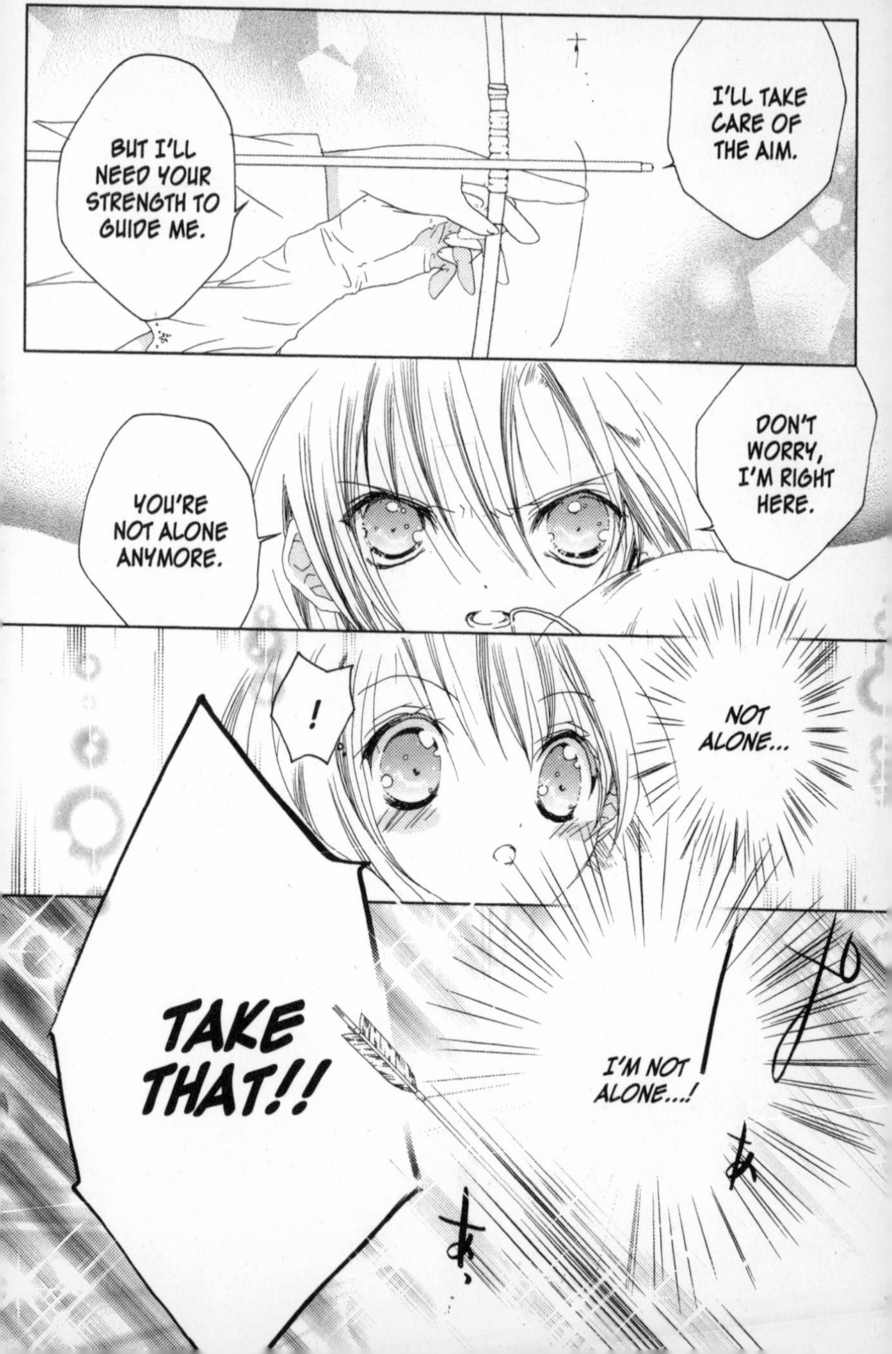
I'LL TAKE CARE OF THE AIM.
BUT I'LL NEED YOUR STRENGTH TO GUIDE ME.
DON'T WORRY, I'M RIGHT HERE.
YOU'RE NOT ALONE ANYMORE.
!
NOT ALONE...
I'M NOT ALONE...!
TAKE THAT!!

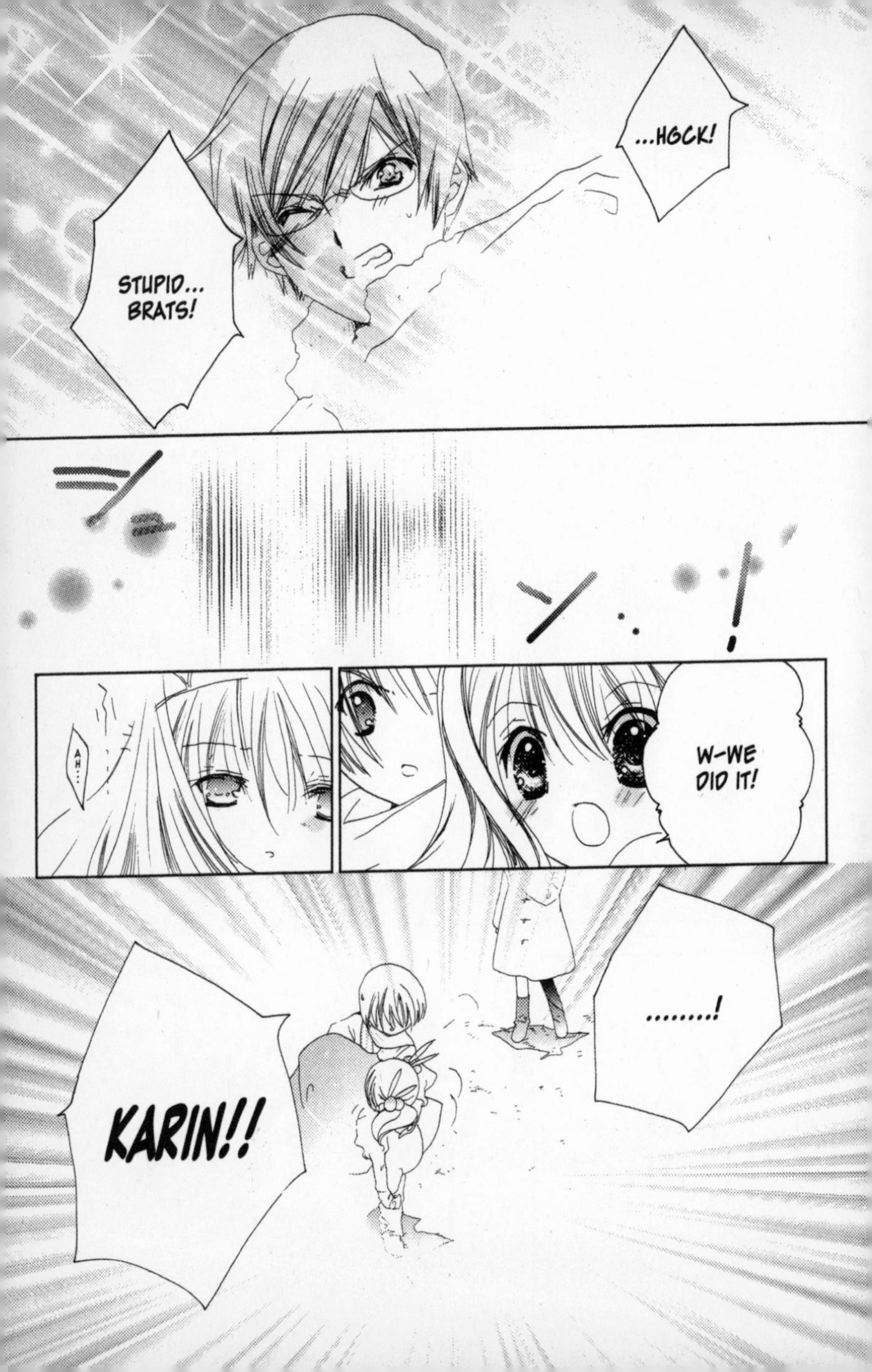
...HGCK!
STUPID... BRATS!
W-WE DID IT!
AH...
........!
KARIN!!

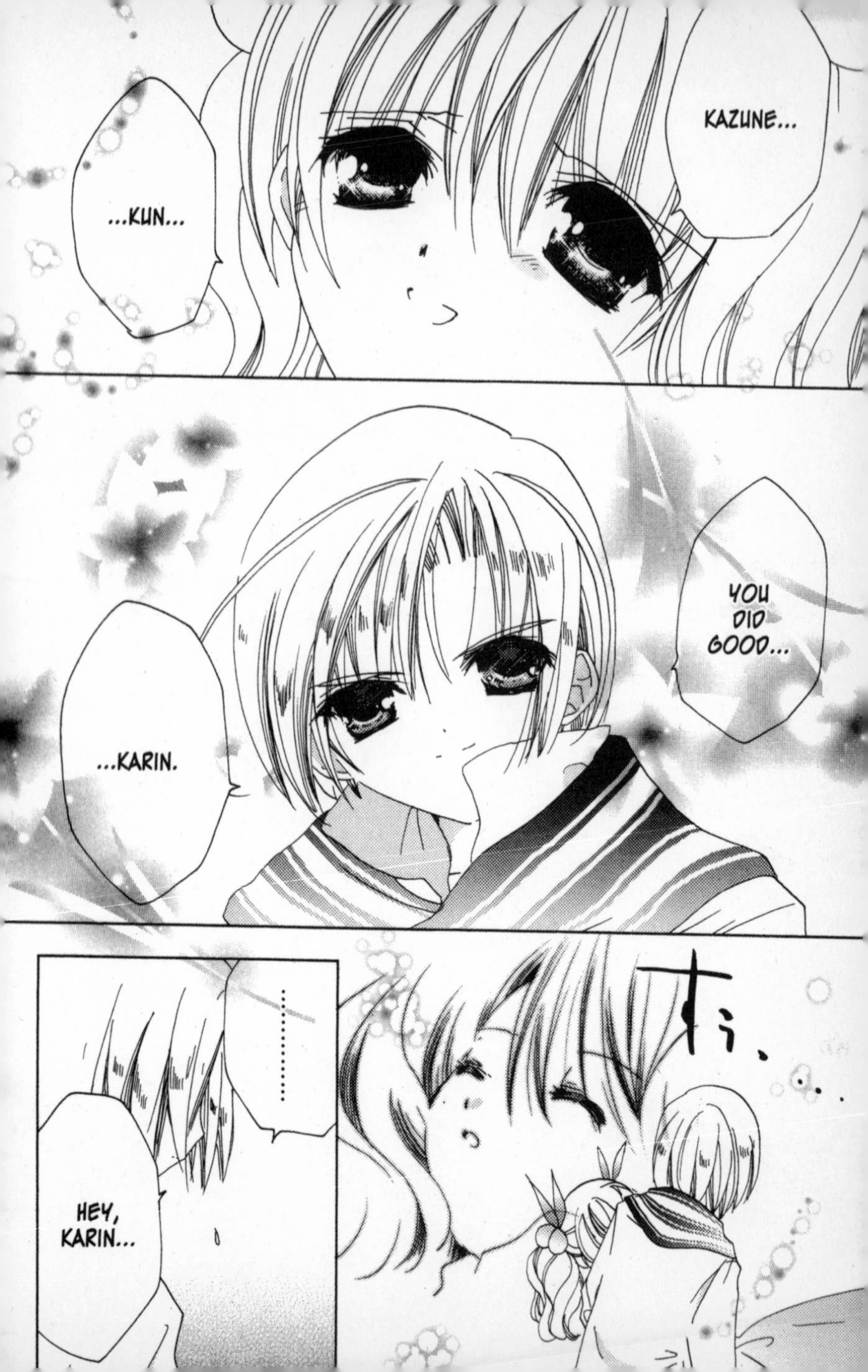
KAZUNE...
...KUN...
YOU DID GOOD...
...KARIN.
......
HEY, KARIN...

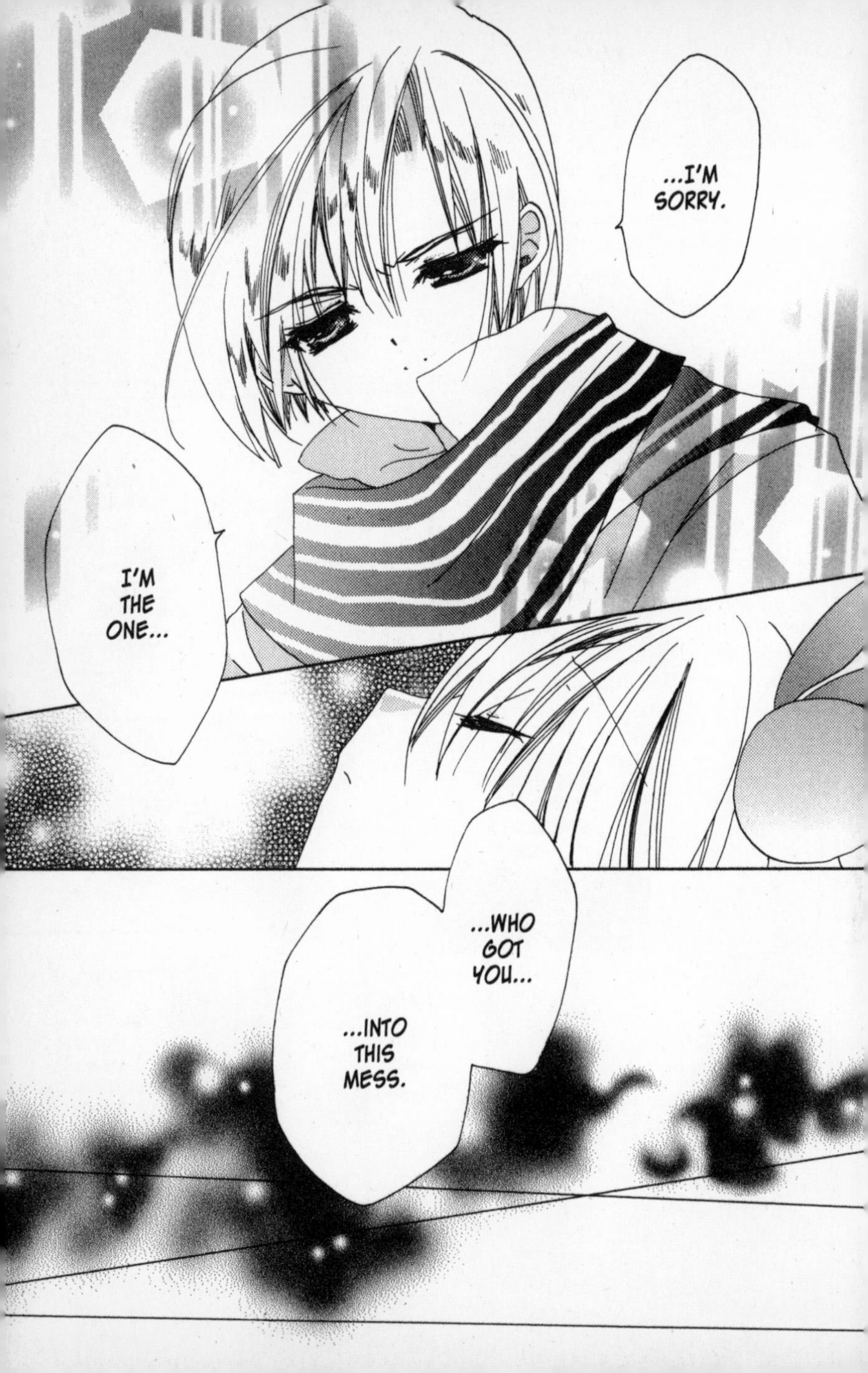
...I'M SORRY.
I'M THE ONE...
...WHO GOT YOU...
...INTO THIS MESS.

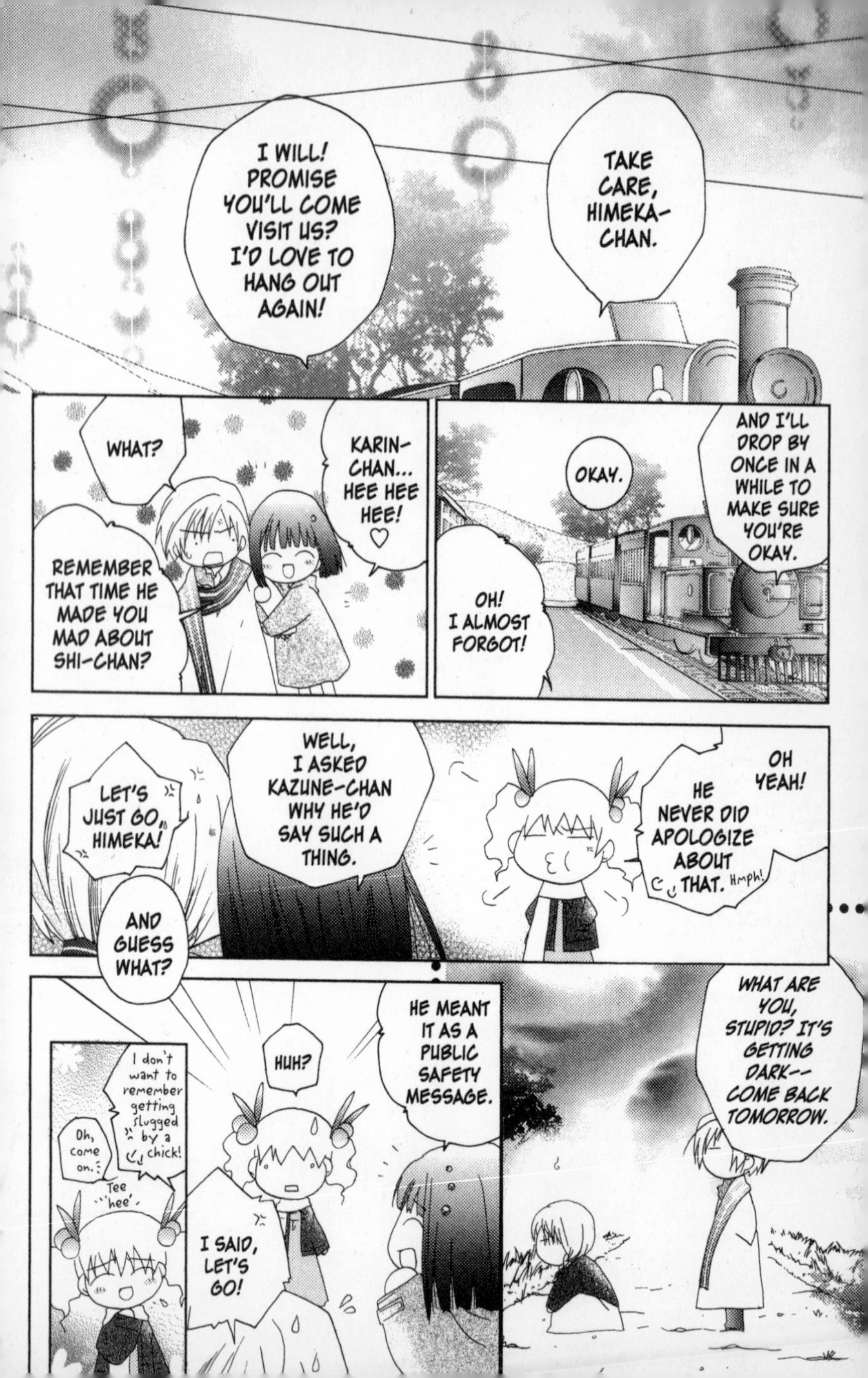
TAKE CARE, HIMEKA-CHAN.
I WILL! PROMISE YOU'LL COME VISIT US? I'D LOVE TO HANG OUT AGAIN!
AND I'LL DROP BY ONCE IN A WHILE TO MAKE SURE YOU'RE OKAY.
OKAY.
OH! I ALMOST FORGOT!
KARIN-CHAN... HEE HEE HEE!
WHAT?
REMEMBER THAT TIME HE MADE YOU MAD ABOUT SHI-CHAN?
OH YEAH!
HE NEVER DID APOLOGIZE ABOUT THAT.
Hmph!
WELL, I ASKED KAZUNE-CHAN WHY HE'D SAY SUCH A THING.
LET'S JUST GO, HIMEKA!
AND GUESS WHAT?
WHAT ARE YOU, STUPID? IT'S GETTING DARK--COME BACK TOMORROW.
HE MEANT IT AS A PUBLIC SAFETY MESSAGE.
HUH?
I SAID, LET'S GO!
I don't want to remember getting slugged by a chick!
Oh, come on.
Tee hee

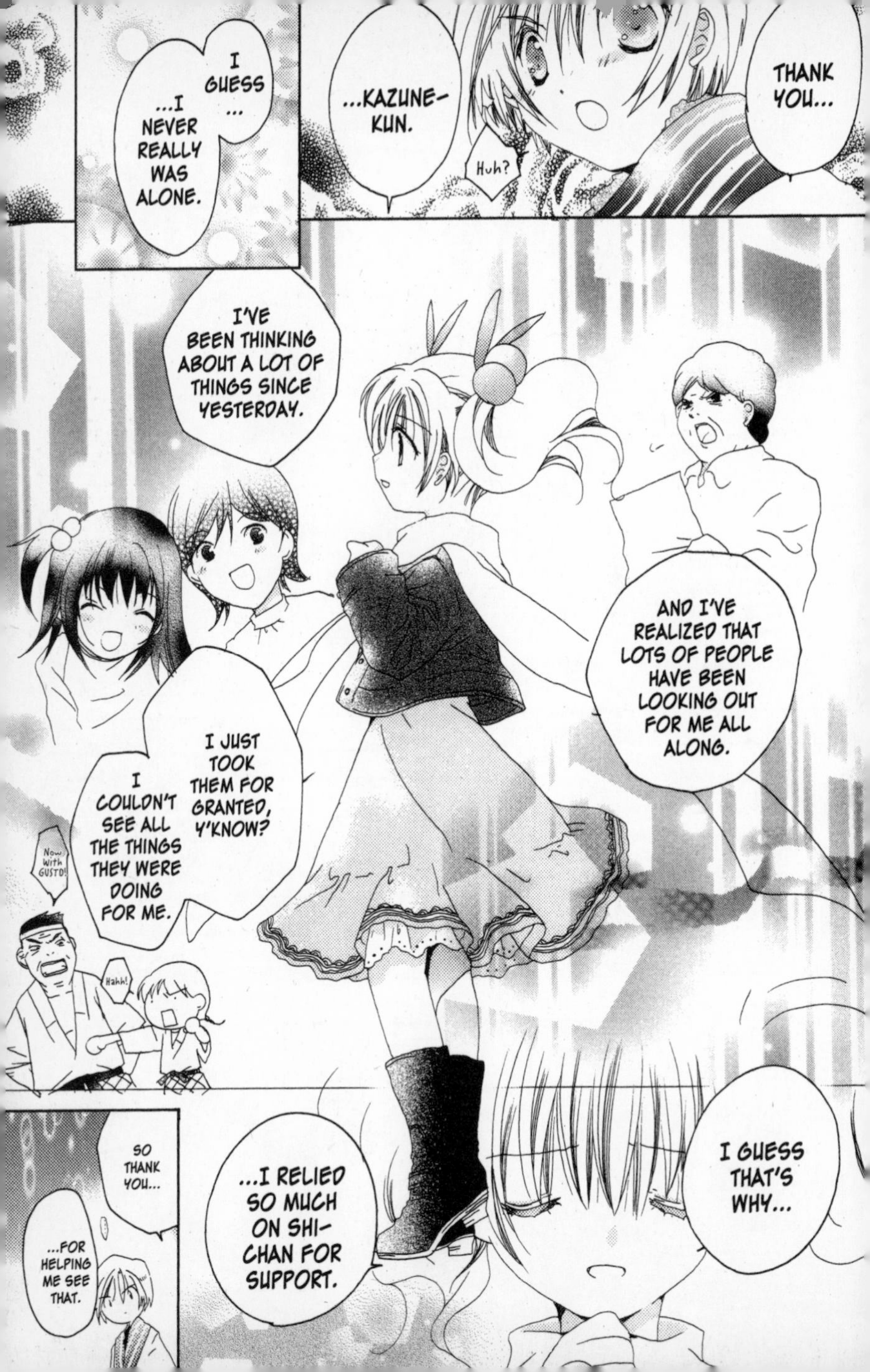
THANK YOU...
Huh?
...KAZUNE-KUN.
I GUESS... ...I NEVER REALLY WAS ALONE.
I'VE BEEN THINKING ABOUT A LOT OF THINGS SINCE YESTERDAY.
AND I'VE REALIZED THAT LOTS OF PEOPLE HAVE BEEN LOOKING OUT FOR ME ALL ALONG.
I JUST TOOK THEM FOR GRANTED, Y'KNOW?
I COULDN'T SEE ALL THE THINGS THEY WERE DOING FOR ME.
Now with GUSTO!
Hahh!
I GUESS THAT'S WHY...
...I RELIED SO MUCH ON SHI-CHAN FOR SUPPORT.
SO THANK YOU...
...FOR HELPING ME SEE THAT.

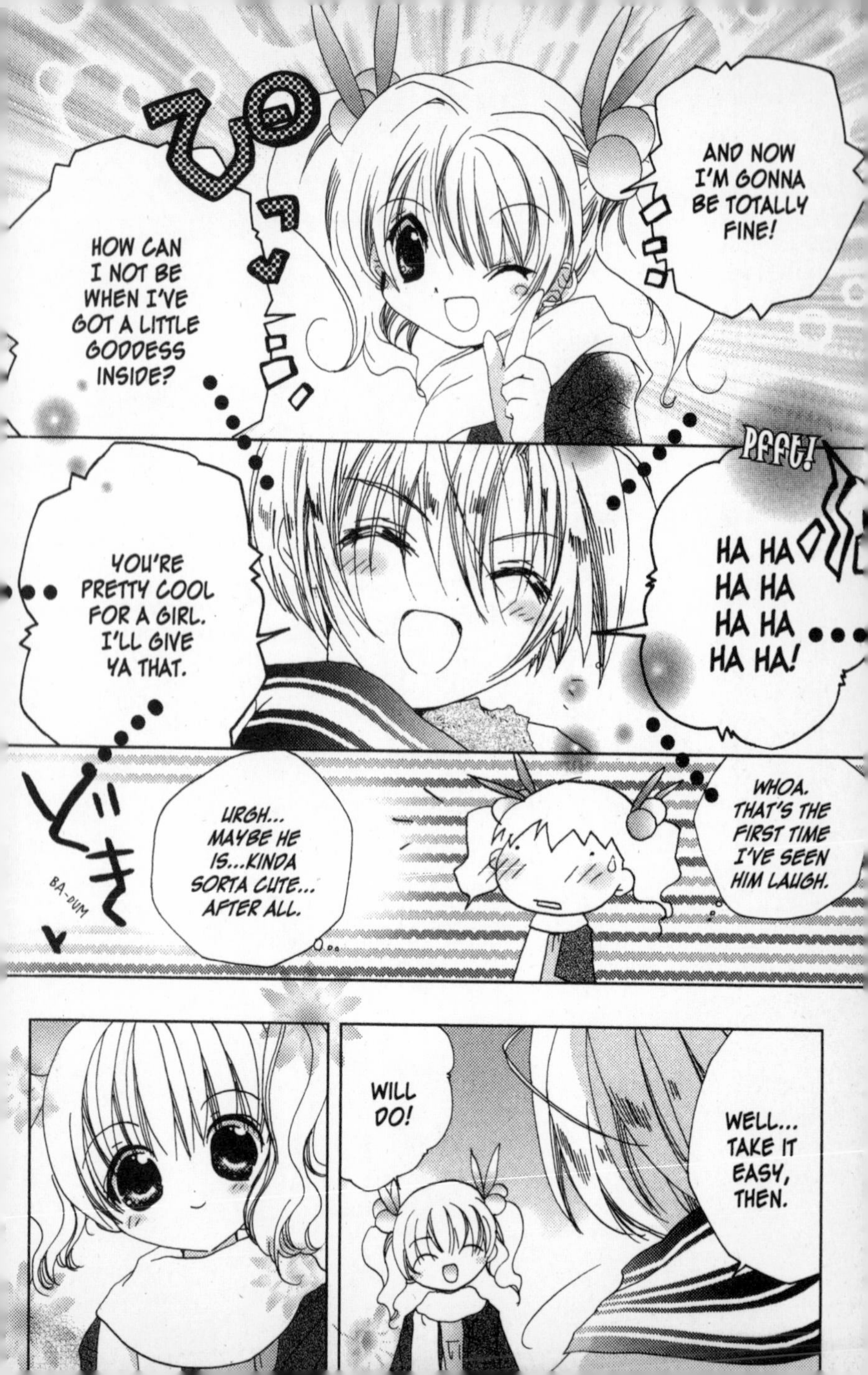
AND NOW I'M GONNA BE TOTALLY FINE!
HOW CAN I NOT BE WHEN I'VE GOT A LITTLE GODDESS INSIDE?
PFFT!
HA HA HA HA HA HA HA HA!
YOU'RE PRETTY COOL FOR A GIRL. I'LL GIVE YA THAT.
WHOA. THAT'S THE FIRST TIME I'VE SEEN HIM LAUGH.
URGH... MAYBE HE IS...KINDA SORTA CUTE... AFTER ALL.
どき
BA-DUM
WELL... TAKE IT EASY, THEN.
WILL DO!

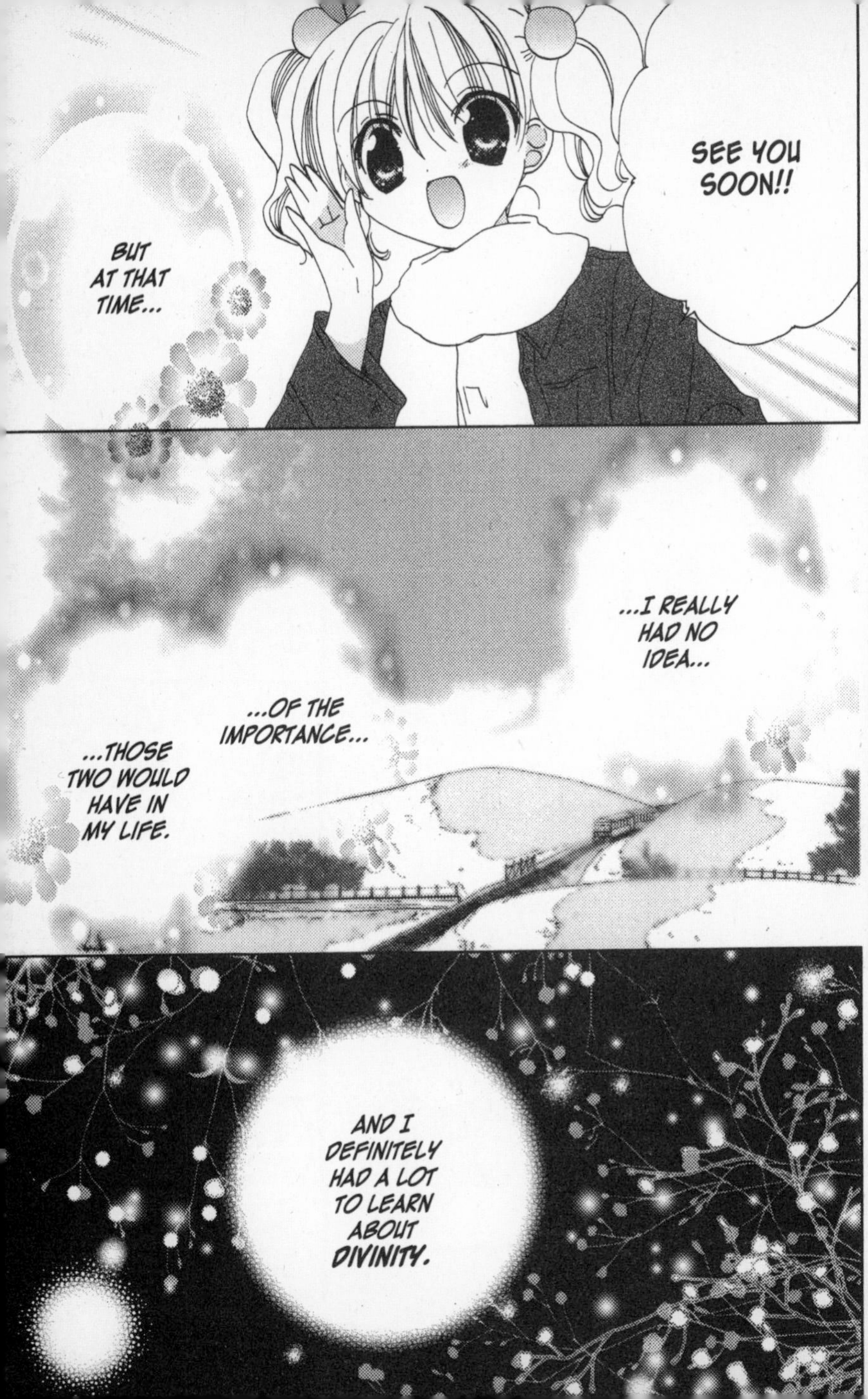
SEE YOU SOON!!
BUT AT THAT TIME...
...I REALLY HAD NO IDEA...
...OF THE IMPORTANCE...
...THOSE TWO WOULD HAVE IN MY LIFE.
AND I DEFINITELY HAD A LOT TO LEARN ABOUT DIVINITY.

+Potpourri!

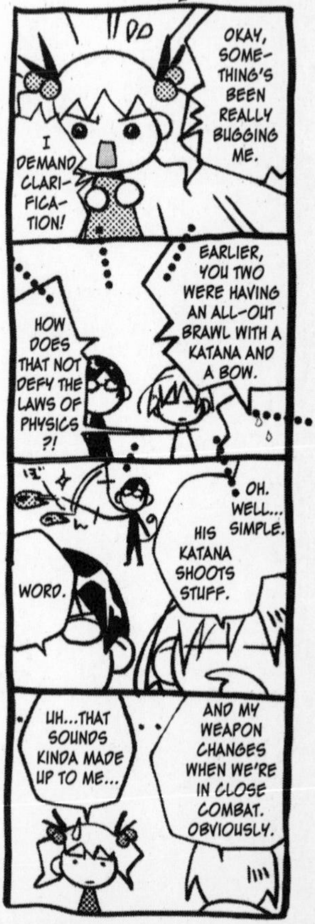
OKAY, SOMETHING'S BEEN REALLY BUGGING ME.
I DEMAND CLARIFICATION!
EARLIER, YOU TWO WERE HAVING AN ALL-OUT BRAWL WITH A KATANA AND A BOW.
HOW DOES THAT NOT DEFY THE LAWS OF PHYSICS?!
OH. WELL... SIMPLE.
HIS KATANA SHOOTS STUFF.
WORD.
AND MY WEAPON CHANGES WHEN WE'RE IN CLOSE COMBAT. OBVIOUSLY.
UH...THAT SOUNDS KINDA MADE UP TO ME...

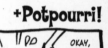

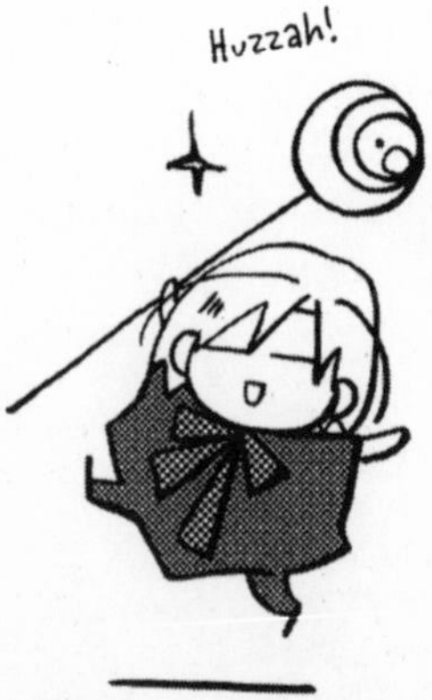
Huzzah!

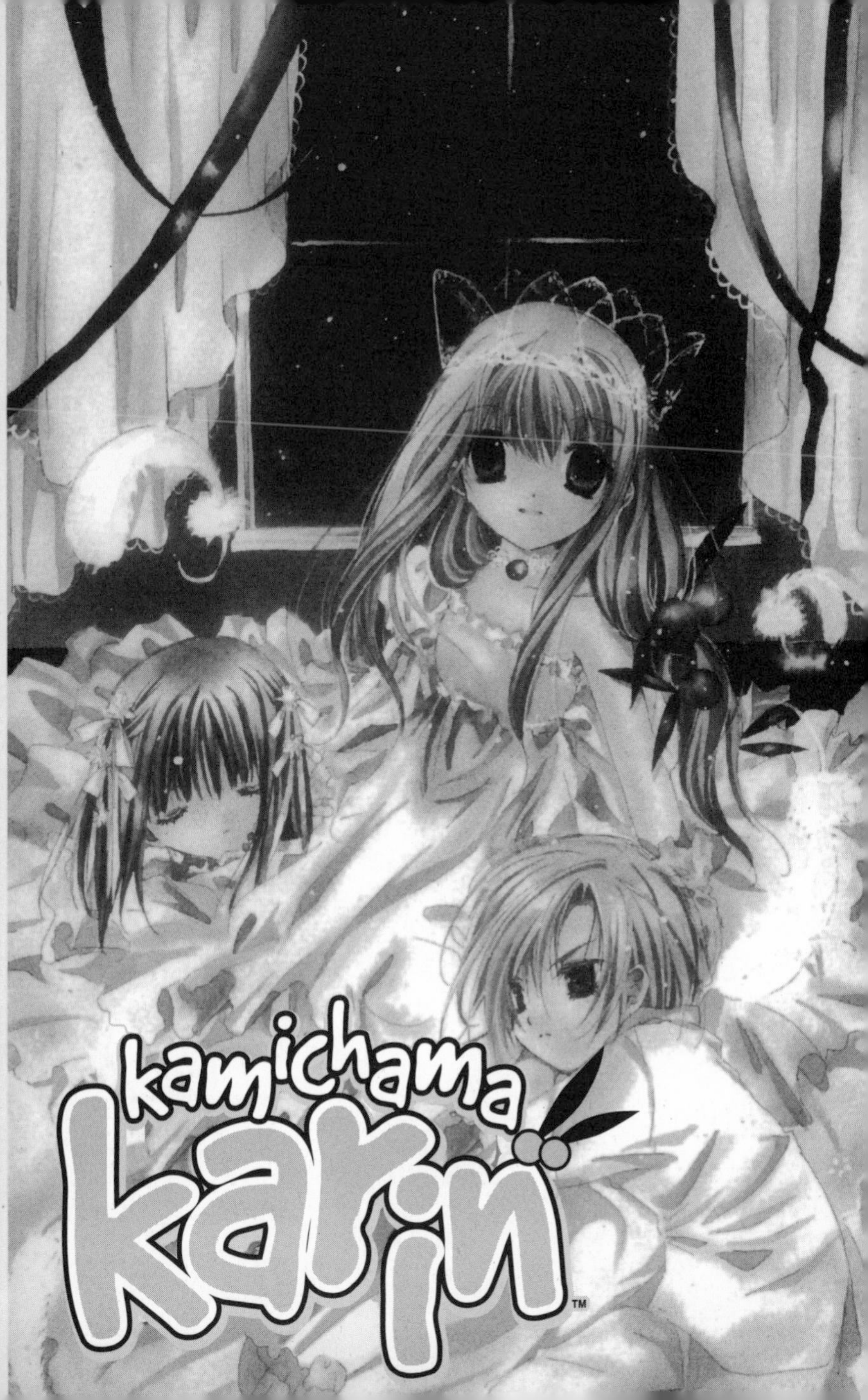
kamichama
karin™

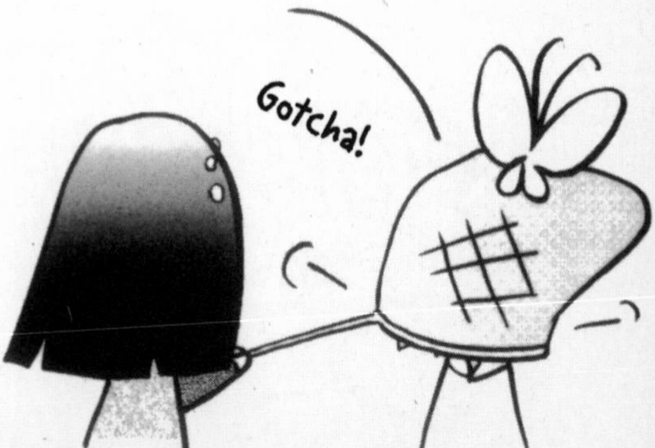
Gotcha!

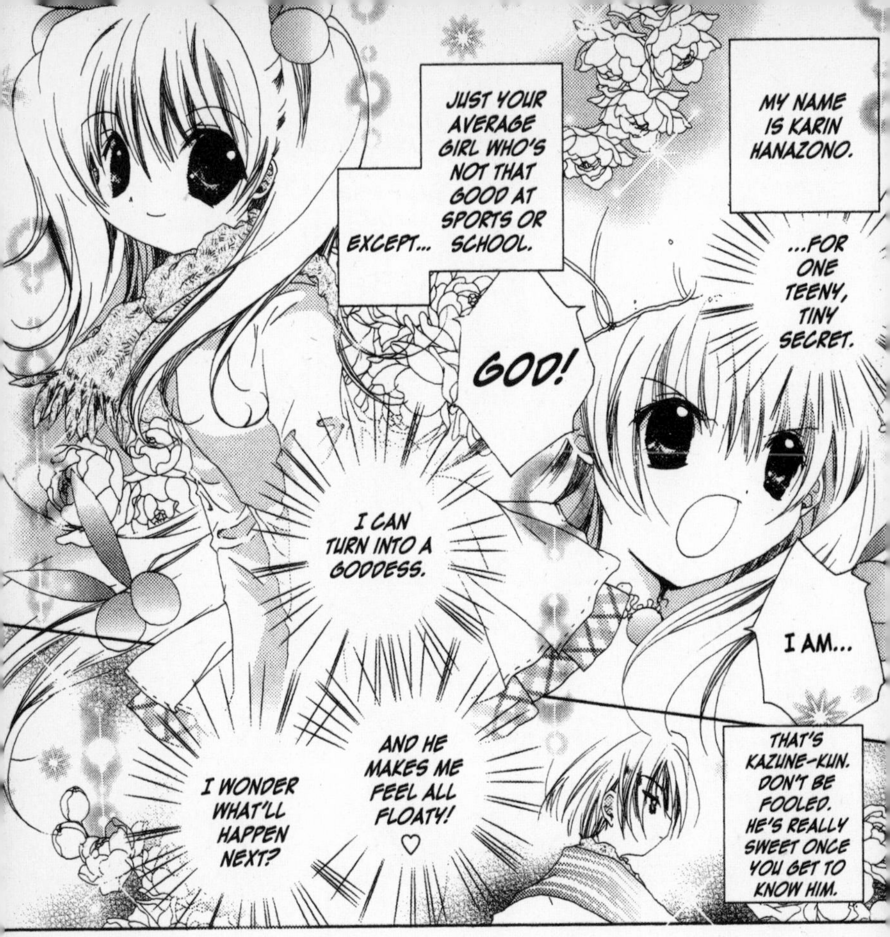
MY NAME IS KARIN HANAZONO.
JUST YOUR AVERAGE GIRL WHO'S NOT THAT GOOD AT SPORTS OR SCHOOL.
EXCEPT...
...FOR ONE TEENY, TINY SECRET.
I AM...
GOD!
I CAN TURN INTO A GODDESS.
THAT'S KAZUNE-KUN. DON'T BE FOOLED. HE'S REALLY SWEET ONCE YOU GET TO KNOW HIM.
AND HE MAKES ME FEEL ALL FLOATY! ♡
I WONDER WHAT'LL HAPPEN NEXT?

There used to be a synopsis here, but now it's gone, gone, gone!

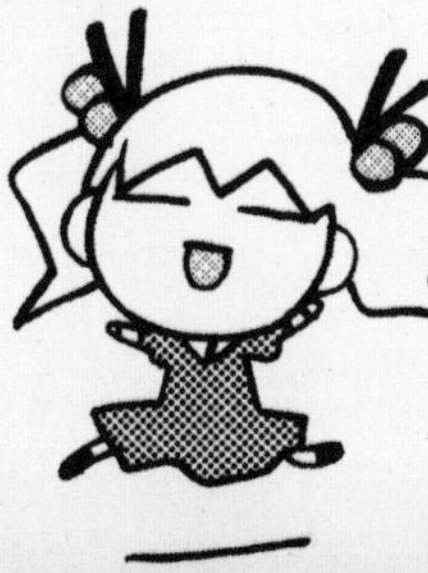

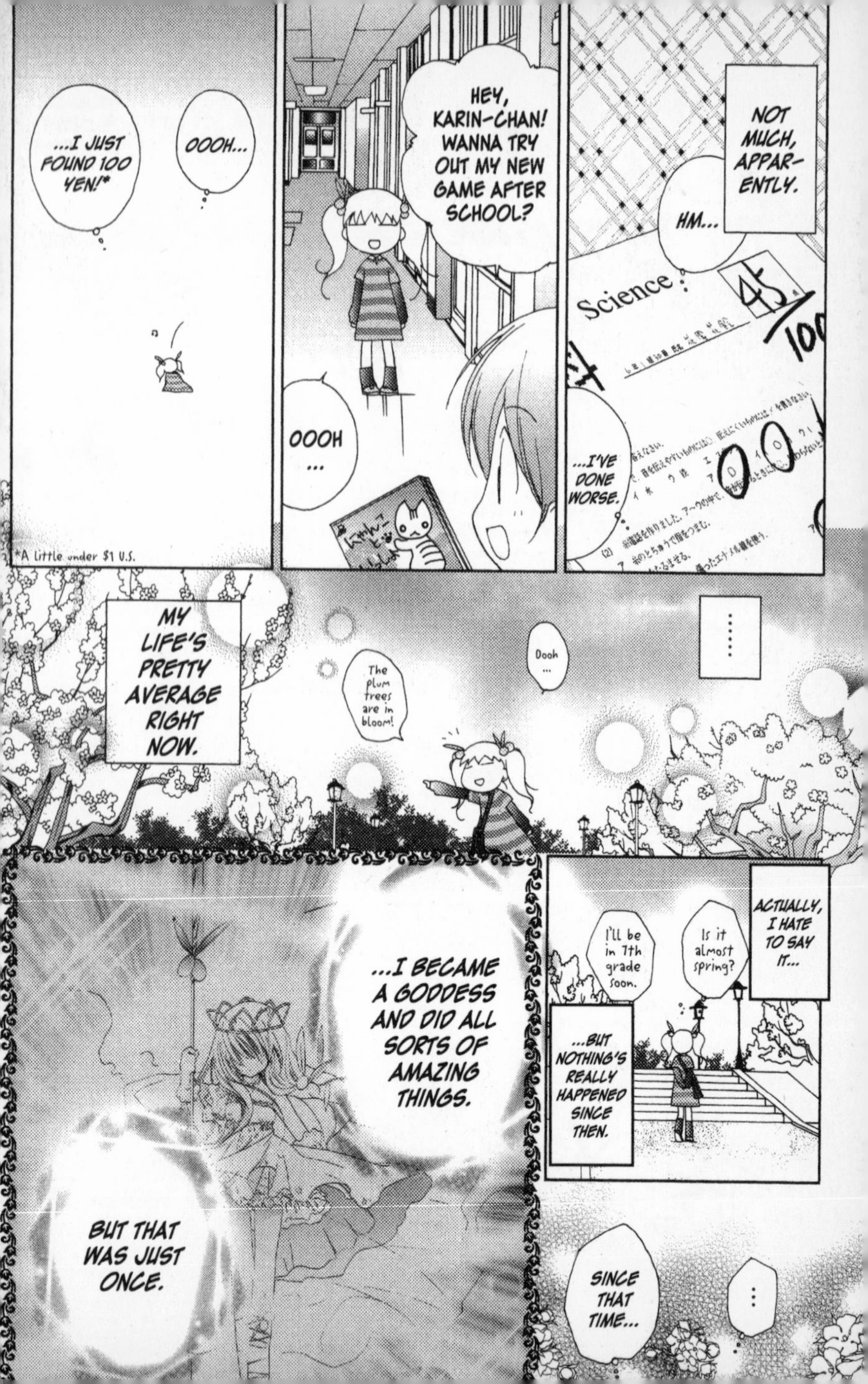
NOT MUCH, APPARENTLY.
HM...
Science
45/100
...I'VE DONE WORSE.
HEY, KARIN-CHAN! WANNA TRY OUT MY NEW GAME AFTER SCHOOL?
OOOH ...
OOOH...
...I JUST FOUND 100 YEN!*
*A little under $1 U.S.
......
Oooh ...
The plum trees are in bloom!
MY LIFE'S PRETTY AVERAGE RIGHT NOW.
ACTUALLY, I HATE TO SAY IT...
Is it almost spring?
I'll be in 7th grade soon.
...BUT NOTHING'S REALLY HAPPENED SINCE THEN.
...
SINCE THAT TIME...
...I BECAME A GODDESS AND DID ALL SORTS OF AMAZING THINGS.
BUT THAT WAS JUST ONCE.

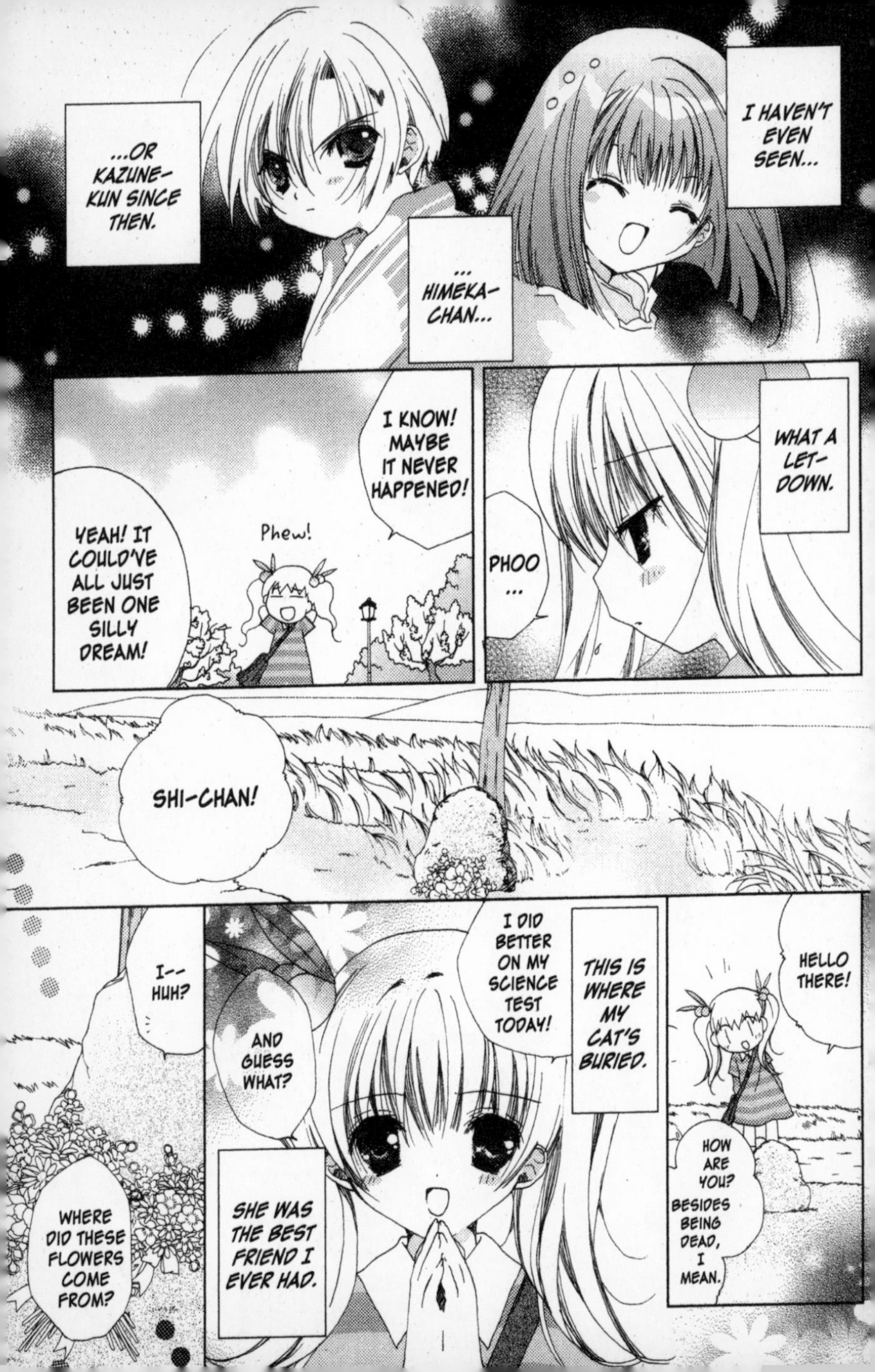
I HAVEN'T EVEN SEEN...
... HIMEKA-CHAN...
...OR KAZUNE-KUN SINCE THEN.
WHAT A LET-DOWN.
PHOO ...
I KNOW! MAYBE IT NEVER HAPPENED!
Phew!
YEAH! IT COULD'VE ALL JUST BEEN ONE SILLY DREAM!
SHI-CHAN!
HELLO THERE!
HOW ARE YOU?
BESIDES BEING DEAD, I MEAN.
THIS IS WHERE MY CAT'S BURIED.
I DID BETTER ON MY SCIENCE TEST TODAY!
AND GUESS WHAT?
SHE WAS THE BEST FRIEND I EVER HAD.
I-- HUH?
WHERE DID THESE FLOWERS COME FROM?

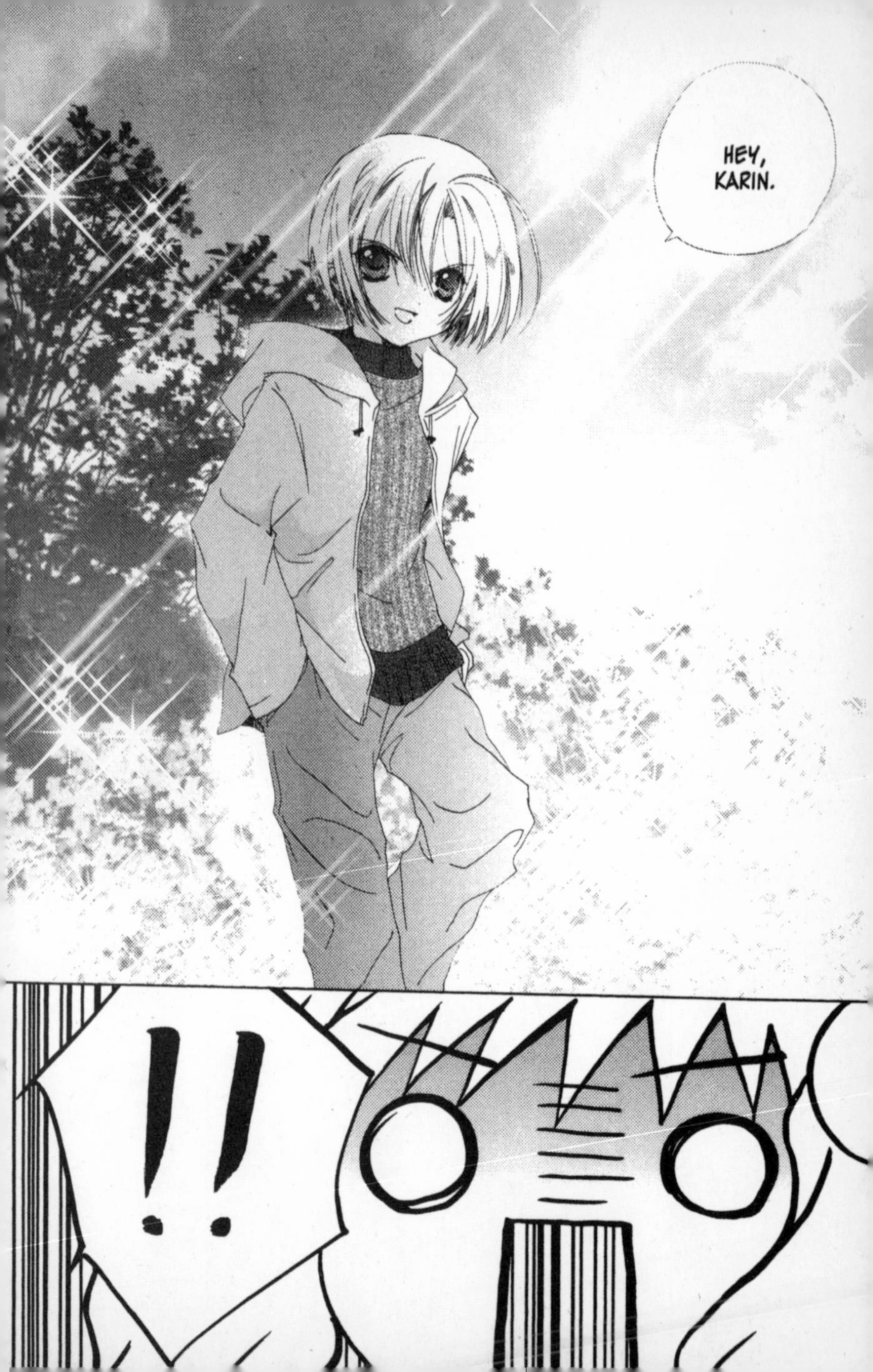
HEY, KARIN.
!!

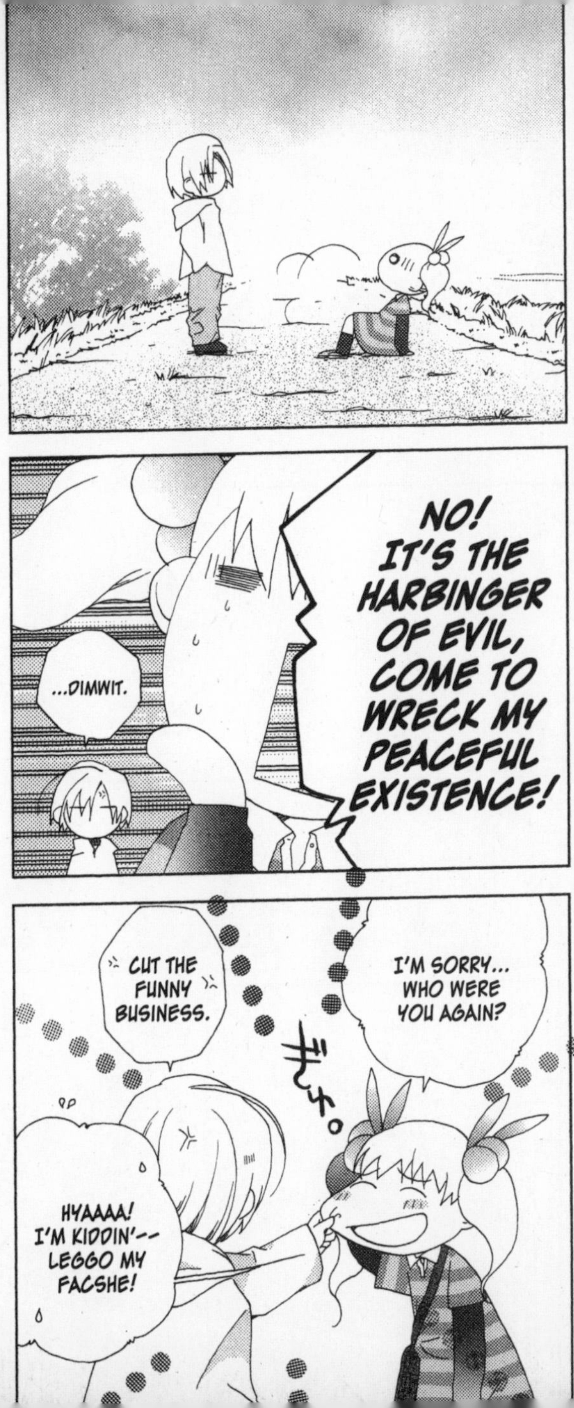
NO! IT'S THE HARBINGER OF EVIL, COME TO WRECK MY PEACEFUL EXISTENCE!
...DIMWIT.
I'M SORRY... WHO WERE YOU AGAIN?
ぎゅっ
CUT THE FUNNY BUSINESS.
HYAAAA! I'M KIDDIN'-- LEGGO MY FACSHE!

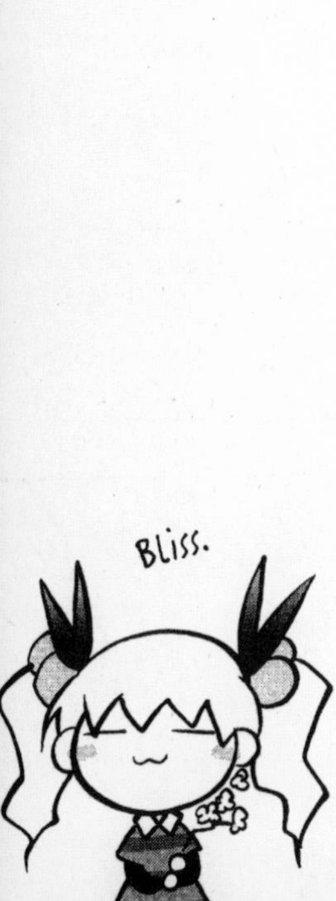
BLISS.

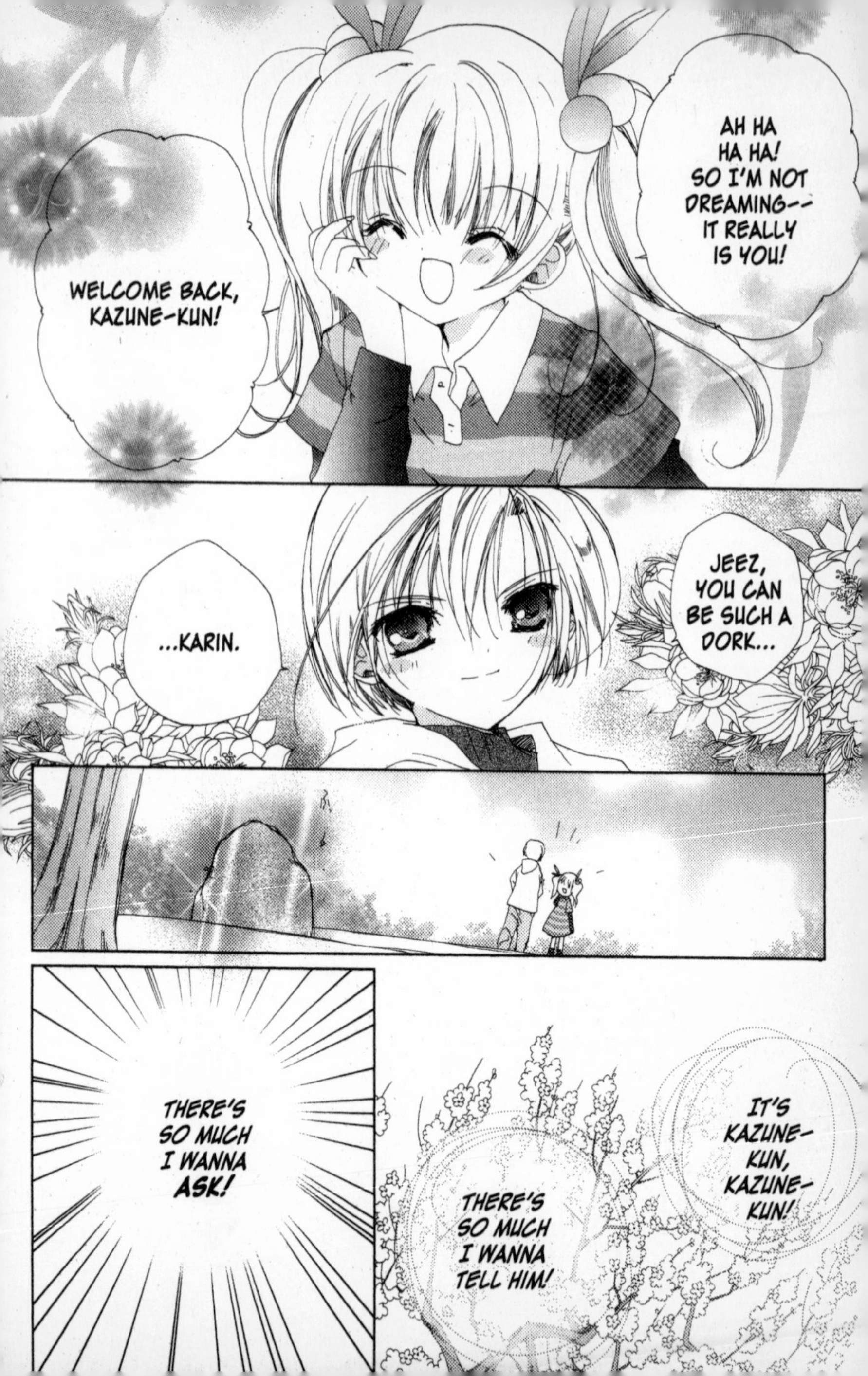
AH HA HA HA! SO I'M NOT DREAMING-- IT REALLY IS YOU!
WELCOME BACK, KAZUNE-KUN!
JEEZ, YOU CAN BE SUCH A DORK...
...KARIN.
IT'S KAZUNE-KUN, KAZUNE-KUN!
THERE'S SO MUCH I WANNA TELL HIM!
THERE'S SO MUCH I WANNA ASK!

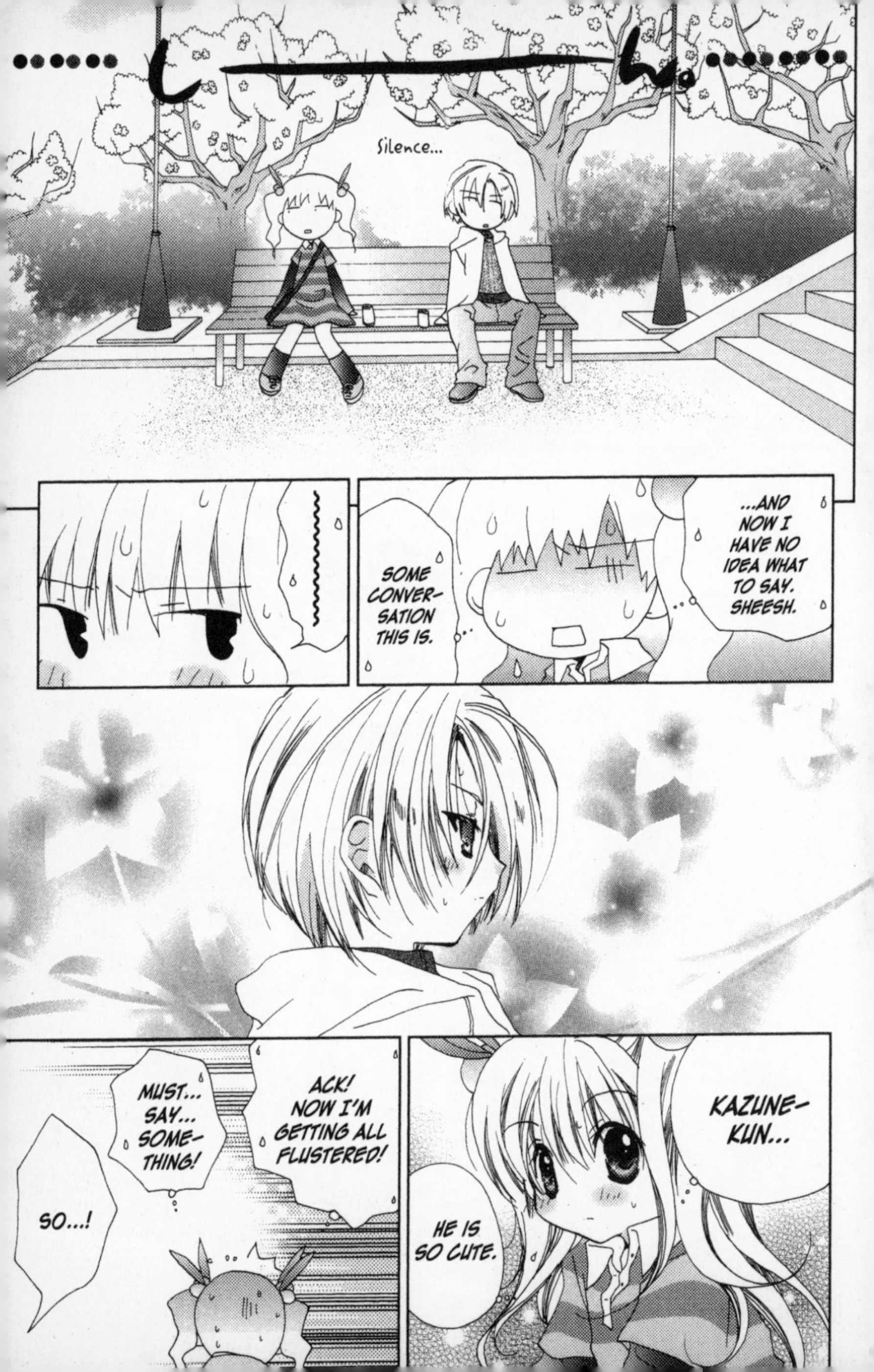
......し―――ん......
Silence...
...AND NOW I HAVE NO IDEA WHAT TO SAY. SHEESH.
SOME CONVERSATION THIS IS.
KAZUNE-KUN...
HE IS SO CUTE.
ACK! NOW I'M GETTING ALL FLUSTERED!
MUST... SAY... SOMETHING!
SO...!

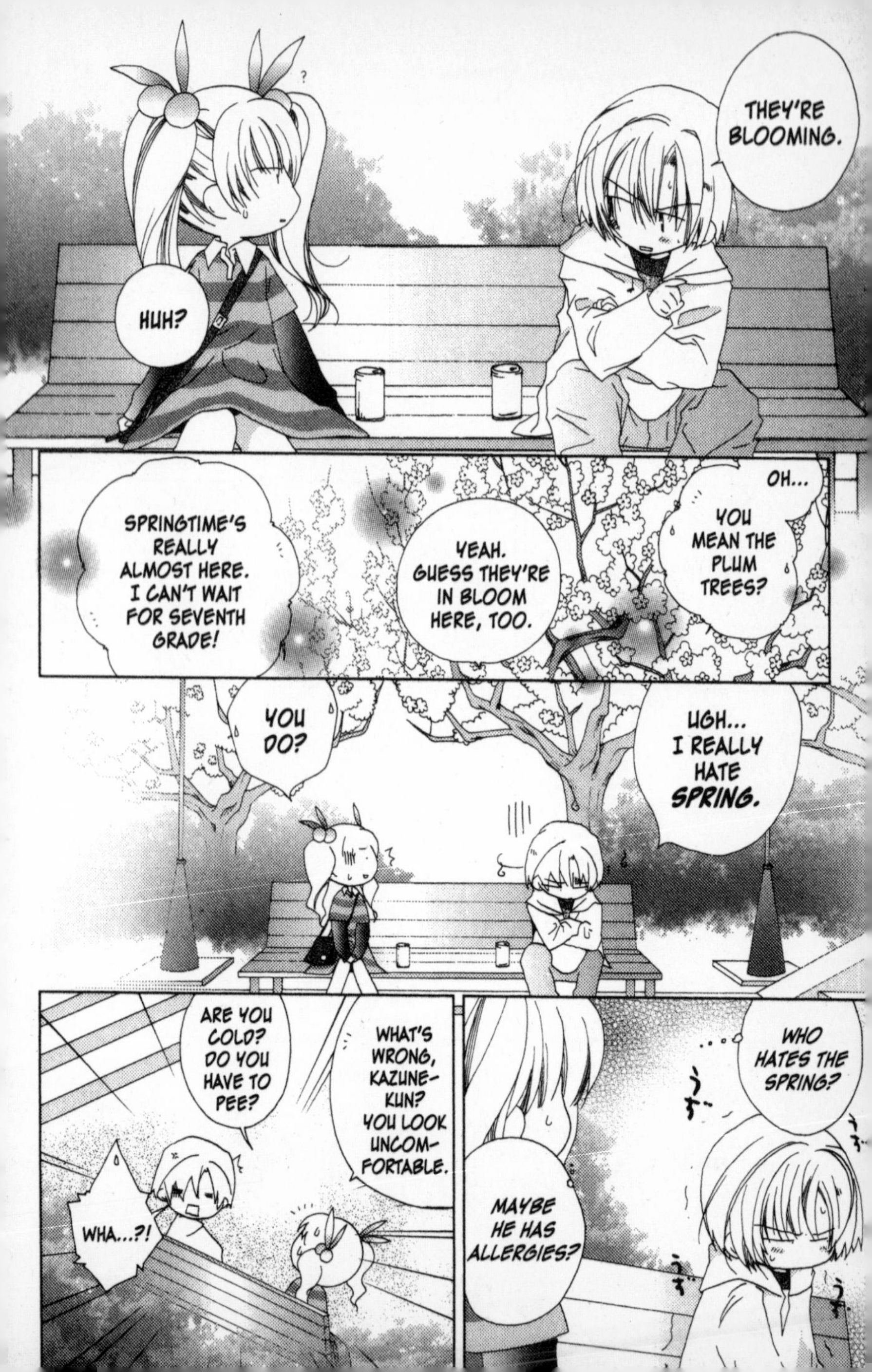
THEY'RE BLOOMING.
HUH?
OH... YOU MEAN THE PLUM TREES?
YEAH. GUESS THEY'RE IN BLOOM HERE, TOO.
SPRINGTIME'S REALLY ALMOST HERE. I CAN'T WAIT FOR SEVENTH GRADE!
UGH... I REALLY HATE SPRING.
YOU DO?
WHO HATES THE SPRING?
MAYBE HE HAS ALLERGIES?
WHAT'S WRONG, KAZUNE-KUN? YOU LOOK UNCOMFORTABLE.
ARE YOU COLD? DO YOU HAVE TO PEE?
WHA...?!

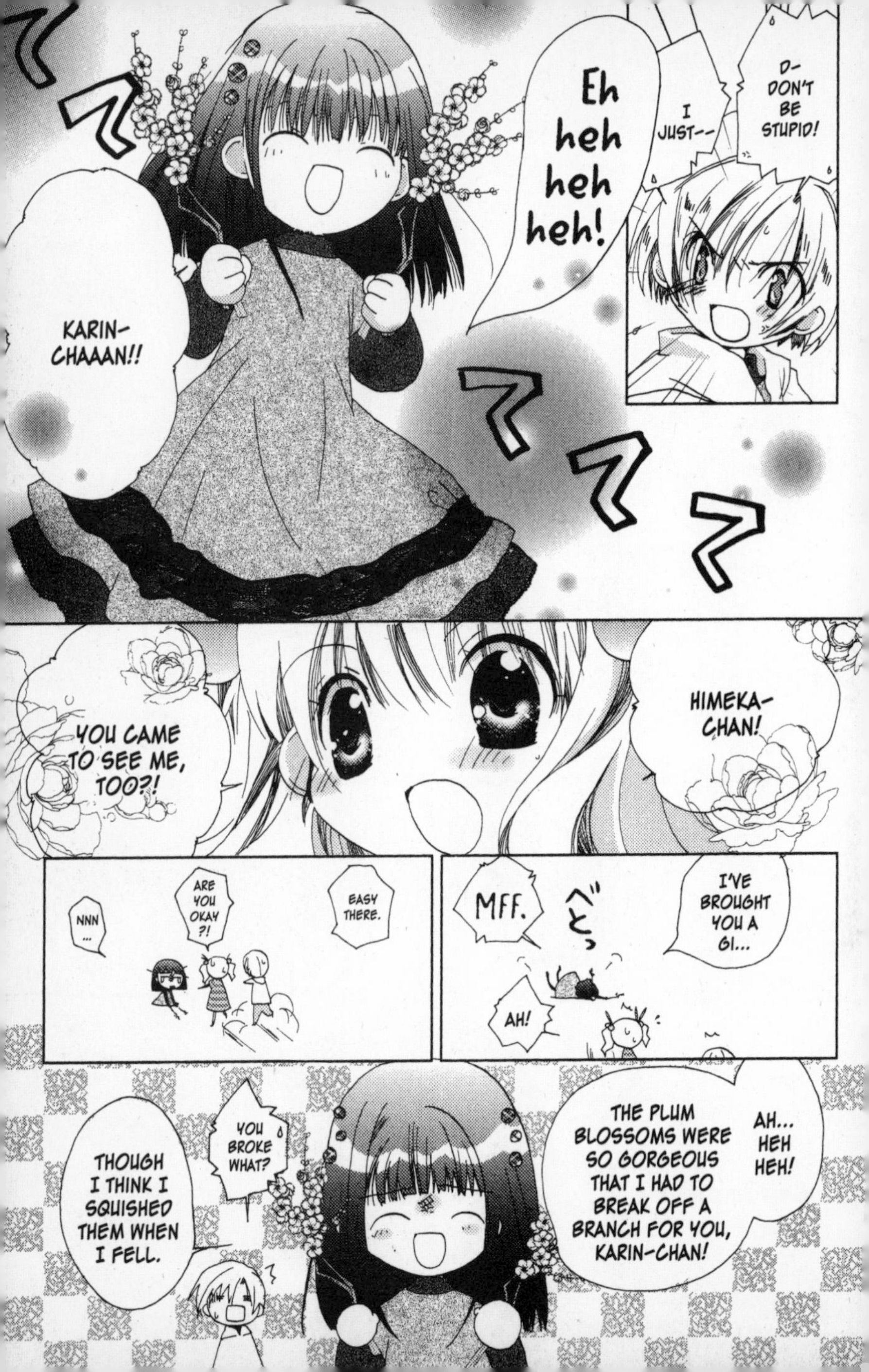
D-DON'T BE STUPID!
I JUST--
Eh heh heh heh!
KARIN-CHAAAN!!
HIMEKA-CHAN!
YOU CAME TO SEE ME, TOO?!
I'VE BROUGHT YOU A GI...
MFF.
べとっ
AH!
EASY THERE.
ARE YOU OKAY?!
NNN...
AH... HEH HEH!
THE PLUM BLOSSOMS WERE SO GORGEOUS THAT I HAD TO BREAK OFF A BRANCH FOR YOU, KARIN-CHAN!
YOU BROKE WHAT?
THOUGH I THINK I SQUISHED THEM WHEN I FELL.

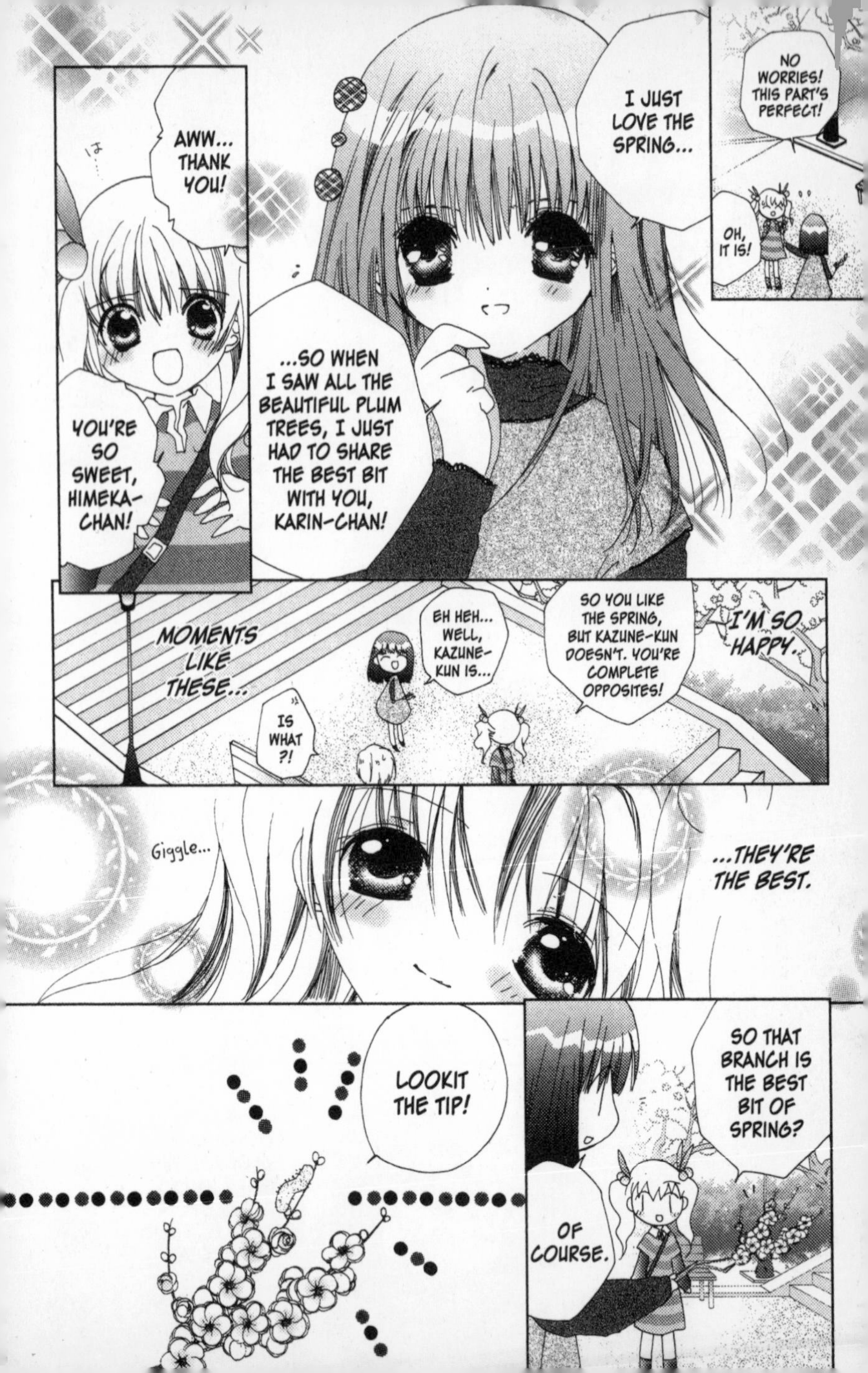
NO WORRIES! THIS PART'S PERFECT!
OH, IT IS!
I JUST LOVE THE SPRING...
...SO WHEN I SAW ALL THE BEAUTIFUL PLUM TREES, I JUST HAD TO SHARE THE BEST BIT WITH YOU, KARIN-CHAN!
AWW... THANK YOU!
YOU'RE SO SWEET, HIMEKA-CHAN!
I'M SO HAPPY.
SO YOU LIKE THE SPRING, BUT KAZUNE-KUN DOESN'T. YOU'RE COMPLETE OPPOSITES!
EH HEH... WELL, KAZUNE-KUN IS...
IS WHAT ?!
MOMENTS LIKE THESE...
...THEY'RE THE BEST.
Giggle...
SO THAT BRANCH IS THE BEST BIT OF SPRING?
OF COURSE.
LOOKIT THE TIP!

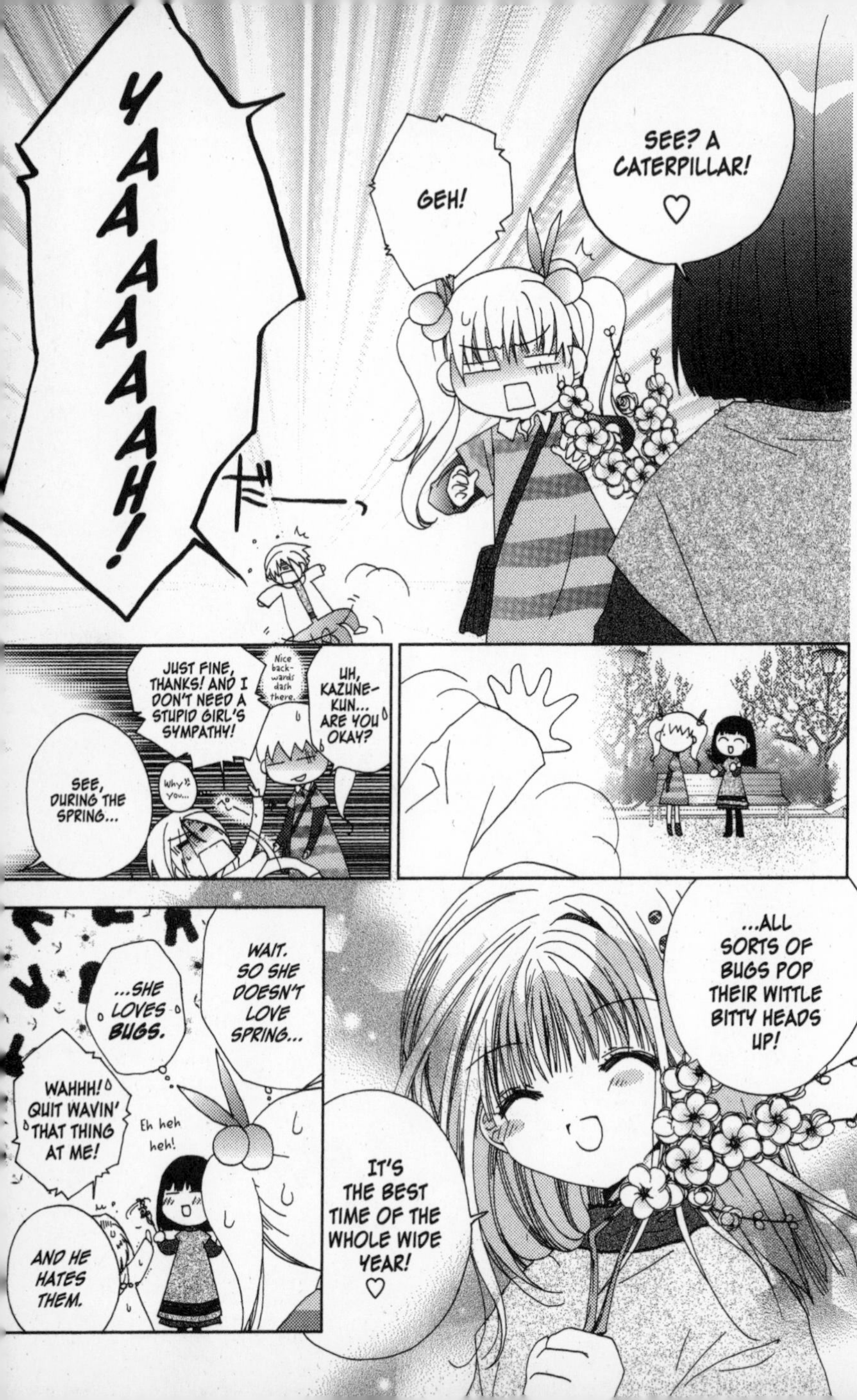
SEE? A CATERPILLAR! ♡
GEH!
YAAAAAAH!
UH, KAZUNE-KUN... ARE YOU OKAY?
Nice back-wards dash there.
JUST FINE, THANKS! AND I DON'T NEED A STUPID GIRL'S SYMPATHY!
Why you...
SEE, DURING THE SPRING...
...ALL SORTS OF BUGS POP THEIR WITTLE BITTY HEADS UP!
IT'S THE BEST TIME OF THE WHOLE WIDE YEAR! ♡
WAIT. SO SHE DOESN'T LOVE SPRING...
...SHE LOVES BUGS.
WAHHH! QUIT WAVIN' THAT THING AT ME!
Eh heh heh!
AND HE HATES THEM.

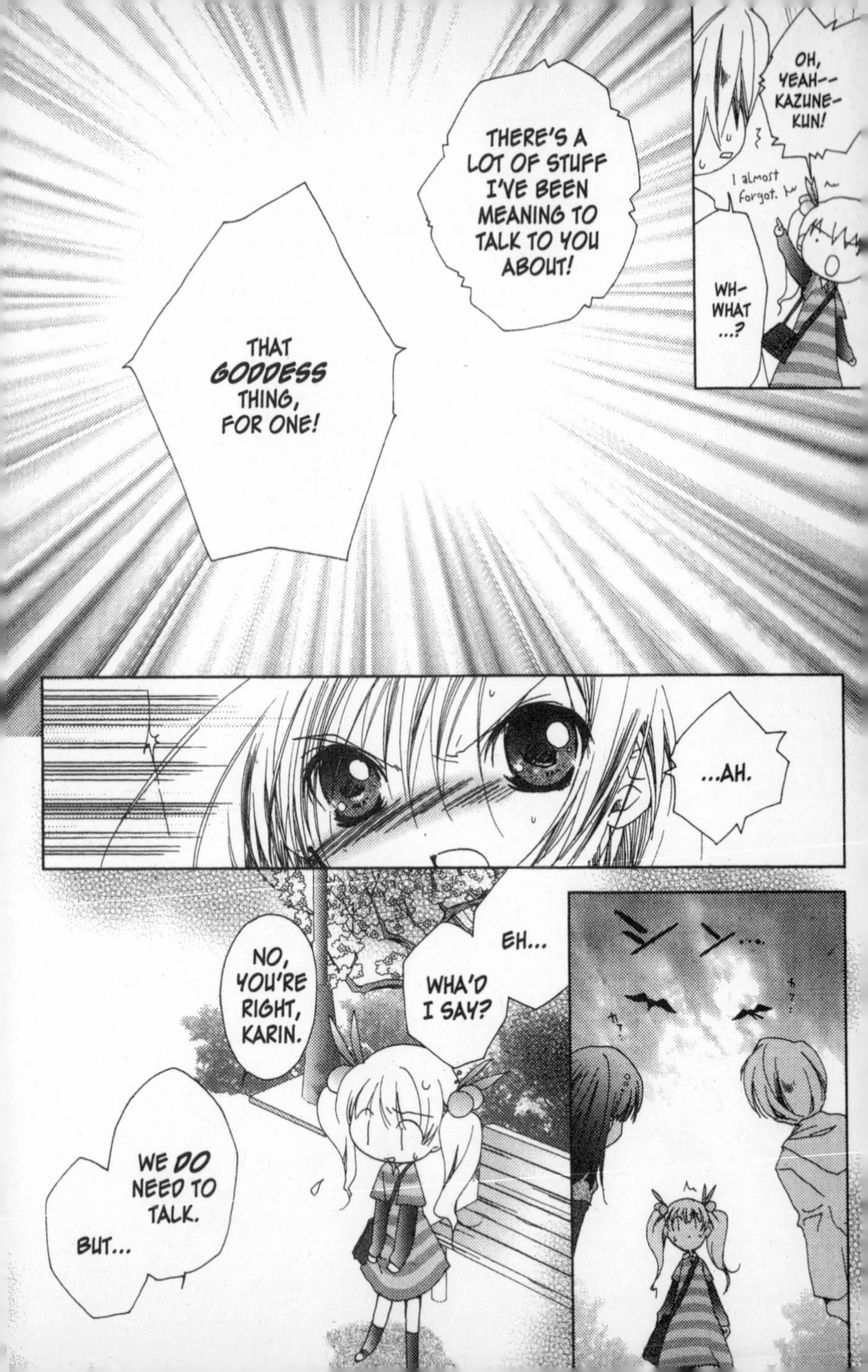
OH, YEAH--KAZUNE-KUN!
I almost forgot.
WH-WHAT...?
THERE'S A LOT OF STUFF I'VE BEEN MEANING TO TALK TO YOU ABOUT!
THAT *GODDESS* THING, FOR ONE!
...AH.
EH...
WHA'D I SAY?
NO, YOU'RE RIGHT, KARIN.
WE *DO* NEED TO TALK.
BUT...

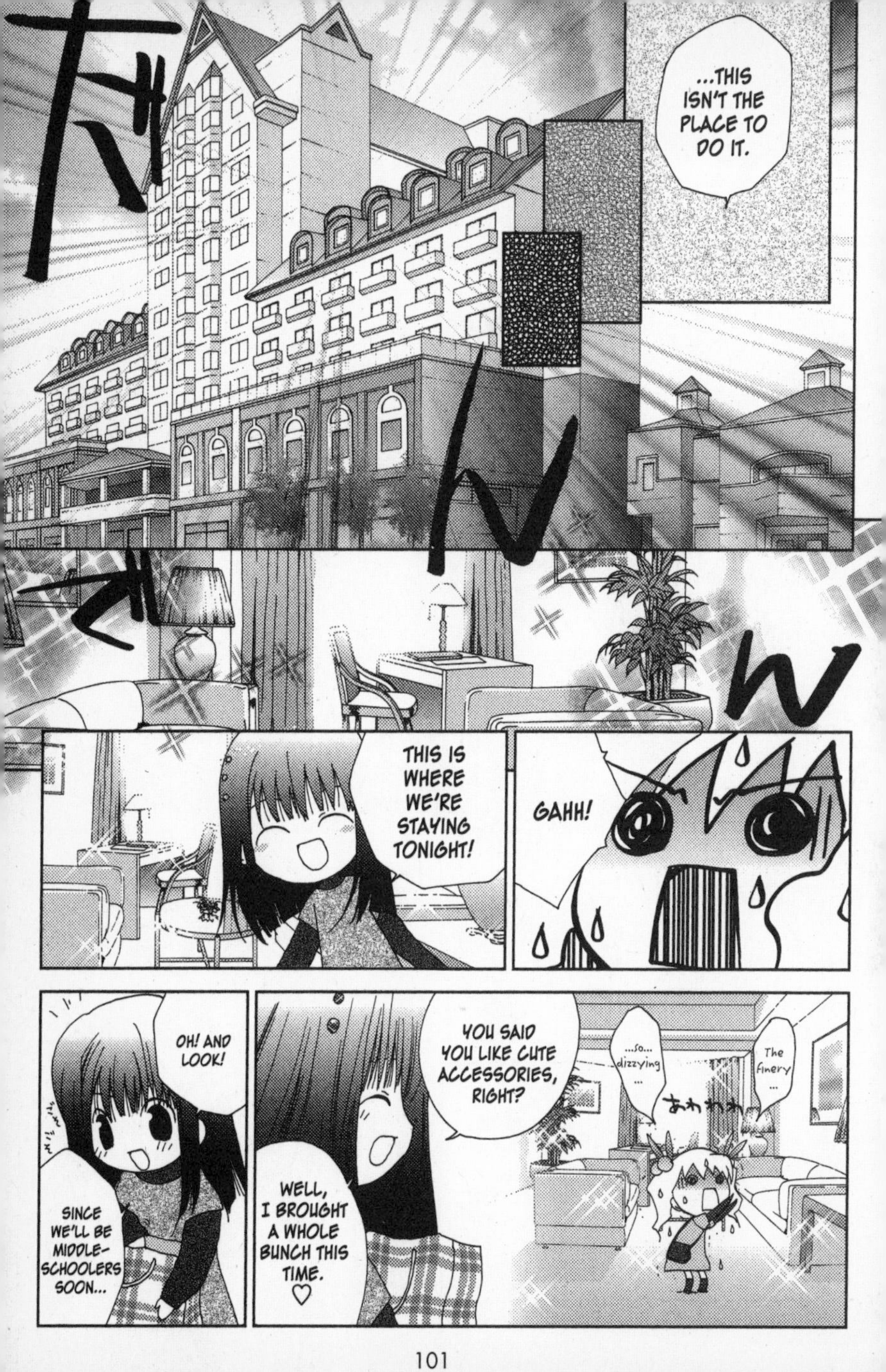
...THIS ISN'T THE PLACE TO DO IT.
GAHH!
THIS IS WHERE WE'RE STAYING TONIGHT!
The finery ...
...so... dizzying ...
YOU SAID YOU LIKE CUTE ACCESSORIES, RIGHT?
あわわわ
WELL, I BROUGHT A WHOLE BUNCH THIS TIME. ♡
OH! AND LOOK!
SINCE WE'LL BE MIDDLE-SCHOOLERS SOON...

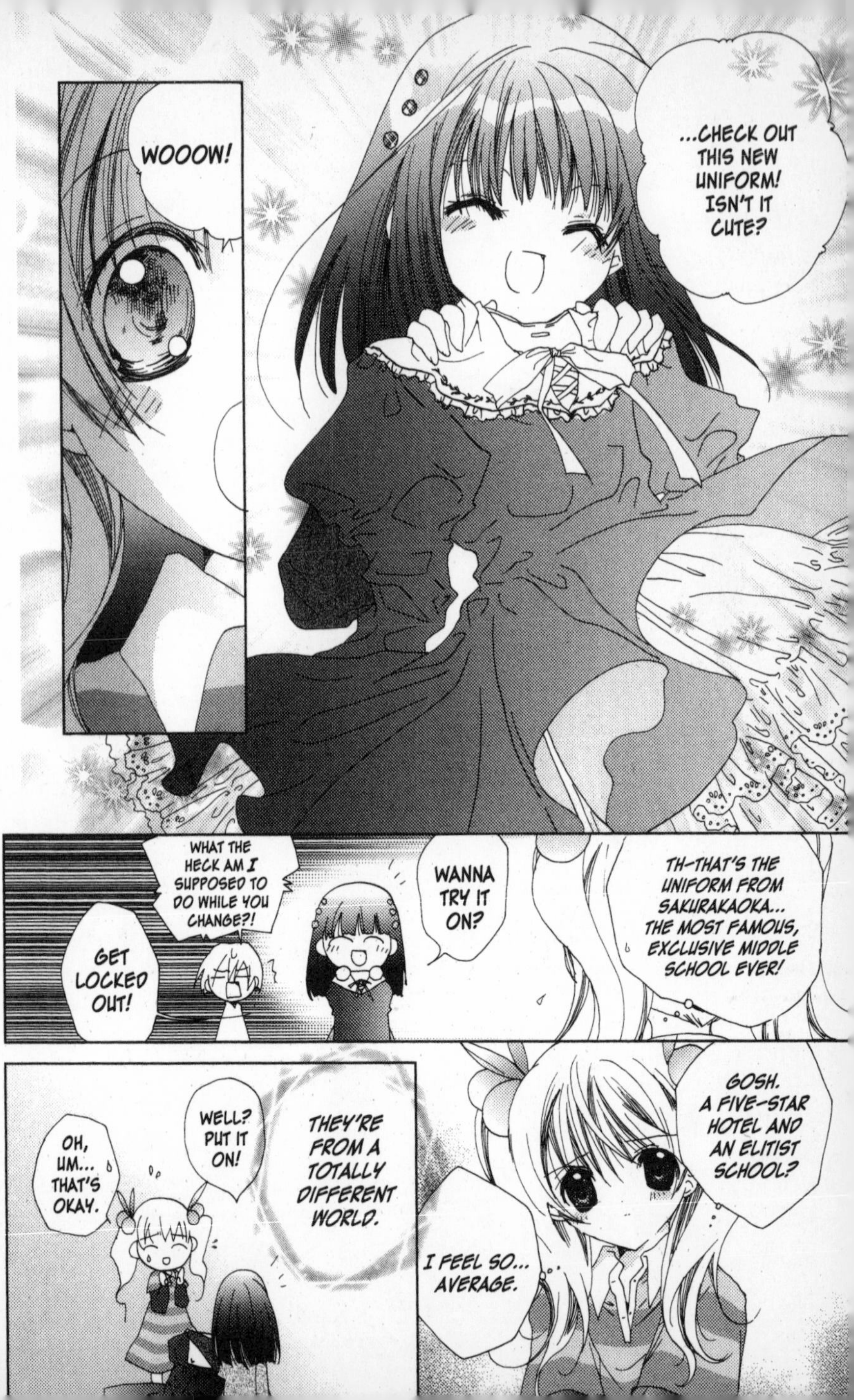
...CHECK OUT THIS NEW UNIFORM! ISN'T IT CUTE?
WOOOW!
TH-THAT'S THE UNIFORM FROM SAKURAKAOKA... THE MOST FAMOUS, EXCLUSIVE MIDDLE SCHOOL EVER!
WANNA TRY IT ON?
WHAT THE HECK AM I SUPPOSED TO DO WHILE YOU CHANGE?!
GET LOCKED OUT!
GOSH. A FIVE-STAR HOTEL AND AN ELITIST SCHOOL?
I FEEL SO... AVERAGE.
THEY'RE FROM A TOTALLY DIFFERENT WORLD.
WELL? PUT IT ON!
OH, UM... THAT'S OKAY.

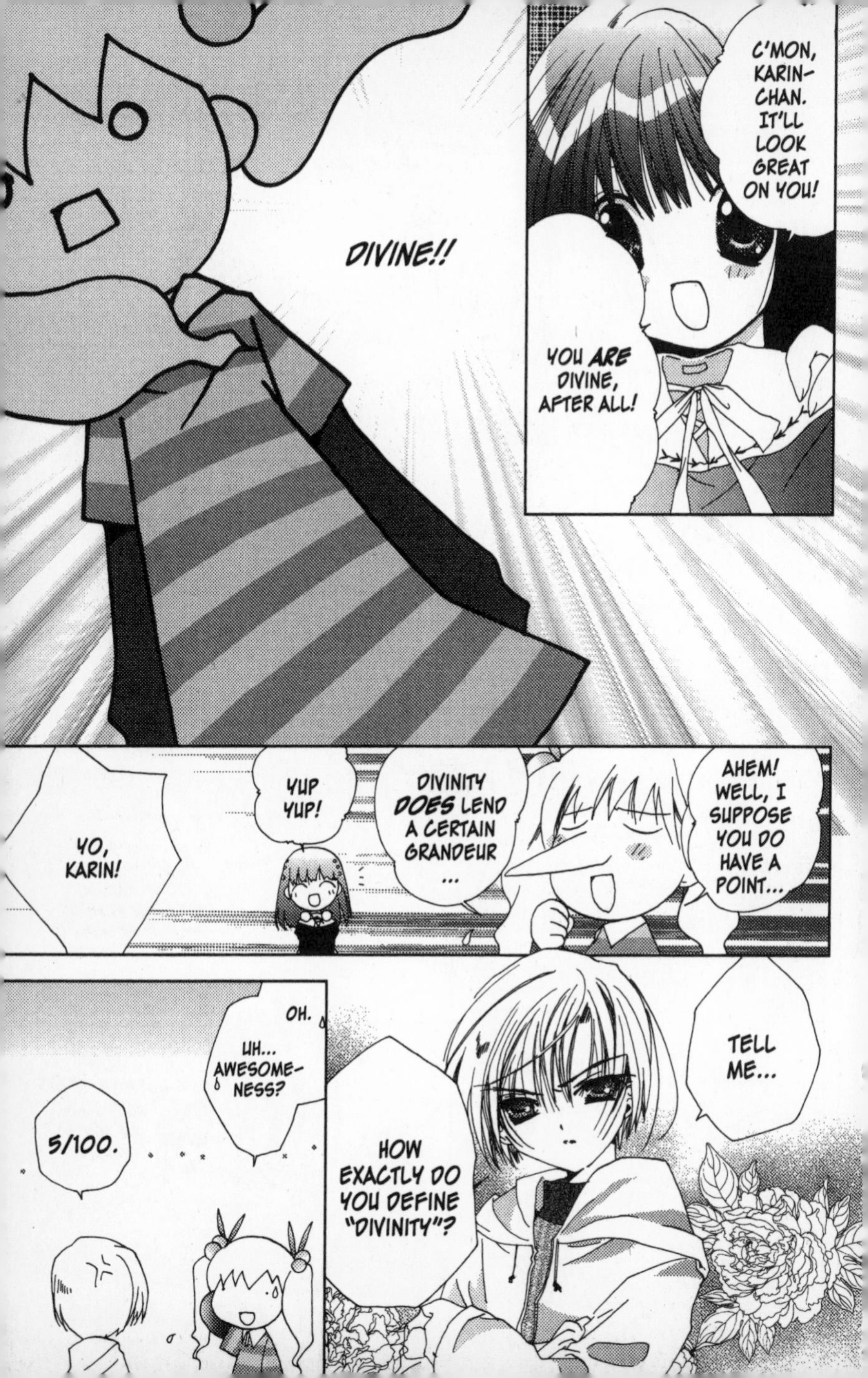
C'MON, KARIN-CHAN. IT'LL LOOK GREAT ON YOU!
YOU **ARE** DIVINE, AFTER ALL!
DIVINE!!
AHEM! WELL, I SUPPOSE YOU DO HAVE A POINT...
DIVINITY **DOES** LEND A CERTAIN GRANDEUR ...
YUP YUP!
YO, KARIN!
TELL ME...
HOW EXACTLY DO YOU DEFINE "DIVINITY"?
OH.
UH... AWESOMENESS?
5/100.

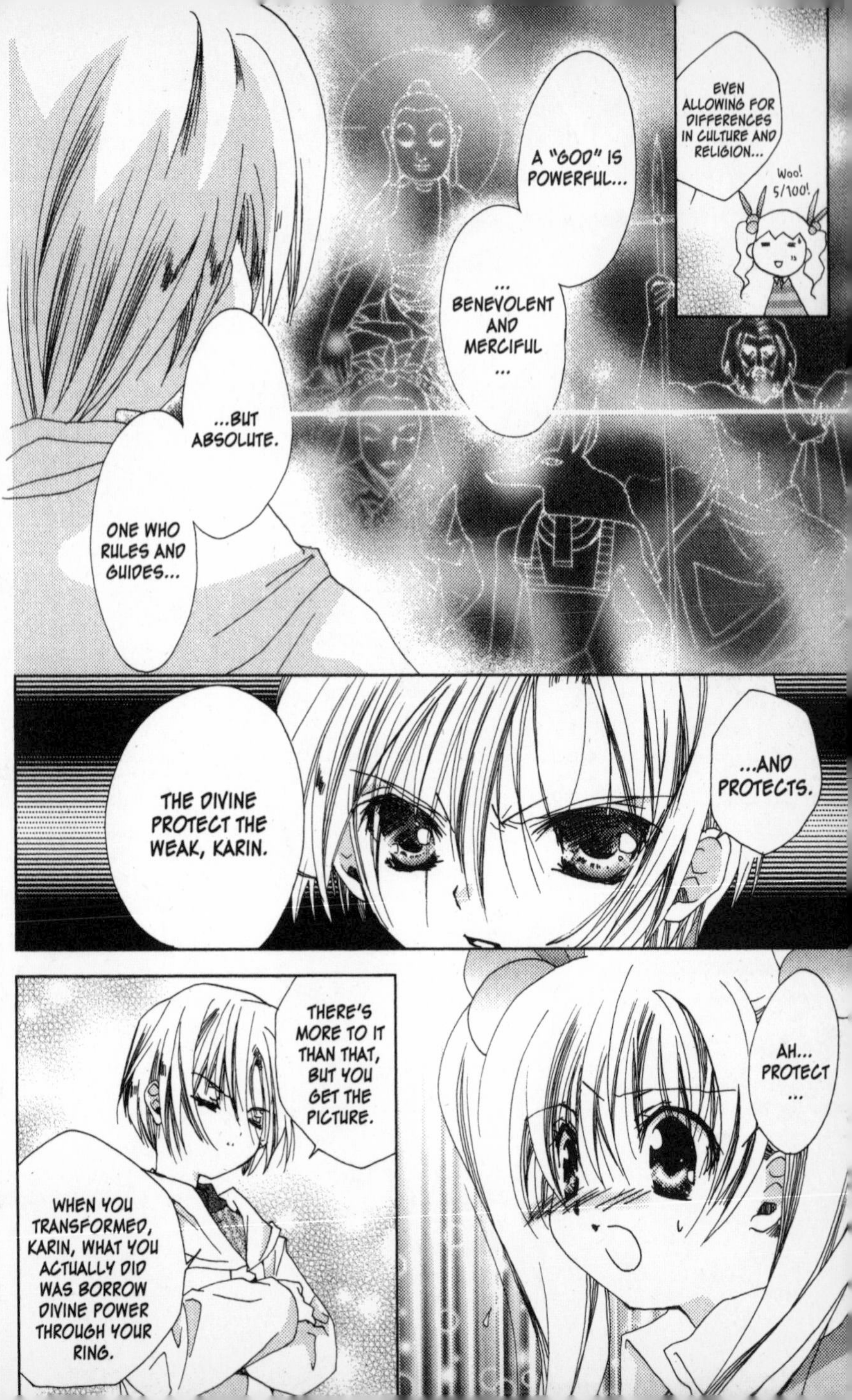
EVEN ALLOWING FOR DIFFERENCES IN CULTURE AND RELIGION...
Woo! 5/100!
A "GOD" IS POWERFUL...
... BENEVOLENT AND MERCIFUL ...
...BUT ABSOLUTE.
ONE WHO RULES AND GUIDES...
...AND PROTECTS.
THE DIVINE PROTECT THE WEAK, KARIN.
AH... PROTECT ...
THERE'S MORE TO IT THAN THAT, BUT YOU GET THE PICTURE.
WHEN YOU TRANSFORMED, KARIN, WHAT YOU ACTUALLY DID WAS BORROW DIVINE POWER THROUGH YOUR RING.

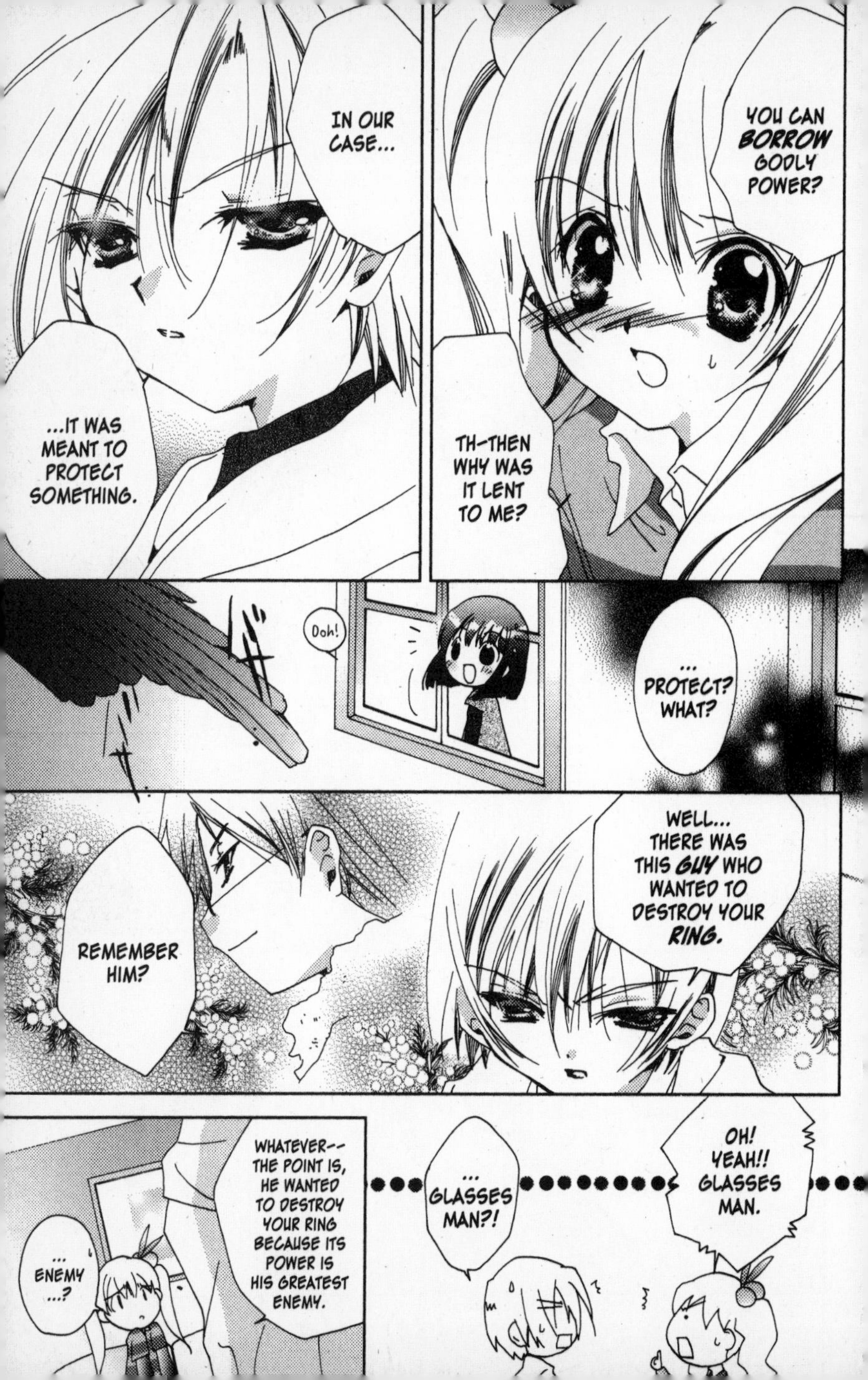
YOU CAN BORROW GODLY POWER?
TH-THEN WHY WAS IT LENT TO ME?
IN OUR CASE...
...IT WAS MEANT TO PROTECT SOMETHING.
...PROTECT? WHAT?
Ooh!
WELL... THERE WAS THIS GUY WHO WANTED TO DESTROY YOUR RING.
REMEMBER HIM?
OH! YEAH!! GLASSES MAN.
...GLASSES MAN?!
WHATEVER--THE POINT IS, HE WANTED TO DESTROY YOUR RING BECAUSE ITS POWER IS HIS GREATEST ENEMY.
...ENEMY...?

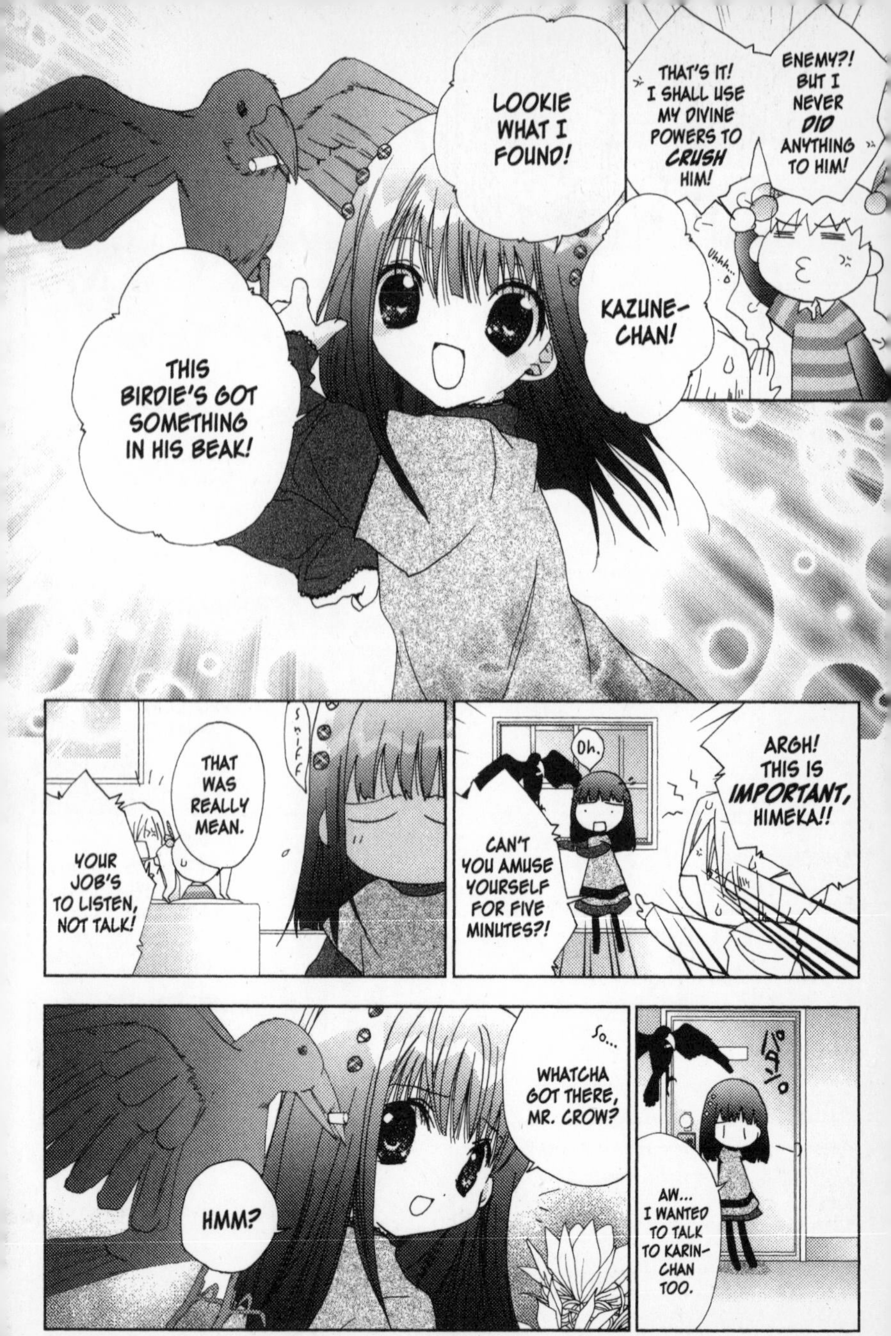
ENEMY?! BUT I NEVER DID ANYTHING TO HIM!
THAT'S IT! I SHALL USE MY DIVINE POWERS TO CRUSH HIM!
Uhhh...
LOOKIE WHAT I FOUND!
KAZUNE-CHAN!
THIS BIRDIE'S GOT SOMETHING IN HIS BEAK!
ARGH! THIS IS IMPORTANT, HIMEKA!!
Oh.
CAN'T YOU AMUSE YOURSELF FOR FIVE MINUTES?!
sniff
THAT WAS REALLY MEAN.
YOUR JOB'S TO LISTEN, NOT TALK!
AW... I WANTED TO TALK TO KARIN-CHAN TOO.
So...
WHATCHA GOT THERE, MR. CROW?
HMM?

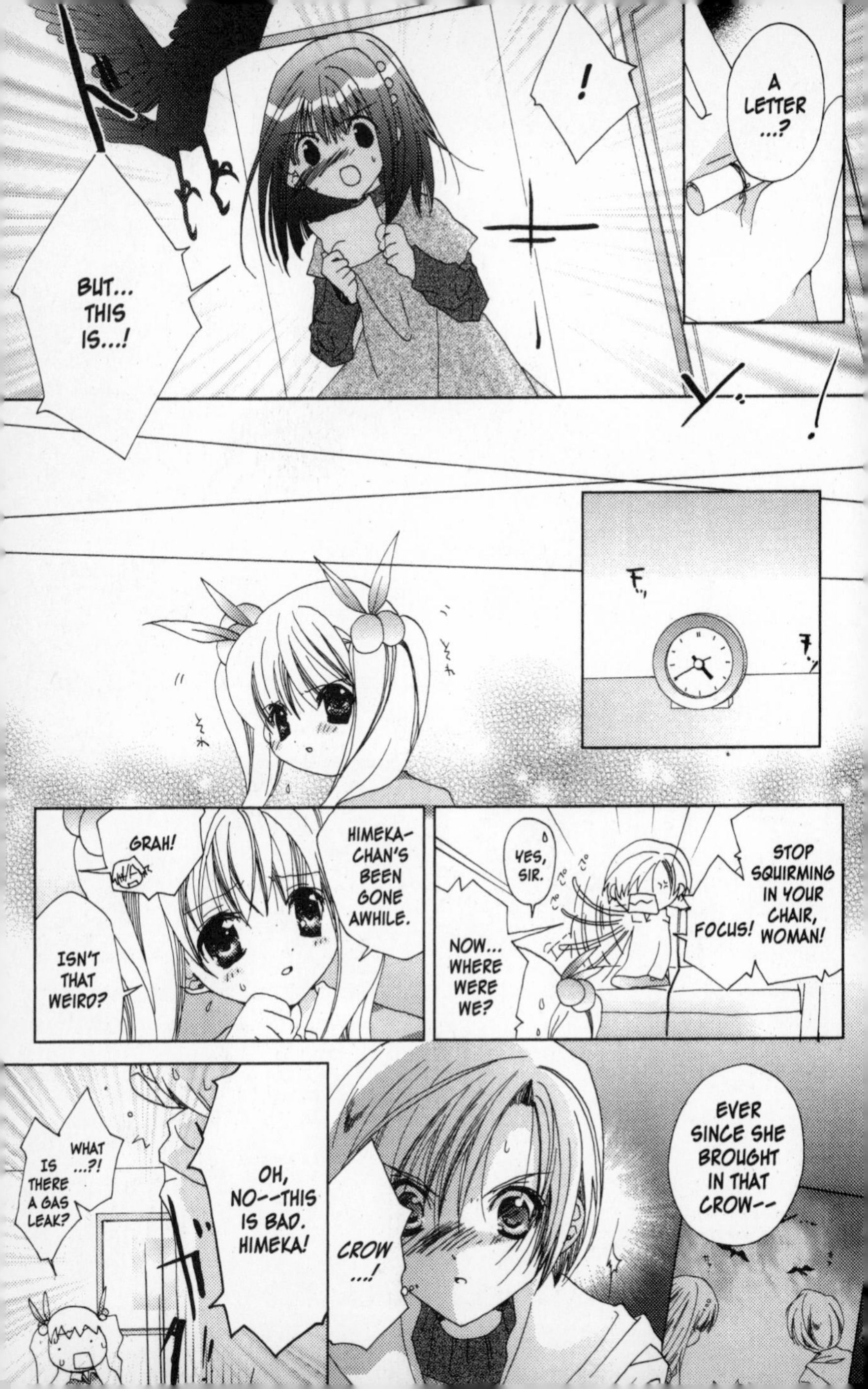
A LETTER ...?
!
BUT... THIS IS...!
STOP SQUIRMING IN YOUR CHAIR, WOMAN!
FOCUS!
YES, SIR.
NOW... WHERE WERE WE?
HIMEKA-CHAN'S BEEN GONE AWHILE.
GRAH!
ISN'T THAT WEIRD?
EVER SINCE SHE BROUGHT IN THAT CROW--
CROW ...!
OH, NO--THIS IS BAD. HIMEKA!
WHAT ...?!
IS THERE A GAS LEAK?

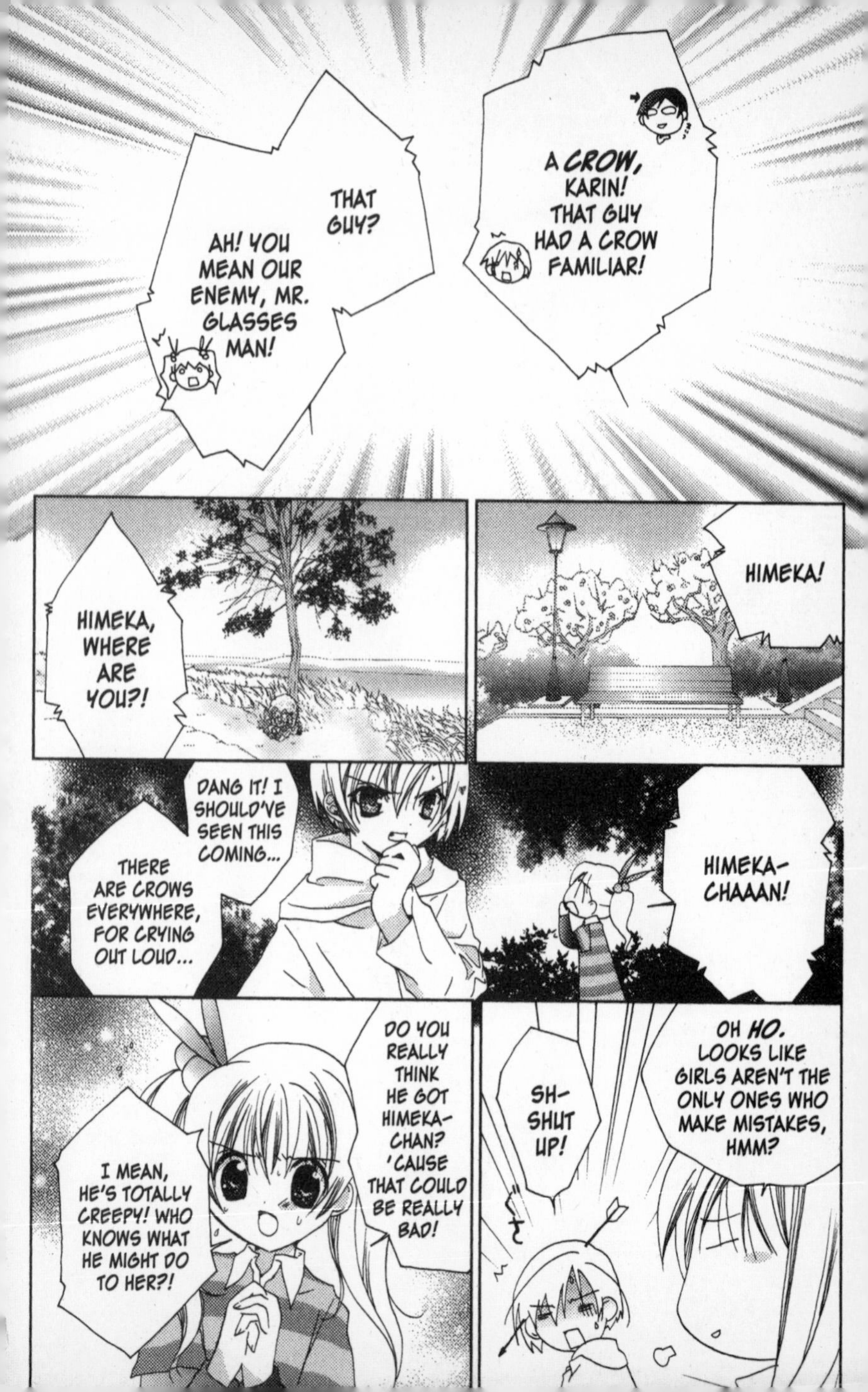
A CROW, KARIN! THAT GUY HAD A CROW FAMILIAR!
THAT GUY?
AH! YOU MEAN OUR ENEMY, MR. GLASSES MAN!
HIMEKA!
HIMEKA, WHERE ARE YOU?!
HIMEKA-CHAAAN!
DANG IT! I SHOULD'VE SEEN THIS COMING...
THERE ARE CROWS EVERYWHERE, FOR CRYING OUT LOUD...
OH HO. LOOKS LIKE GIRLS AREN'T THE ONLY ONES WHO MAKE MISTAKES, HMM?
SH-SHUT UP!
DO YOU REALLY THINK HE GOT HIMEKA-CHAN? 'CAUSE THAT COULD BE REALLY BAD!
I MEAN, HE'S TOTALLY CREEPY! WHO KNOWS WHAT HE MIGHT DO TO HER?!

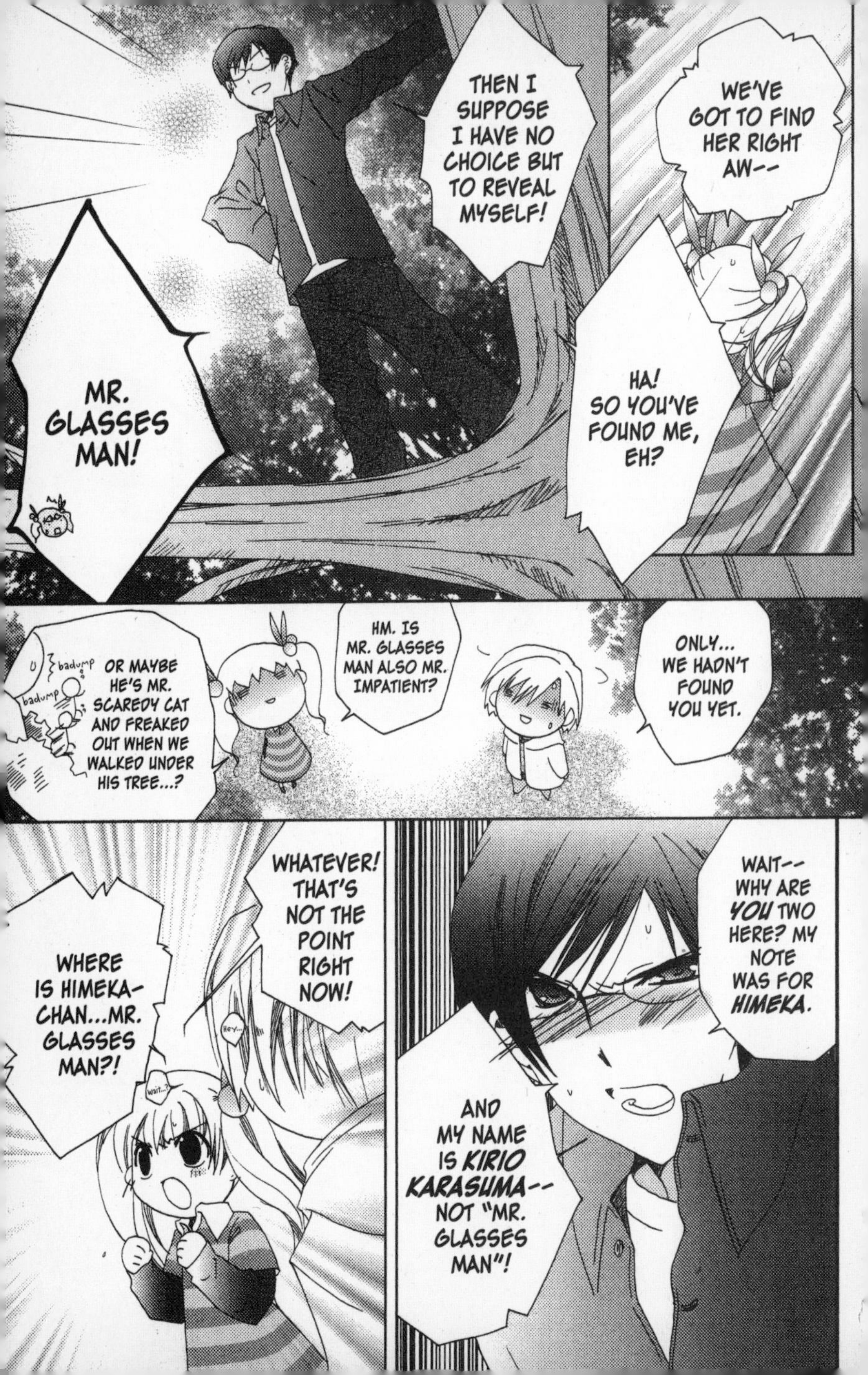
WE'VE GOT TO FIND HER RIGHT AW--
HA! SO YOU'VE FOUND ME, EH?
THEN I SUPPOSE I HAVE NO CHOICE BUT TO REVEAL MYSELF!
MR. GLASSES MAN!
ONLY... WE HADN'T FOUND YOU YET.
HM. IS MR. GLASSES MAN ALSO MR. IMPATIENT?
OR MAYBE HE'S MR. SCAREDY CAT AND FREAKED OUT WHEN WE WALKED UNDER HIS TREE...?
badump
badump
WAIT--WHY ARE *YOU* TWO HERE? MY NOTE WAS FOR *HIMEKA*.
AND MY NAME IS *KIRIO KARASUMA*--NOT "MR. GLASSES MAN"!
WHATEVER! THAT'S NOT THE POINT RIGHT NOW!
Hey...
WHERE IS HIMEKA-CHAN...MR. GLASSES MAN?!
wait...?

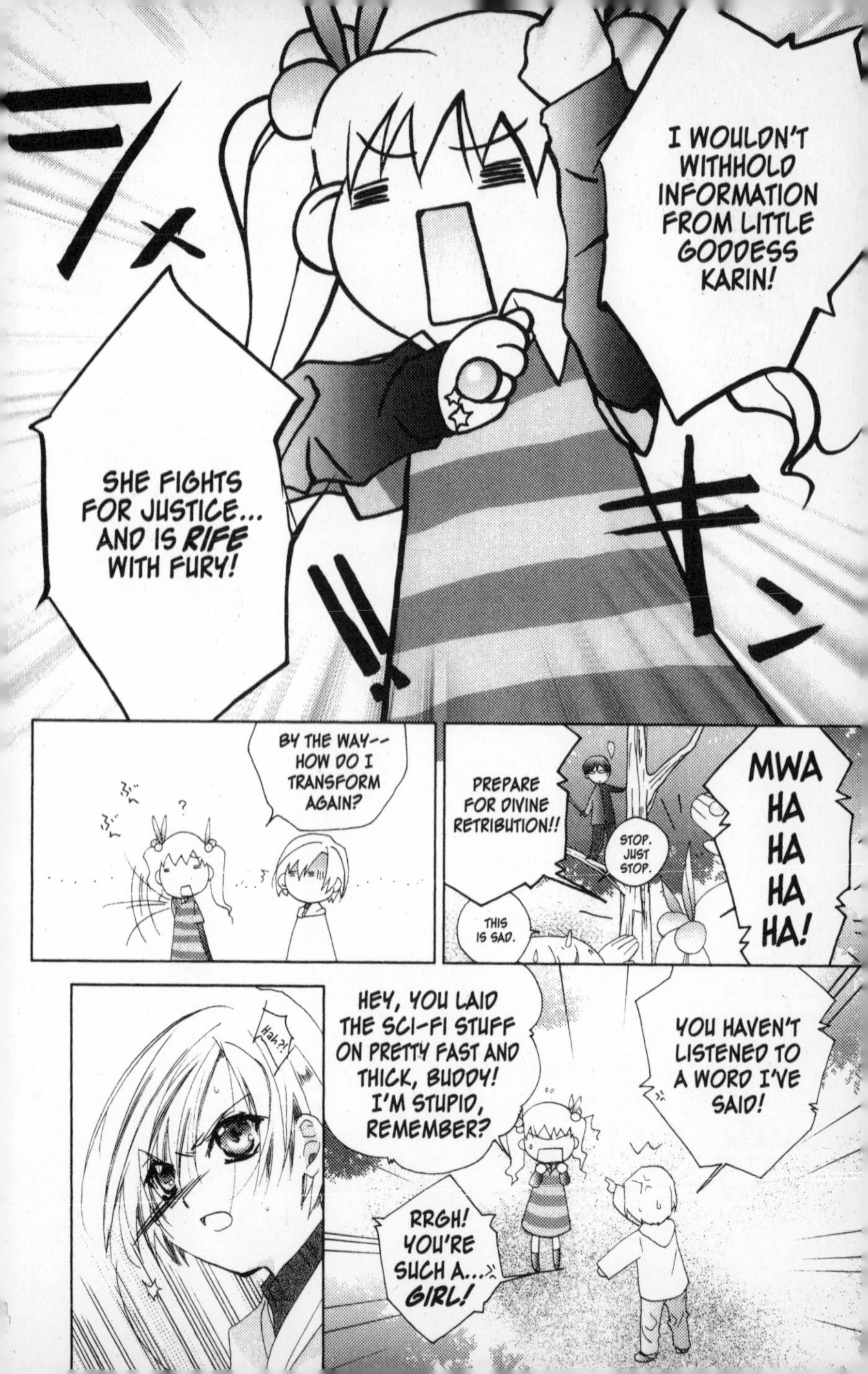
I WOULDN'T WITHHOLD INFORMATION FROM LITTLE GODDESS KARIN!
SHE FIGHTS FOR JUSTICE... AND IS *RIFE* WITH FURY!
MWA HA HA HA HA HA!
PREPARE FOR DIVINE RETRIBUTION!!
STOP. JUST STOP.
THIS IS SAD.
BY THE WAY-- HOW DO I TRANSFORM AGAIN?
YOU HAVEN'T LISTENED TO A WORD I'VE SAID!
HEY, YOU LAID THE SCI-FI STUFF ON PRETTY FAST AND THICK, BUDDY! I'M STUPID, REMEMBER?
RRGH! YOU'RE SUCH A... *GIRL!*
Hah?!

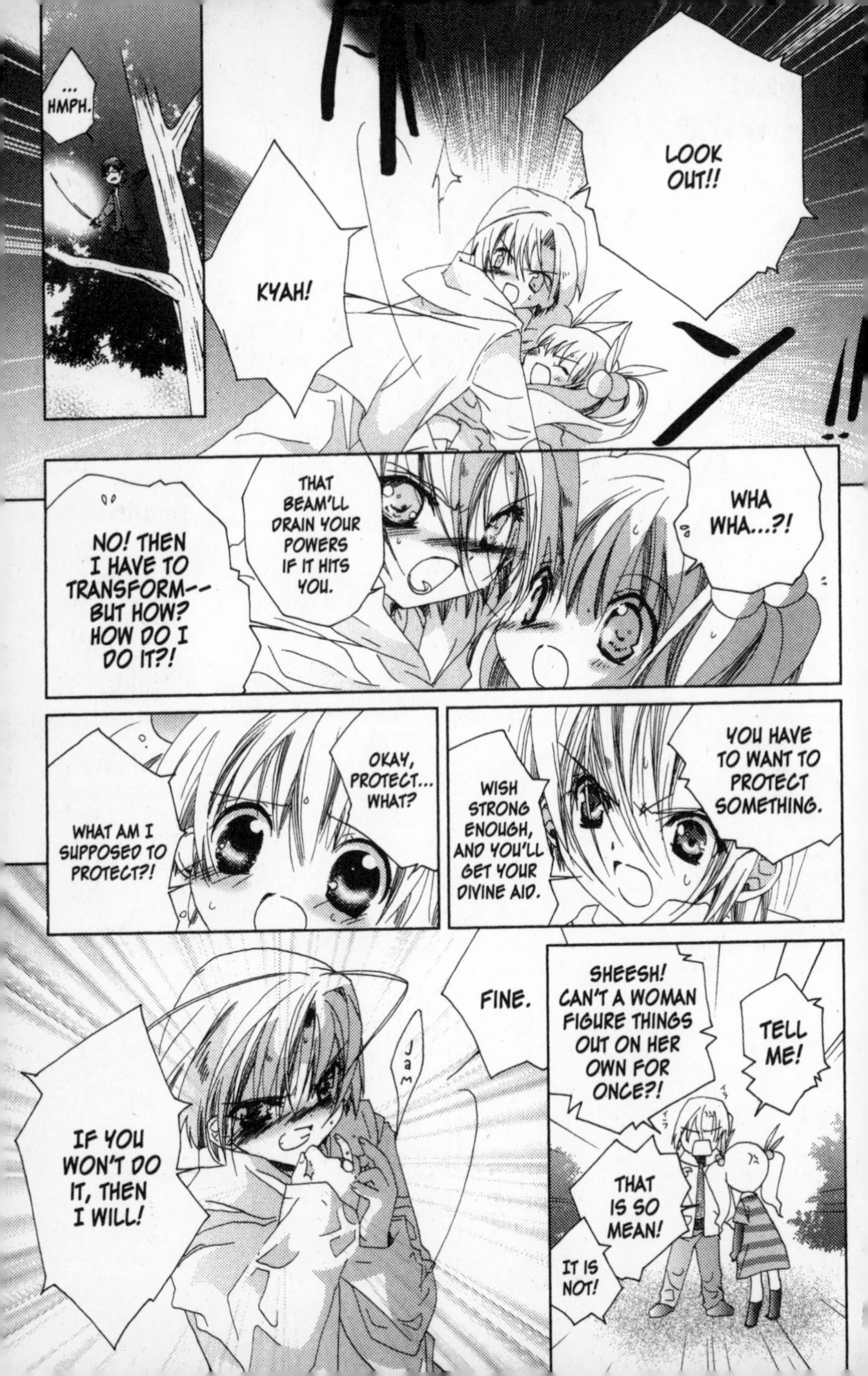
LOOK OUT!!
KYAH!
... HMPH.
WHA WHA...?!
THAT BEAM'LL DRAIN YOUR POWERS IF IT HITS YOU.
NO! THEN I HAVE TO TRANSFORM--BUT HOW? HOW DO I DO IT?!
YOU HAVE TO WANT TO PROTECT SOMETHING.
WISH STRONG ENOUGH, AND YOU'LL GET YOUR DIVINE AID.
OKAY, PROTECT... WHAT?
WHAT AM I SUPPOSED TO PROTECT?!
TELL ME!
SHEESH! CAN'T A WOMAN FIGURE THINGS OUT ON HER OWN FOR ONCE?!
THAT IS SO MEAN!
IT IS NOT!
FINE.
IF YOU WON'T DO IT, THEN I WILL!

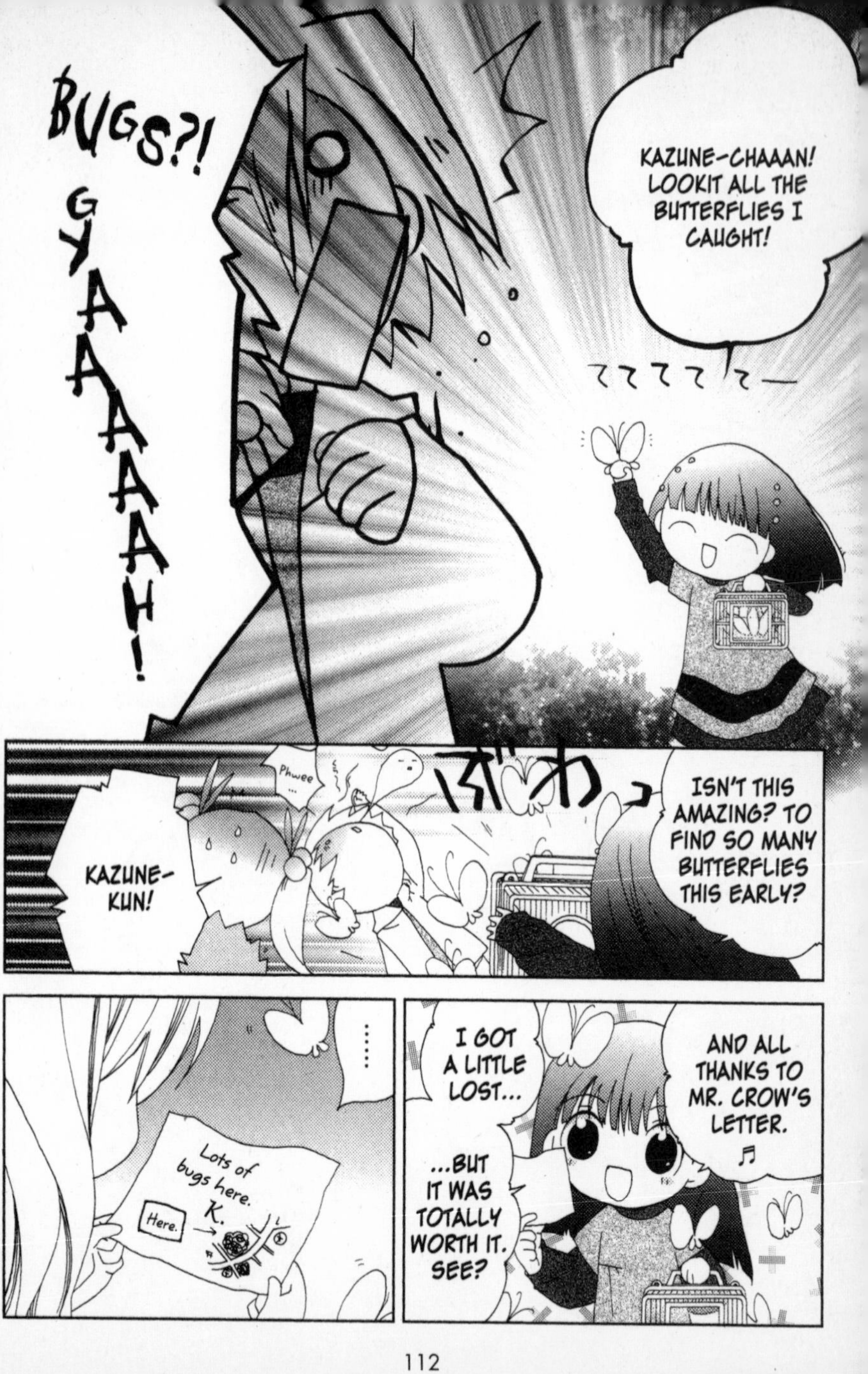
KAZUNE-CHAAAN! LOOKIT ALL THE BUTTERFLIES I CAUGHT!
てててててー
BUGS?!
GYAAAAAH!
ISN'T THIS AMAZING? TO FIND SO MANY BUTTERFLIES THIS EARLY?
ぶわっ
Phwee...
KAZUNE-KUN!
AND ALL THANKS TO MR. CROW'S LETTER. ♪
I GOT A LITTLE LOST...
...BUT IT WAS TOTALLY WORTH IT. SEE?
......
Lots of bugs here. K.
Here.

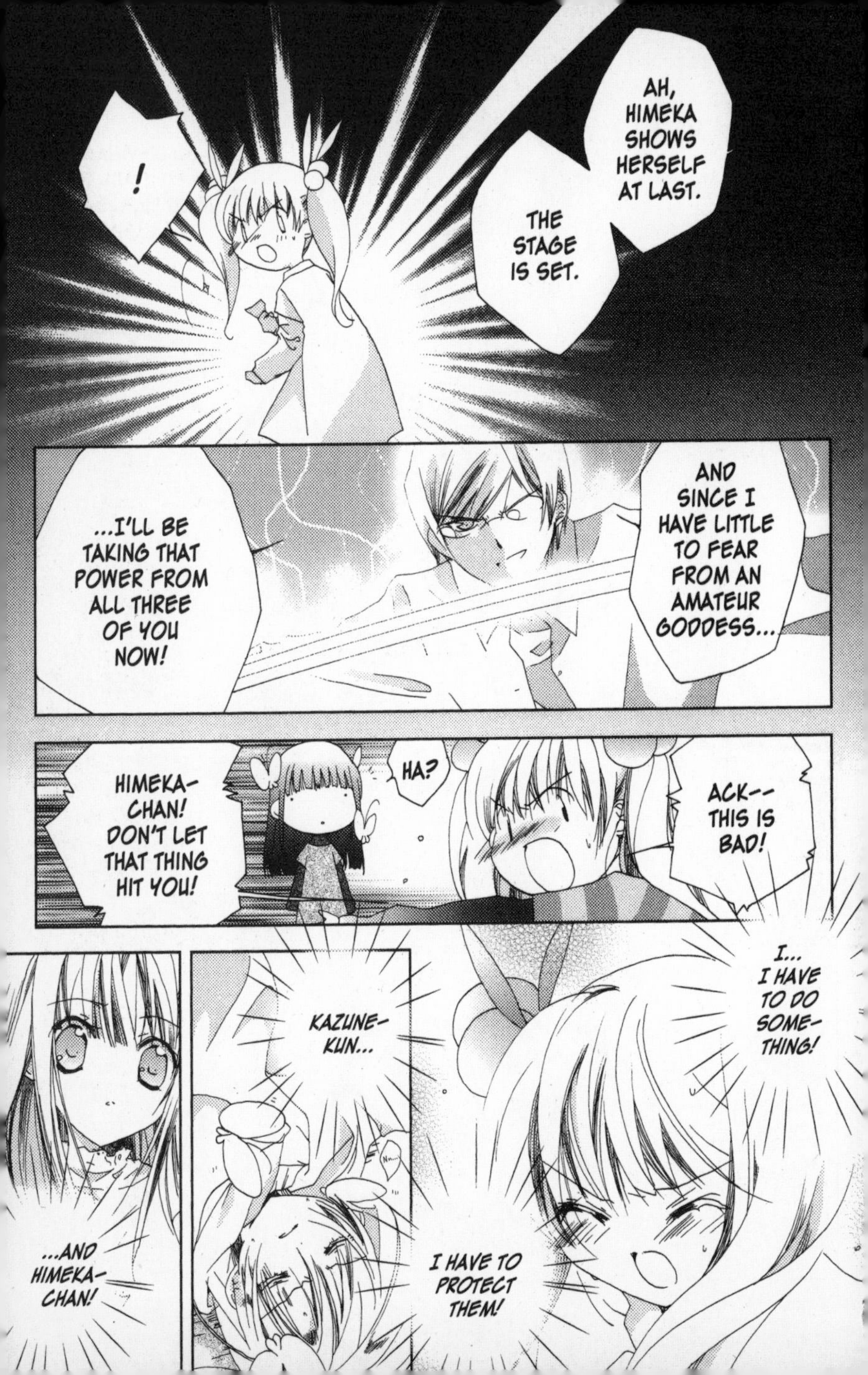
AH, HIMEKA SHOWS HERSELF AT LAST.
THE STAGE IS SET.
!
AND SINCE I HAVE LITTLE TO FEAR FROM AN AMATEUR GODDESS...
...I'LL BE TAKING THAT POWER FROM ALL THREE OF YOU NOW!
ACK--THIS IS BAD!
HA?
HIMEKA-CHAN! DON'T LET THAT THING HIT YOU!
I... I HAVE TO DO SOMETHING!
I HAVE TO PROTECT THEM!
KAZUNE-KUN...
...AND HIMEKA-CHAN!

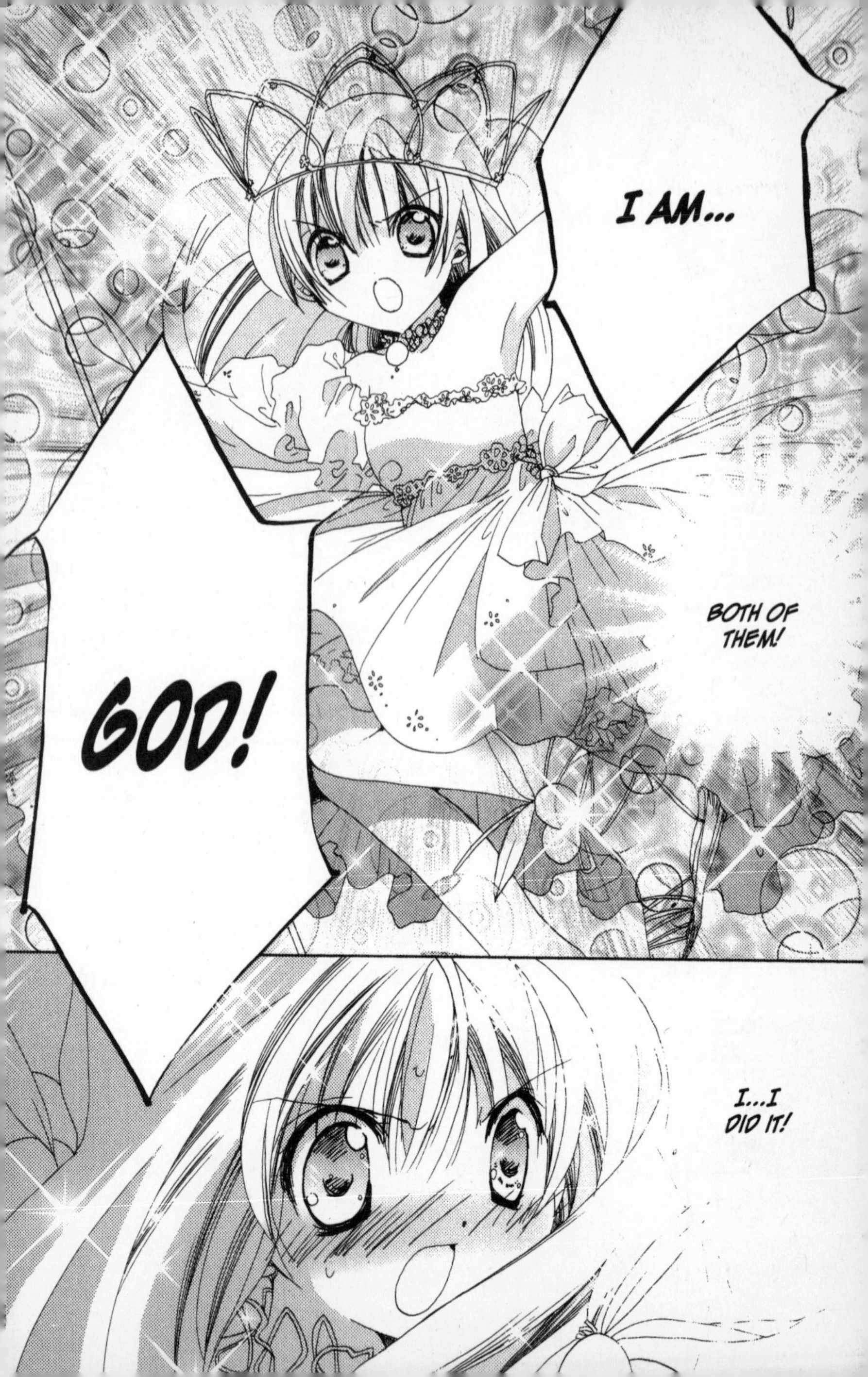
I AM...
GOD!
BOTH OF THEM!
I...I DID IT!

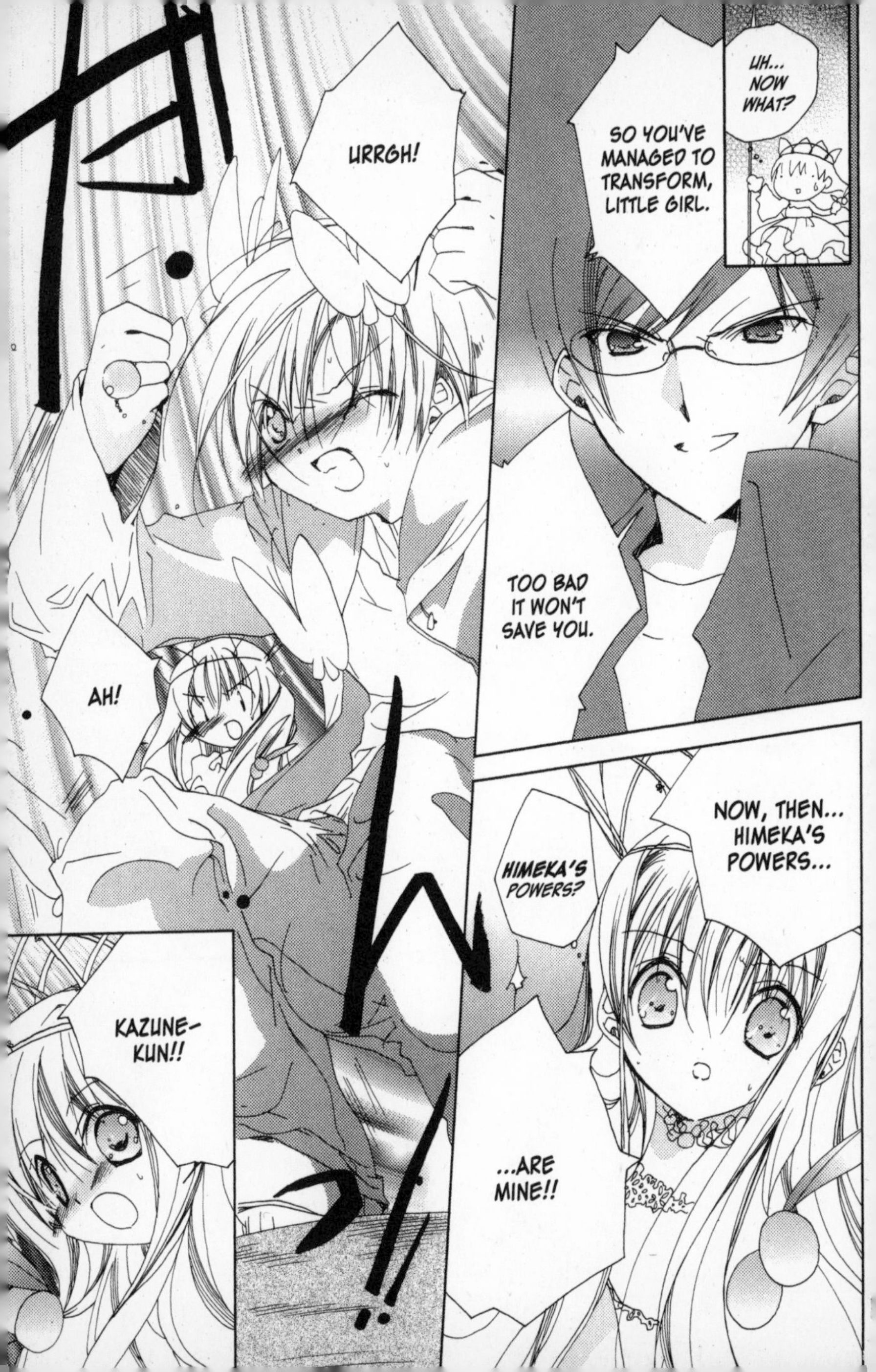
UH... NOW WHAT?
SO YOU'VE MANAGED TO TRANSFORM, LITTLE GIRL.
TOO BAD IT WON'T SAVE YOU.
URRGH!
AH!
NOW, THEN... HIMEKA'S POWERS...
HIMEKA'S POWERS?
...ARE MINE!!
KAZUNE-KUN!!

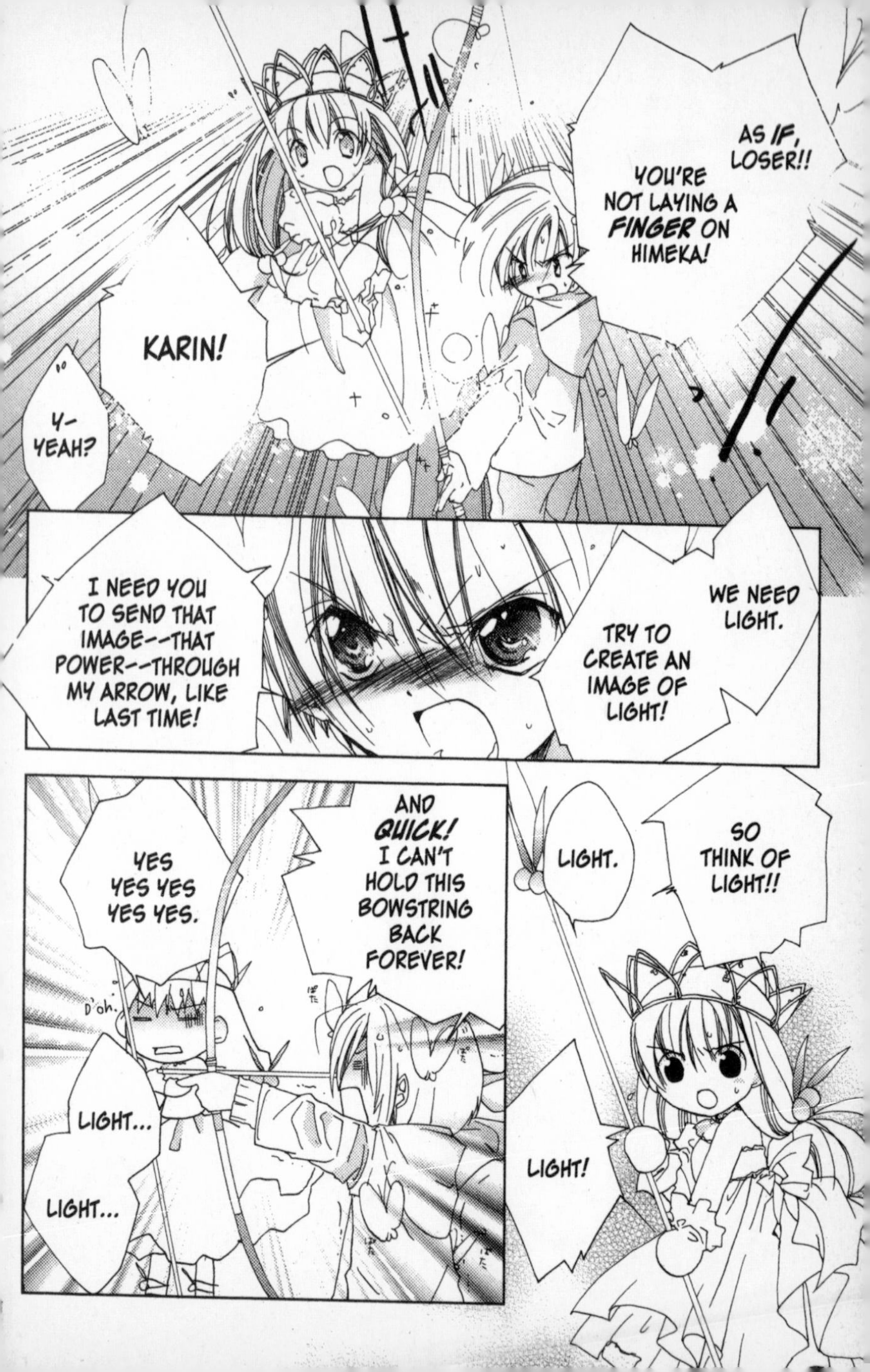
AS *IF*, LOSER!!
YOU'RE NOT LAYING A **FINGER** ON HIMEKA!
KARIN!
Y-YEAH?
WE NEED LIGHT.
TRY TO CREATE AN IMAGE OF LIGHT!
I NEED YOU TO SEND THAT IMAGE--THAT POWER--THROUGH MY ARROW, LIKE LAST TIME!
SO THINK OF LIGHT!!
LIGHT.
LIGHT!
AND ***QUICK!*** I CAN'T HOLD THIS BOWSTRING BACK FOREVER!
YES YES YES YES YES.
D'oh.
LIGHT...
LIGHT...

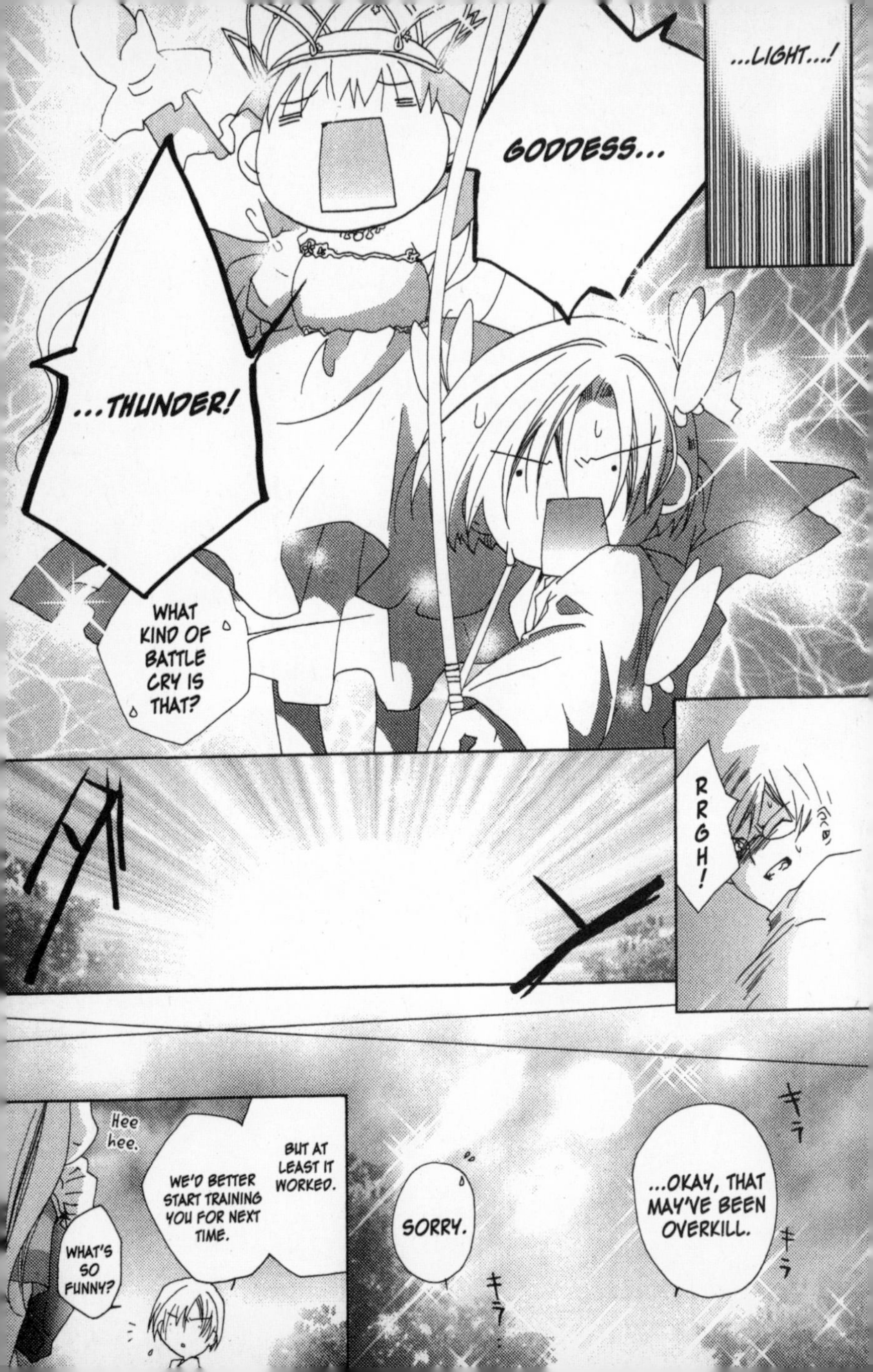
...LIGHT...!
GODDESS...
...THUNDER!
WHAT KIND OF BATTLE CRY IS THAT?
RRGH!
...OKAY, THAT MAY'VE BEEN OVERKILL.
SORRY.
BUT AT LEAST IT WORKED.
WE'D BETTER START TRAINING YOU FOR NEXT TIME.
Hee hee.
WHAT'S SO FUNNY?

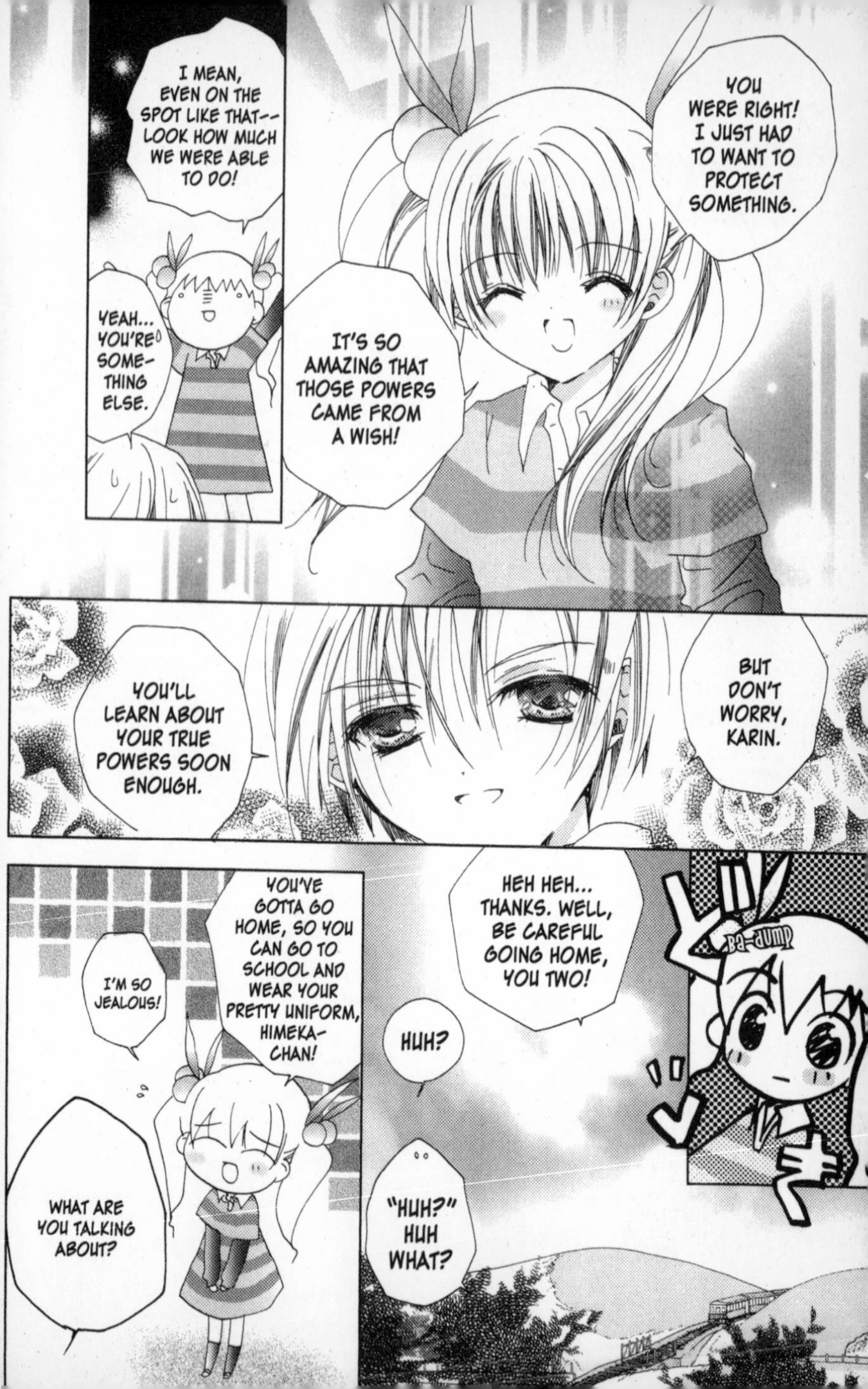
YOU WERE RIGHT! I JUST HAD TO WANT TO PROTECT SOMETHING.
IT'S SO AMAZING THAT THOSE POWERS CAME FROM A WISH!
I MEAN, EVEN ON THE SPOT LIKE THAT-- LOOK HOW MUCH WE WERE ABLE TO DO!
YEAH... YOU'RE SOME-THING ELSE.
BUT DON'T WORRY, KARIN.
YOU'LL LEARN ABOUT YOUR TRUE POWERS SOON ENOUGH.
BA-dUMP
HEH HEH... THANKS. WELL, BE CAREFUL GOING HOME, YOU TWO!
HUH?
"HUH?" HUH WHAT?
YOU'VE GOTTA GO HOME, SO YOU CAN GO TO SCHOOL AND WEAR YOUR PRETTY UNIFORM, HIMEKA-CHAN!
I'M SO JEALOUS!
WHAT ARE YOU TALKING ABOUT?

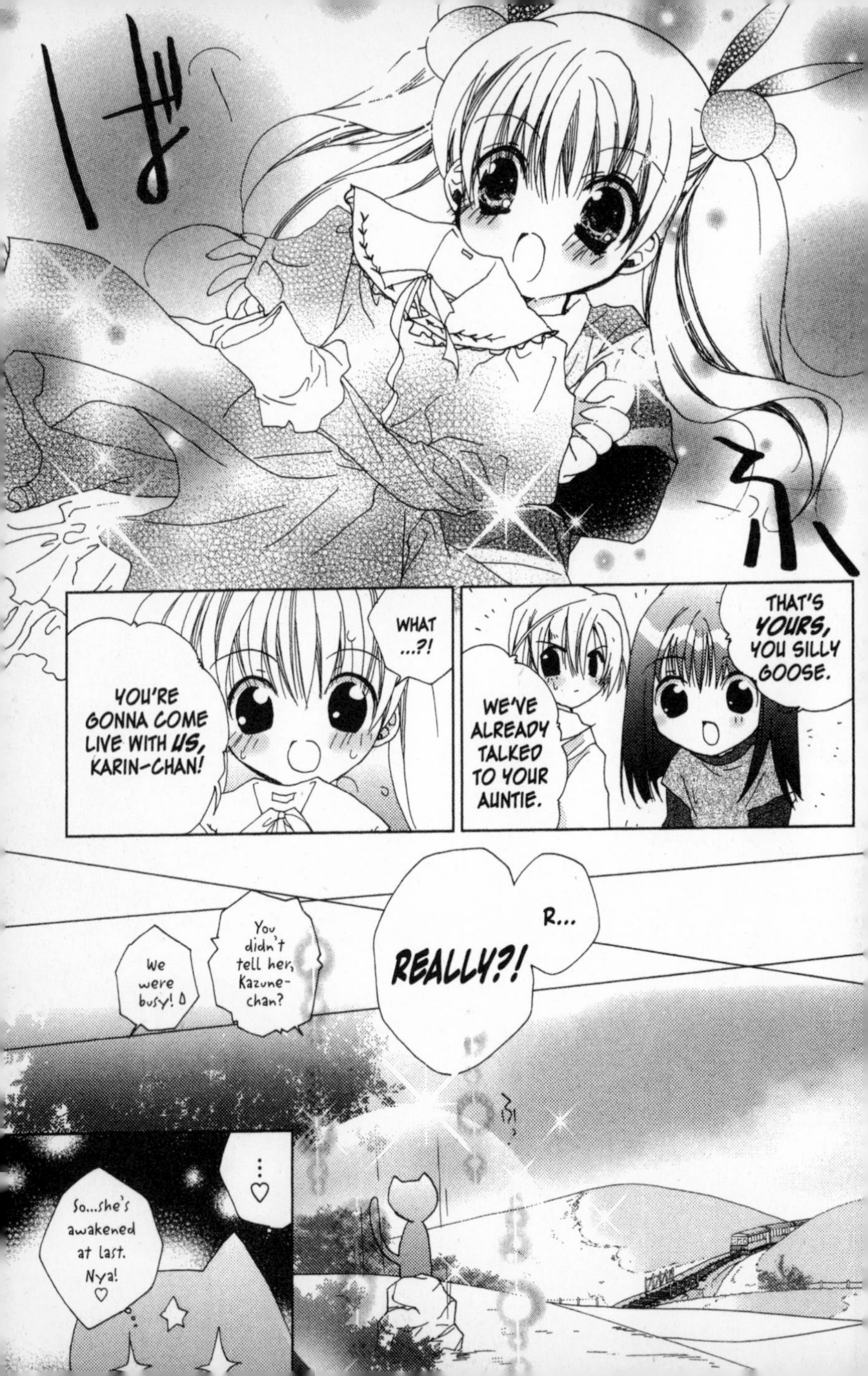
THAT'S *YOURS,* YOU SILLY GOOSE.
WE'VE ALREADY TALKED TO YOUR AUNTIE.
WHAT ...?!
YOU'RE GONNA COME LIVE WITH *US,* KARIN-CHAN!
R... *REALLY?!*
You didn't tell her, Kazune-chan?
We were busy! ♪
...♡
So...she's awakened at last. Nya! ♡

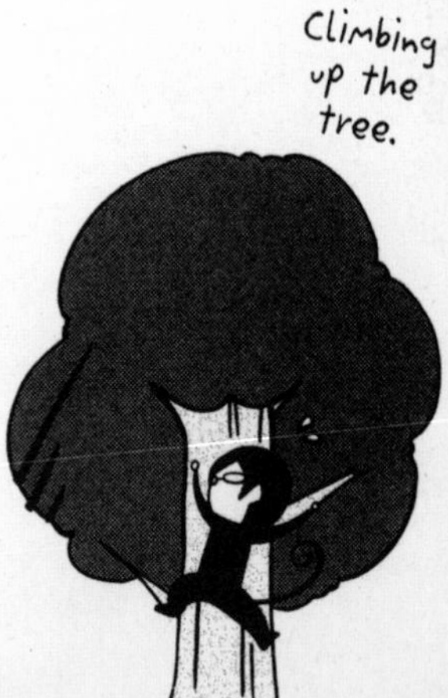
Climbing up the tree.

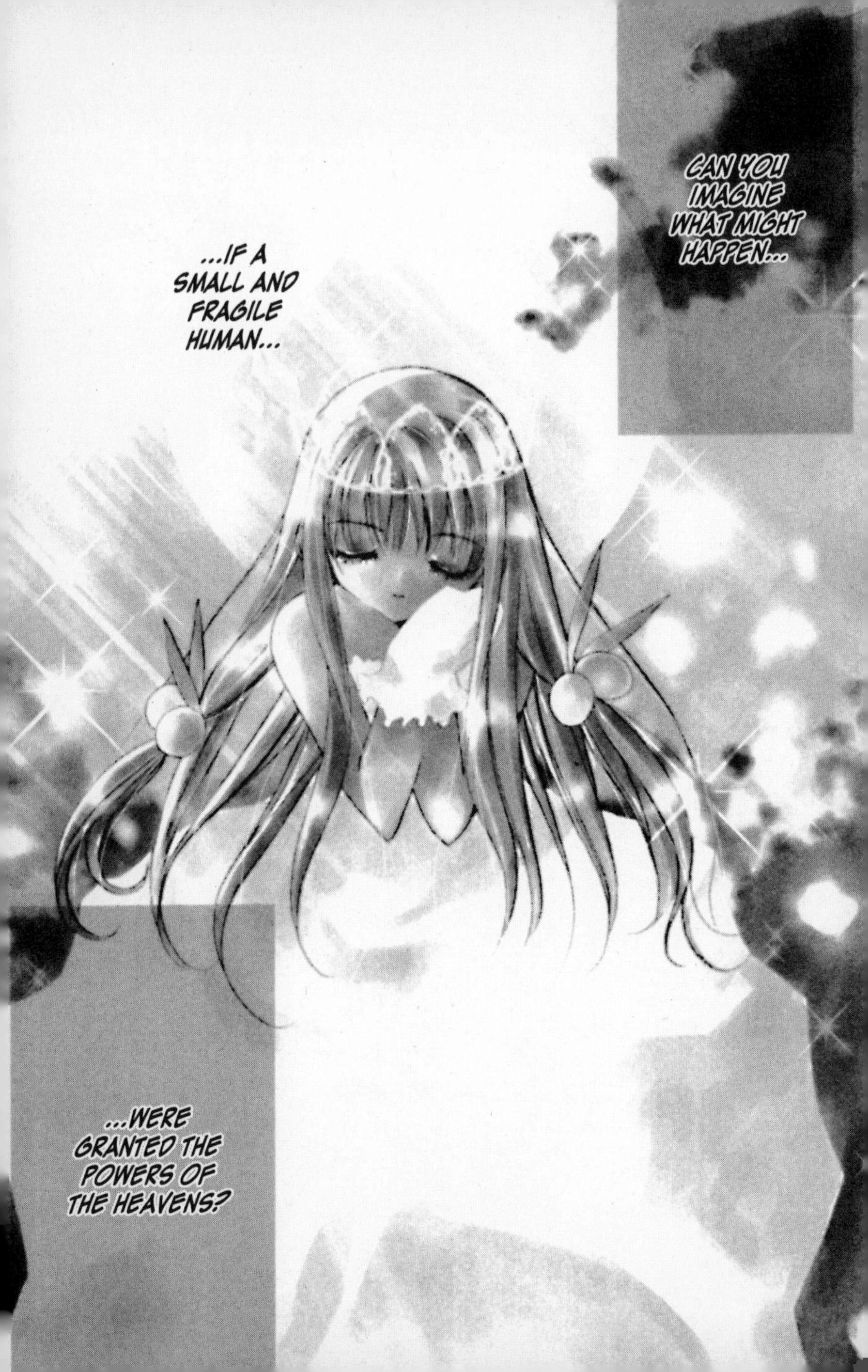
CAN YOU IMAGINE WHAT MIGHT HAPPEN...
...IF A SMALL AND FRAGILE HUMAN...
...WERE GRANTED THE POWERS OF THE HEAVENS?

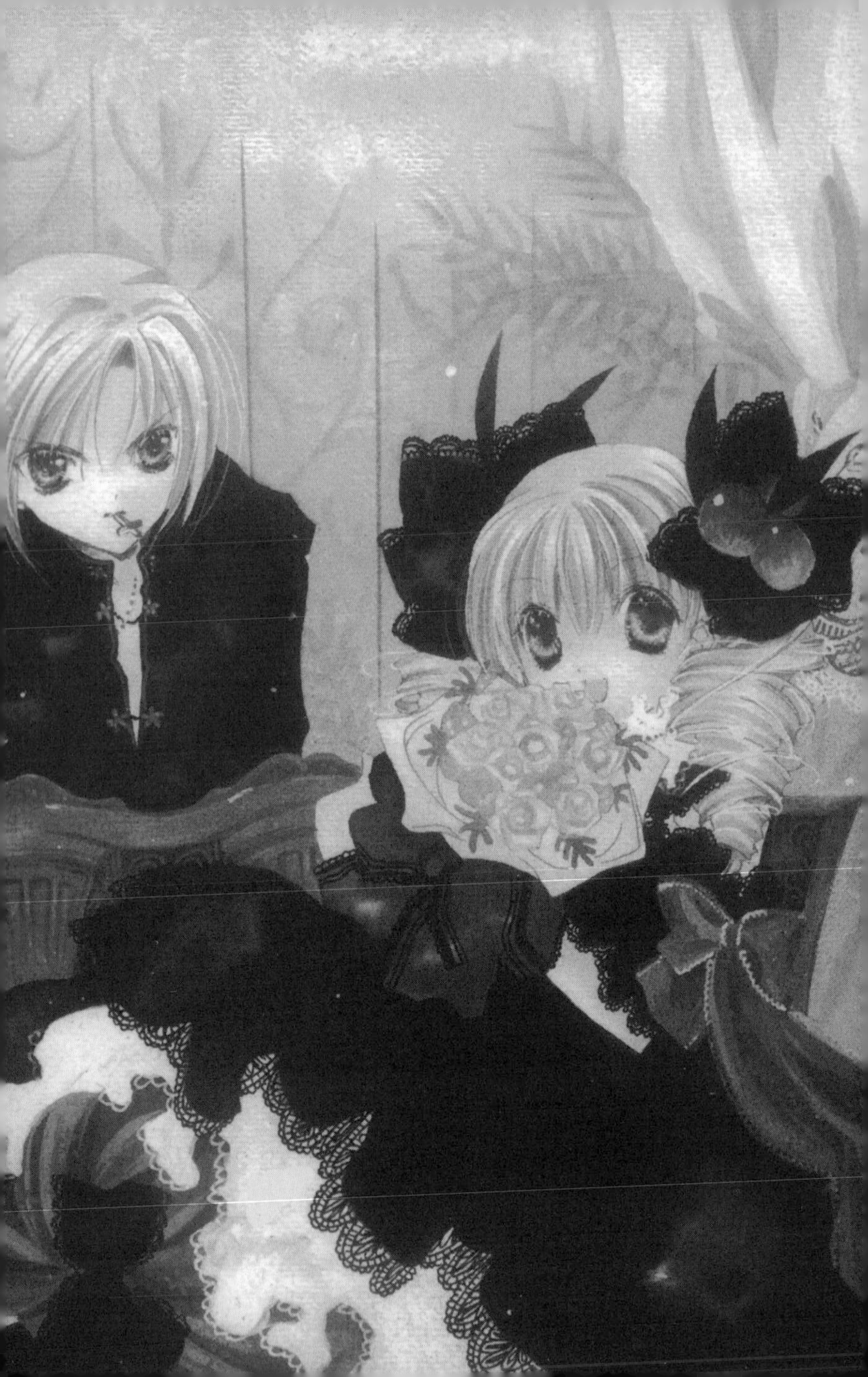

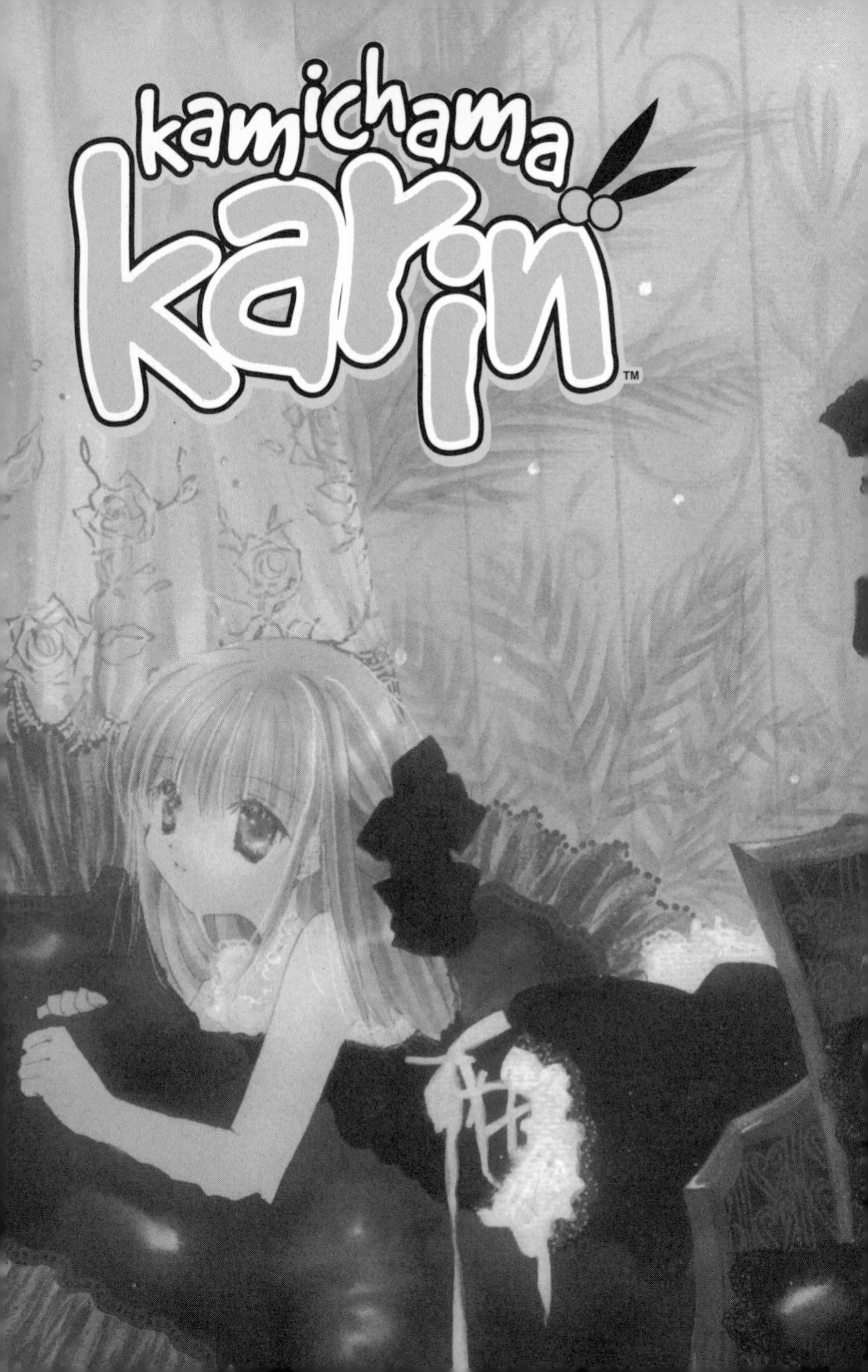
kamichama
karin™

Go!

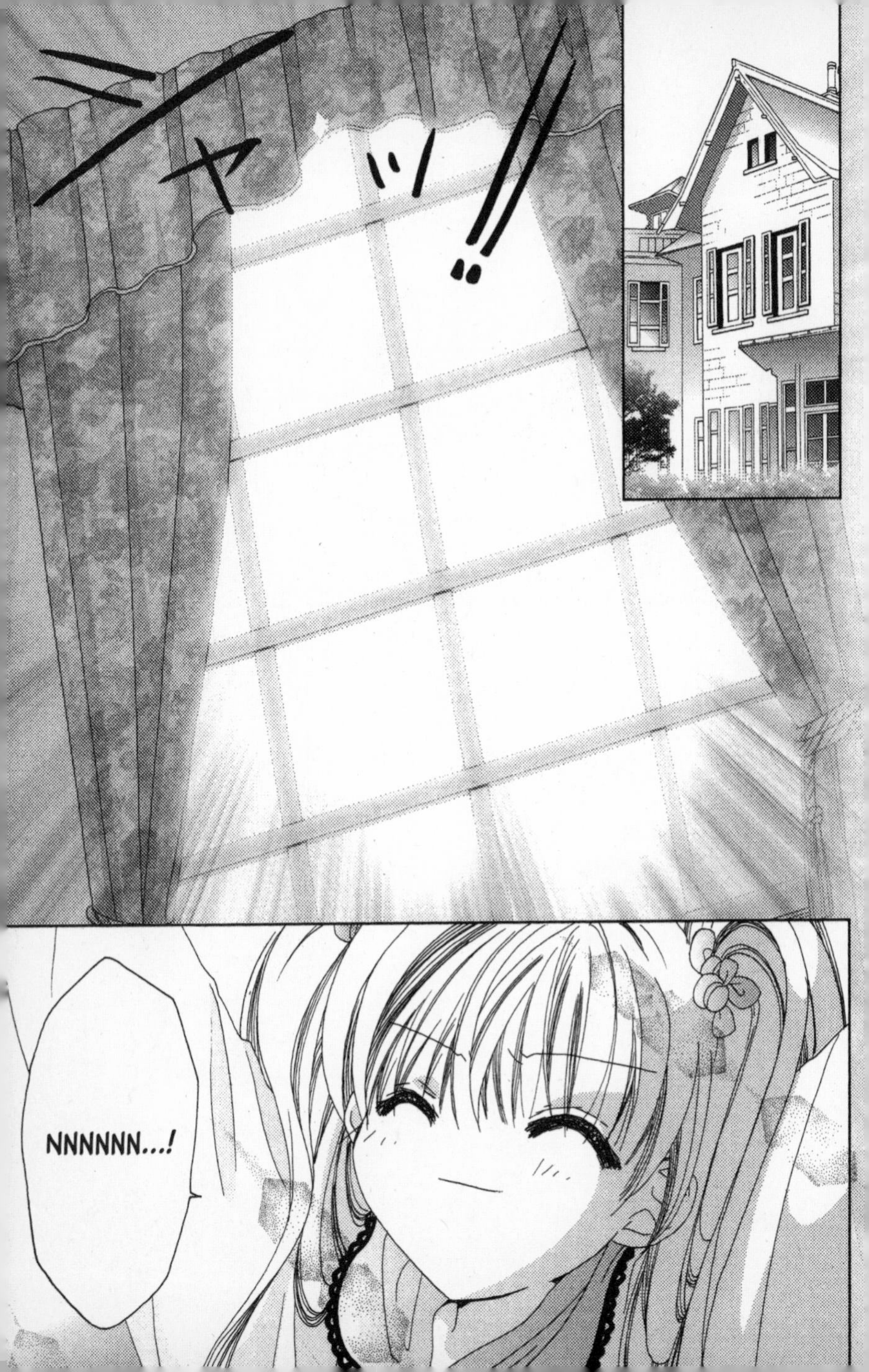
シャッ!!
NNNNNN...!

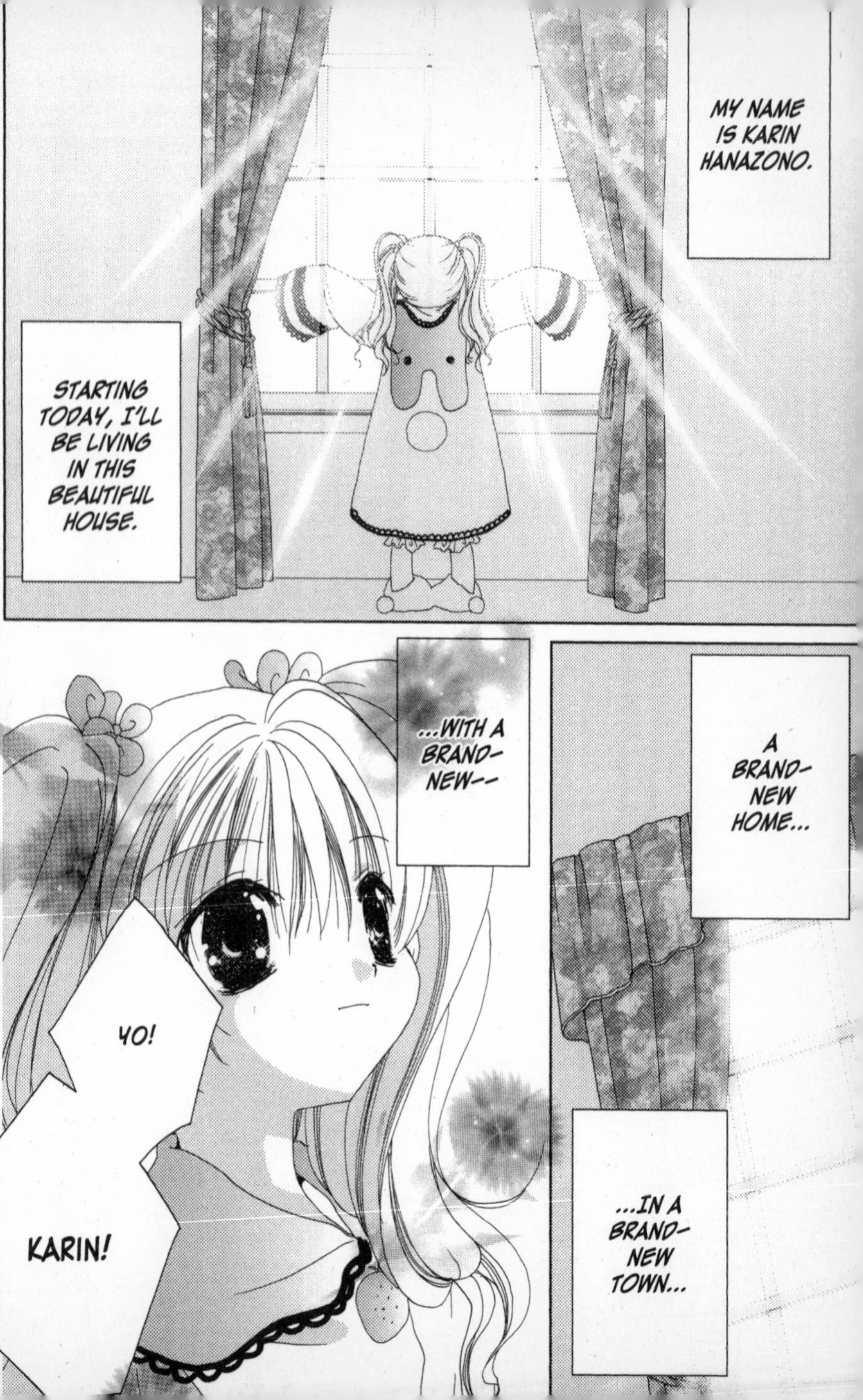
MY NAME IS KARIN HANAZONO.
STARTING TODAY, I'LL BE LIVING IN THIS BEAUTIFUL HOUSE.
A BRAND-NEW HOME...
...IN A BRAND-NEW TOWN...
...WITH A BRAND-NEW--
YO!
KARIN!

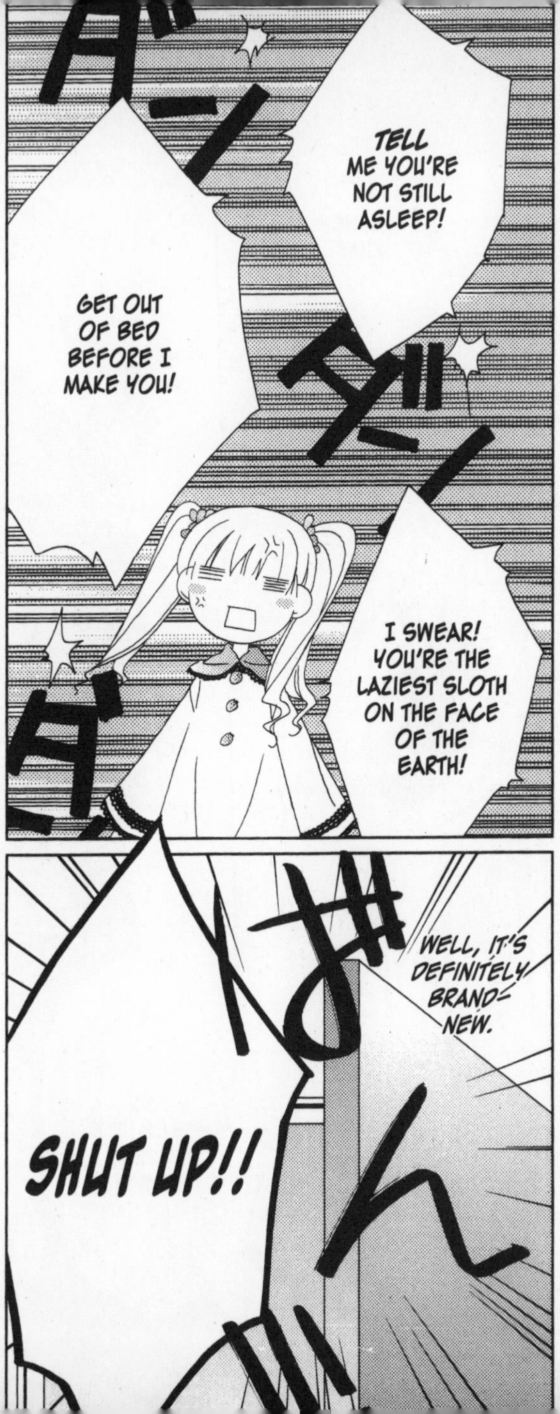
TELL ME YOU'RE NOT STILL ASLEEP!
GET OUT OF BED BEFORE I MAKE YOU!
I SWEAR! YOU'RE THE LAZIEST SLOTH ON THE FACE OF THE EARTH!
WELL, IT'S DEFINITELY BRAND-NEW.
SHUT UP!!

A noble vote for Karasuma.

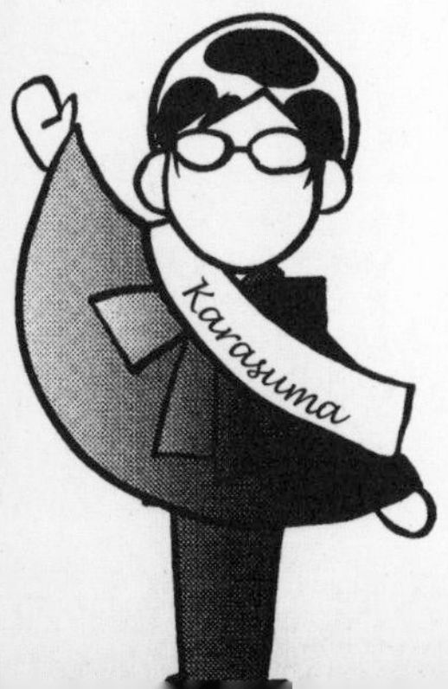
Karasuma

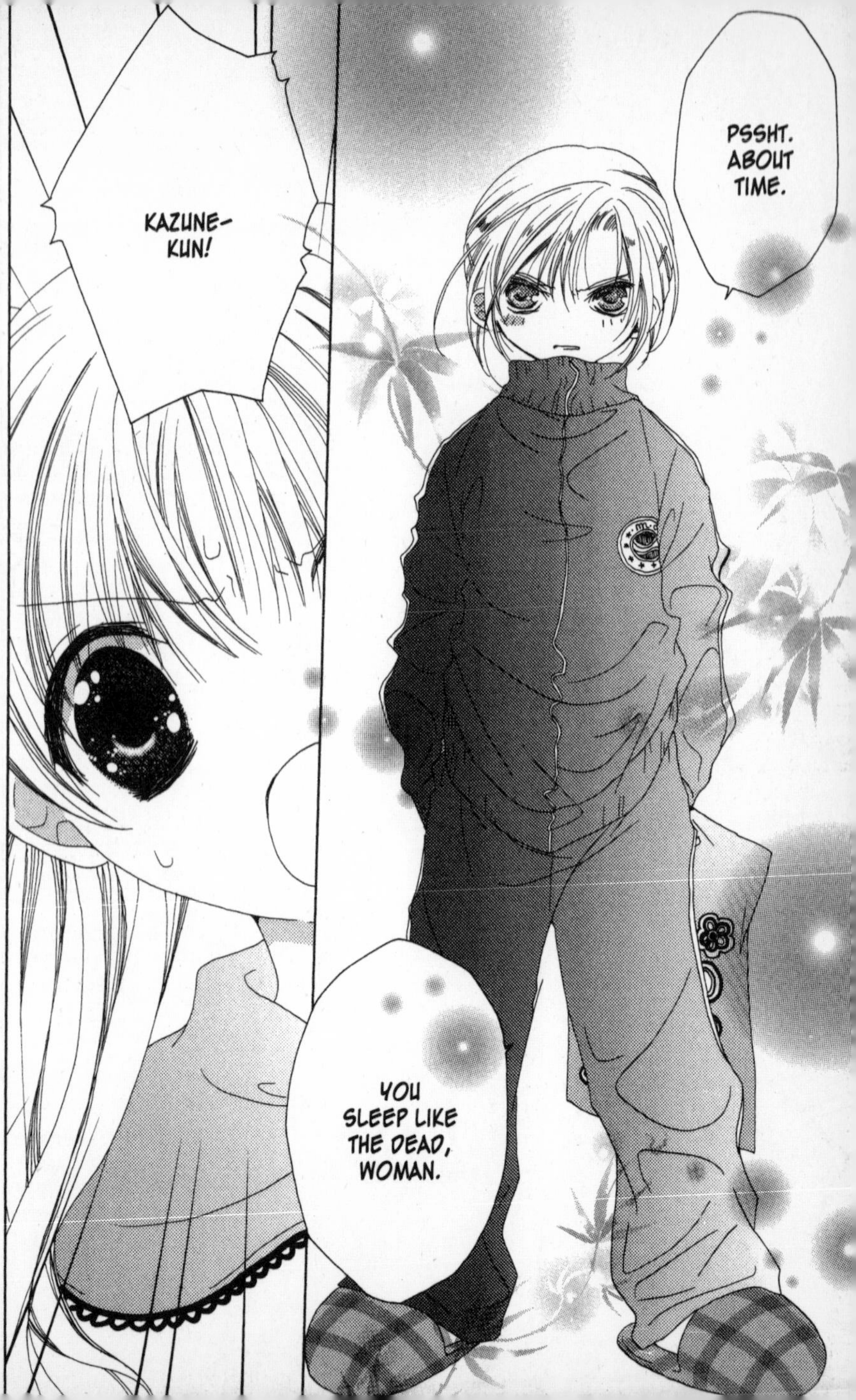
PSSHT. ABOUT TIME.
YOU SLEEP LIKE THE DEAD, WOMAN.
KAZUNE-KUN!

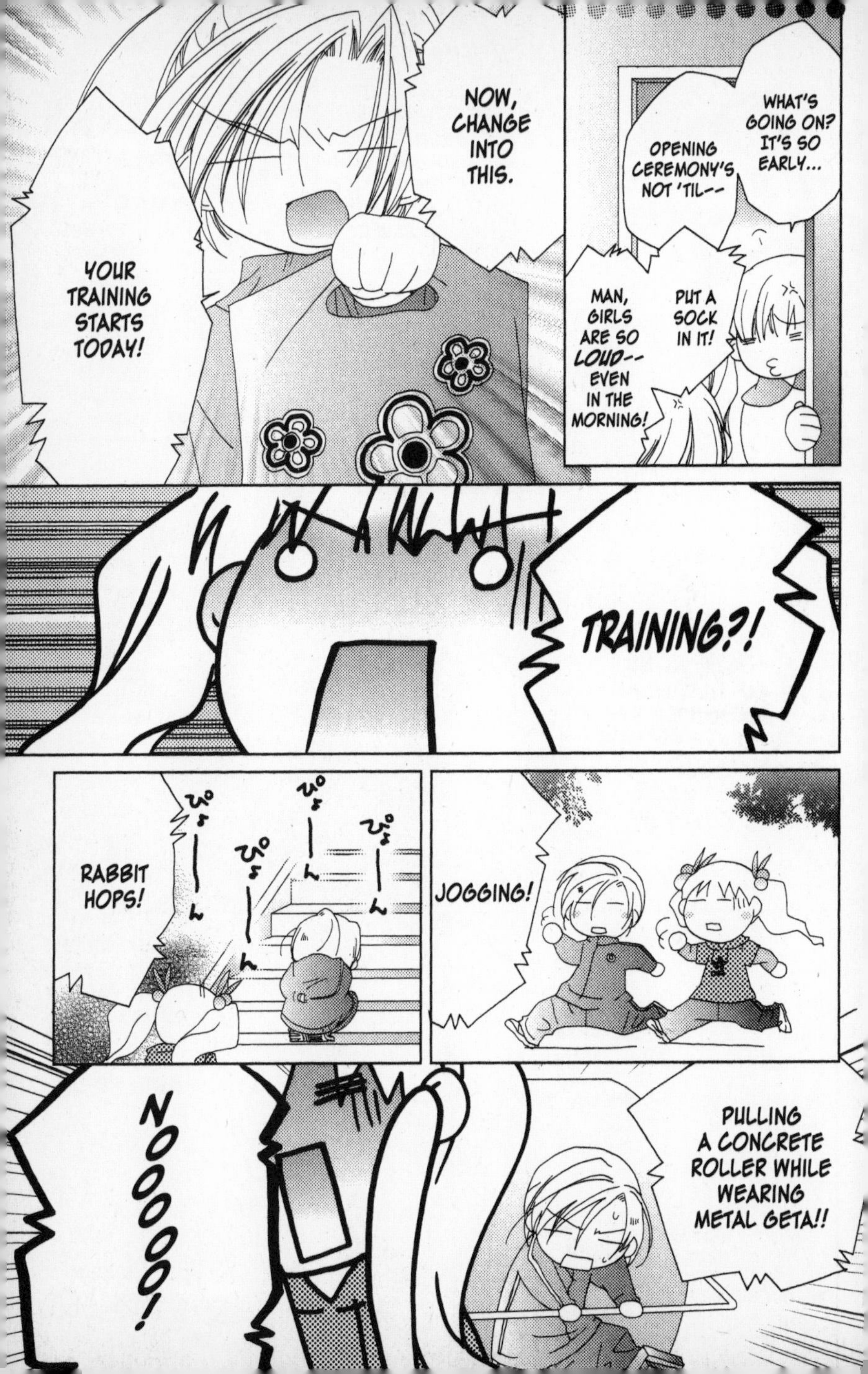

WHAT'S GOING ON? IT'S SO EARLY...
OPENING CEREMONY'S NOT 'TIL--
PUT A SOCK IN IT!
MAN, GIRLS ARE SO *LOUD*-- EVEN IN THE MORNING!
NOW, CHANGE INTO THIS.
YOUR TRAINING STARTS TODAY!
TRAINING?!
JOGGING!
ぴょーん
ぴょーん
ぴょーん
ぴょーん
RABBIT HOPS!
PULLING A CONCRETE ROLLER WHILE WEARING METAL GETA!!
NOOOOO!

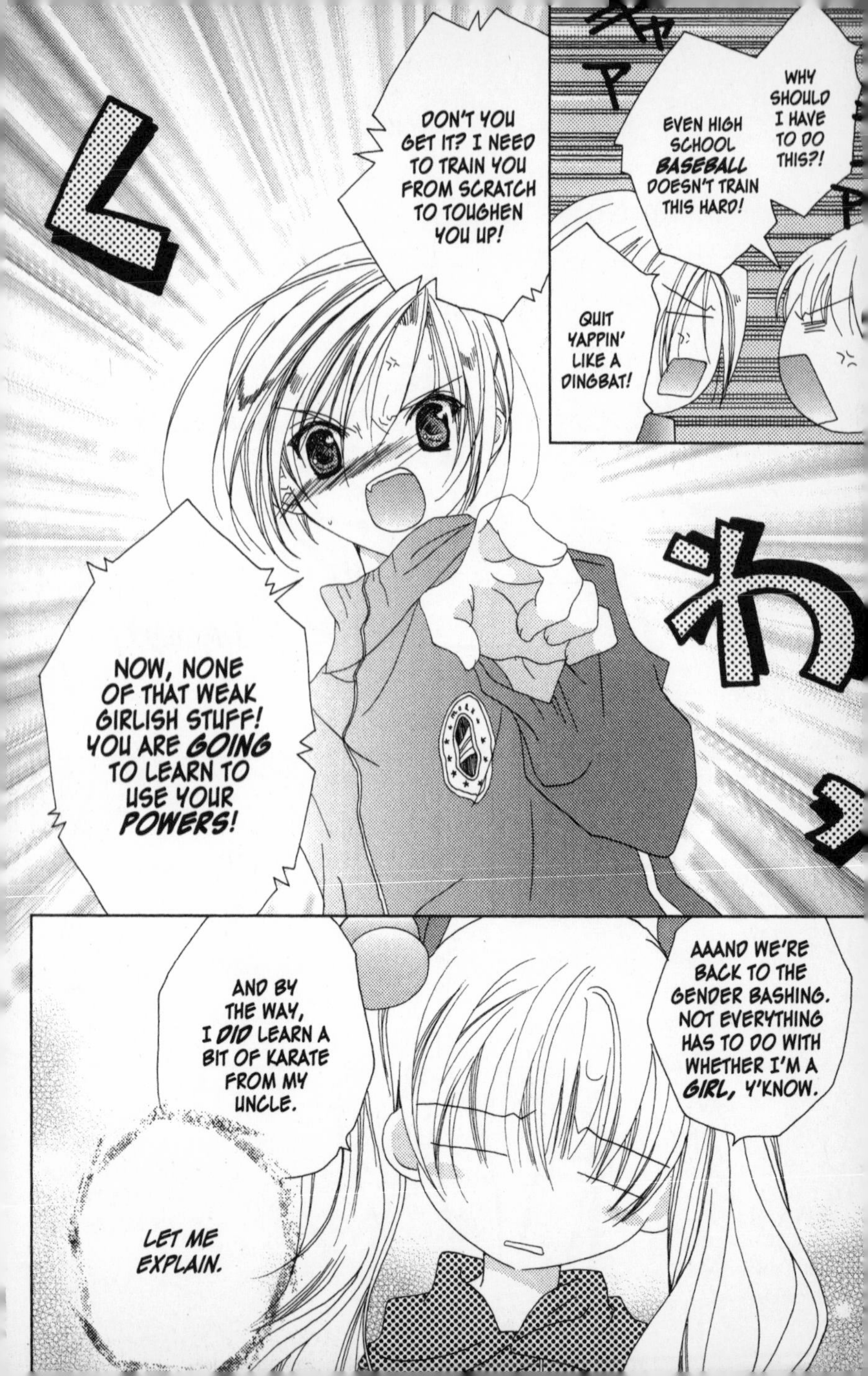
WHY SHOULD I HAVE TO DO THIS?!
EVEN HIGH SCHOOL BASEBALL DOESN'T TRAIN THIS HARD!
QUIT YAPPIN' LIKE A DINGBAT!
DON'T YOU GET IT? I NEED TO TRAIN YOU FROM SCRATCH TO TOUGHEN YOU UP!
ム
わ
NOW, NONE OF THAT WEAK GIRLISH STUFF! YOU ARE GOING TO LEARN TO USE YOUR POWERS!
AAAND WE'RE BACK TO THE GENDER BASHING. NOT EVERYTHING HAS TO DO WITH WHETHER I'M A GIRL, Y'KNOW.
AND BY THE WAY, I DID LEARN A BIT OF KARATE FROM MY UNCLE.
LET ME EXPLAIN.

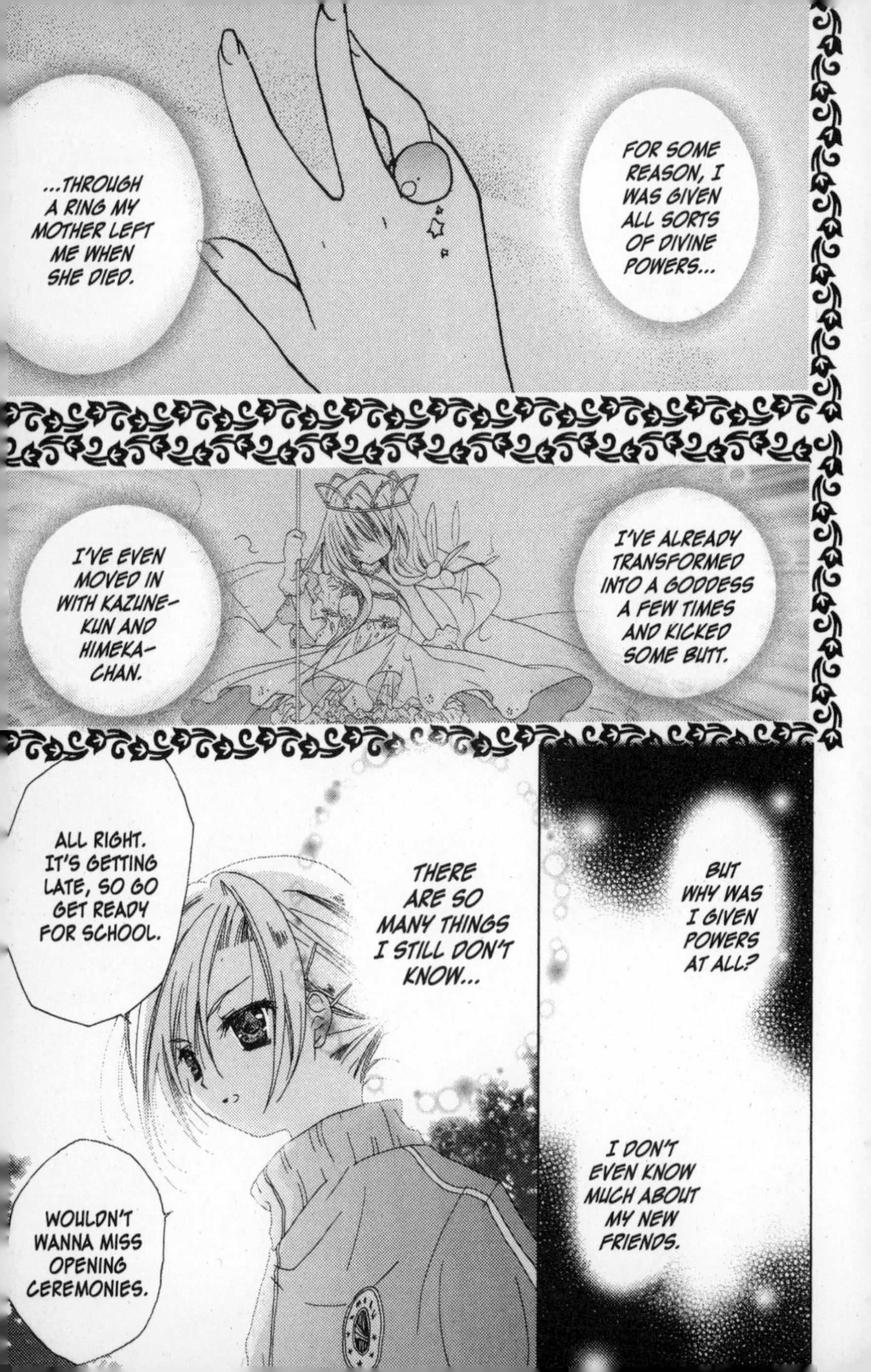
FOR SOME REASON, I WAS GIVEN ALL SORTS OF DIVINE POWERS...
...THROUGH A RING MY MOTHER LEFT ME WHEN SHE DIED.
I'VE ALREADY TRANSFORMED INTO A GODDESS A FEW TIMES AND KICKED SOME BUTT.
I'VE EVEN MOVED IN WITH KAZUNE-KUN AND HIMEKA-CHAN.
BUT WHY WAS I GIVEN POWERS AT ALL?
I DON'T EVEN KNOW MUCH ABOUT MY NEW FRIENDS.
THERE ARE SO MANY THINGS I STILL DON'T KNOW...
ALL RIGHT. IT'S GETTING LATE, SO GO GET READY FOR SCHOOL.
WOULDN'T WANNA MISS OPENING CEREMONIES.

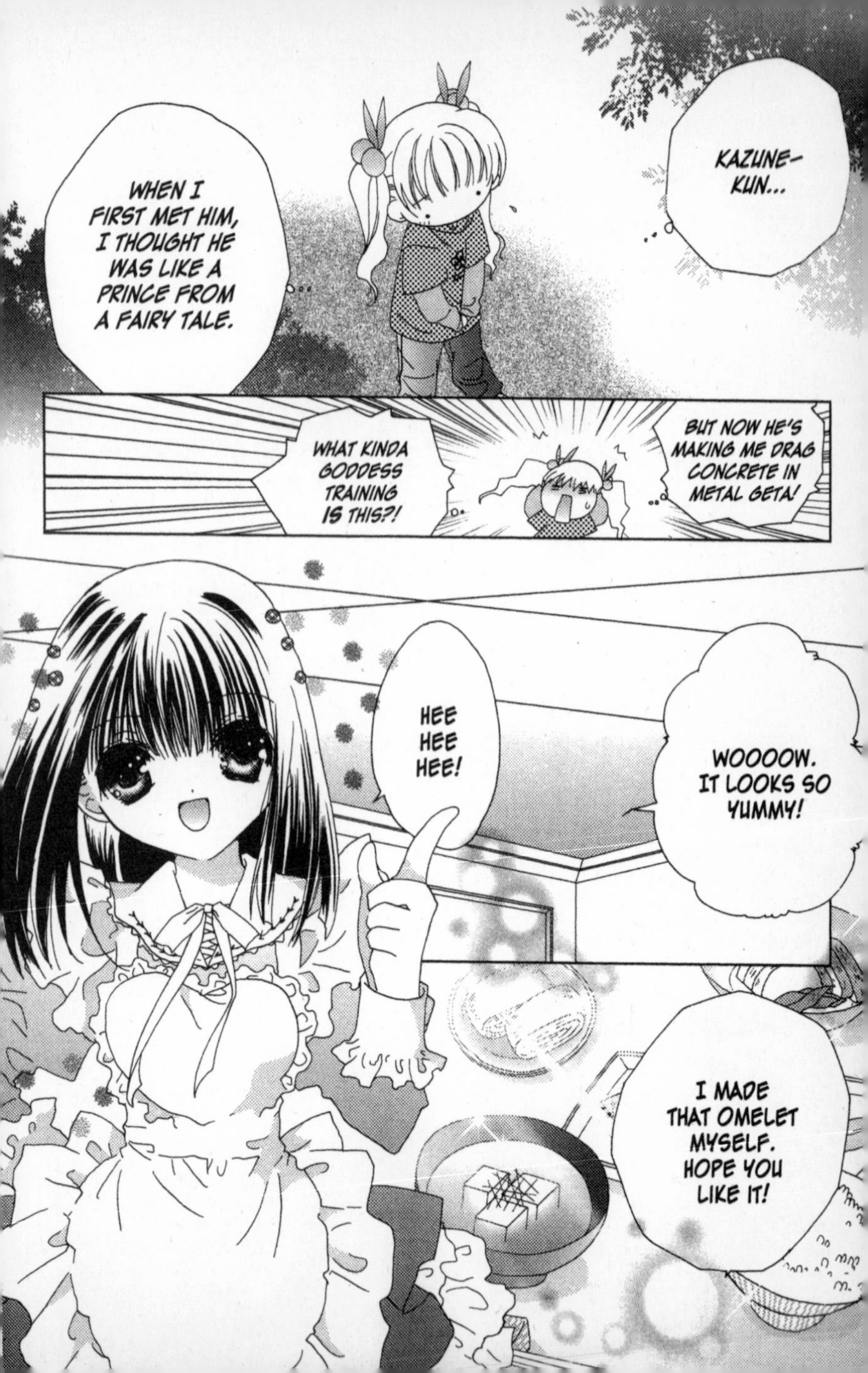
KAZUNE-KUN...
WHEN I FIRST MET HIM, I THOUGHT HE WAS LIKE A PRINCE FROM A FAIRY TALE.
BUT NOW HE'S MAKING ME DRAG CONCRETE IN METAL GETA!
WHAT KINDA GODDESS TRAINING IS THIS?!
WOOOOW. IT LOOKS SO YUMMY!
HEE HEE HEE!
I MADE THAT OMELET MYSELF. HOPE YOU LIKE IT!

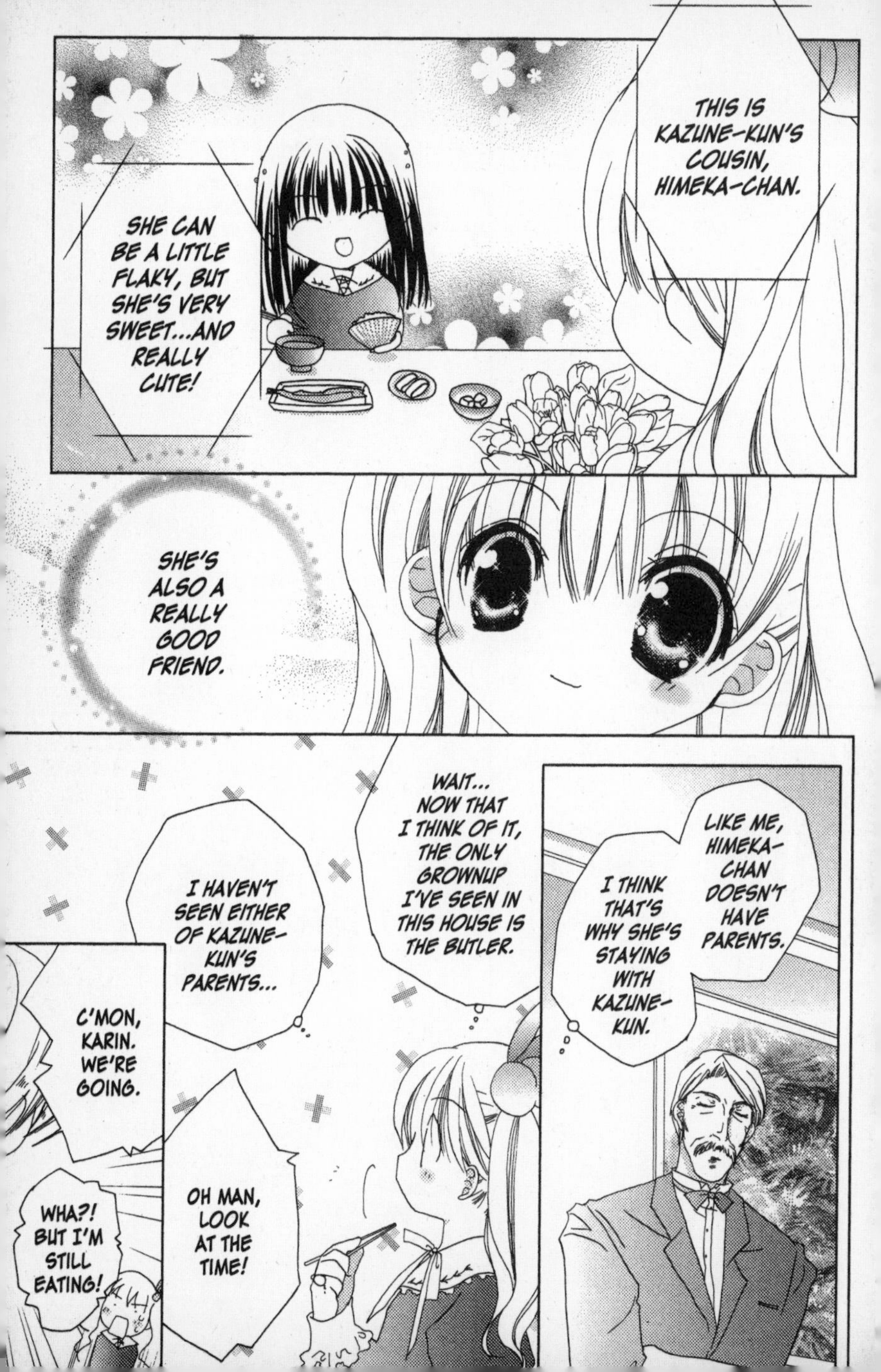
THIS IS KAZUNE-KUN'S COUSIN, HIMEKA-CHAN.
SHE CAN BE A LITTLE FLAKY, BUT SHE'S VERY SWEET...AND REALLY CUTE!
SHE'S ALSO A REALLY GOOD FRIEND.
LIKE ME, HIMEKA-CHAN DOESN'T HAVE PARENTS.
I THINK THAT'S WHY SHE'S STAYING WITH KAZUNE-KUN.
WAIT... NOW THAT I THINK OF IT, THE ONLY GROWNUP I'VE SEEN IN THIS HOUSE IS THE BUTLER.
I HAVEN'T SEEN EITHER OF KAZUNE-KUN'S PARENTS...
C'MON, KARIN. WE'RE GOING.
OH MAN, LOOK AT THE TIME!
WHA?! BUT I'M STILL EATING!

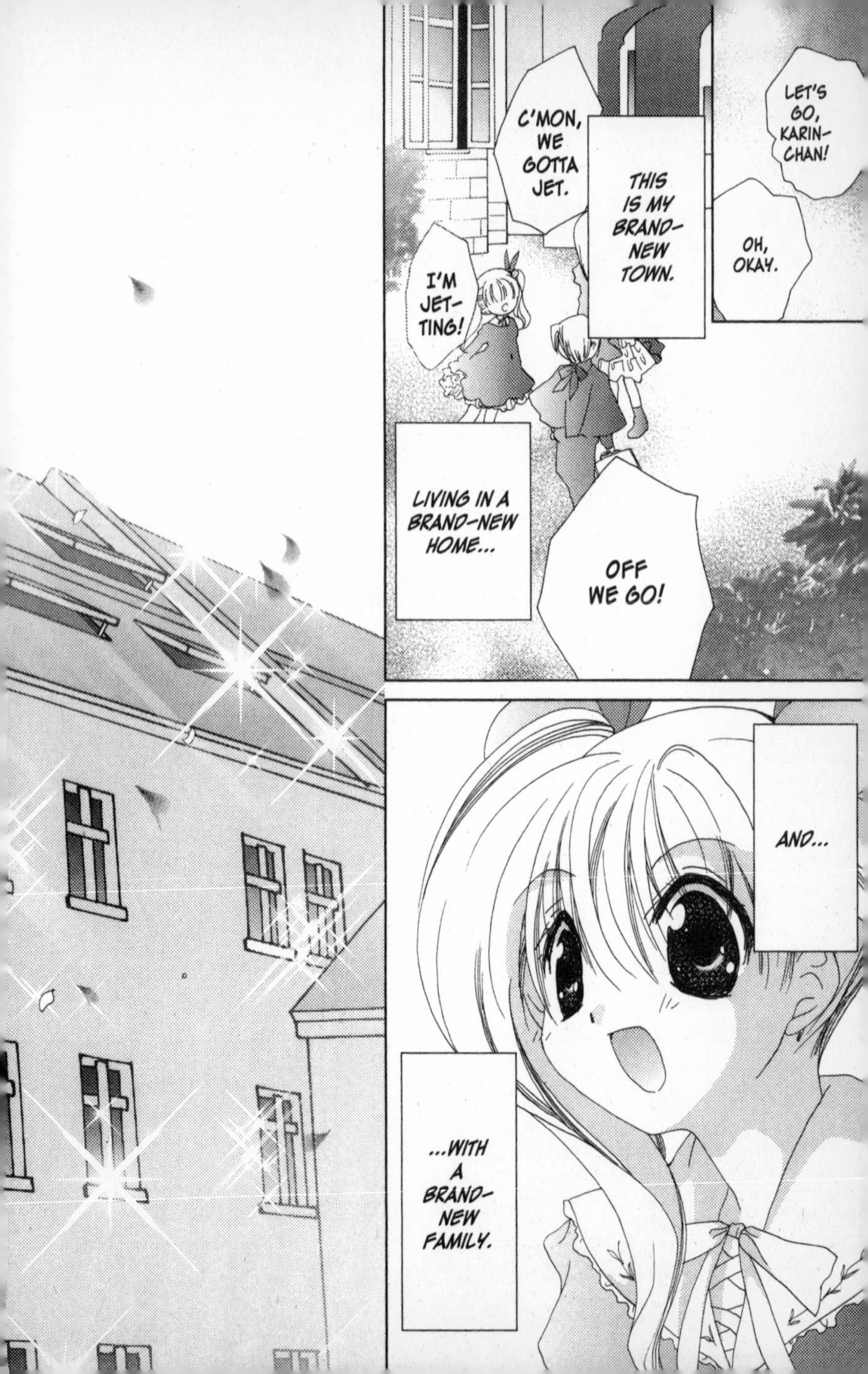
LET'S GO, KARIN-CHAN!
OH, OKAY.
THIS IS MY BRAND-NEW TOWN.
C'MON, WE GOTTA JET.
I'M JET-TING!
OFF WE GO!
LIVING IN A BRAND-NEW HOME...
AND...
...WITH A BRAND-NEW FAMILY.

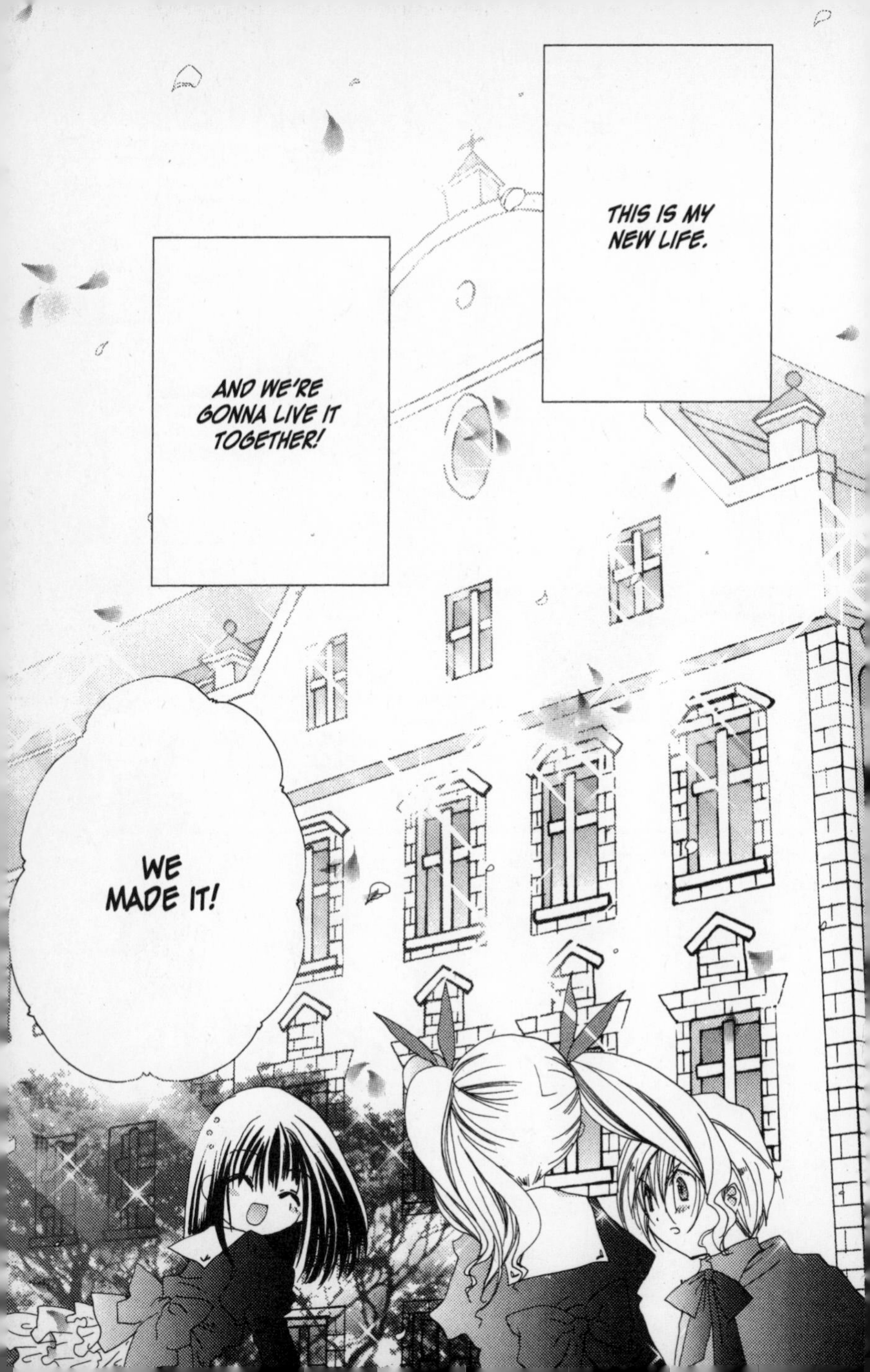
THIS IS MY NEW LIFE.
AND WE'RE GONNA LIVE IT TOGETHER!
WE MADE IT!

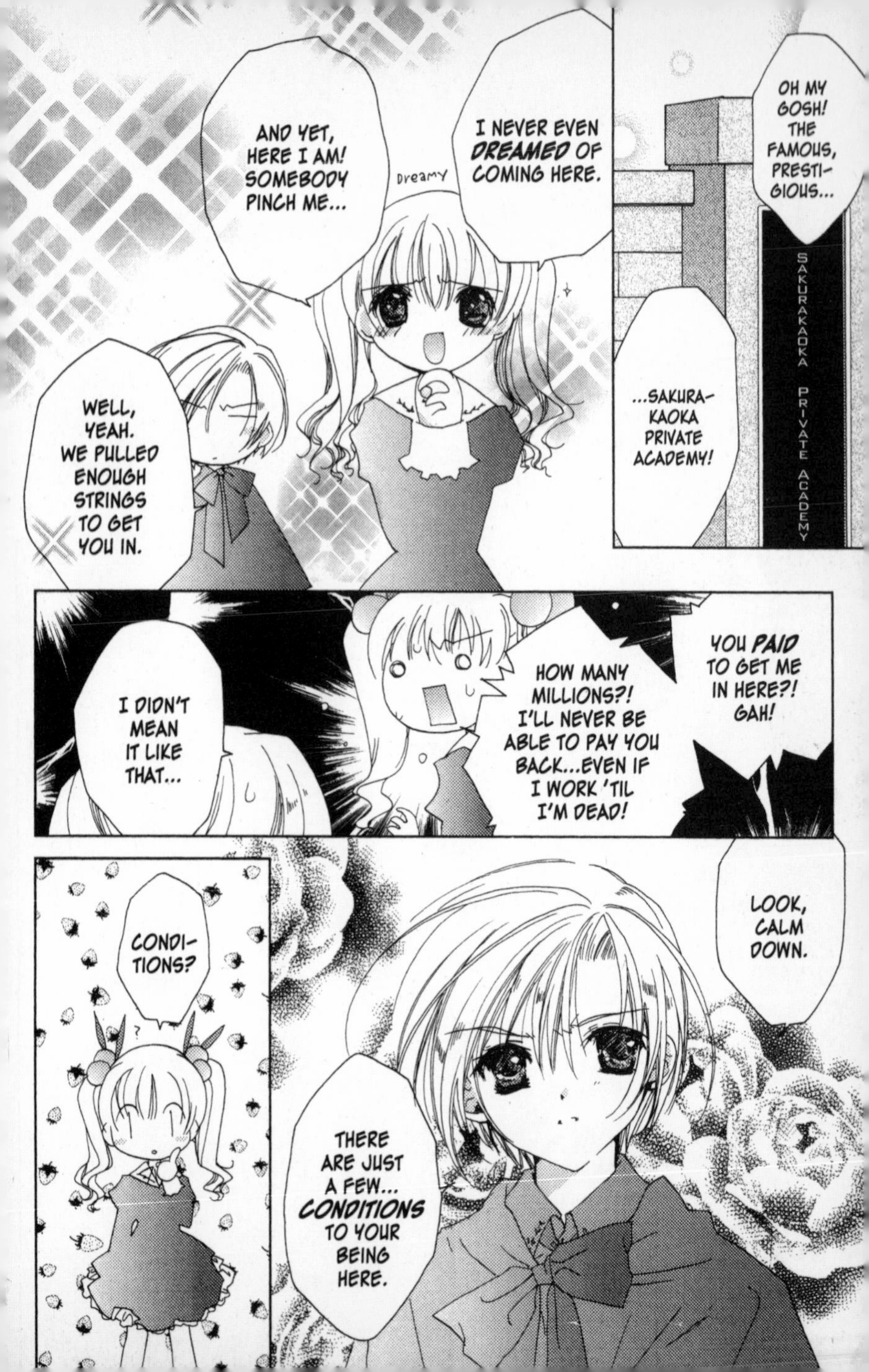
OH MY GOSH! THE FAMOUS, PRESTI-GIOUS...
SAKURAKAOKA PRIVATE ACADEMY
...SAKURA-KAOKA PRIVATE ACADEMY!
I NEVER EVEN **DREAMED** OF COMING HERE.
Dreamy
AND YET, HERE I AM! SOMEBODY PINCH ME...
WELL, YEAH. WE PULLED ENOUGH STRINGS TO GET YOU IN.
YOU **PAID** TO GET ME IN HERE?! GAH!
HOW MANY MILLIONS?! I'LL NEVER BE ABLE TO PAY YOU BACK...EVEN IF I WORK 'TIL I'M DEAD!
I DIDN'T MEAN IT LIKE THAT...
LOOK, CALM DOWN.
THERE ARE JUST A FEW... **CONDITIONS** TO YOUR BEING HERE.
CONDI-TIONS?

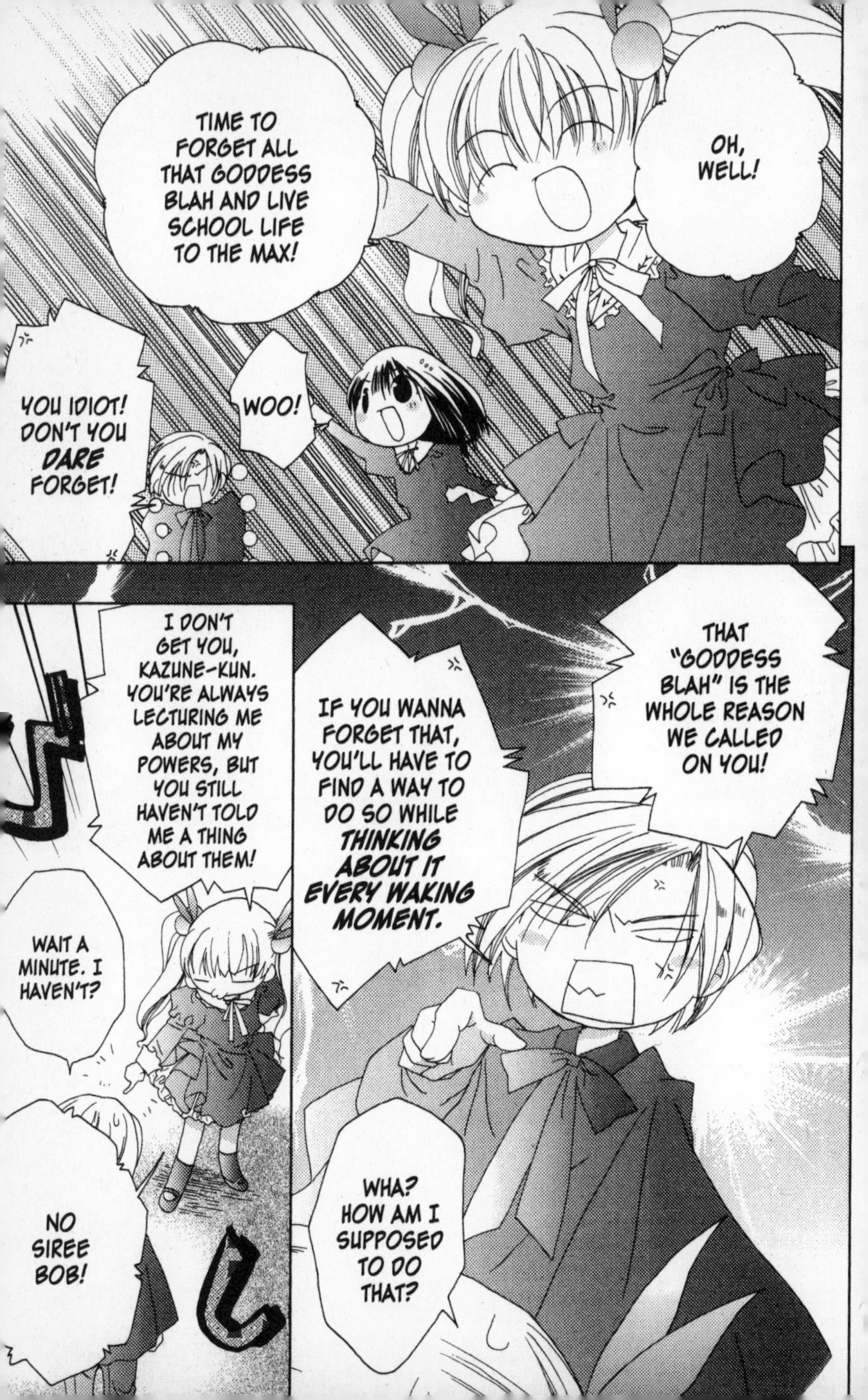
OH, WELL!
TIME TO FORGET ALL THAT GODDESS BLAH AND LIVE SCHOOL LIFE TO THE MAX!
WOO!
YOU IDIOT! DON'T YOU DARE FORGET!
THAT "GODDESS BLAH" IS THE WHOLE REASON WE CALLED ON YOU!
IF YOU WANNA FORGET THAT, YOU'LL HAVE TO FIND A WAY TO DO SO WHILE THINKING ABOUT IT EVERY WAKING MOMENT.
WHA? HOW AM I SUPPOSED TO DO THAT?
I DON'T GET YOU, KAZUNE-KUN. YOU'RE ALWAYS LECTURING ME ABOUT MY POWERS, BUT YOU STILL HAVEN'T TOLD ME A THING ABOUT THEM!
WAIT A MINUTE. I HAVEN'T?
NO SIREE BOB!

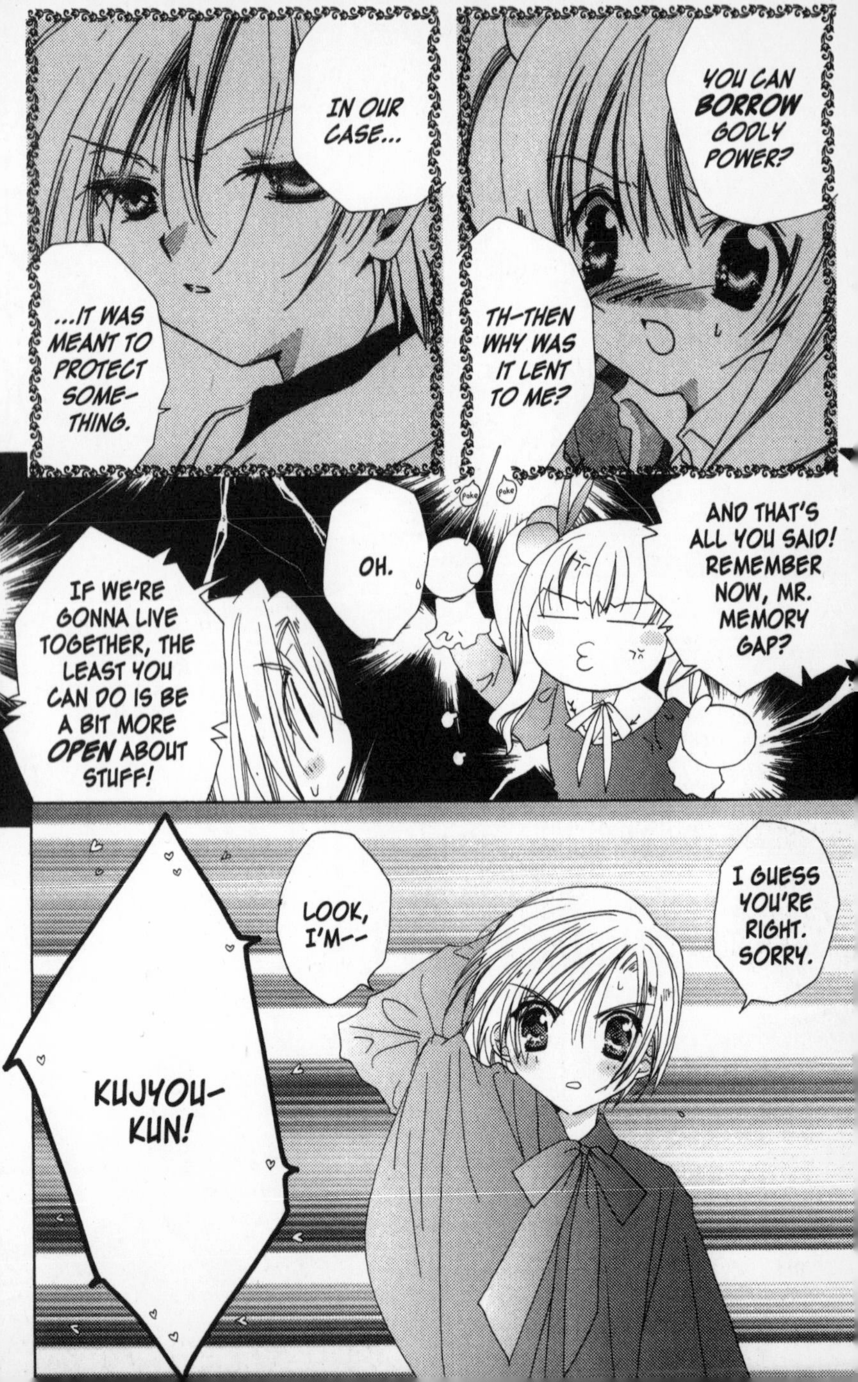
YOU CAN BORROW GODLY POWER?
TH-THEN WHY WAS IT LENT TO ME?
IN OUR CASE...
...IT WAS MEANT TO PROTECT SOME-THING.
AND THAT'S ALL YOU SAID! REMEMBER NOW, MR. MEMORY GAP?
Poke
Poke
OH.
IF WE'RE GONNA LIVE TOGETHER, THE LEAST YOU CAN DO IS BE A BIT MORE OPEN ABOUT STUFF!
I GUESS YOU'RE RIGHT. SORRY.
LOOK, I'M--
KUJYOU-KUN!

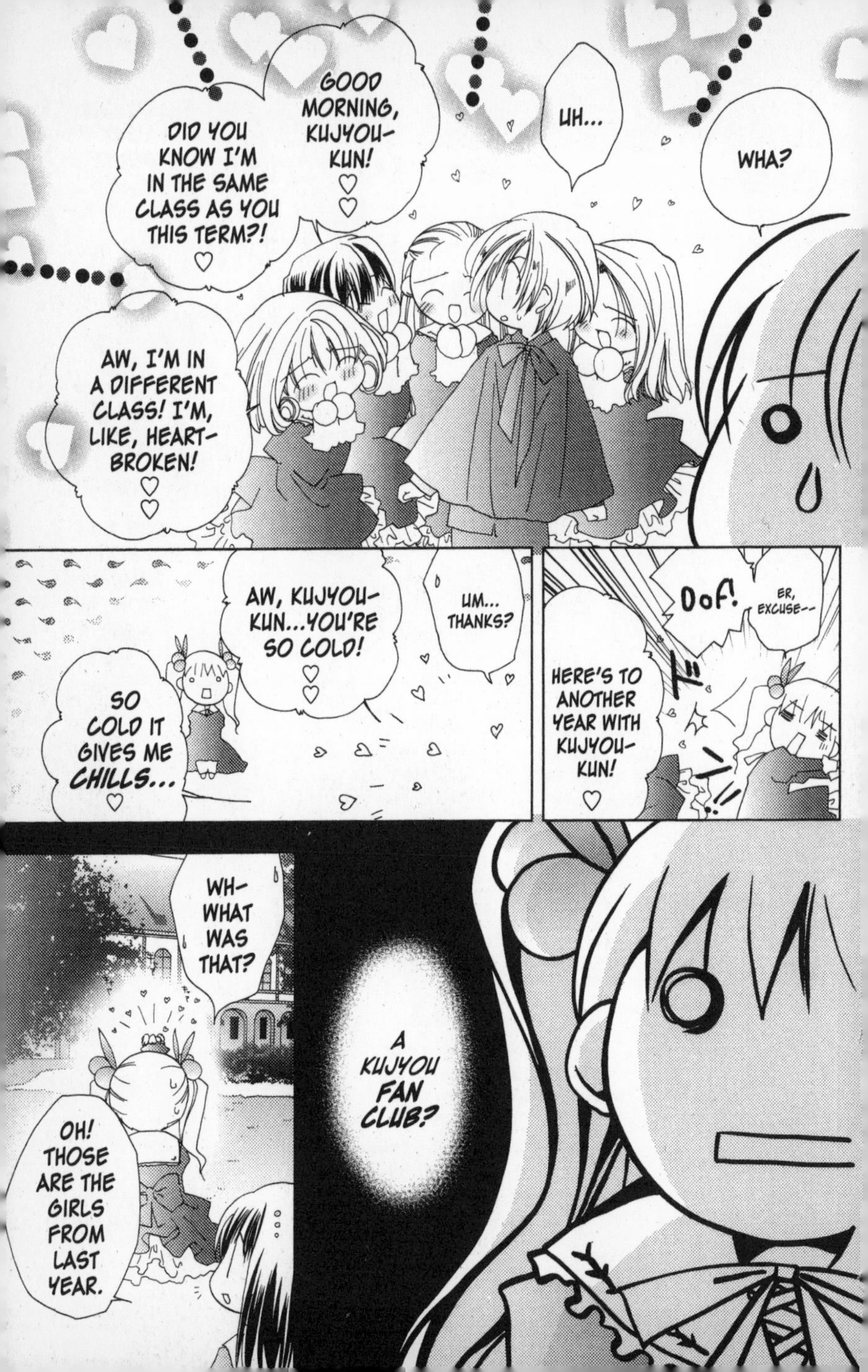
WHA?
UH...
GOOD MORNING, KUJYOU-KUN!
DID YOU KNOW I'M IN THE SAME CLASS AS YOU THIS TERM?!
AW, I'M IN A DIFFERENT CLASS! I'M, LIKE, HEART-BROKEN!
Dof!
ER, EXCUSE--
HERE'S TO ANOTHER YEAR WITH KUJYOU-KUN!
UM... THANKS?
AW, KUJYOU-KUN...YOU'RE SO COLD!
SO COLD IT GIVES ME *CHILLS...*
A KUJYOU FAN CLUB?
WH-WHAT WAS THAT?
OH! THOSE ARE THE GIRLS FROM LAST YEAR.

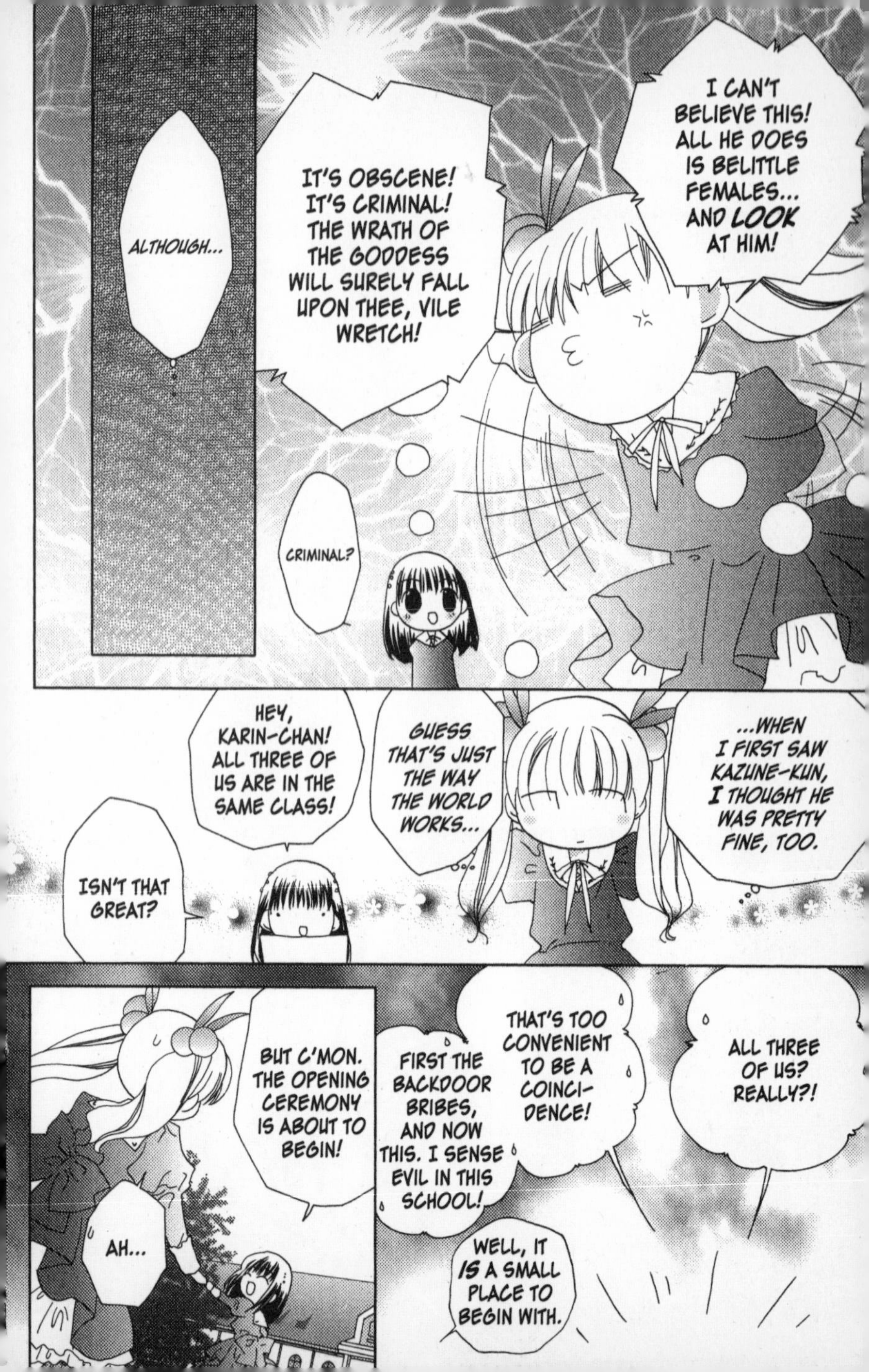
I CAN'T BELIEVE THIS! ALL HE DOES IS BELITTLE FEMALES... AND **LOOK** AT HIM!
IT'S OBSCENE! IT'S CRIMINAL! THE WRATH OF THE GODDESS WILL SURELY FALL UPON THEE, VILE WRETCH!
CRIMINAL?
ALTHOUGH...
...WHEN I FIRST SAW KAZUNE-KUN, I THOUGHT HE WAS PRETTY FINE, TOO.
GUESS THAT'S JUST THE WAY THE WORLD WORKS...
HEY, KARIN-CHAN! ALL THREE OF US ARE IN THE SAME CLASS!
ISN'T THAT GREAT?
ALL THREE OF US? REALLY?!
THAT'S TOO CONVENIENT TO BE A COINCI-DENCE!
FIRST THE BACKDOOR BRIBES, AND NOW THIS. I SENSE EVIL IN THIS SCHOOL!
WELL, IT *IS* A SMALL PLACE TO BEGIN WITH.
BUT C'MON. THE OPENING CEREMONY IS ABOUT TO BEGIN!
AH...

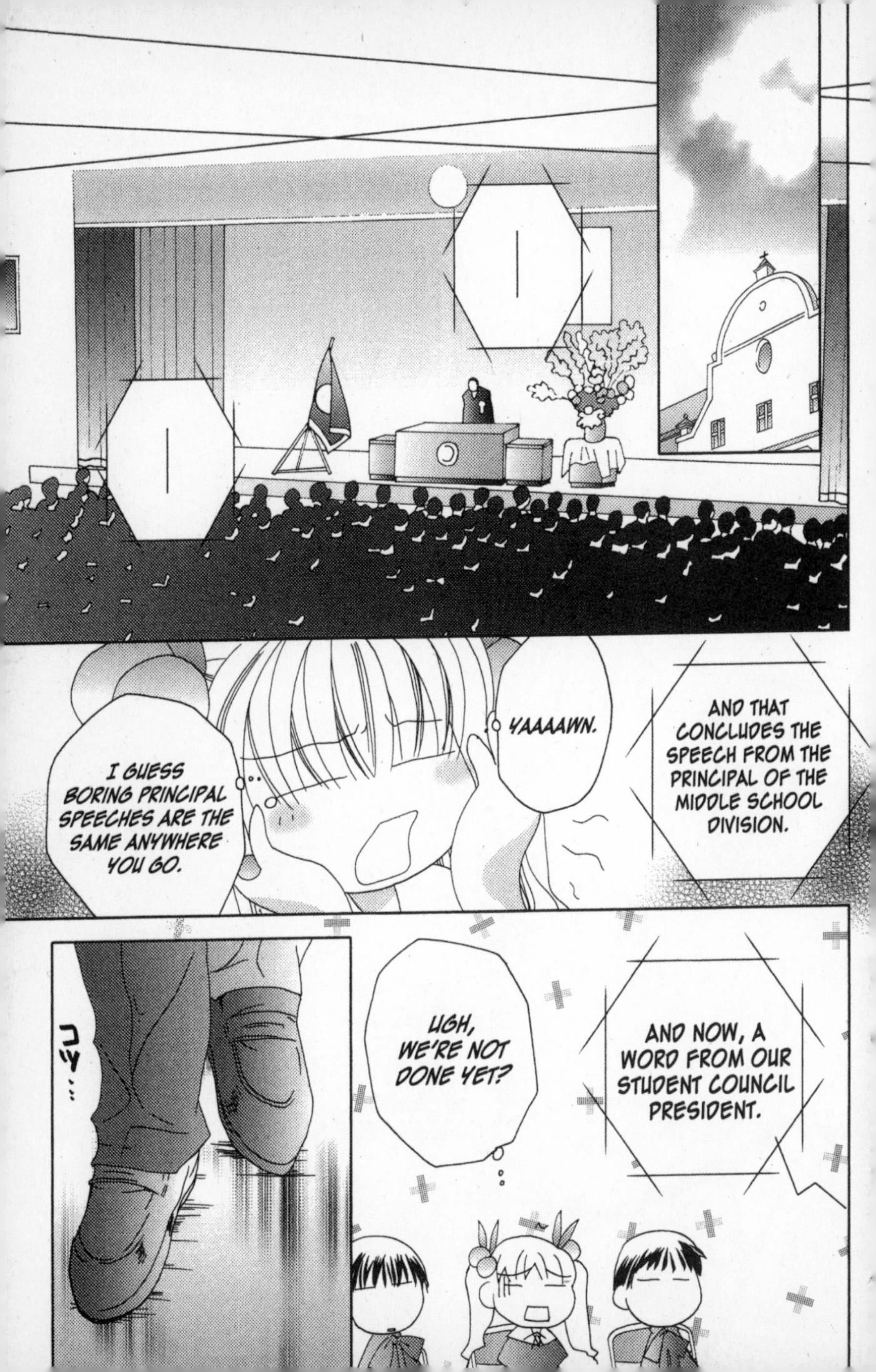
AND THAT CONCLUDES THE SPEECH FROM THE PRINCIPAL OF THE MIDDLE SCHOOL DIVISION.
YAAAAWN.
I GUESS BORING PRINCIPAL SPEECHES ARE THE SAME ANYWHERE YOU GO.
AND NOW, A WORD FROM OUR STUDENT COUNCIL PRESIDENT.
UGH, WE'RE NOT DONE YET?
コツ…

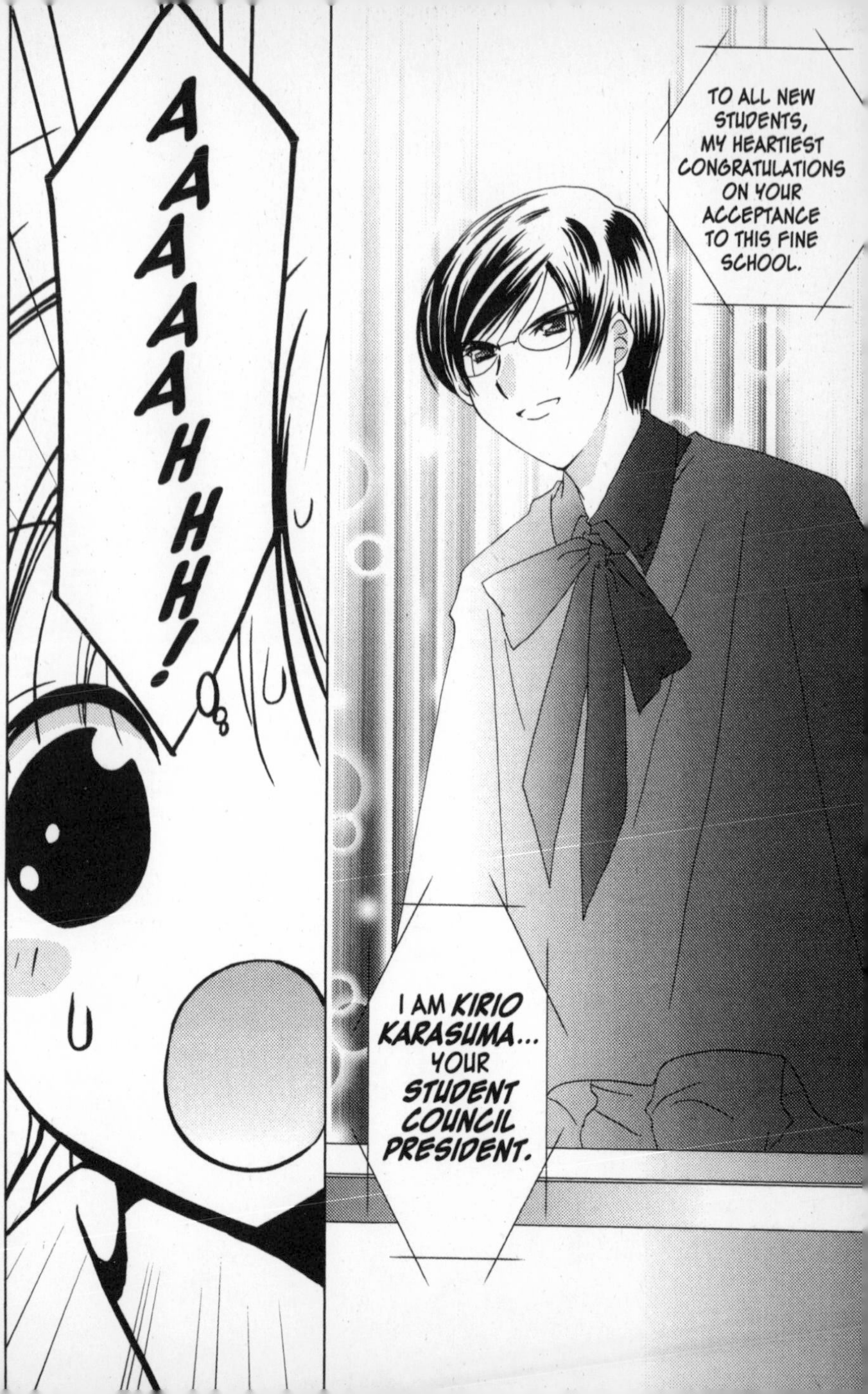
TO ALL NEW STUDENTS, MY HEARTIEST CONGRATULATIONS ON YOUR ACCEPTANCE TO THIS FINE SCHOOL.
I AM KIRIO KARASUMA... YOUR STUDENT COUNCIL PRESIDENT.
AAAAHHH!

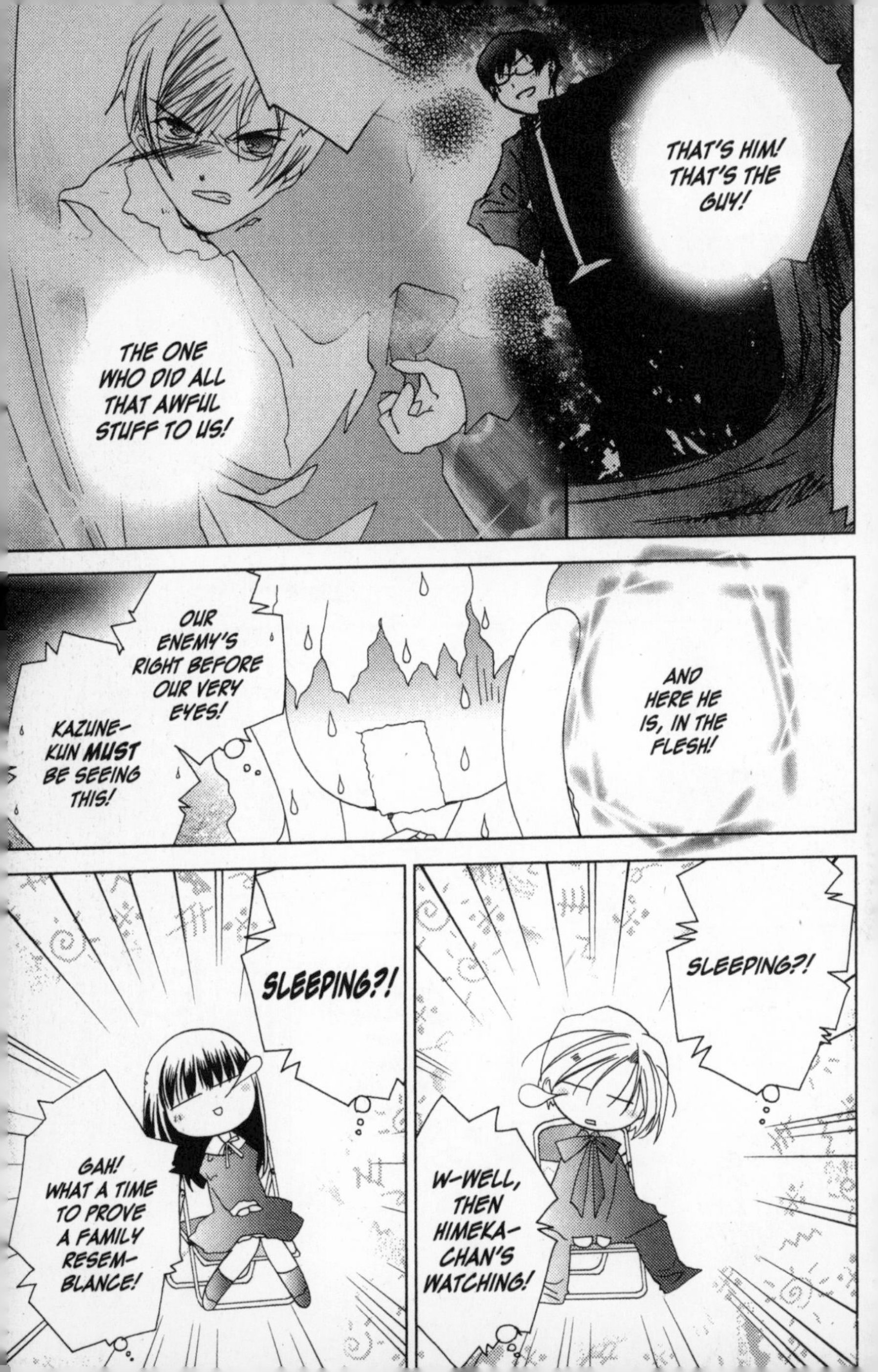
THAT'S HIM! THAT'S THE GUY!
THE ONE WHO DID ALL THAT AWFUL STUFF TO US!
AND HERE HE IS, IN THE FLESH!
OUR ENEMY'S RIGHT BEFORE OUR VERY EYES!
KAZUNE-KUN MUST BE SEEING THIS!
SLEEPING?!
W-WELL, THEN HIMEKA-CHAN'S WATCHING!
SLEEPING?!
GAH! WHAT A TIME TO PROVE A FAMILY RESEMBLANCE!

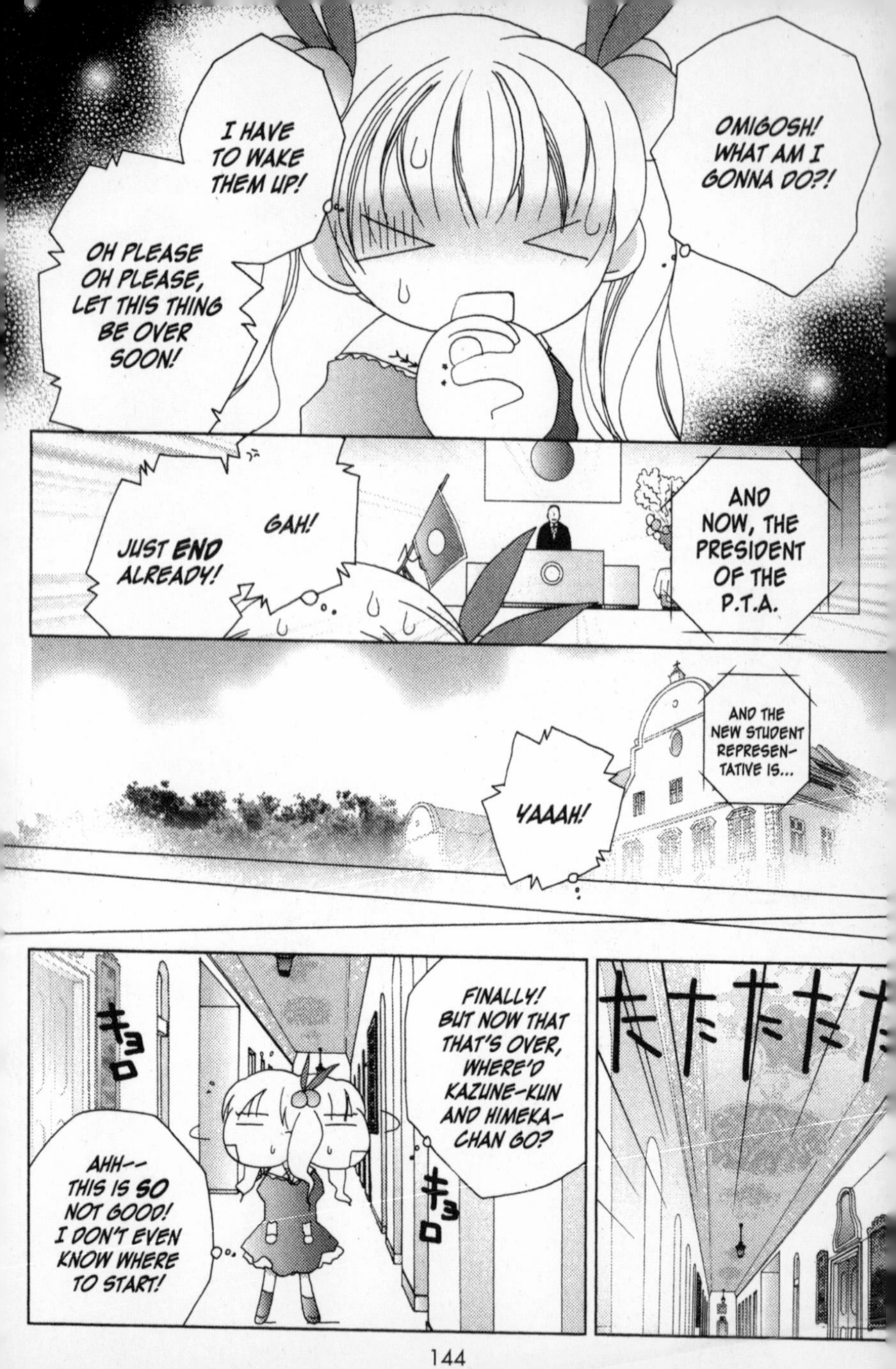

OMIGOSH! WHAT AM I GONNA DO?!
I HAVE TO WAKE THEM UP!
OH PLEASE OH PLEASE, LET THIS THING BE OVER SOON!
AND NOW, THE PRESIDENT OF THE P.T.A.
GAH!
JUST **END** ALREADY!
AND THE NEW STUDENT REPRESENTATIVE IS...
YAAAH!
たたたたた
FINALLY! BUT NOW THAT THAT'S OVER, WHERE'D KAZUNE-KUN AND HIMEKA-CHAN GO?
キョロ
キョロ
AHH-- THIS IS **SO** NOT GOOD! I DON'T EVEN KNOW WHERE TO START!

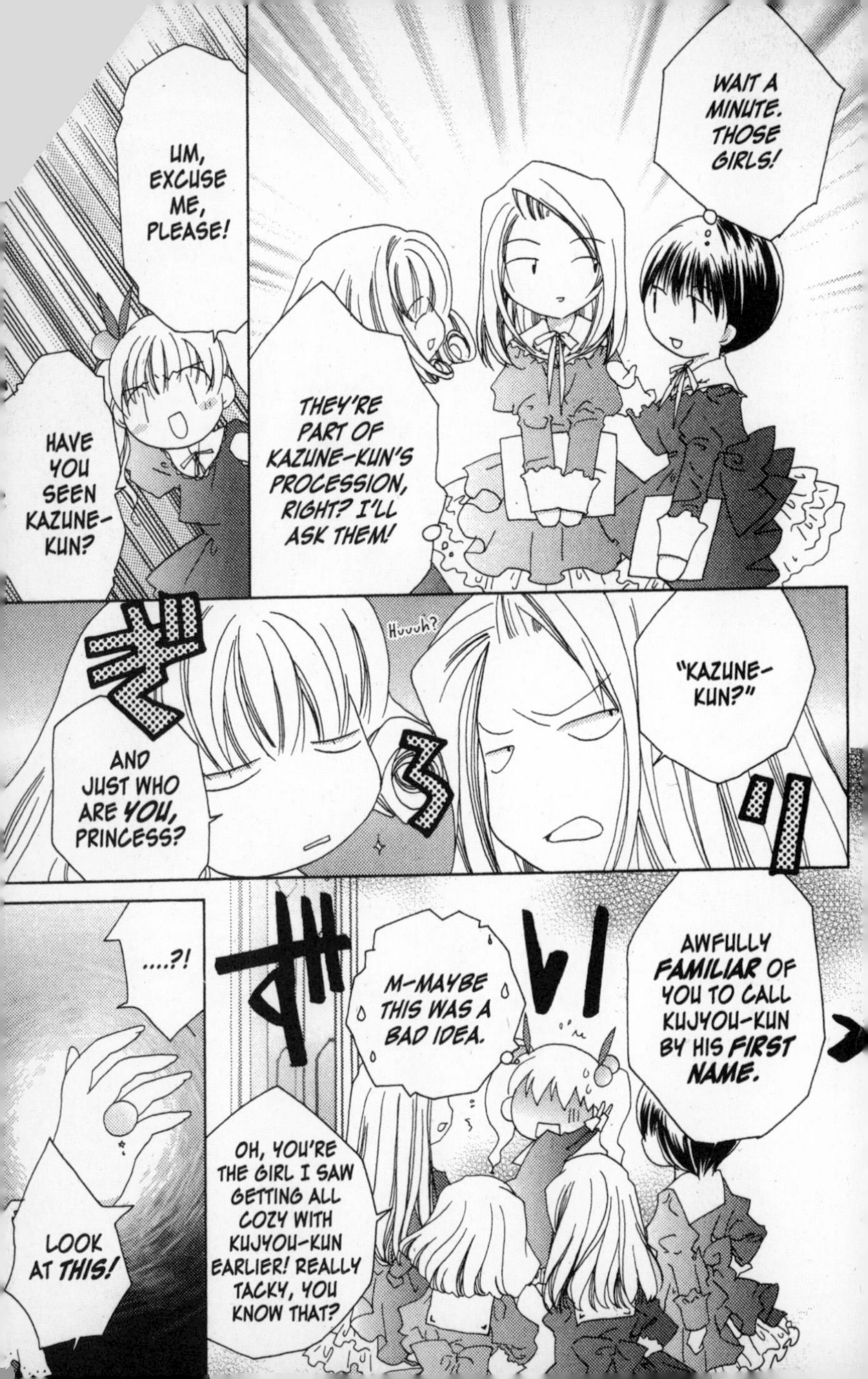
WAIT A MINUTE. THOSE GIRLS!
THEY'RE PART OF KAZUNE-KUN'S PROCESSION, RIGHT? I'LL ASK THEM!
UM, EXCUSE ME, PLEASE!
HAVE YOU SEEN KAZUNE-KUN?
"KAZUNE-KUN?"
Huuuh?
AND JUST WHO ARE YOU, PRINCESS?
AWFULLY FAMILIAR OF YOU TO CALL KUJYOU-KUN BY HIS FIRST NAME.
M-MAYBE THIS WAS A BAD IDEA.
OH, YOU'RE THE GIRL I SAW GETTING ALL COZY WITH KUJYOU-KUN EARLIER! REALLY TACKY, YOU KNOW THAT?
....?!
LOOK AT THIS!

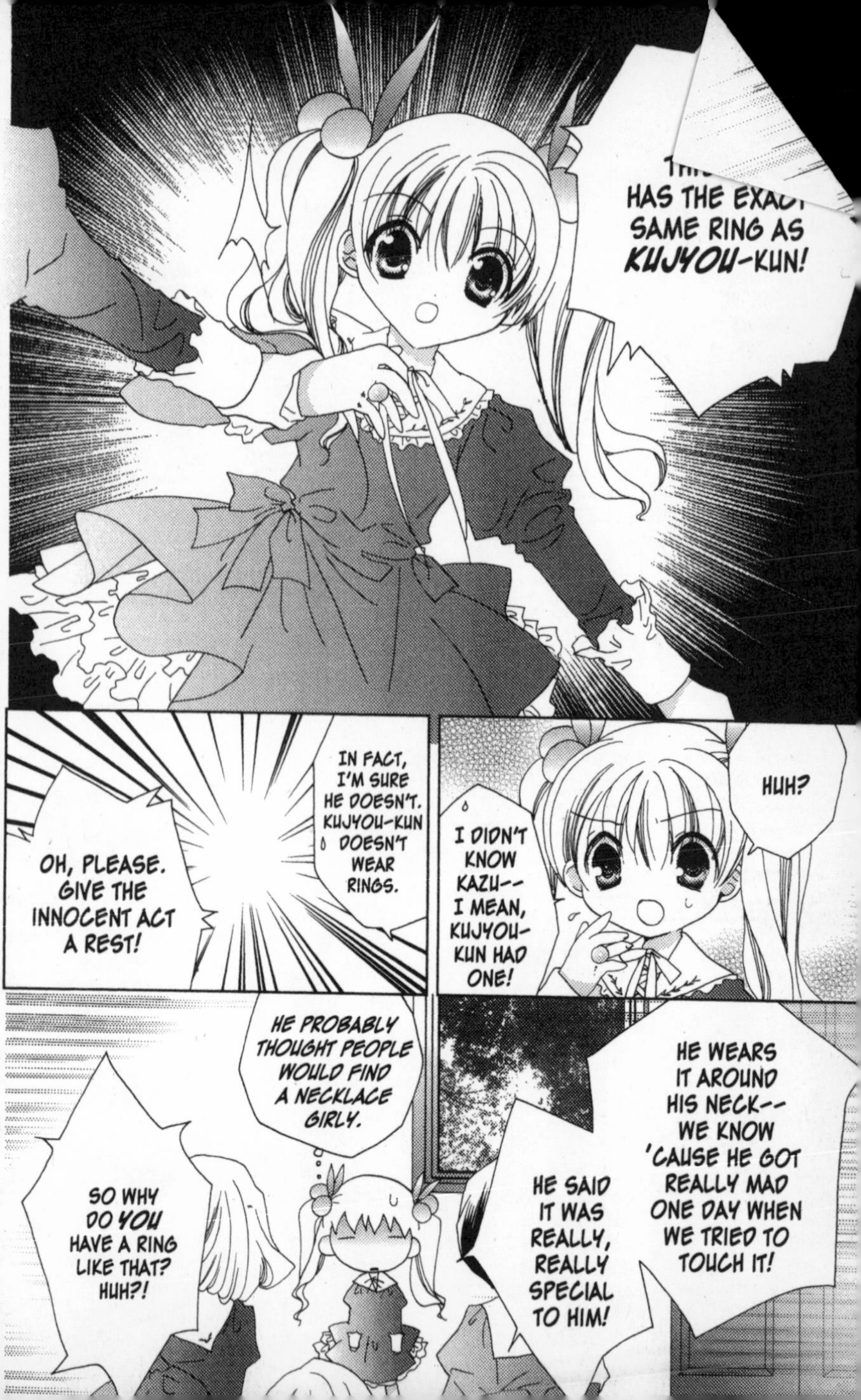
HAS THE EXACT SAME RING AS KUJYOU-KUN!
HUH?
I DIDN'T KNOW KAZU-- I MEAN, KUJYOU-KUN HAD ONE!
IN FACT, I'M SURE HE DOESN'T. KUJYOU-KUN DOESN'T WEAR RINGS.
OH, PLEASE. GIVE THE INNOCENT ACT A REST!
HE WEARS IT AROUND HIS NECK-- WE KNOW 'CAUSE HE GOT REALLY MAD ONE DAY WHEN WE TRIED TO TOUCH IT!
HE SAID IT WAS REALLY, REALLY SPECIAL TO HIM!
HE PROBABLY THOUGHT PEOPLE WOULD FIND A NECKLACE GIRLY.
SO WHY DO YOU HAVE A RING LIKE THAT? HUH?!

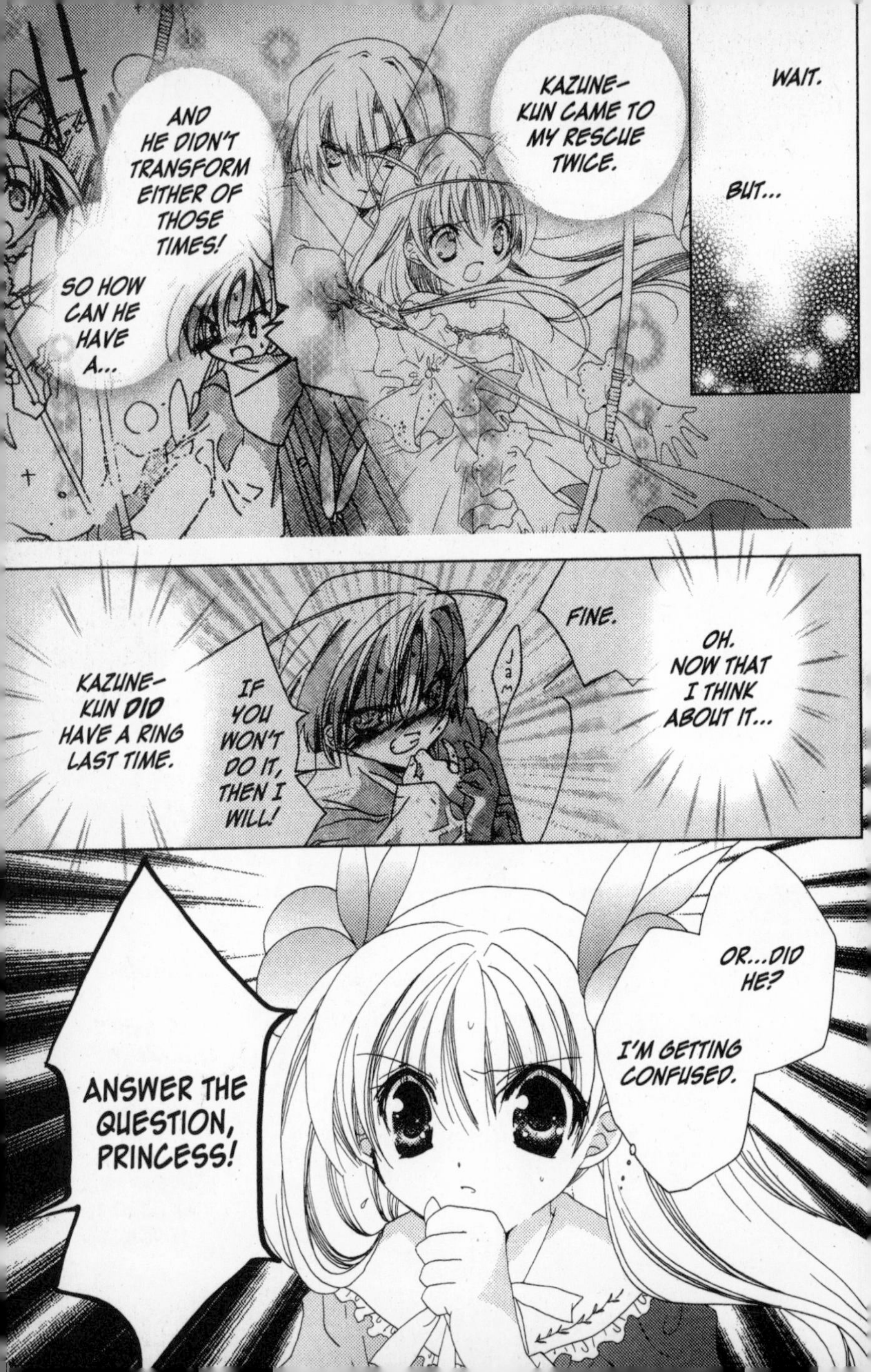
WAIT.
BUT...
KAZUNE-KUN CAME TO MY RESCUE TWICE.
AND HE DIDN'T TRANSFORM EITHER OF THOSE TIMES!
SO HOW CAN HE HAVE A...
OH. NOW THAT I THINK ABOUT IT...
FINE.
IF YOU WON'T DO IT, THEN I WILL!
KAZUNE-KUN DID HAVE A RING LAST TIME.
OR...DID HE?
I'M GETTING CONFUSED.
ANSWER THE QUESTION, PRINCESS!

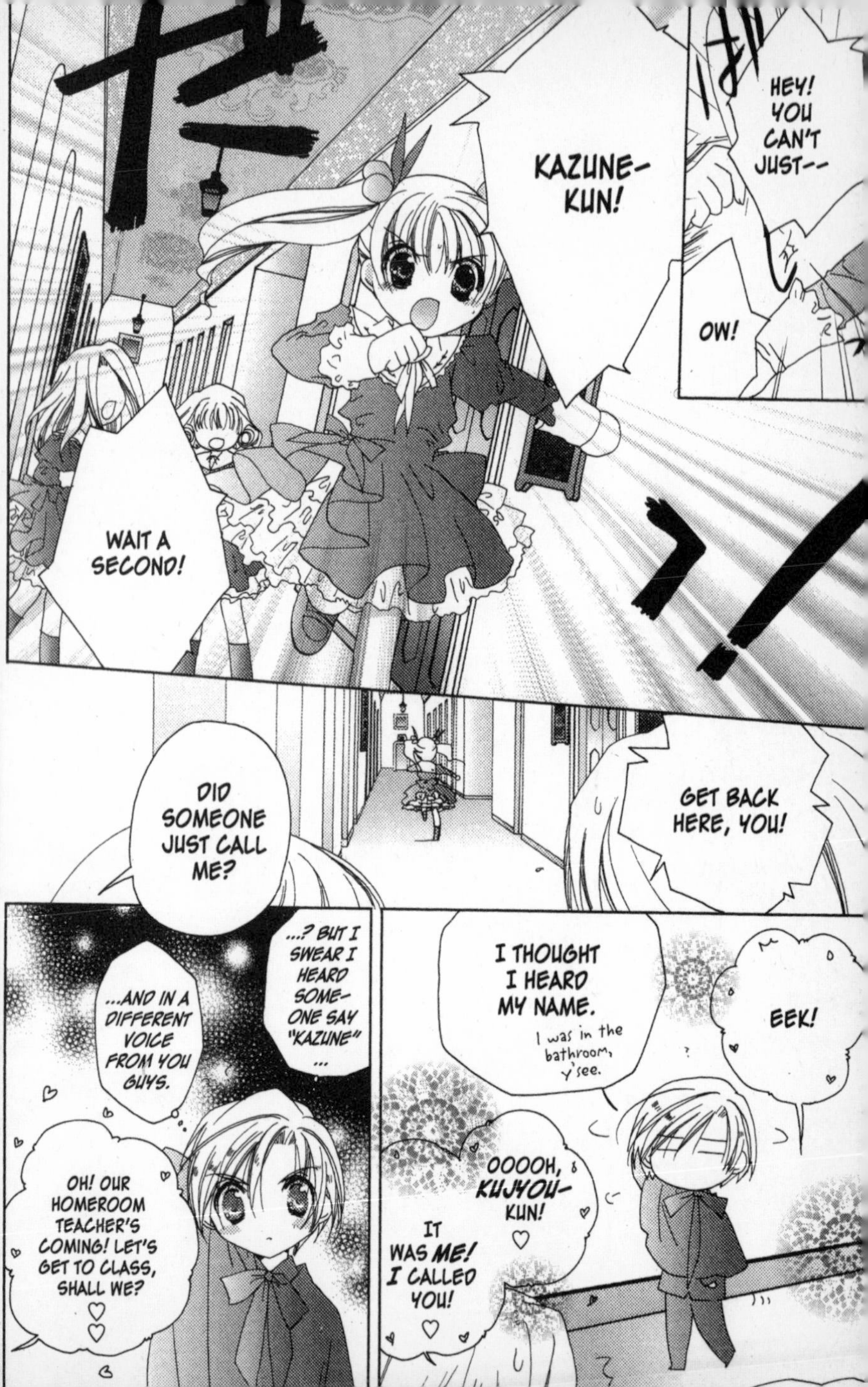
HEY! YOU CAN'T JUST--
OW!
KAZUNE-KUN!
WAIT A SECOND!
GET BACK HERE, YOU!
DID SOMEONE JUST CALL ME?
EEK!
I THOUGHT I HEARD MY NAME.
I was in the bathroom, y'see.
OOOOH, KUJYOU-KUN!
IT WAS ME! I CALLED YOU!
...? BUT I SWEAR I HEARD SOME-ONE SAY "KAZUNE"...
...AND IN A DIFFERENT VOICE FROM YOU GUYS.
OH! OUR HOMEROOM TEACHER'S COMING! LET'S GET TO CLASS, SHALL WE?

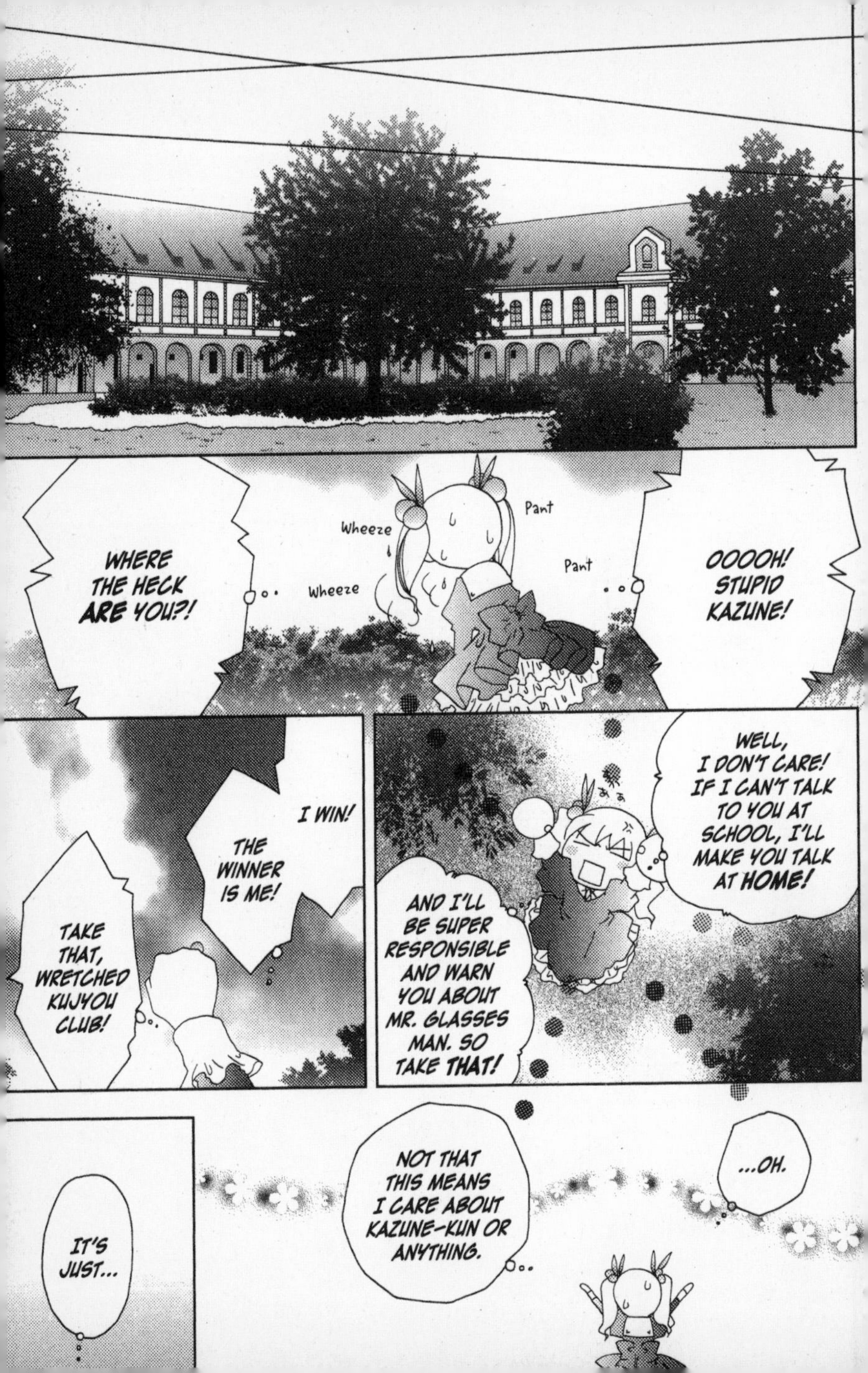
OOOOH! STUPID KAZUNE!
Pant
Pant
Wheeze
Wheeze
WHERE THE HECK ARE YOU?!
WELL, I DON'T CARE! IF I CAN'T TALK TO YOU AT SCHOOL, I'LL MAKE YOU TALK AT HOME!
AND I'LL BE SUPER RESPONSIBLE AND WARN YOU ABOUT MR. GLASSES MAN. SO TAKE THAT!
I WIN!
THE WINNER IS ME!
TAKE THAT, WRETCHED KUJYOU CLUB!
...OH.
NOT THAT THIS MEANS I CARE ABOUT KAZUNE-KUN OR ANYTHING.
IT'S JUST...

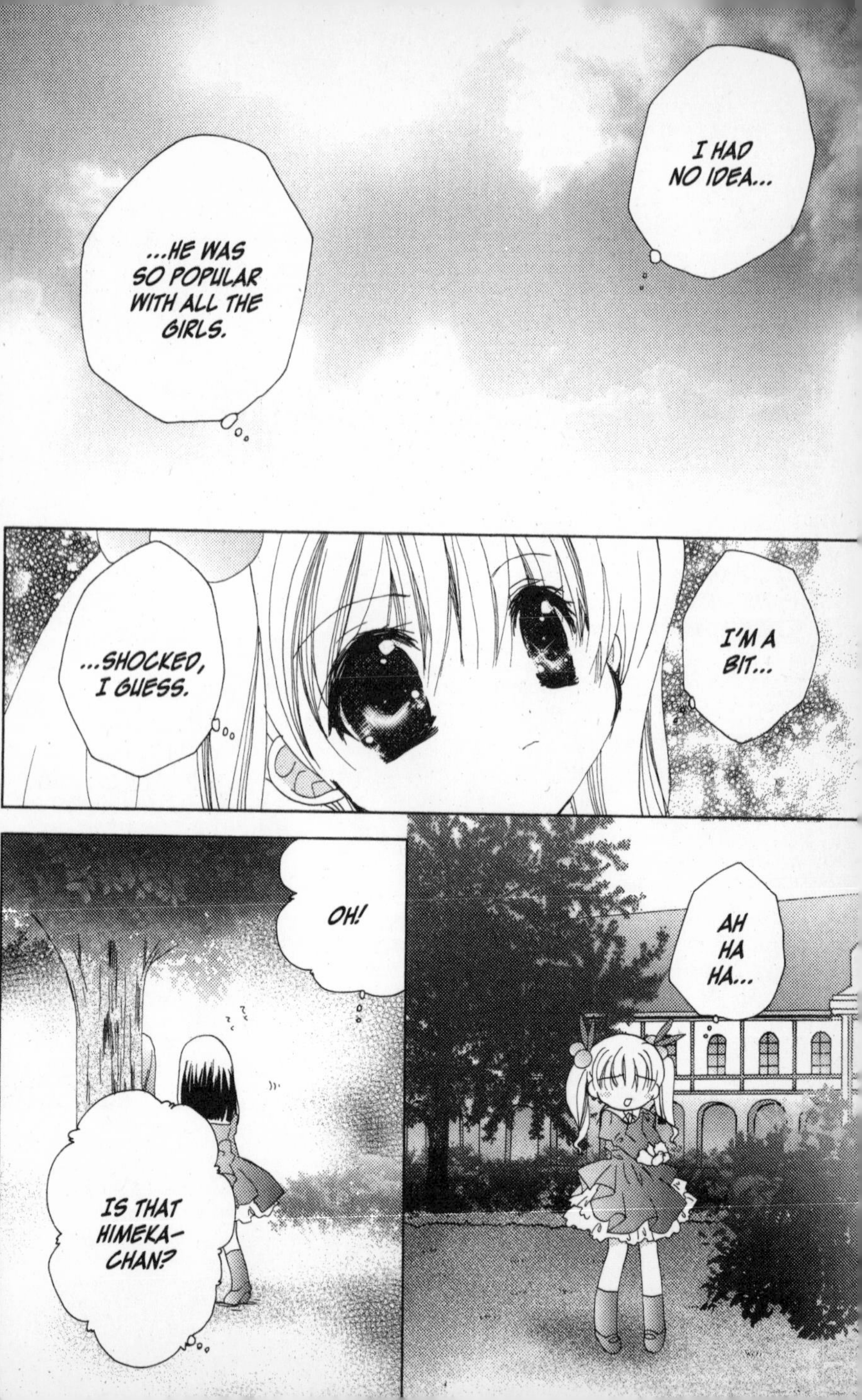
I HAD NO IDEA...
...HE WAS SO POPULAR WITH ALL THE GIRLS.
I'M A BIT...
...SHOCKED, I GUESS.
AH HA HA...
OH!
IS THAT HIMEKA-CHAN?

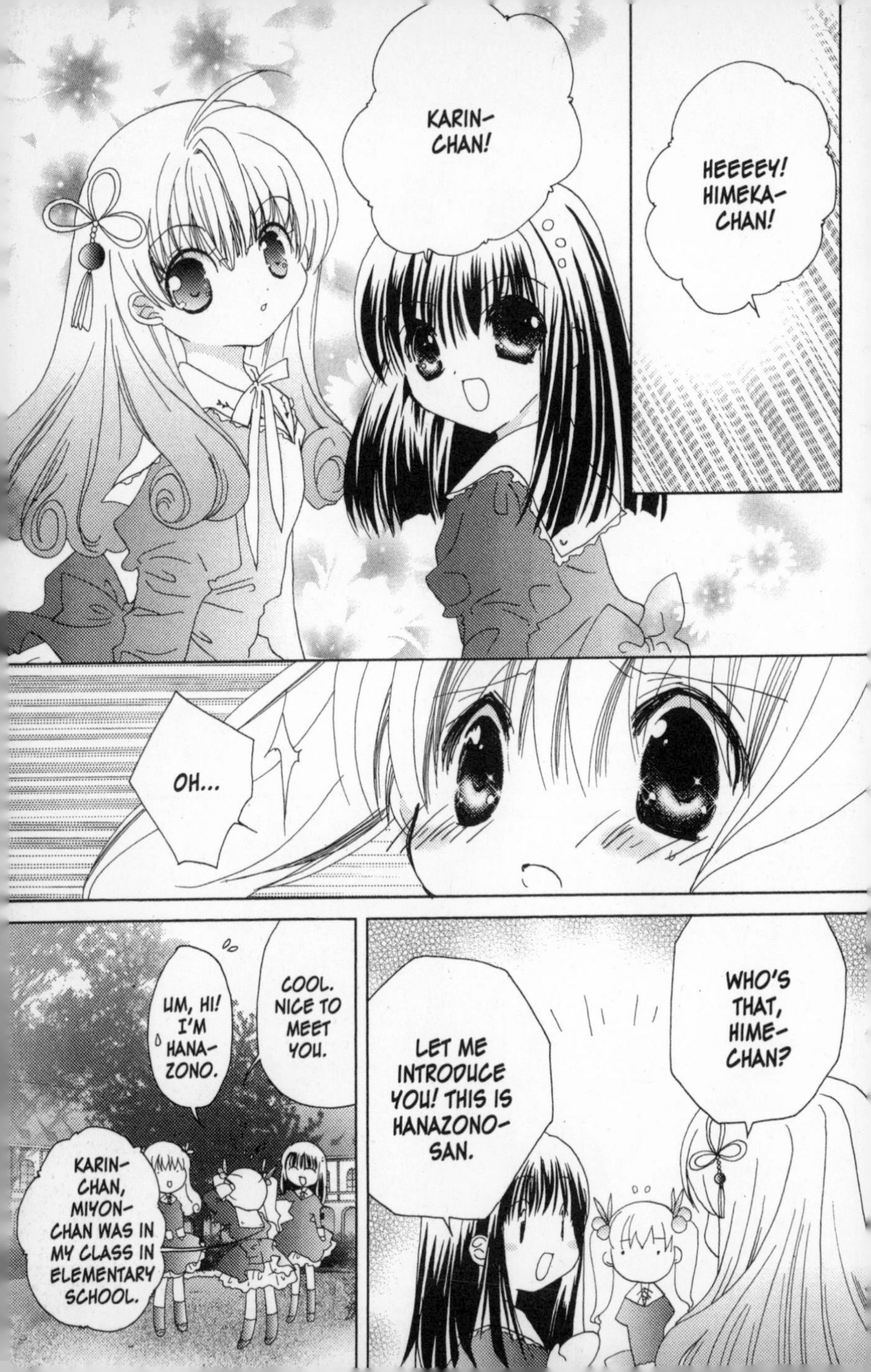
HEEEEY! HIMEKA-CHAN!
KARIN-CHAN!
OH...
WHO'S THAT, HIME-CHAN?
LET ME INTRODUCE YOU! THIS IS HANAZONO-SAN.
COOL. NICE TO MEET YOU.
UM, HI! I'M HANA-ZONO.
KARIN-CHAN, MIYON-CHAN WAS IN MY CLASS IN ELEMENTARY SCHOOL.

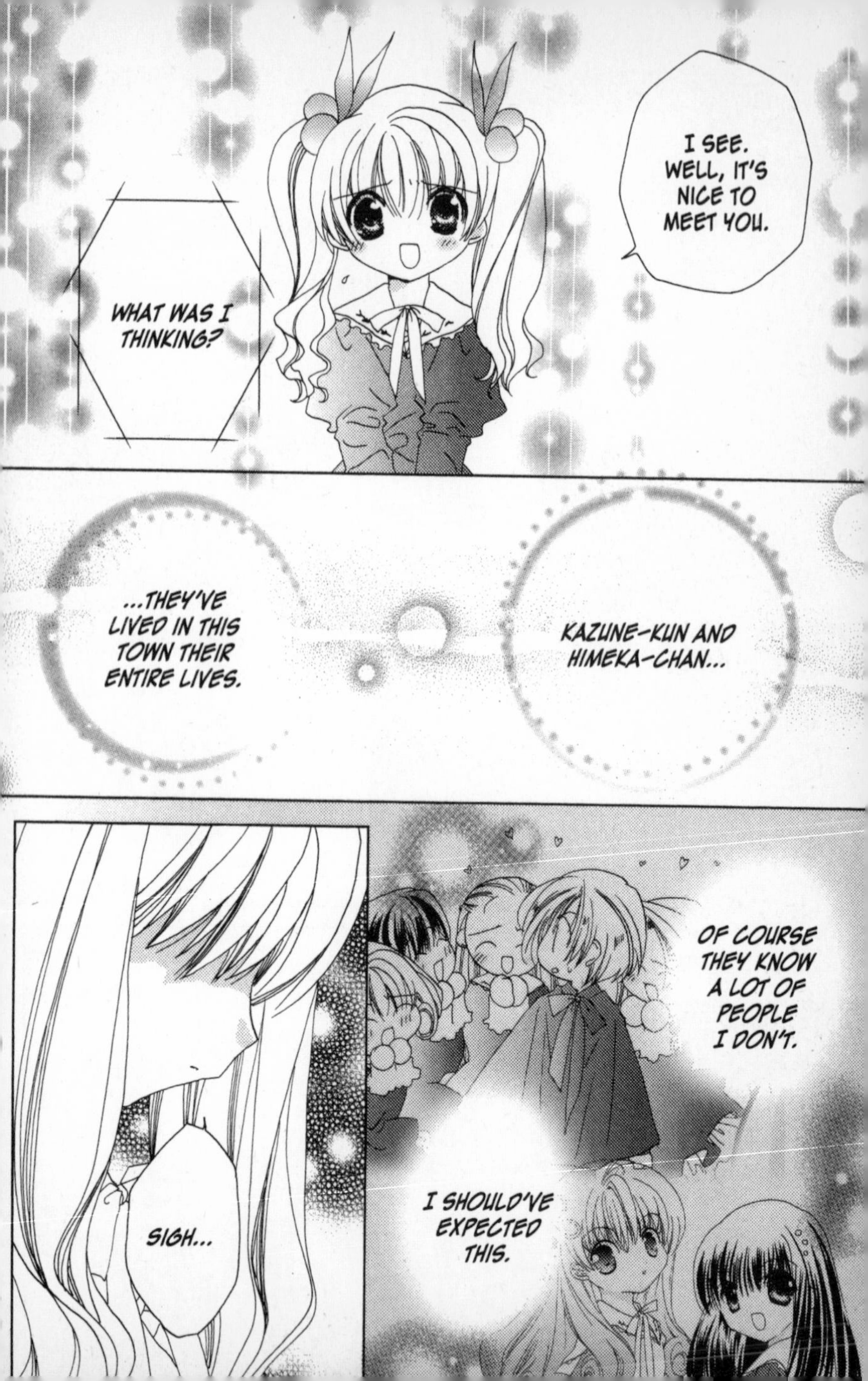
I SEE. WELL, IT'S NICE TO MEET YOU.
WHAT WAS I THINKING?
KAZUNE-KUN AND HIMEKA-CHAN...
...THEY'VE LIVED IN THIS TOWN THEIR ENTIRE LIVES.
OF COURSE THEY KNOW A LOT OF PEOPLE I DON'T.
I SHOULD'VE EXPECTED THIS.
SIGH...

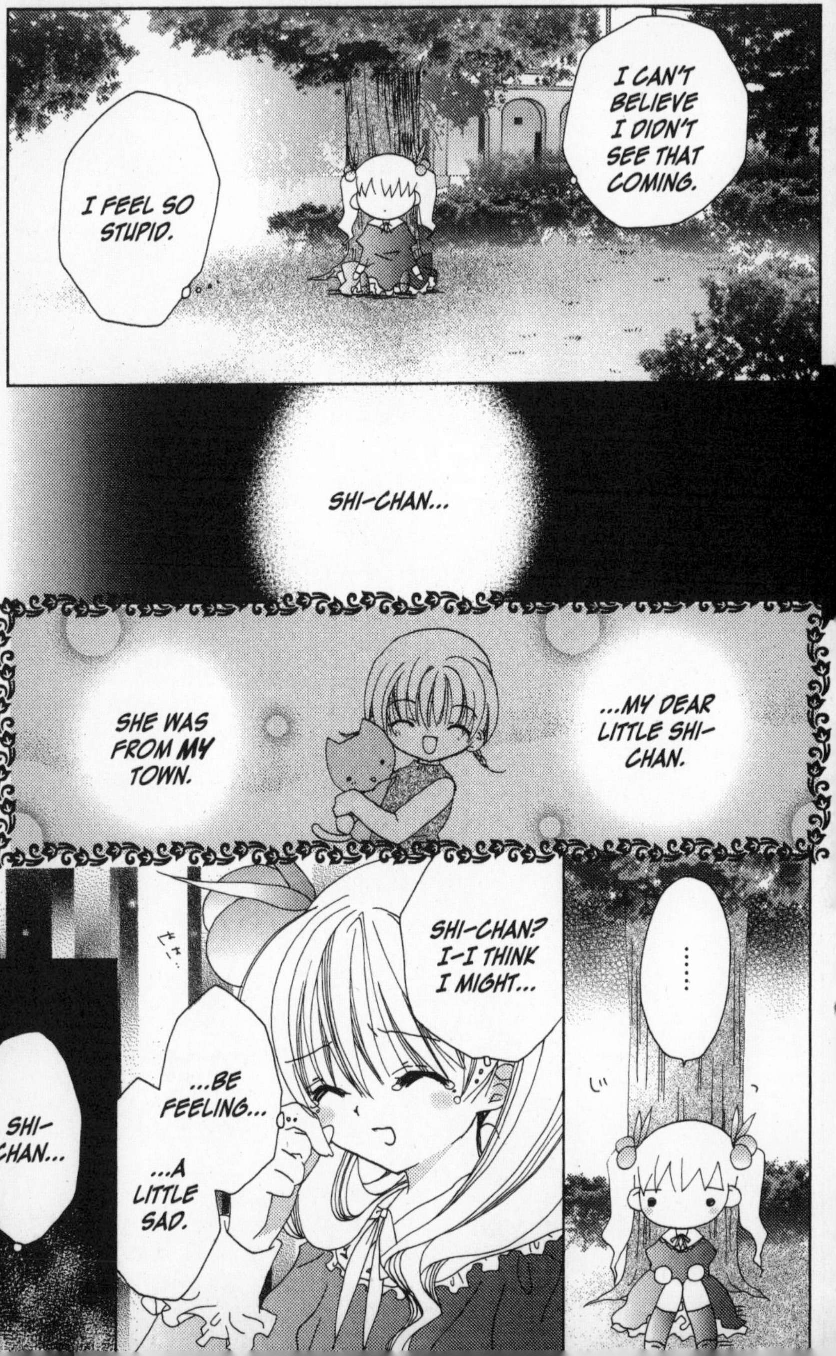
I CAN'T BELIEVE I DIDN'T SEE THAT COMING.
I FEEL SO STUPID.
SHI-CHAN...
...MY DEAR LITTLE SHI-CHAN.
SHE WAS FROM MY TOWN.
......
SHI-CHAN? I-I THINK I MIGHT...
...BE FEELING...
...A LITTLE SAD.
SHI-CHAN...

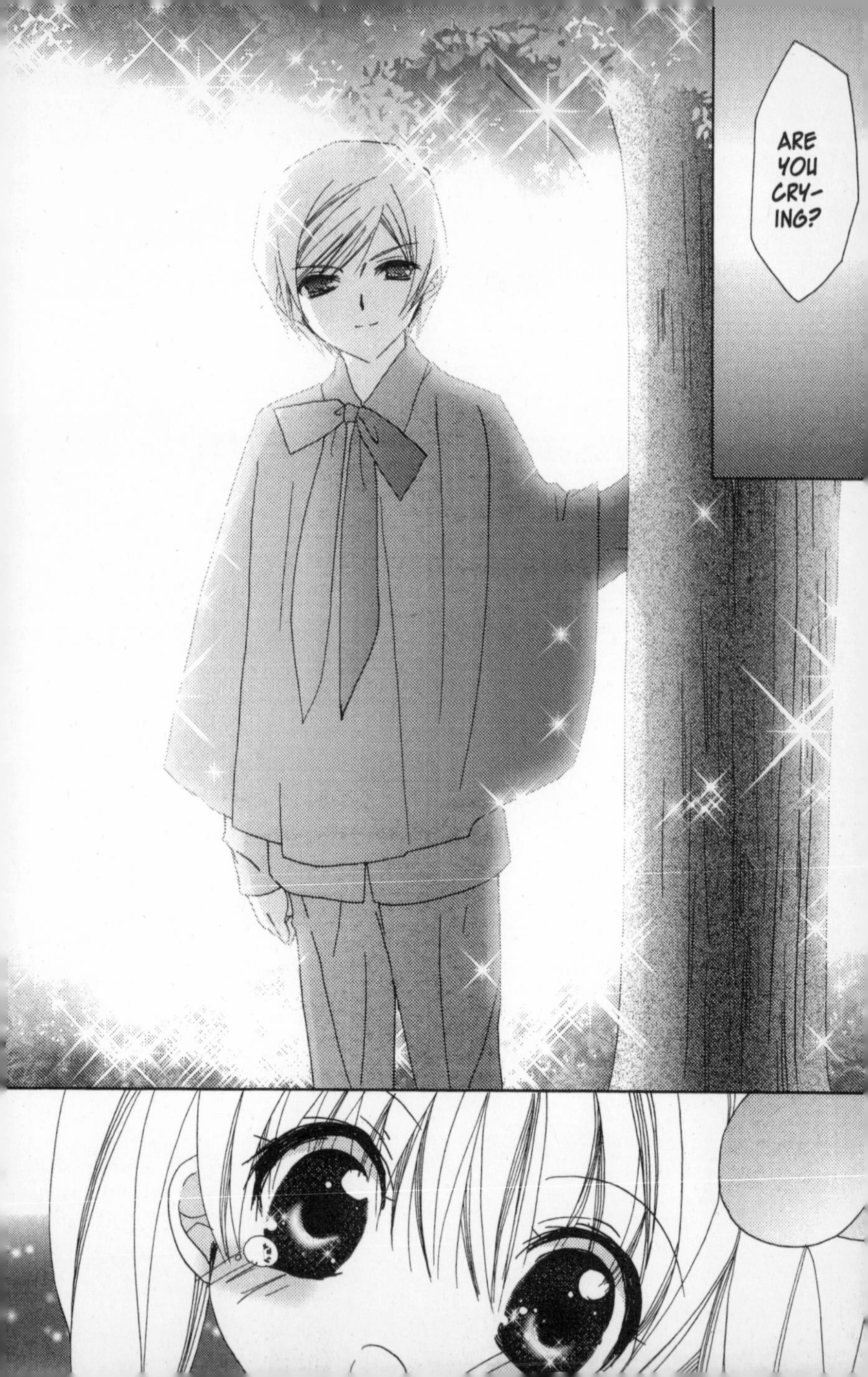
ARE YOU CRY-ING?

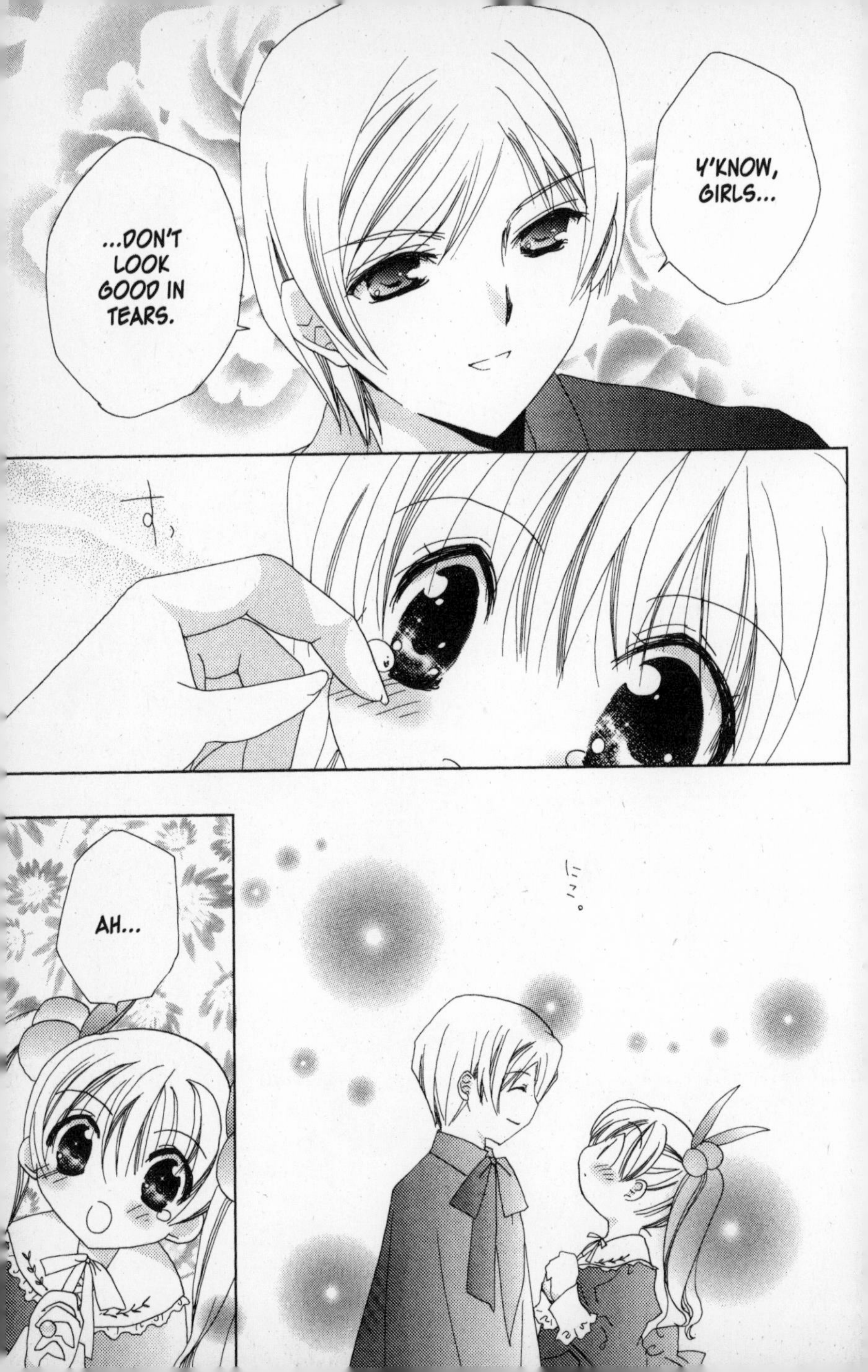
Y'KNOW, GIRLS...
...DON'T LOOK GOOD IN TEARS.
す、
にこ。
AH...

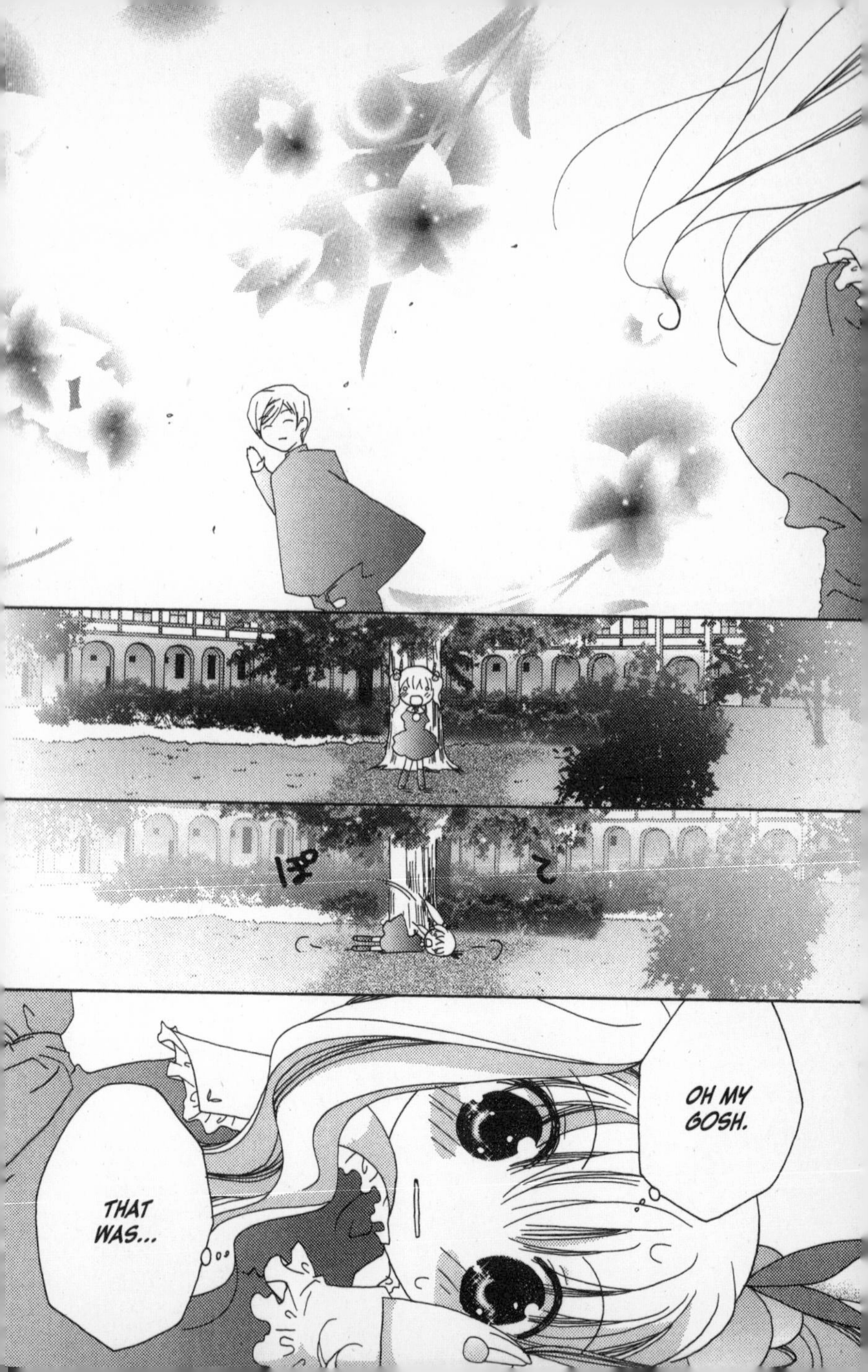
OH MY GOSH.
THAT WAS...

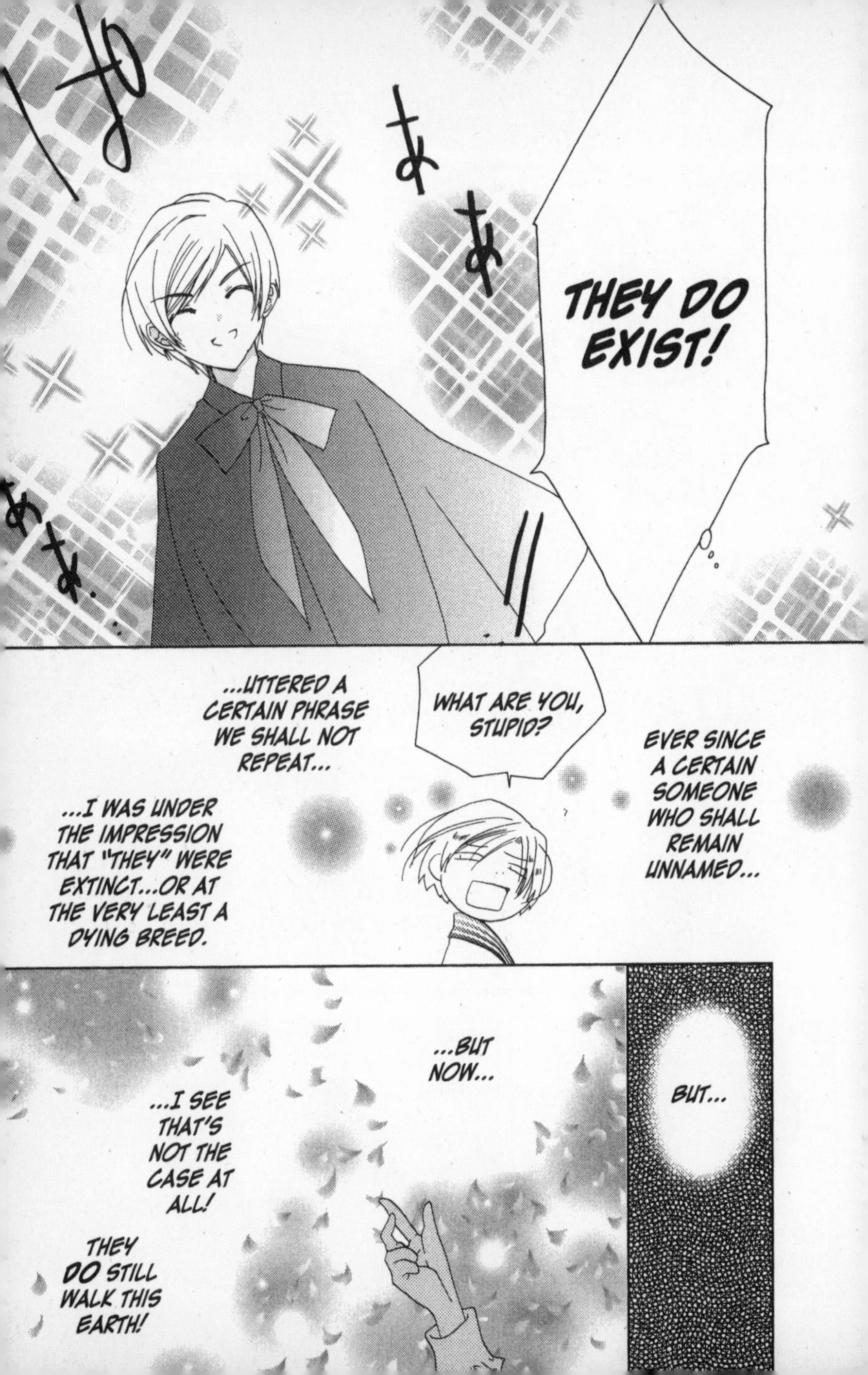
THEY DO EXIST!
EVER SINCE A CERTAIN SOMEONE WHO SHALL REMAIN UNNAMED...
WHAT ARE YOU, STUPID?
...UTTERED A CERTAIN PHRASE WE SHALL NOT REPEAT...
...I WAS UNDER THE IMPRESSION THAT "THEY" WERE EXTINCT...OR AT THE VERY LEAST A DYING BREED.
BUT...
...BUT NOW...
...I SEE THAT'S NOT THE CASE AT ALL!
THEY DO STILL WALK THIS EARTH!

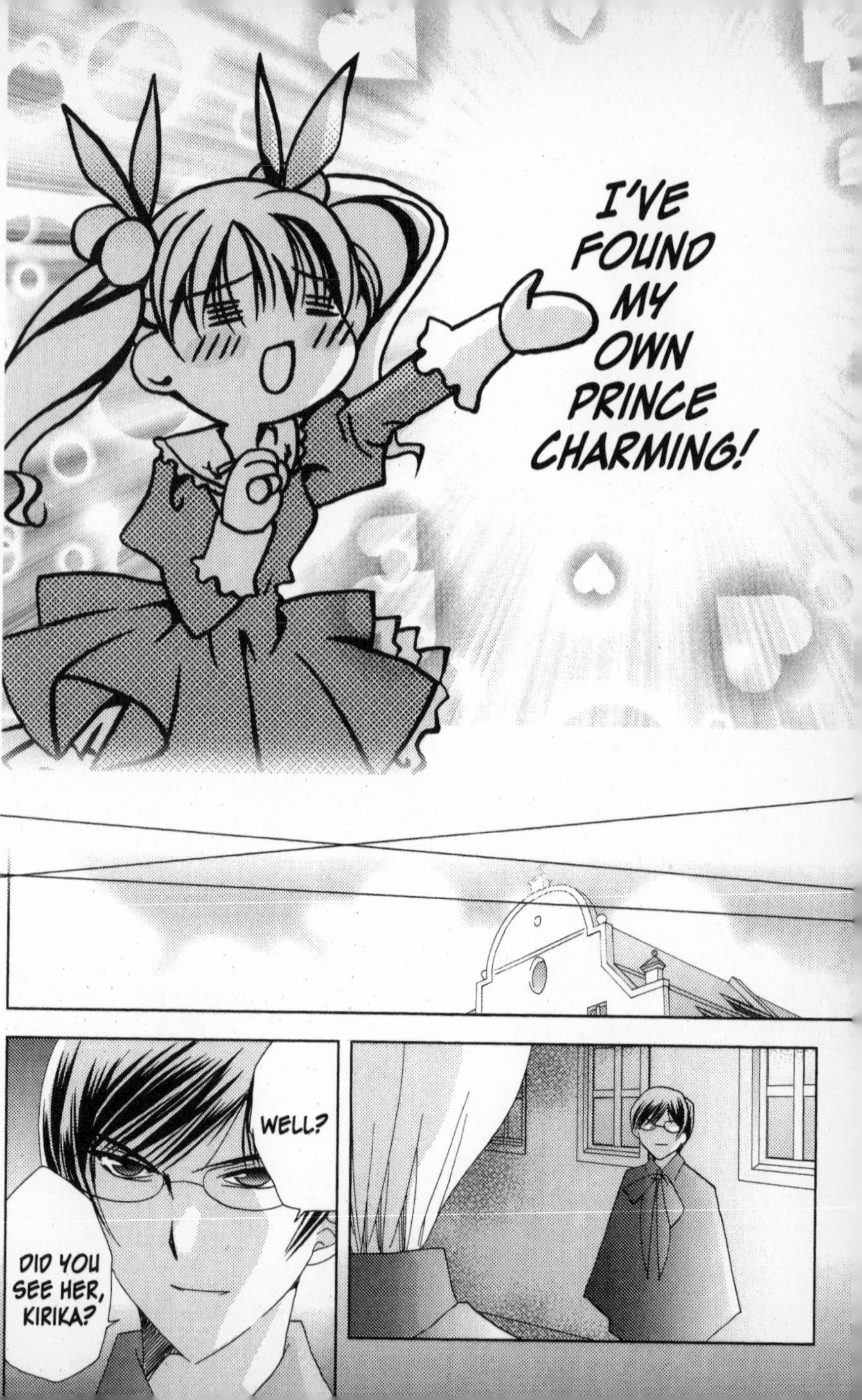
I'VE FOUND MY OWN PRINCE CHARMING!
WELL?
DID YOU SEE HER, KIRIKA?

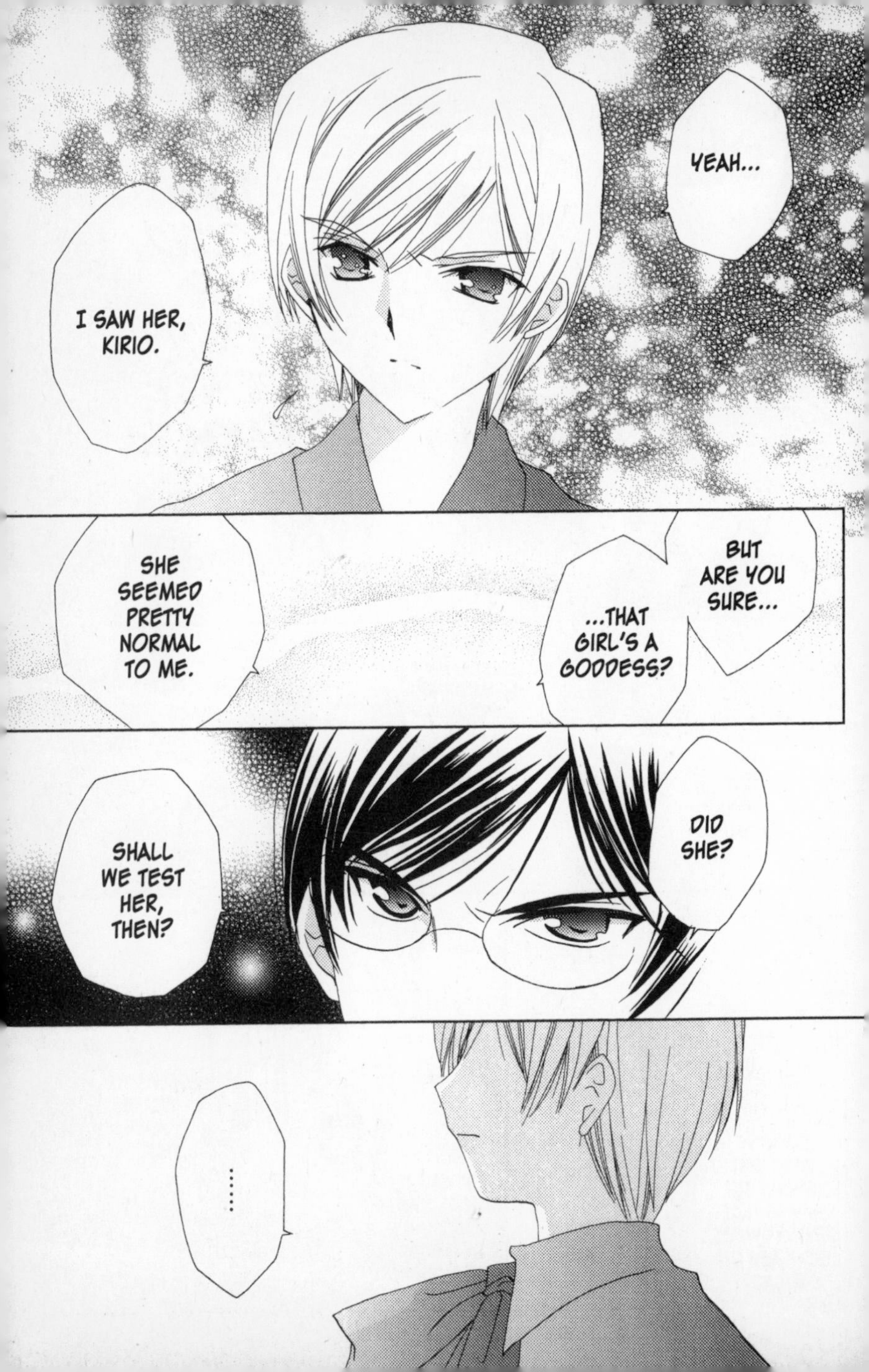
YEAH...
I SAW HER, KIRIO.
BUT ARE YOU SURE...
...THAT GIRL'S A GODDESS?
SHE SEEMED PRETTY NORMAL TO ME.
DID SHE?
SHALL WE TEST HER, THEN?
......

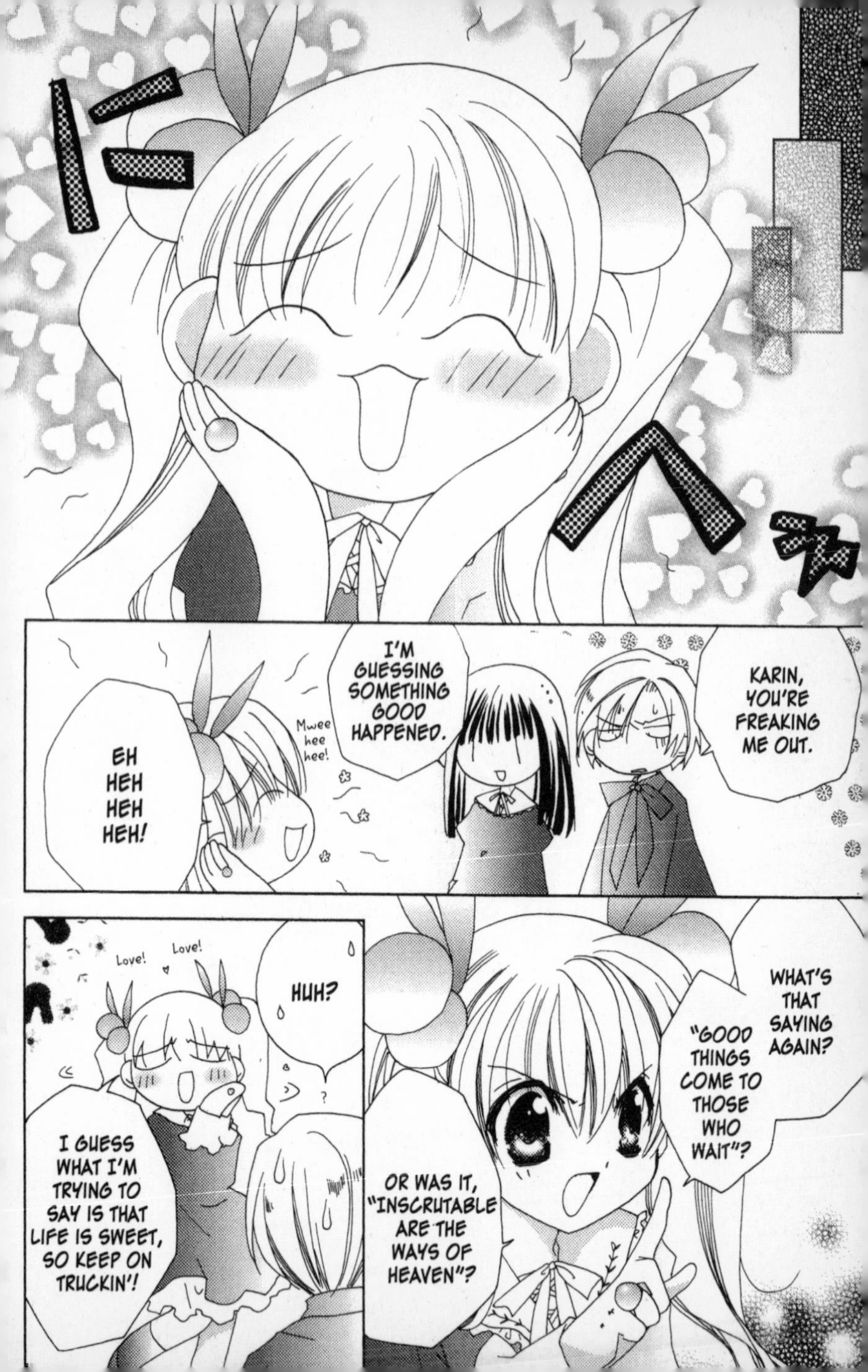
KARIN, YOU'RE FREAKING ME OUT.
I'M GUESSING SOMETHING GOOD HAPPENED.
Mwee hee hee!
EH HEH HEH HEH!
WHAT'S THAT SAYING AGAIN?
"GOOD THINGS COME TO THOSE WHO WAIT"?
OR WAS IT, "INSCRUTABLE ARE THE WAYS OF HEAVEN"?
HUH?
Love! Love!
I GUESS WHAT I'M TRYING TO SAY IS THAT LIFE IS SWEET, SO KEEP ON TRUCKIN'!

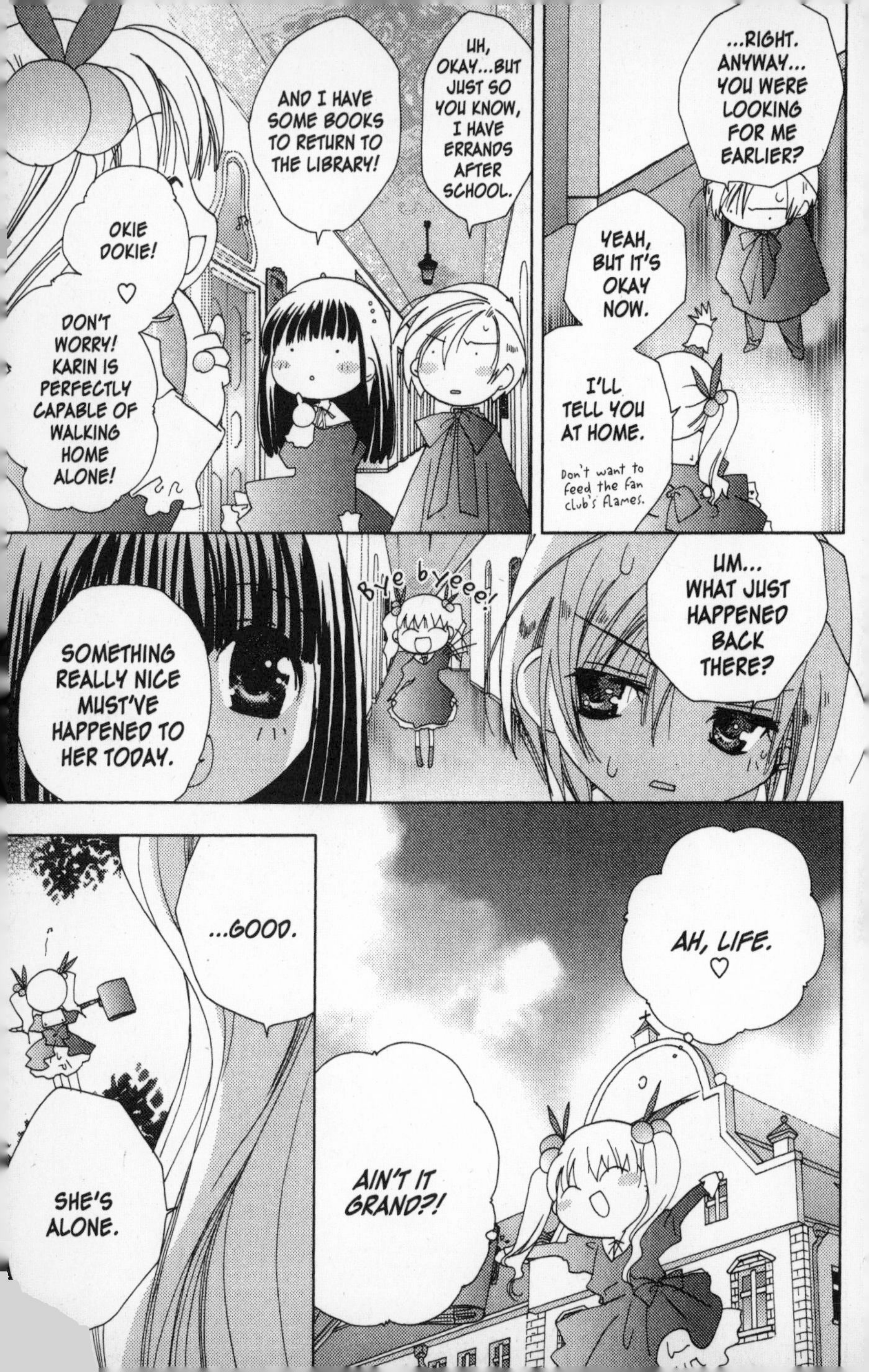
...RIGHT. ANYWAY... YOU WERE LOOKING FOR ME EARLIER?
YEAH, BUT IT'S OKAY NOW.
I'LL TELL YOU AT HOME.
Don't want to feed the fan club's flames.
UH, OKAY...BUT JUST SO YOU KNOW, I HAVE ERRANDS AFTER SCHOOL.
AND I HAVE SOME BOOKS TO RETURN TO THE LIBRARY!
OKIE DOKIE! ♡
DON'T WORRY! KARIN IS PERFECTLY CAPABLE OF WALKING HOME ALONE!
UM... WHAT JUST HAPPENED BACK THERE?
Bye byeee!
SOMETHING REALLY NICE MUST'VE HAPPENED TO HER TODAY.
AH, LIFE. ♡
AIN'T IT GRAND?!
...GOOD.
SHE'S ALONE.

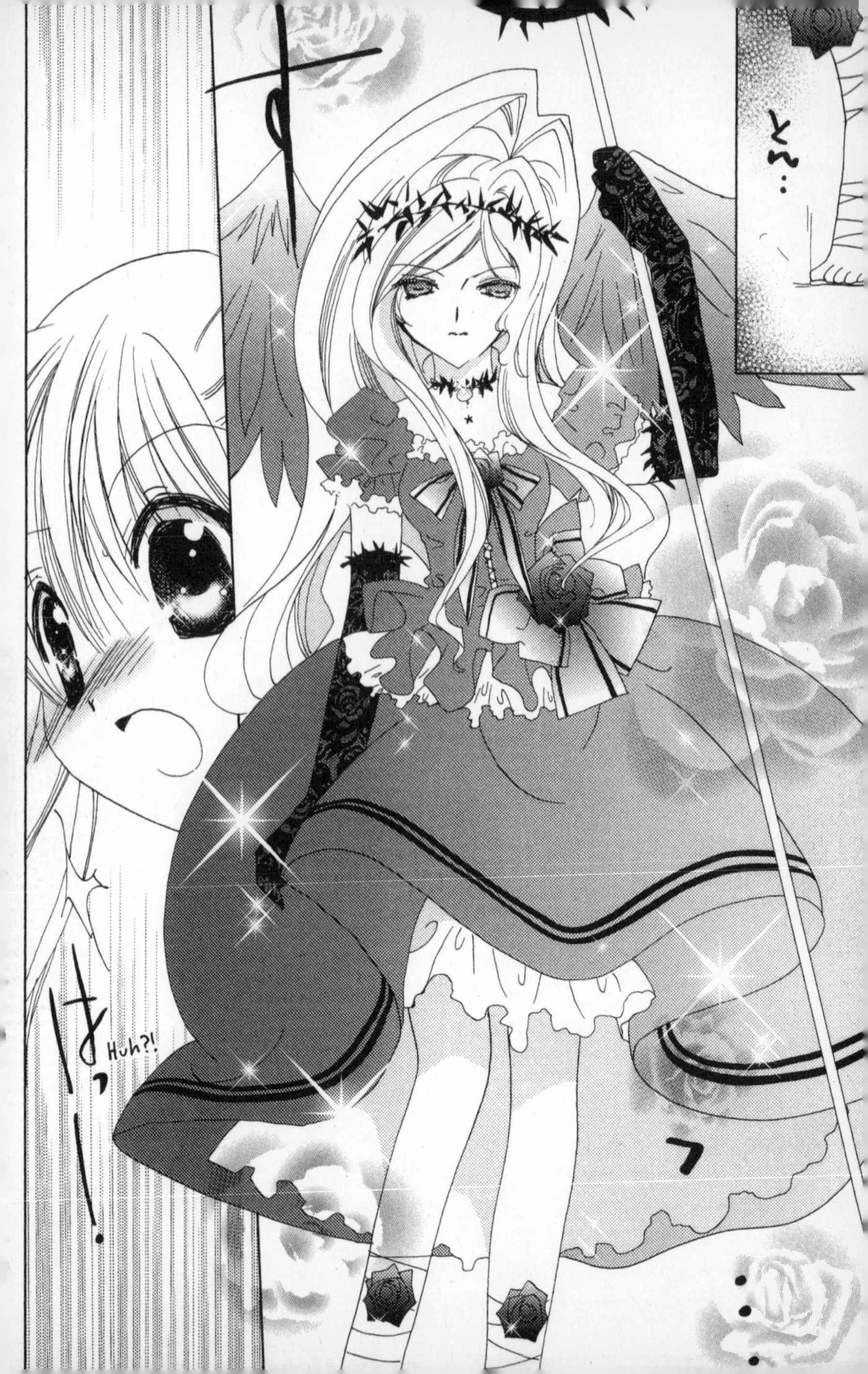
とん‥
はっーー！
Huh?!

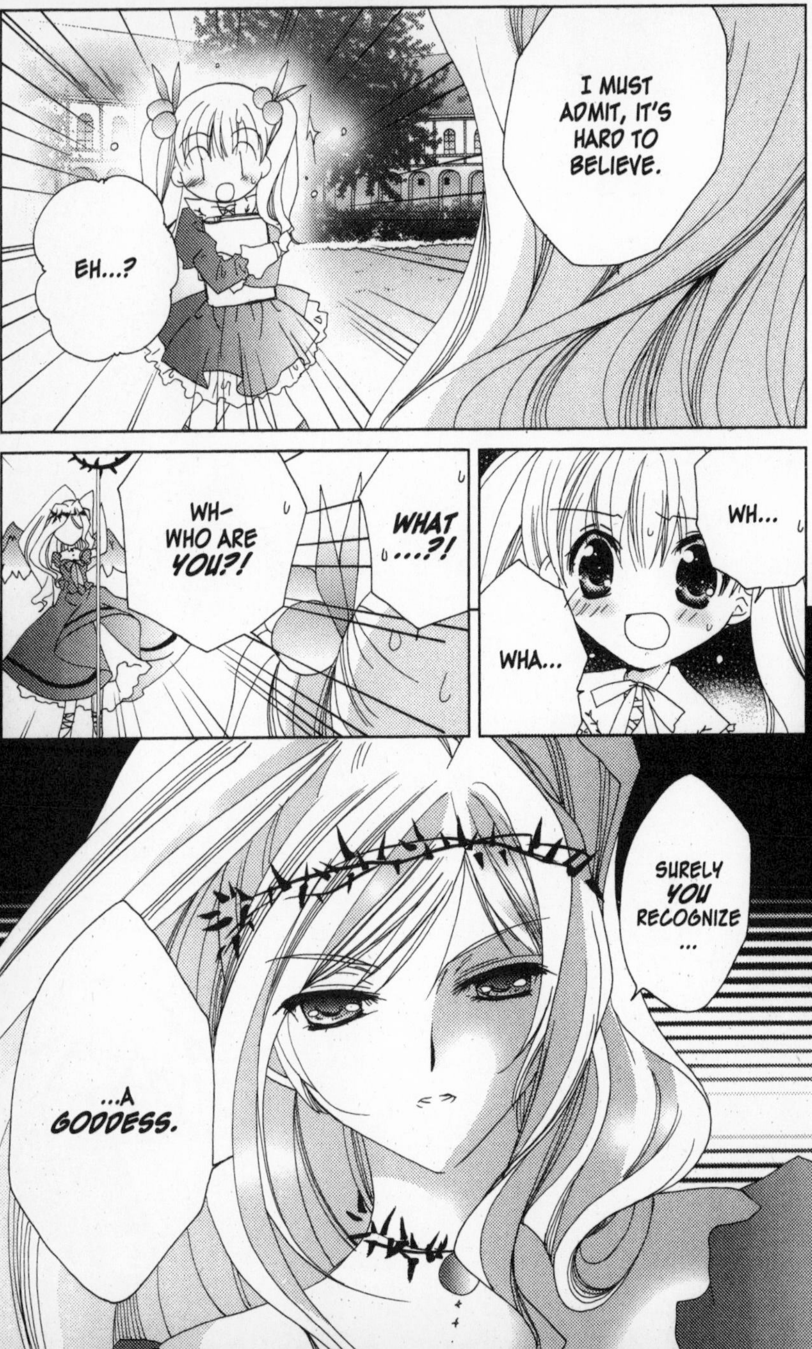
I MUST ADMIT, IT'S HARD TO BELIEVE.
EH...?
WH...
WHA...
WHAT ...?!
WH- WHO ARE YOU?!
SURELY YOU RECOGNIZE ...
...A GODDESS.

Delinquent

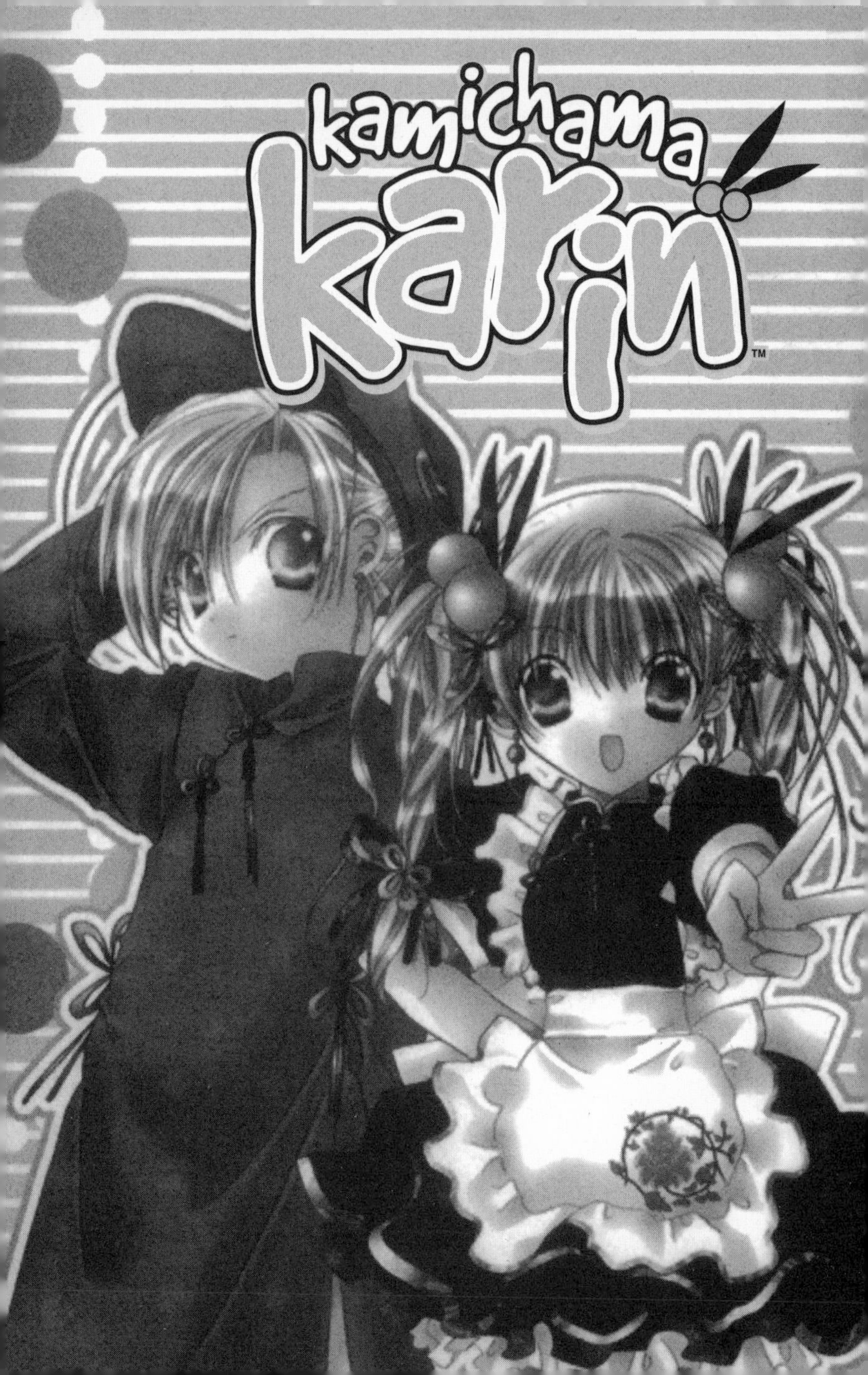
kamichama karin™

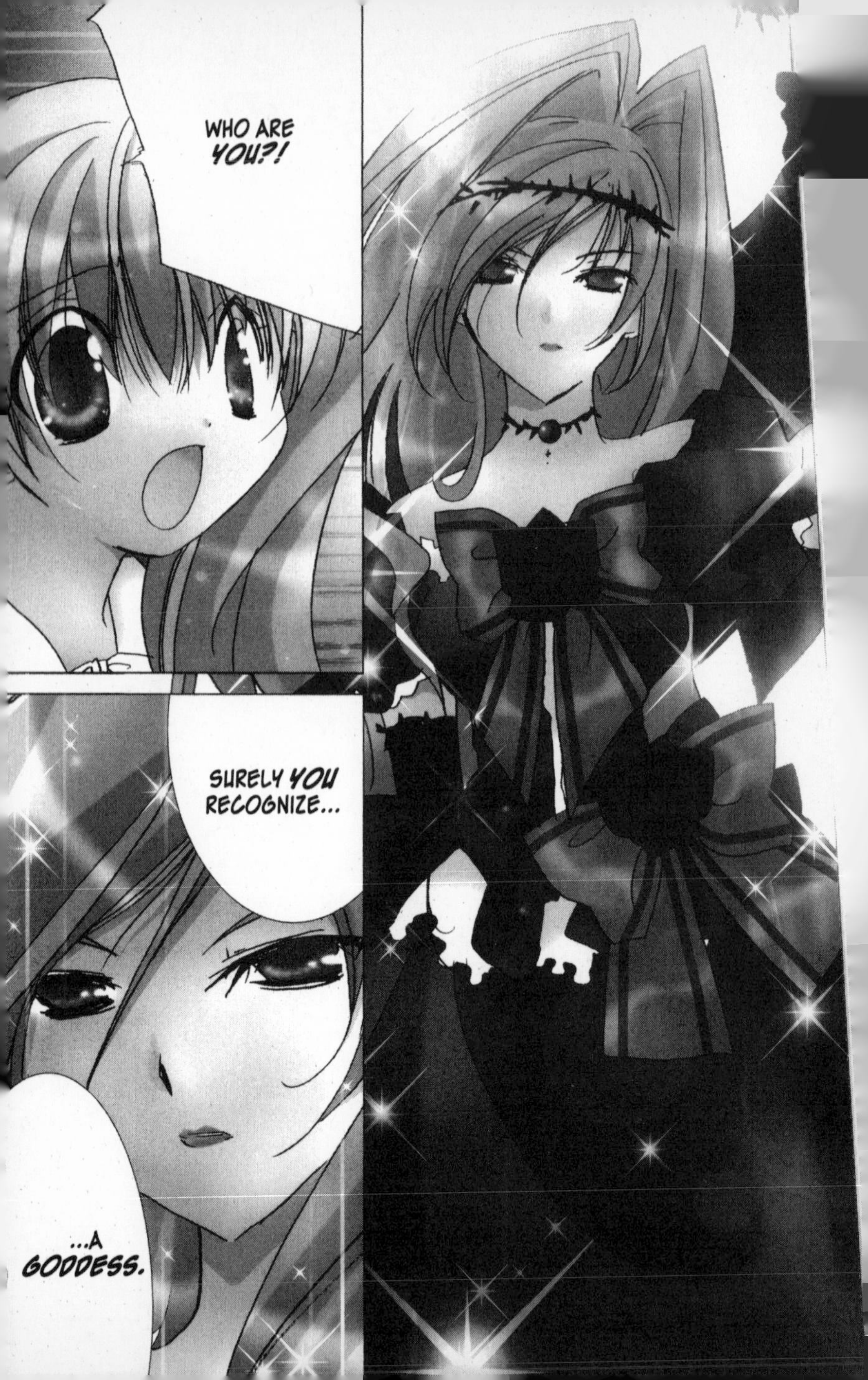
WHO ARE YOU?!
SURELY YOU RECOGNIZE...
...A GODDESS.

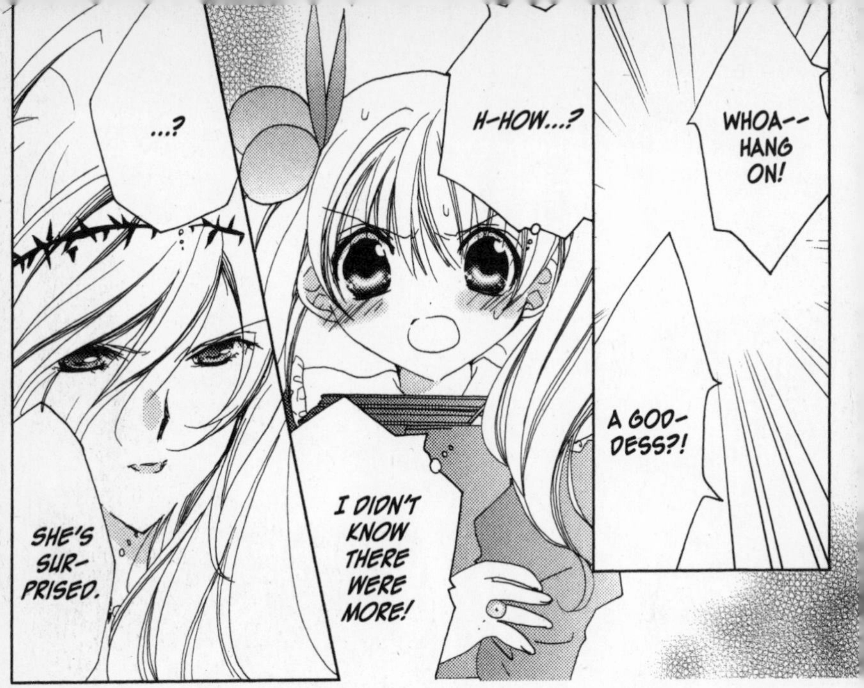
WHOA--HANG ON!
A GOD-DESS?!
H-HOW...?
I DIDN'T KNOW THERE WERE MORE!
...?
SHE'S SUR-PRISED.

I wonder what used to be here. Oh, well-- who cares! Eh heh heh!

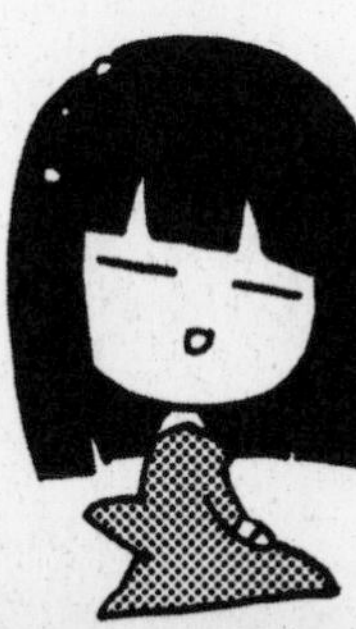

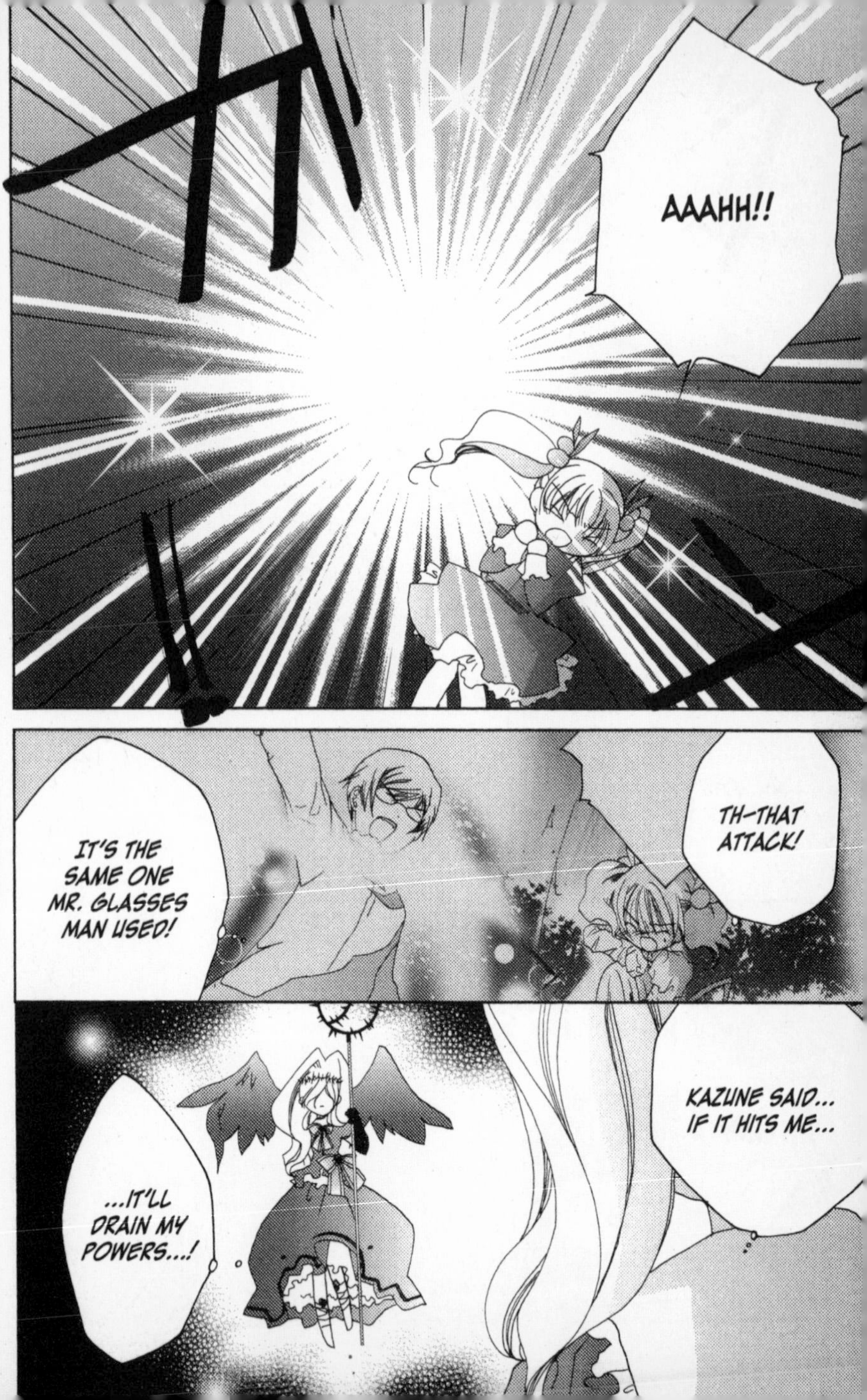
AAAHH!!
TH-THAT ATTACK!
IT'S THE SAME ONE MR. GLASSES MAN USED!
KAZUNE SAID... IF IT HITS ME...
...IT'LL DRAIN MY POWERS...!

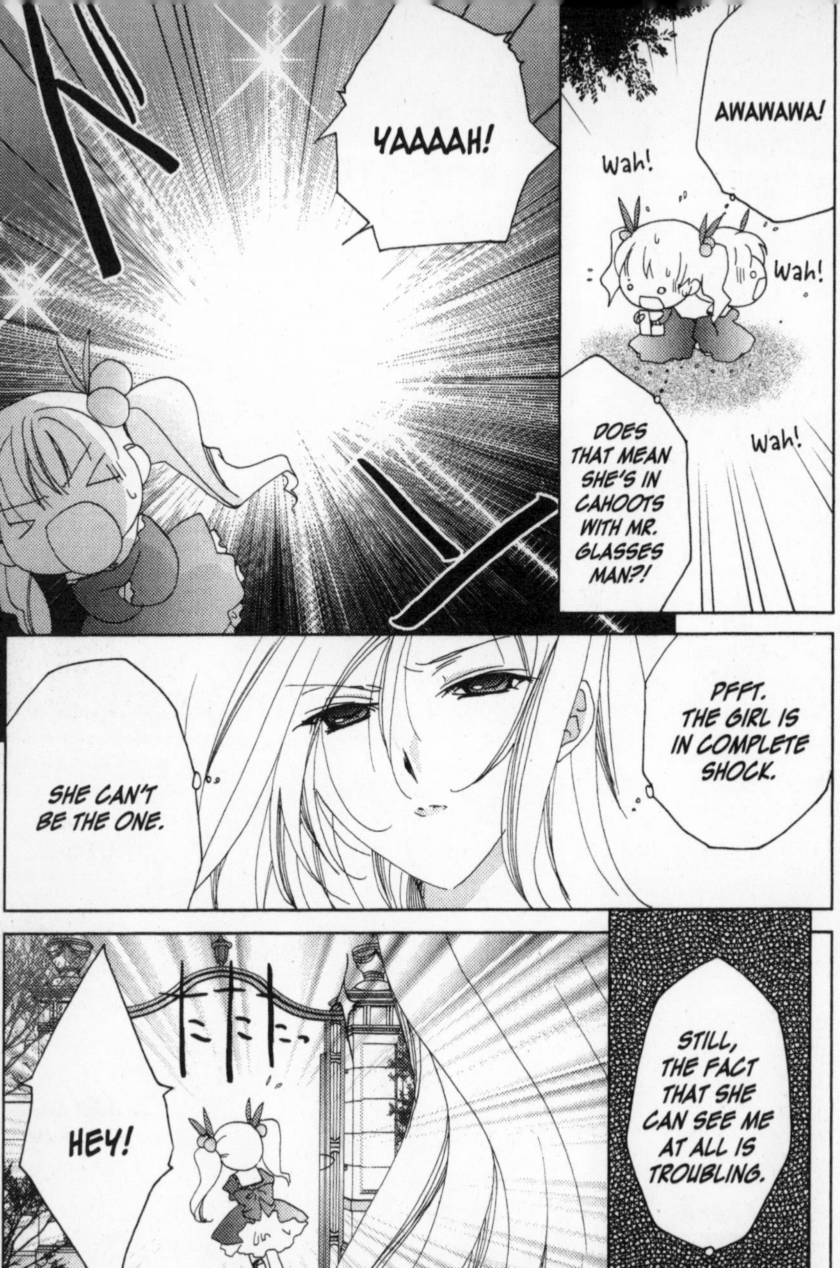
AWAWAWA!
Wah!
Wah!
DOES THAT MEAN SHE'S IN CAHOOTS WITH MR. GLASSES MAN?!
Wah!
YAAAAH!
PFFT. THE GIRL IS IN COMPLETE SHOCK.
SHE CAN'T BE THE ONE.
STILL, THE FACT THAT SHE CAN SEE ME AT ALL IS TROUBLING.
HEY!

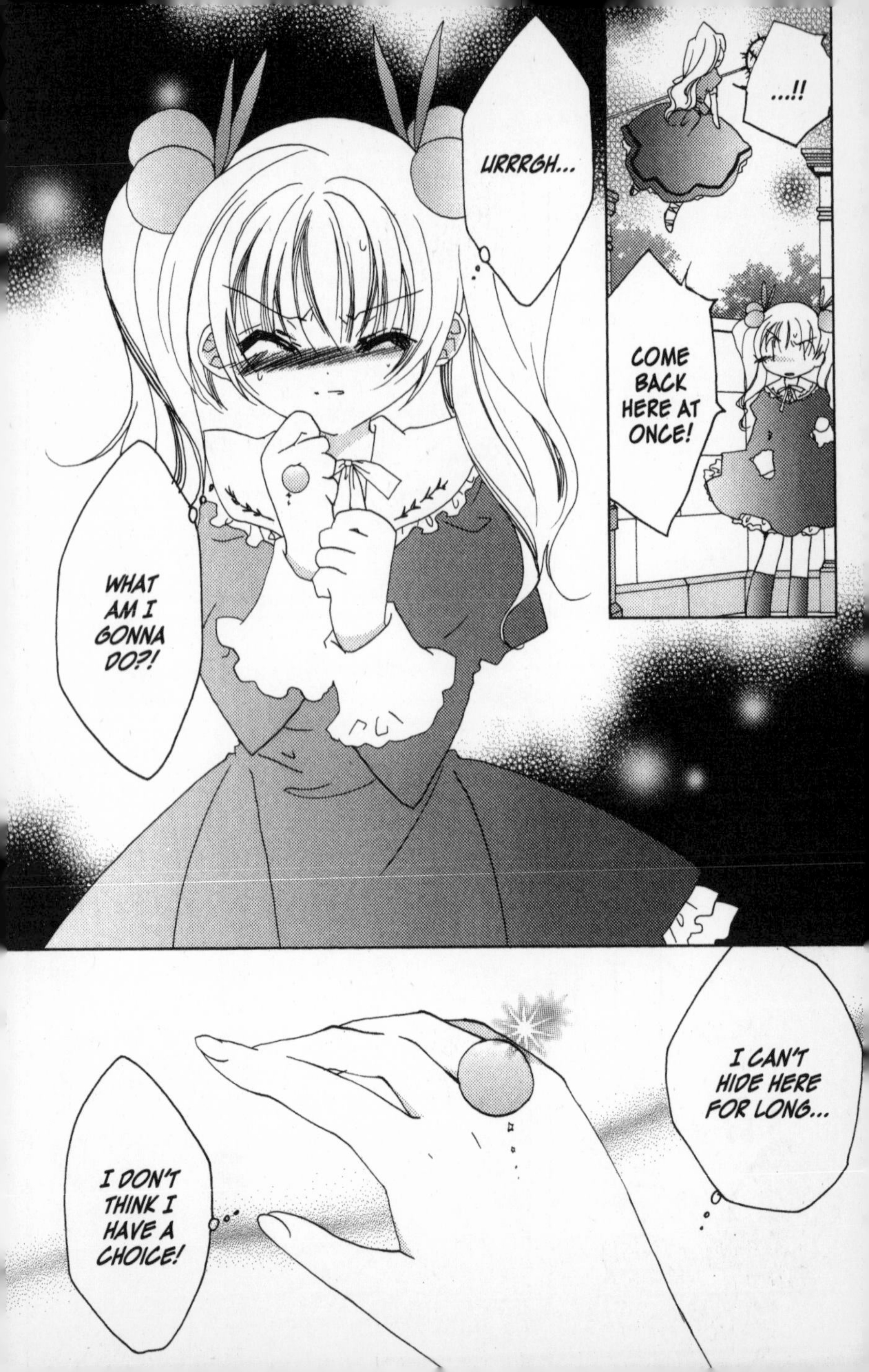
...!!
COME BACK HERE AT ONCE!
URRRGH...
WHAT AM I GONNA DO?!
I CAN'T HIDE HERE FOR LONG...
I DON'T THINK I HAVE A CHOICE!

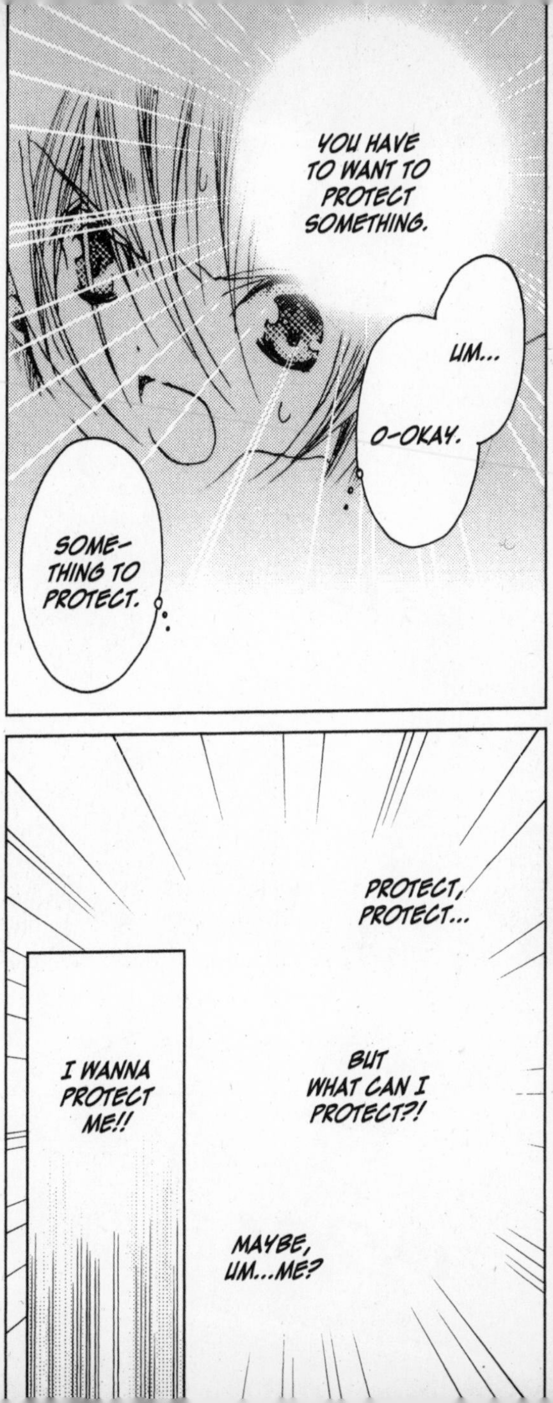
YOU HAVE TO WANT TO PROTECT SOMETHING.
UM...
O-OKAY.
SOME-THING TO PROTECT.
PROTECT, PROTECT...
BUT WHAT CAN I PROTECT?!
MAYBE, UM...ME?
I WANNA PROTECT ME!!
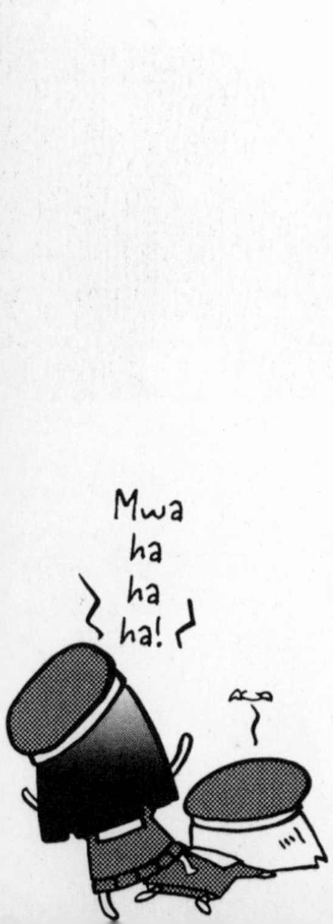
Mwa ha ha ha!

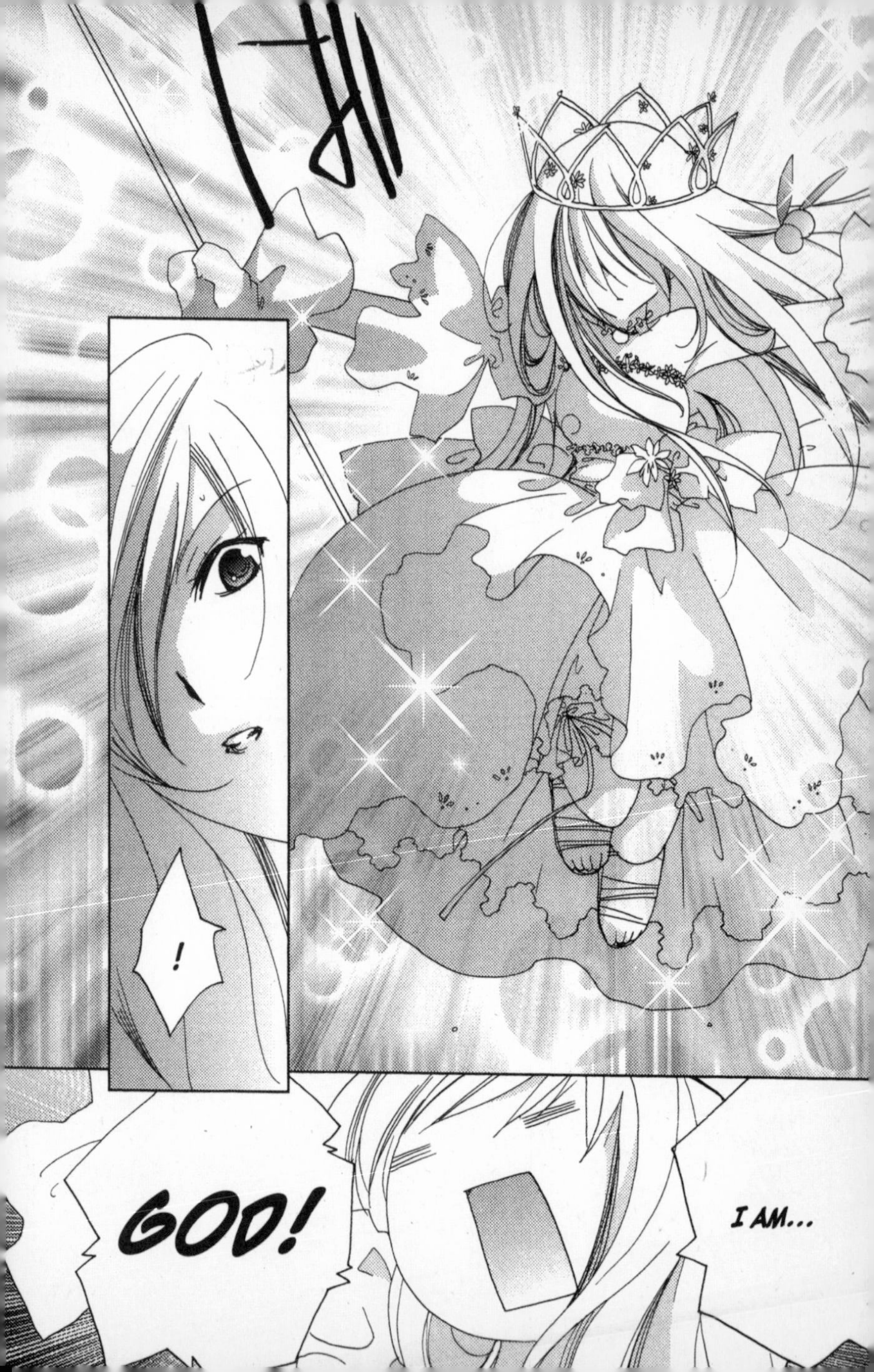
!
I AM...
GOD!

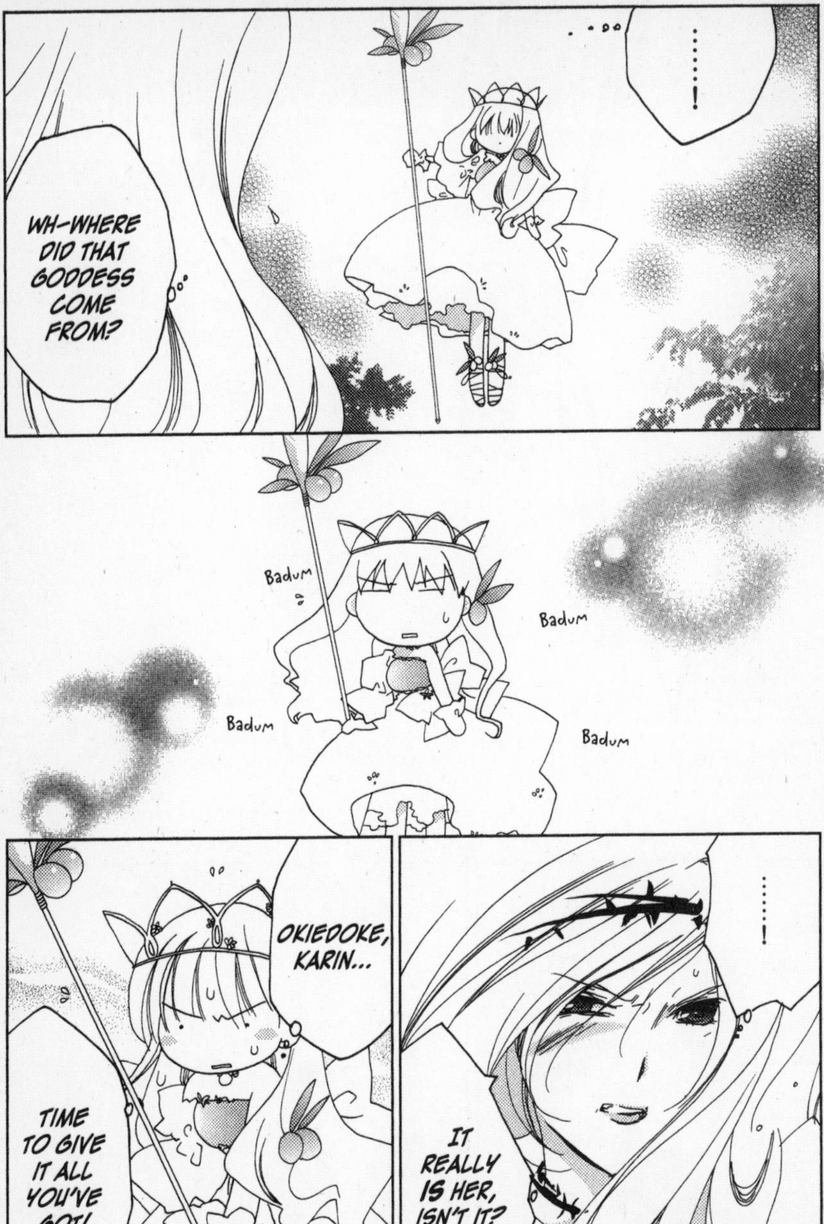
......!
WH-WHERE DID THAT GODDESS COME FROM?
Badum
Badum
Badum
Badum
......!
IT REALLY IS HER, ISN'T IT?
OKIEDOKE, KARIN...
TIME TO GIVE IT ALL YOU'VE GOT!

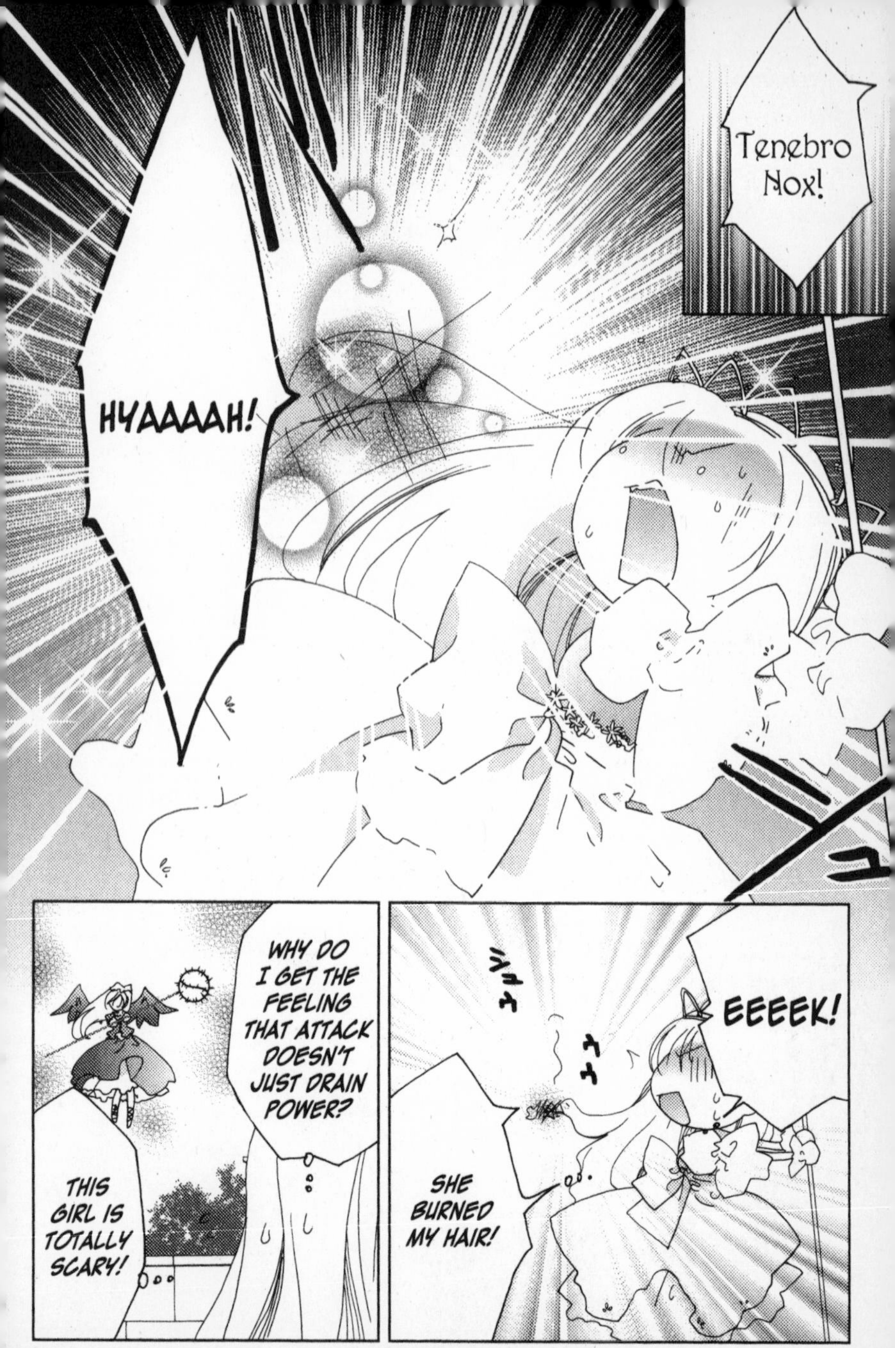
Tenebro Nox!
HYAAAAH!
EEEEK!
SHE BURNED MY HAIR!
WHY DO I GET THE FEELING THAT ATTACK DOESN'T JUST DRAIN POWER?
THIS GIRL IS TOTALLY SCARY!

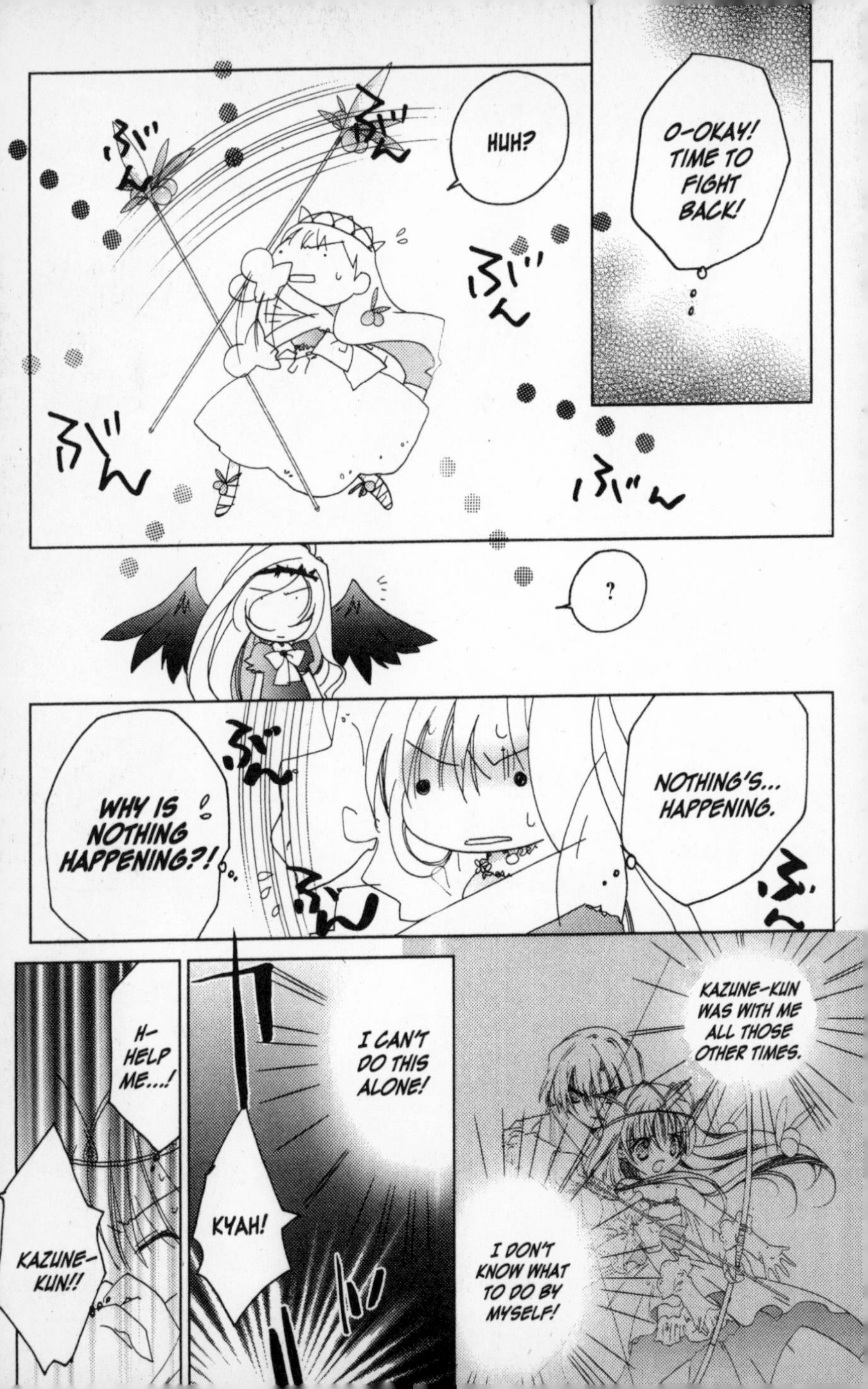
O-OKAY! TIME TO FIGHT BACK!
HUH?
ぶん
ぶん
ぶん
ぶん
ぶん
?
NOTHING'S... HAPPENING.
ぶん
ぶん
WHY IS NOTHING HAPPENING?!
ぶん
KAZUNE-KUN WAS WITH ME ALL THOSE OTHER TIMES.
I DON'T KNOW WHAT TO DO BY MYSELF!
I CAN'T DO THIS ALONE!
KYAH!
H-HELP ME...!
KAZUNE-KUN!!

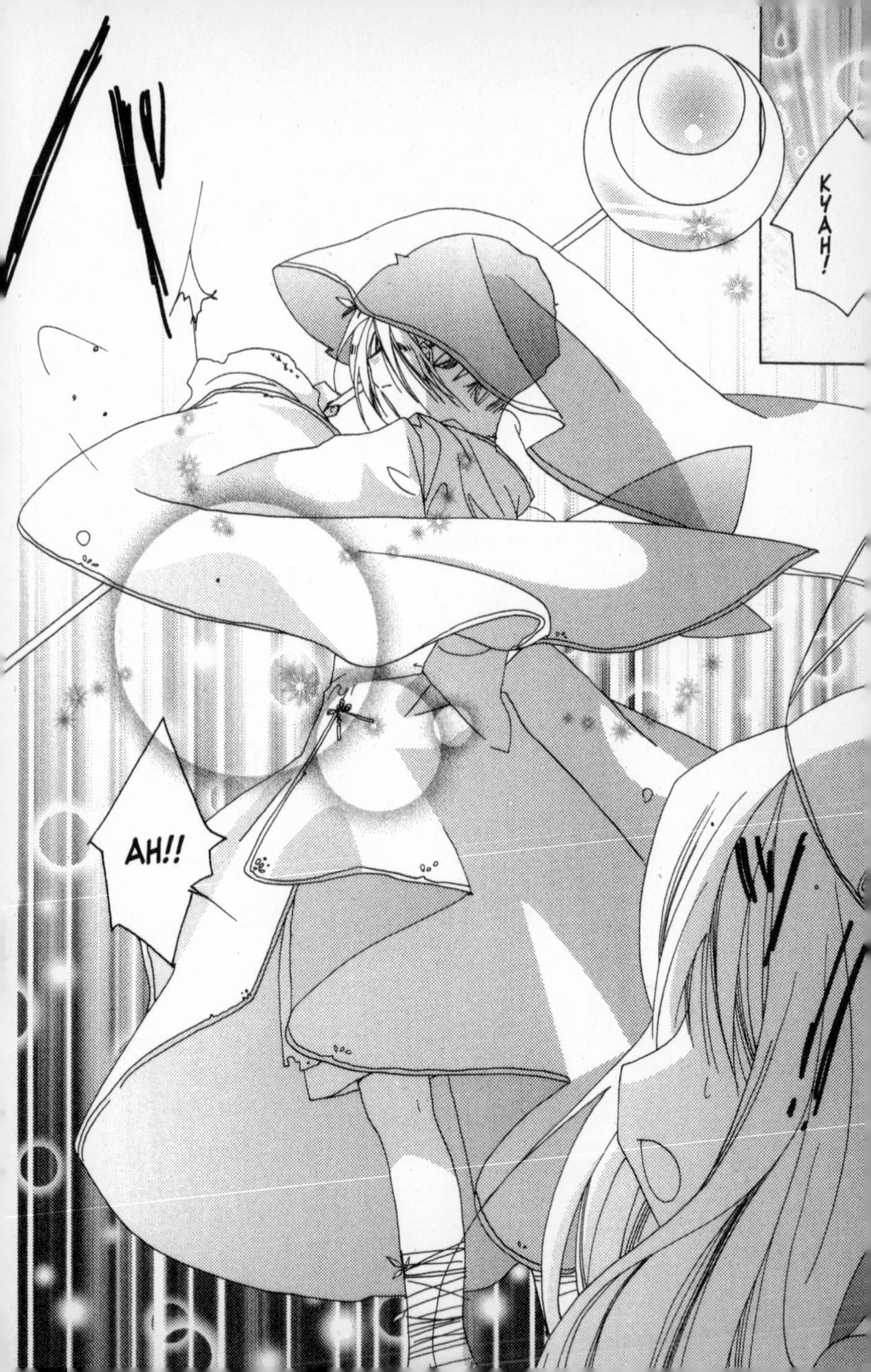
KYAH!
AH!!

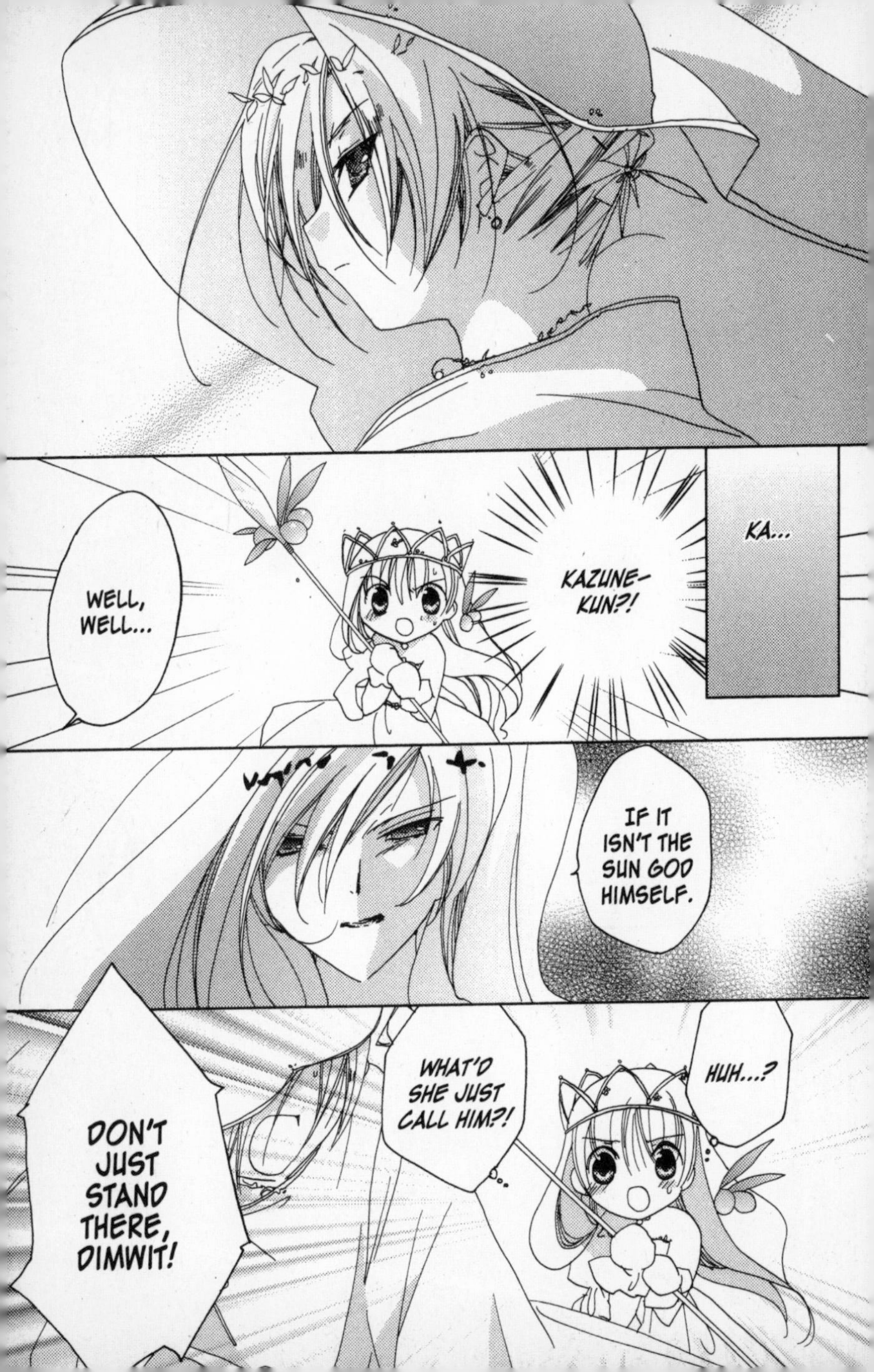
KA...
KAZUNE-KUN?!
WELL, WELL...
IF IT ISN'T THE SUN GOD HIMSELF.
HUH...?
WHAT'D SHE JUST CALL HIM?!
DON'T JUST STAND THERE, DIMWIT!

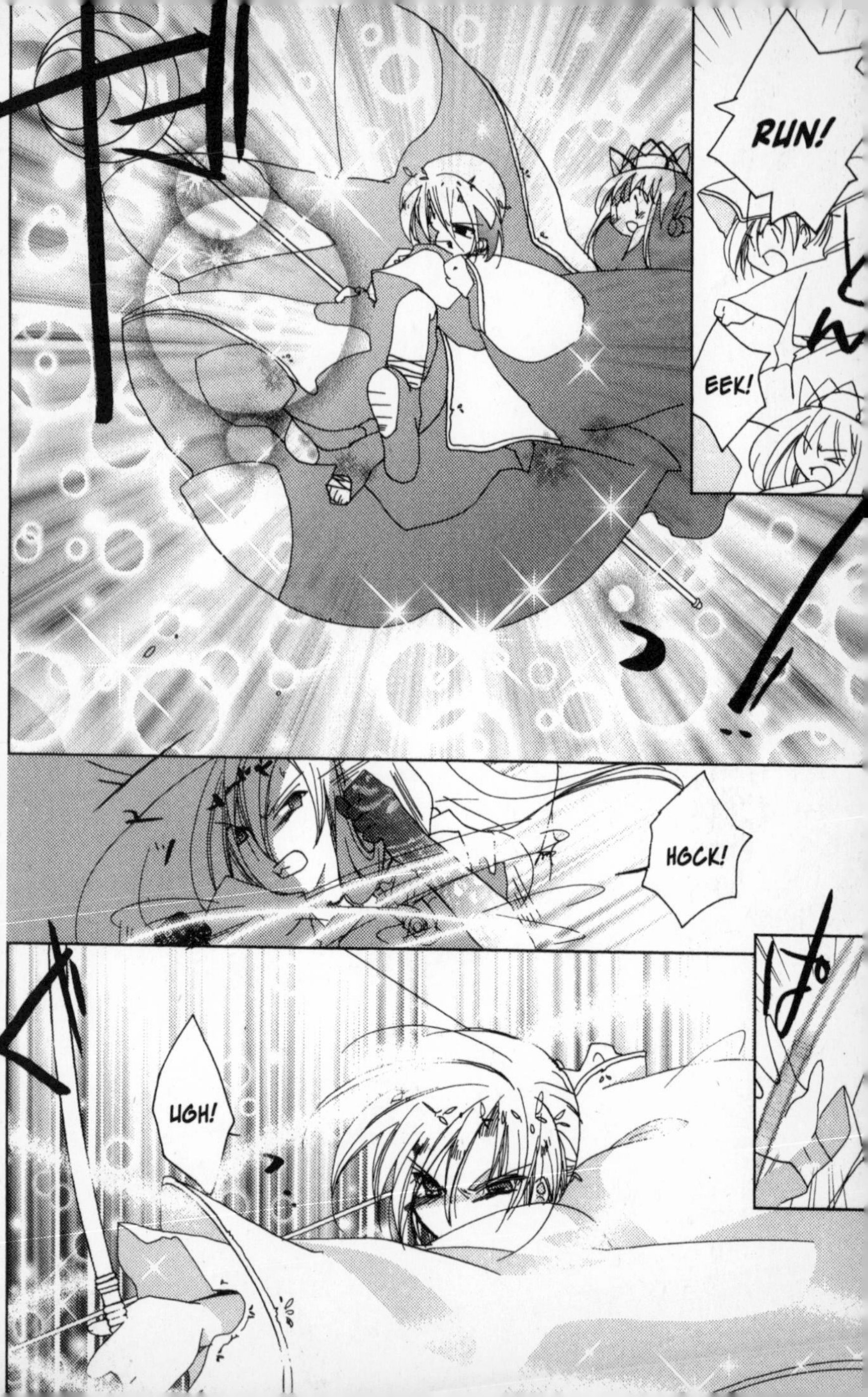
RUN!
EEK!
HGCK!
UGH!

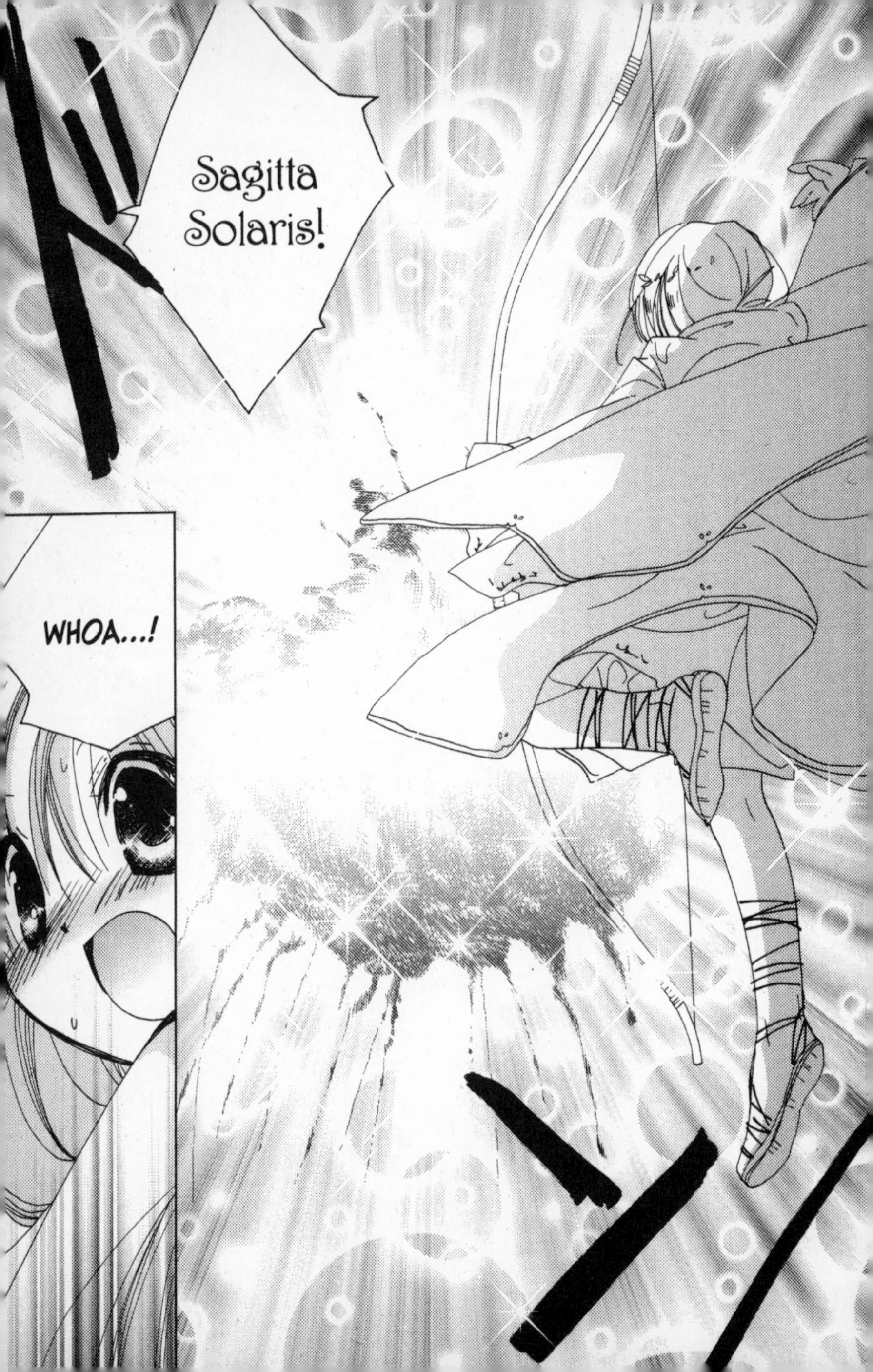
Sagitta Solaris!
WHOA...!

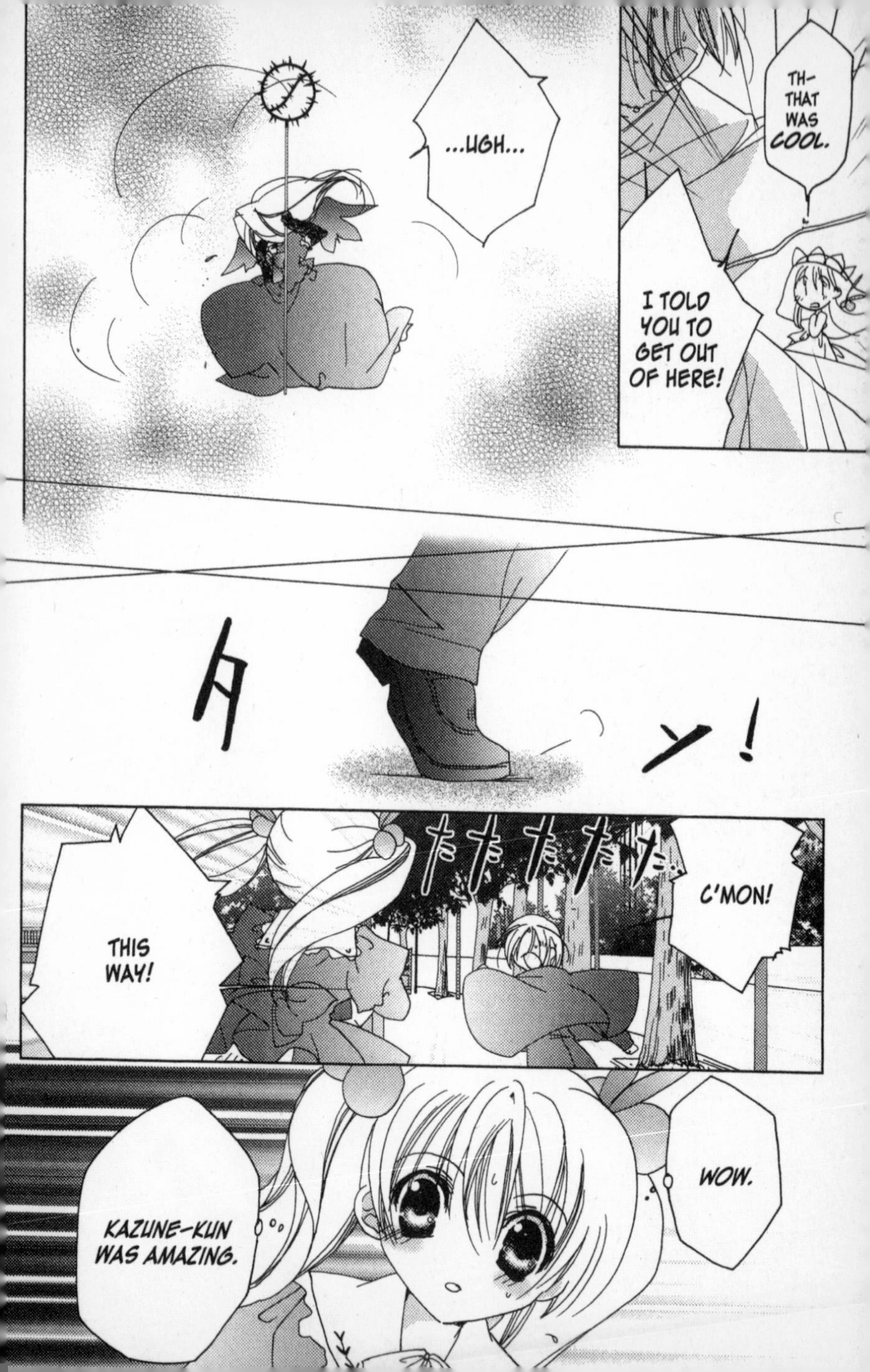
TH-THAT WAS COOL.
I TOLD YOU TO GET OUT OF HERE!
...UGH...
タン!
C'MON!
たたたたた
THIS WAY!
WOW.
KAZUNE-KUN WAS AMAZING.

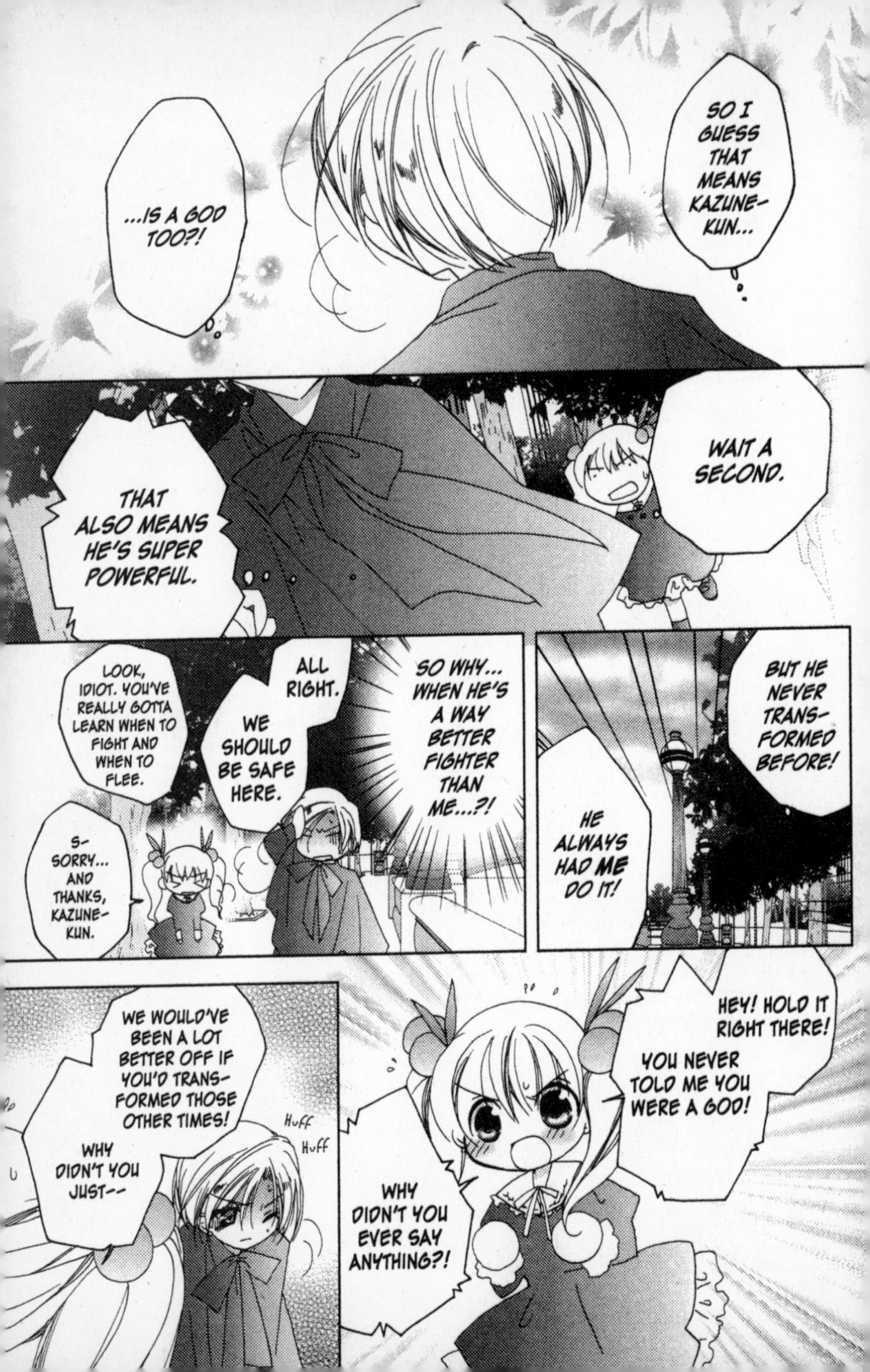
SO I GUESS THAT MEANS KAZUNE-KUN...
...IS A GOD TOO?!
WAIT A SECOND.
THAT ALSO MEANS HE'S SUPER POWERFUL.
BUT HE NEVER TRANS-FORMED BEFORE!
HE ALWAYS HAD ME DO IT!
SO WHY... WHEN HE'S A WAY BETTER FIGHTER THAN ME...?!
ALL RIGHT.
WE SHOULD BE SAFE HERE.
LOOK, IDIOT. YOU'VE REALLY GOTTA LEARN WHEN TO FIGHT AND WHEN TO FLEE.
S-SORRY... AND THANKS, KAZUNE-KUN.
HEY! HOLD IT RIGHT THERE!
YOU NEVER TOLD ME YOU WERE A GOD!
WHY DIDN'T YOU EVER SAY ANYTHING?!
WE WOULD'VE BEEN A LOT BETTER OFF IF YOU'D TRANS-FORMED THOSE OTHER TIMES!
Huff
Huff
WHY DIDN'T YOU JUST--

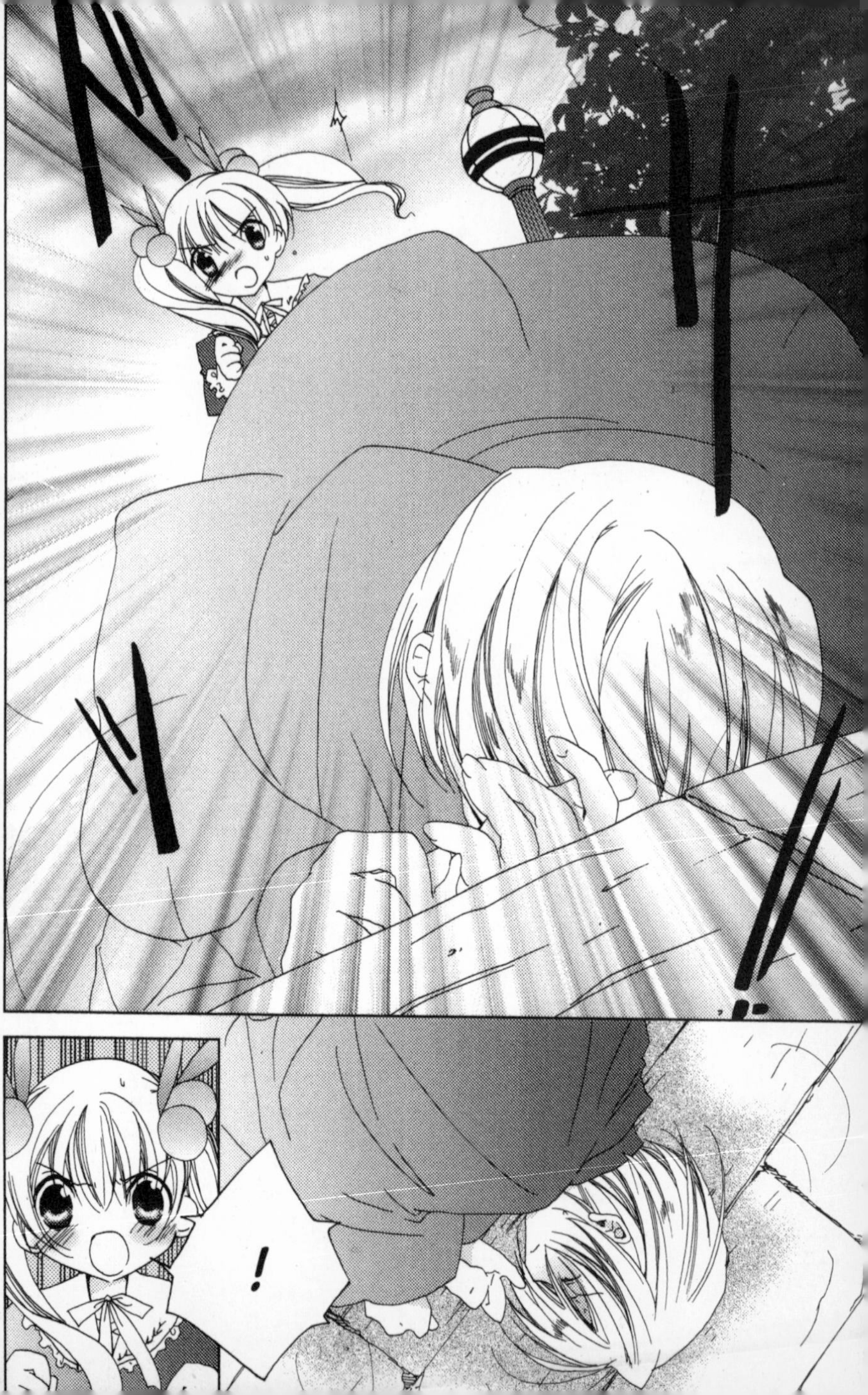
!

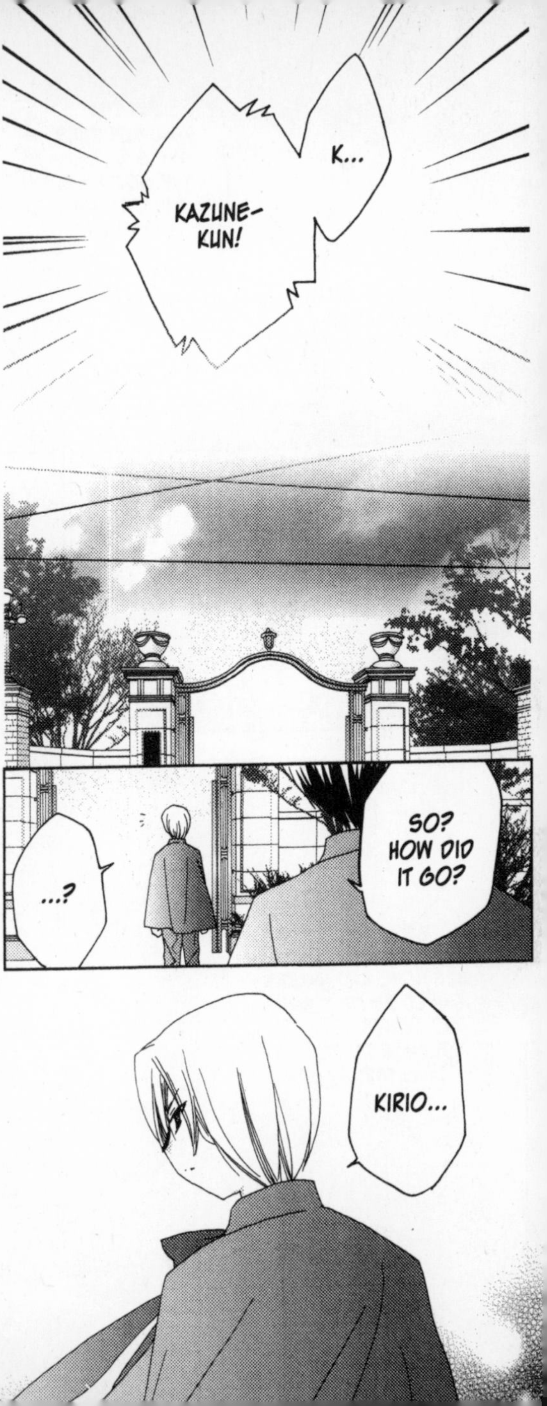
K...
KAZUNE-KUN!
SO? HOW DID IT GO?
...?
KIRIO...

Hi and how are you!!
It's me, Koge-Donbo.

So if you're reading this, you obviously know that *Kamichama Karin* is finally in motion. This is my first (?) shoujo (girls') manga, so I was really flustered and frustrated about it. I mean, my previous project ran in a shounen (boys') manga magazine, so now that I look at it, the pictures I drew for Karin (which actually was originally supposed to be done as a two part one-shot deal) were really boyish. I debated a lot over whether to redo all the artwork, but due to time constraints and the enjoyment of drawing it as it was, I just gave up. (In many ways.)

At any rate, pretty much this whole project began as a one-shot gag when I had Karin, the heroine, say something stupid like, "I AM GOD." Ha ha ha. So if you think that's a stupid catchphrase, well, you're absolutely right.

But later I realized that concept alone wasn't enough to drive the series, so I've been thinking of a lot of other little stories to weave in as time progresses. So please--stick around for the long run!

Note: Well, that's it for now. I'll try my best with Volume 2... ♪ see you then!

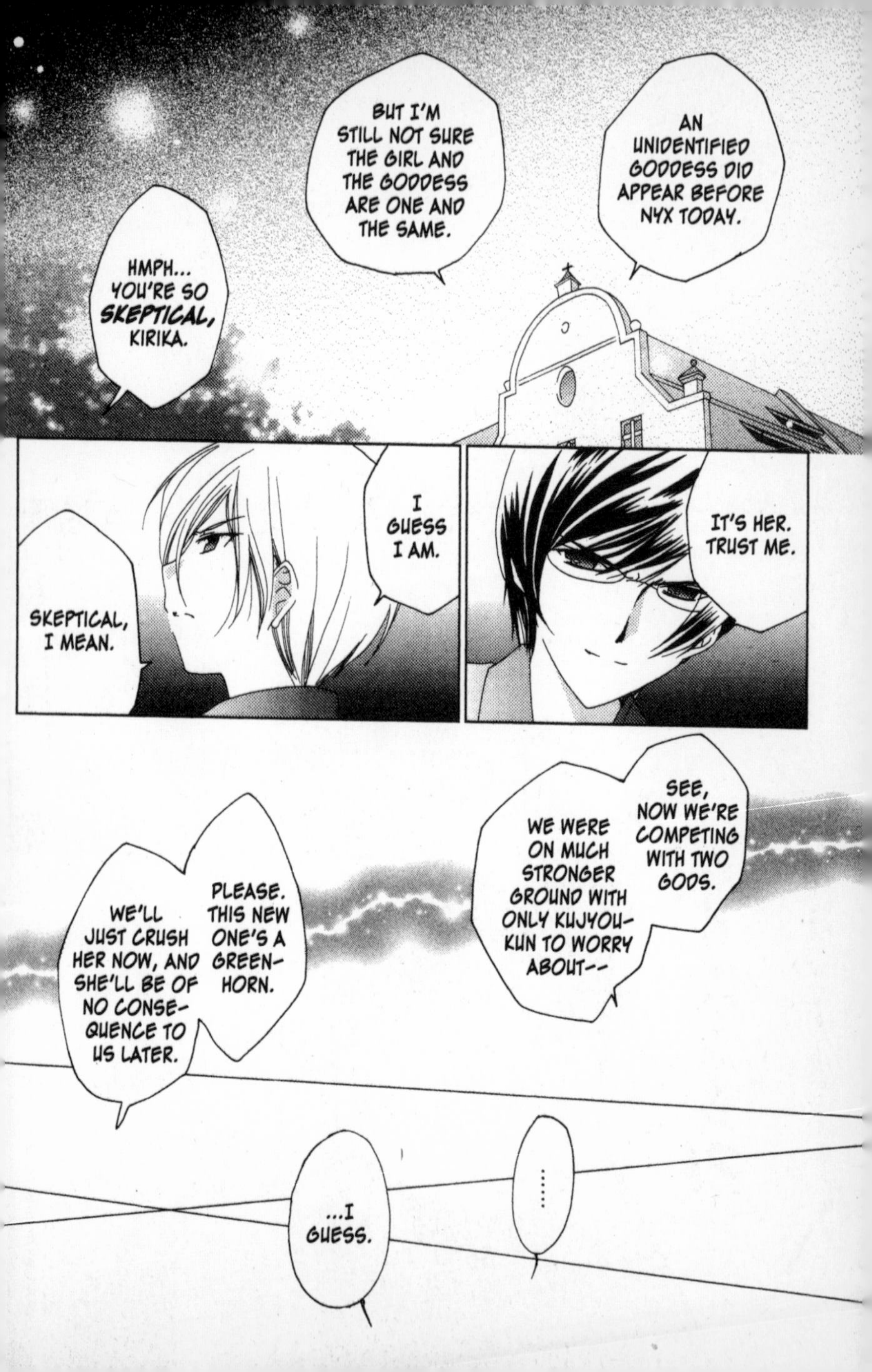
AN UNIDENTIFIED GODDESS DID APPEAR BEFORE NYX TODAY.
BUT I'M STILL NOT SURE THE GIRL AND THE GODDESS ARE ONE AND THE SAME.
HMPH... YOU'RE SO ***SKEPTICAL,*** KIRIKA.
IT'S HER. TRUST ME.
I GUESS I AM.
SKEPTICAL, I MEAN.
SEE, NOW WE'RE COMPETING WITH TWO GODS.
WE WERE ON MUCH STRONGER GROUND WITH ONLY KUJYOU-KUN TO WORRY ABOUT--
PLEASE. THIS NEW ONE'S A GREEN-HORN.
WE'LL JUST CRUSH HER NOW, AND SHE'LL BE OF NO CONSE-QUENCE TO US LATER.
......
...I GUESS.

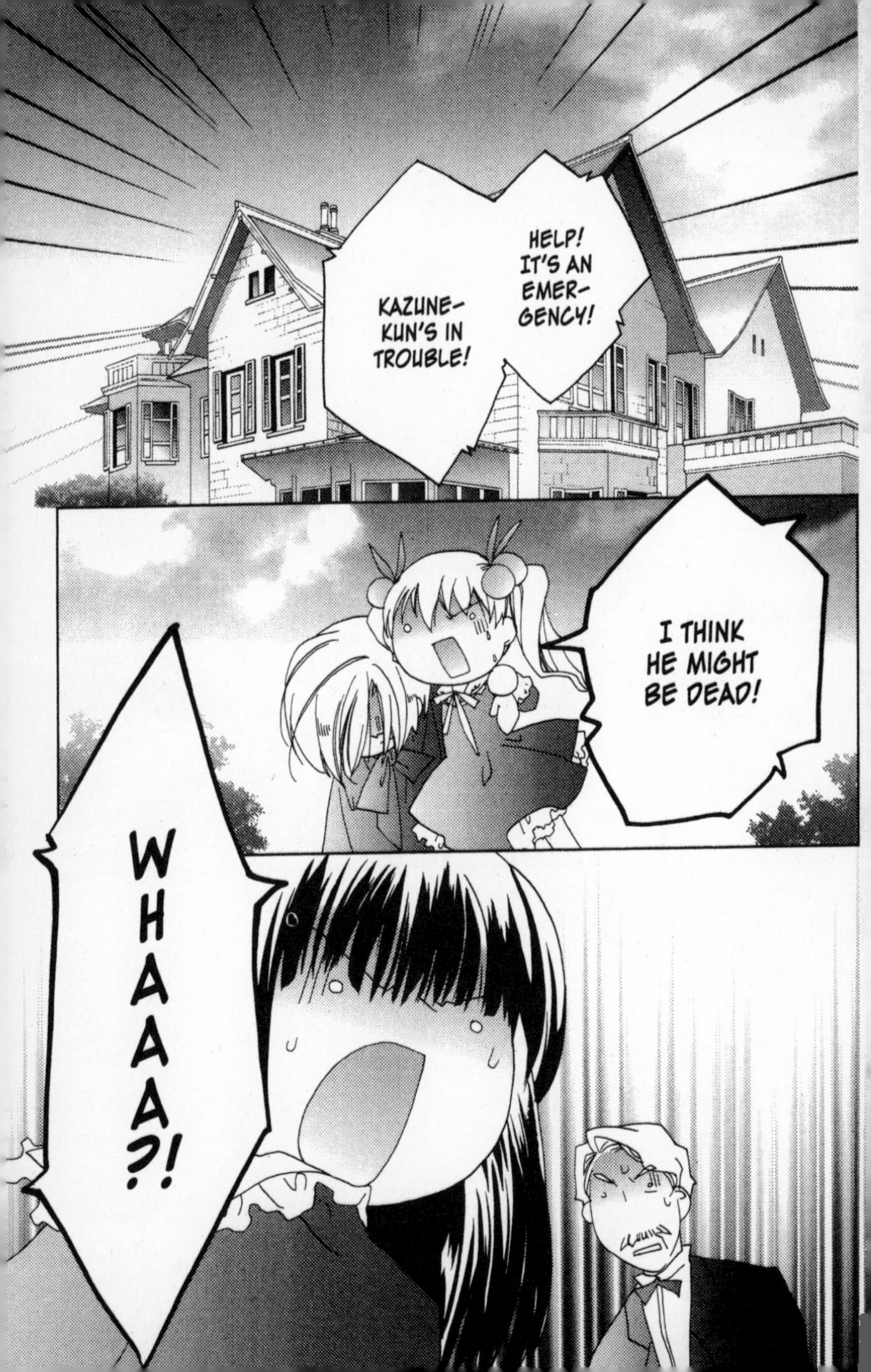
HELP! IT'S AN EMER-GENCY!
KAZUNE-KUN'S IN TROUBLE!
I THINK HE MIGHT BE DEAD!
WHAAA?!

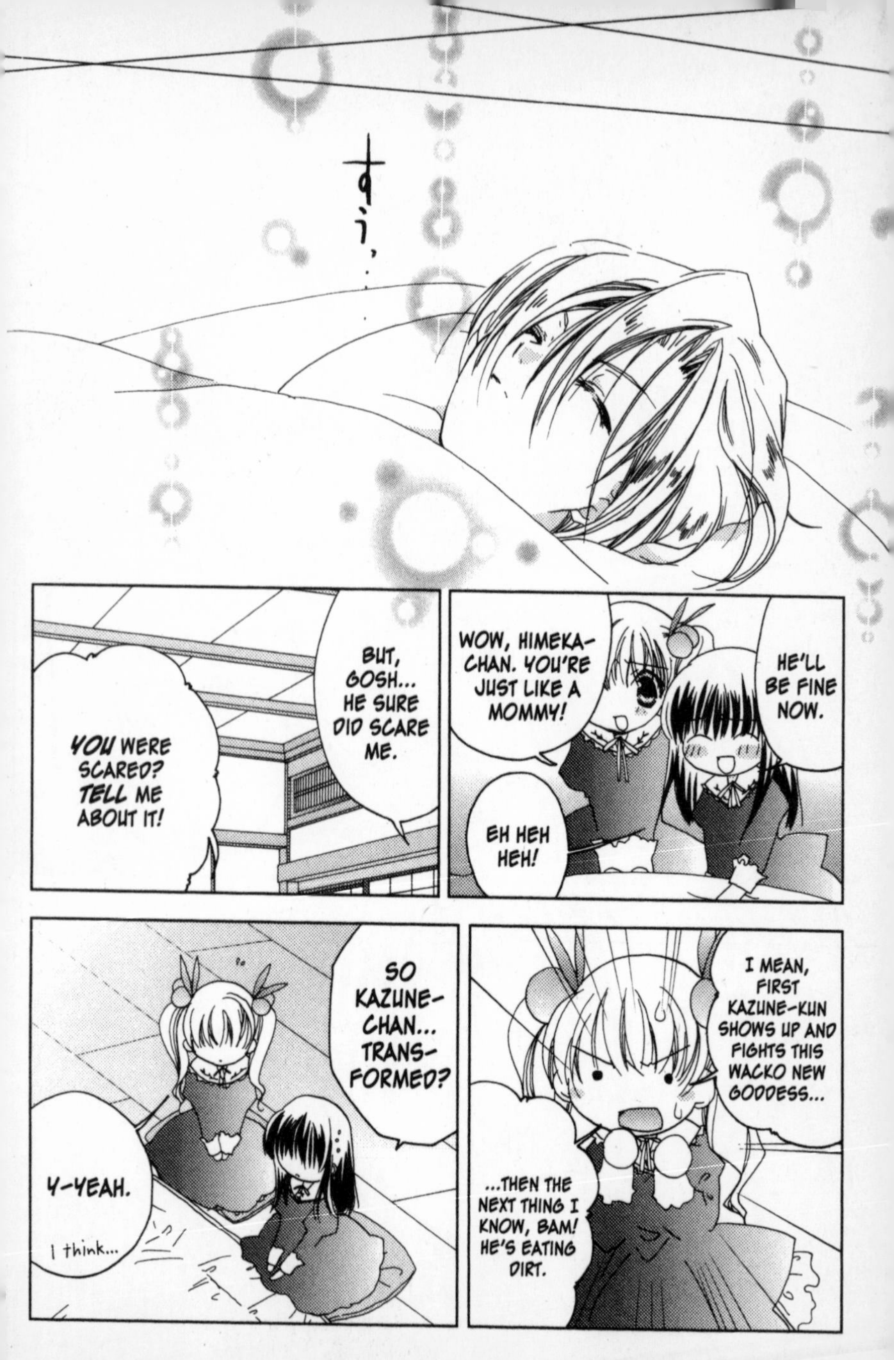
すう、...
HE'LL BE FINE NOW.
WOW, HIMEKA-CHAN. YOU'RE JUST LIKE A MOMMY!
EH HEH HEH!
BUT, GOSH... HE SURE DID SCARE ME.
YOU WERE SCARED? TELL ME ABOUT IT!
I MEAN, FIRST KAZUNE-KUN SHOWS UP AND FIGHTS THIS WACKO NEW GODDESS...
...THEN THE NEXT THING I KNOW, BAM! HE'S EATING DIRT.
SO KAZUNE-CHAN... TRANSFORMED?
Y-YEAH.
I think...

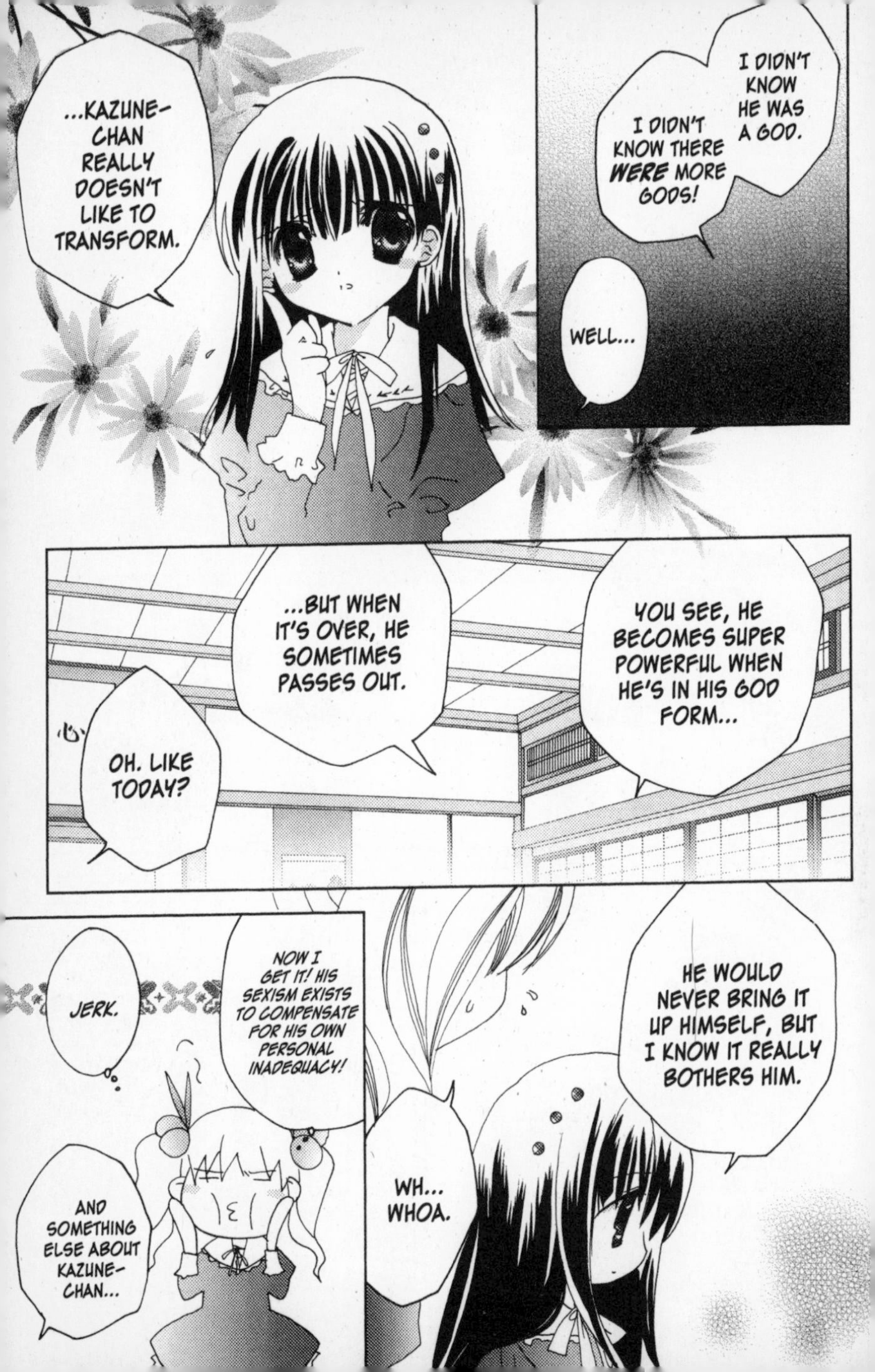
I DIDN'T KNOW HE WAS A GOD.
I DIDN'T KNOW THERE *WERE* MORE GODS!
WELL...
...KAZUNE-CHAN REALLY DOESN'T LIKE TO TRANSFORM.
YOU SEE, HE BECOMES SUPER POWERFUL WHEN HE'S IN HIS GOD FORM...
...BUT WHEN IT'S OVER, HE SOMETIMES PASSES OUT.
OH. LIKE TODAY?
HE WOULD NEVER BRING IT UP HIMSELF, BUT I KNOW IT REALLY BOTHERS HIM.
WH... WHOA.
NOW I GET IT! HIS SEXISM EXISTS TO COMPENSATE FOR HIS OWN PERSONAL INADEQUACY!
JERK.
AND SOMETHING ELSE ABOUT KAZUNE-CHAN...

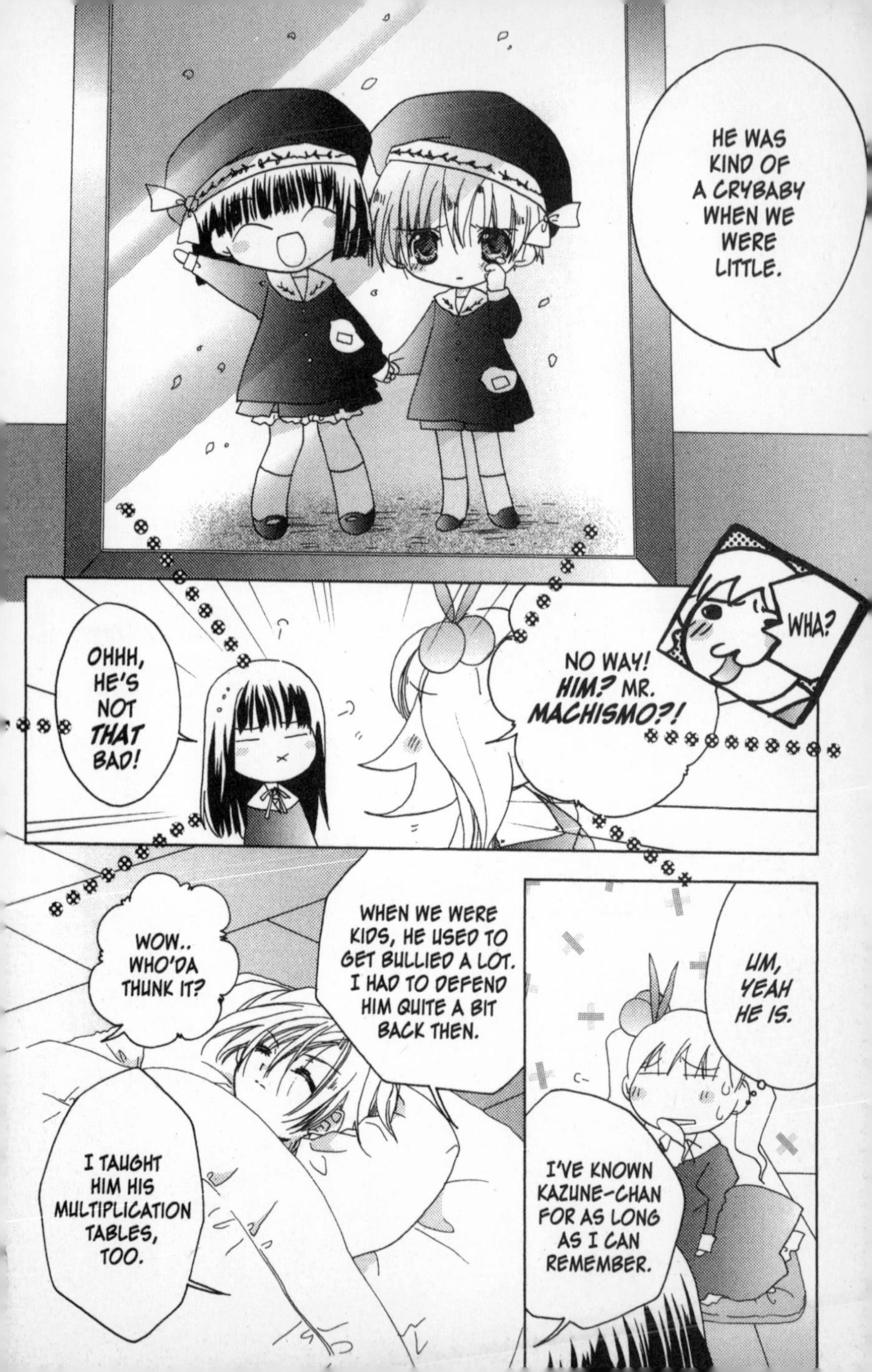
HE WAS KIND OF A CRYBABY WHEN WE WERE LITTLE.
WHA?
NO WAY! HIM? MR. MACHISMO?!
OHHH, HE'S NOT THAT BAD!
UM, YEAH HE IS.
I'VE KNOWN KAZUNE-CHAN FOR AS LONG AS I CAN REMEMBER.
WHEN WE WERE KIDS, HE USED TO GET BULLIED A LOT. I HAD TO DEFEND HIM QUITE A BIT BACK THEN.
WOW.. WHO'DA THUNK IT?
I TAUGHT HIM HIS MULTIPLICATION TABLES, TOO.

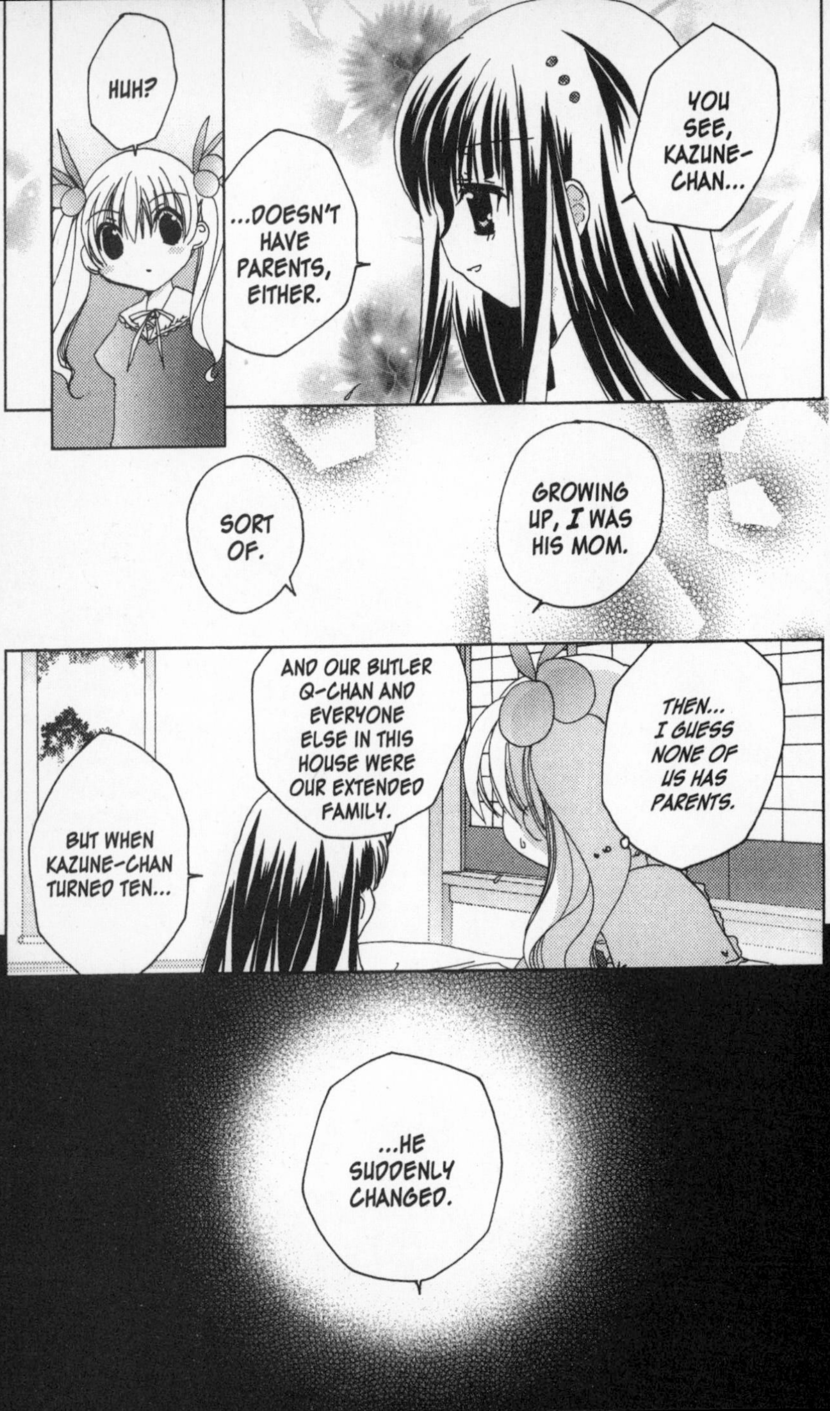
YOU SEE, KAZUNE-CHAN...
...DOESN'T HAVE PARENTS, EITHER.
HUH?
GROWING UP, *I* WAS HIS MOM.
SORT OF.
THEN... *I GUESS NONE OF US HAS PARENTS.*
AND OUR BUTLER Q-CHAN AND EVERYONE ELSE IN THIS HOUSE WERE OUR EXTENDED FAMILY.
BUT WHEN KAZUNE-CHAN TURNED TEN...
...HE SUDDENLY CHANGED.

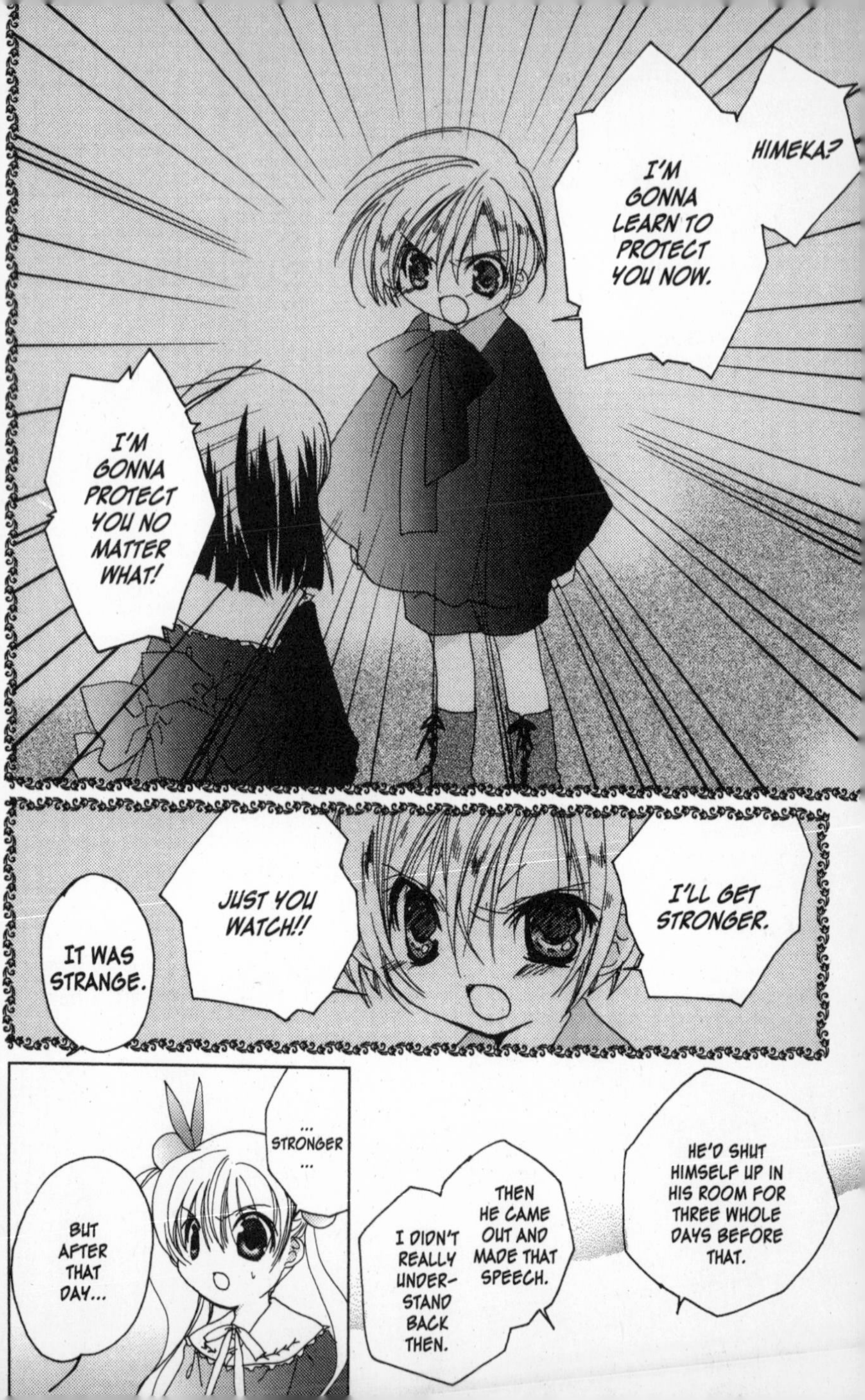
HIMEKA?
I'M GONNA LEARN TO PROTECT YOU NOW.
I'M GONNA PROTECT YOU NO MATTER WHAT!
I'LL GET STRONGER.
JUST YOU WATCH!!
IT WAS STRANGE.
HE'D SHUT HIMSELF UP IN HIS ROOM FOR THREE WHOLE DAYS BEFORE THAT.
THEN HE CAME OUT AND MADE THAT SPEECH.
I DIDN'T REALLY UNDER-STAND BACK THEN.
...STRONGER...
BUT AFTER THAT DAY...

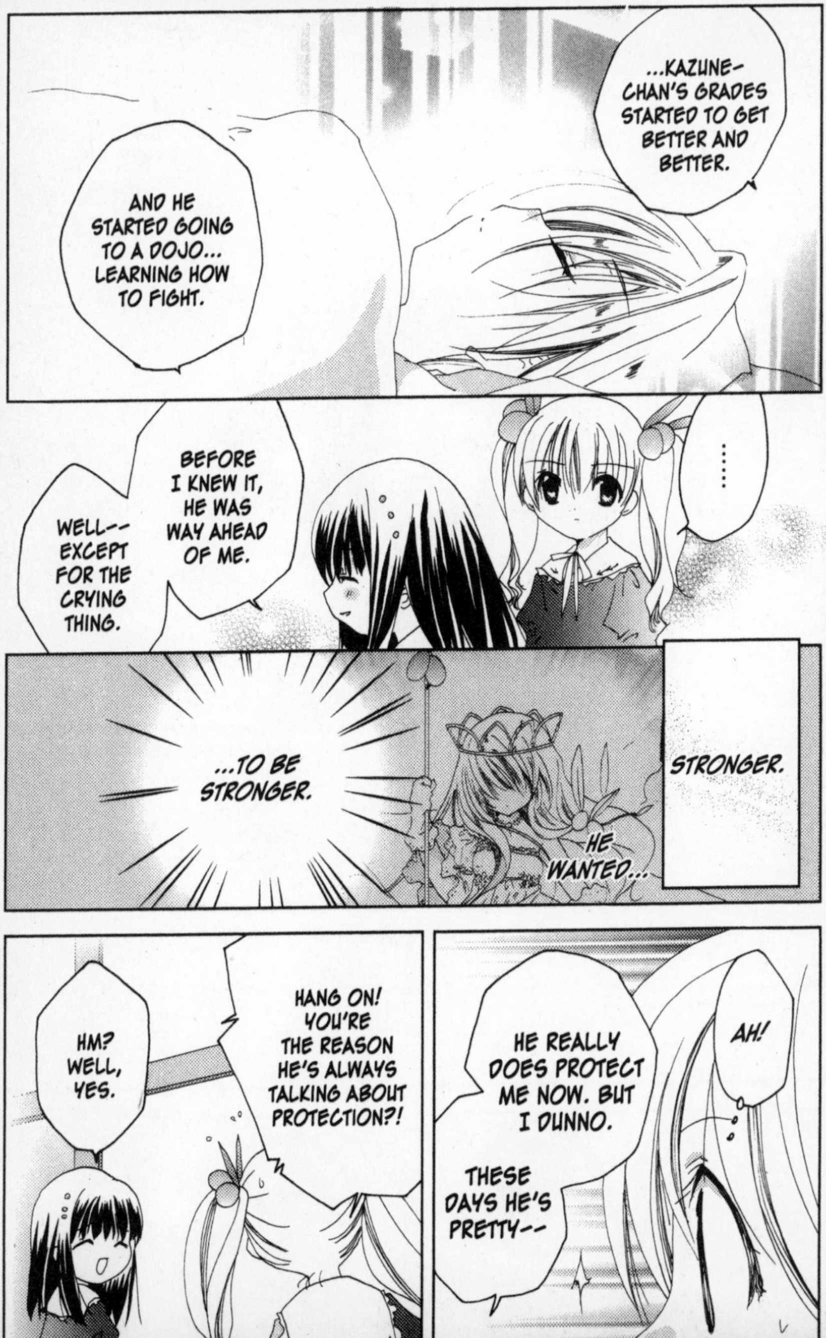
...KAZUNE-CHAN'S GRADES STARTED TO GET BETTER AND BETTER.
AND HE STARTED GOING TO A DOJO... LEARNING HOW TO FIGHT.
......
BEFORE I KNEW IT, HE WAS WAY AHEAD OF ME.
WELL--EXCEPT FOR THE CRYING THING.
STRONGER.
HE WANTED...
...TO BE STRONGER.
AH!
HE REALLY DOES PROTECT ME NOW. BUT I DUNNO.
THESE DAYS HE'S PRETTY--
HANG ON! YOU'RE THE REASON HE'S ALWAYS TALKING ABOUT PROTECTION?!
HM? WELL, YES.

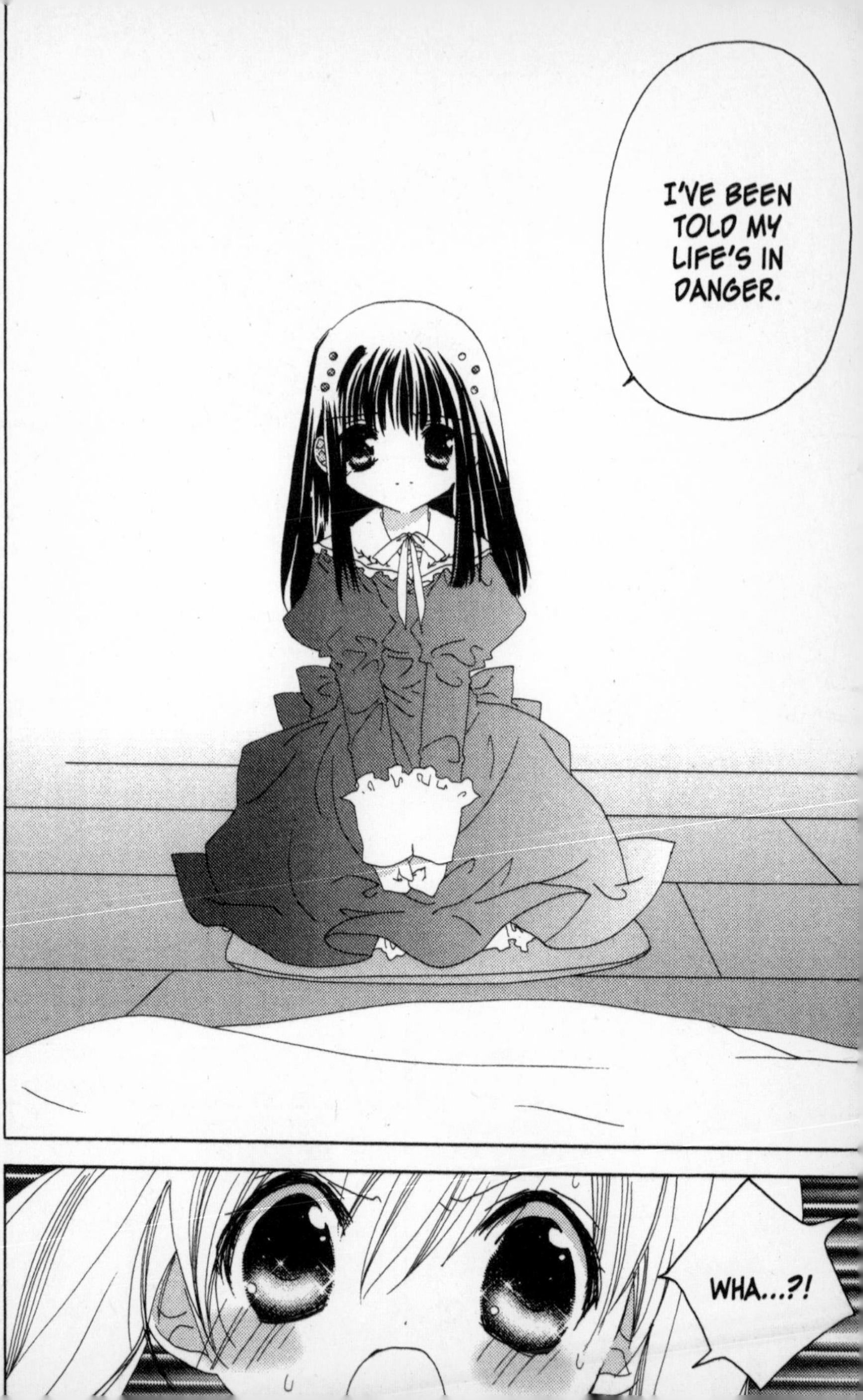
I'VE BEEN TOLD MY LIFE'S IN DANGER.
WHA...?!

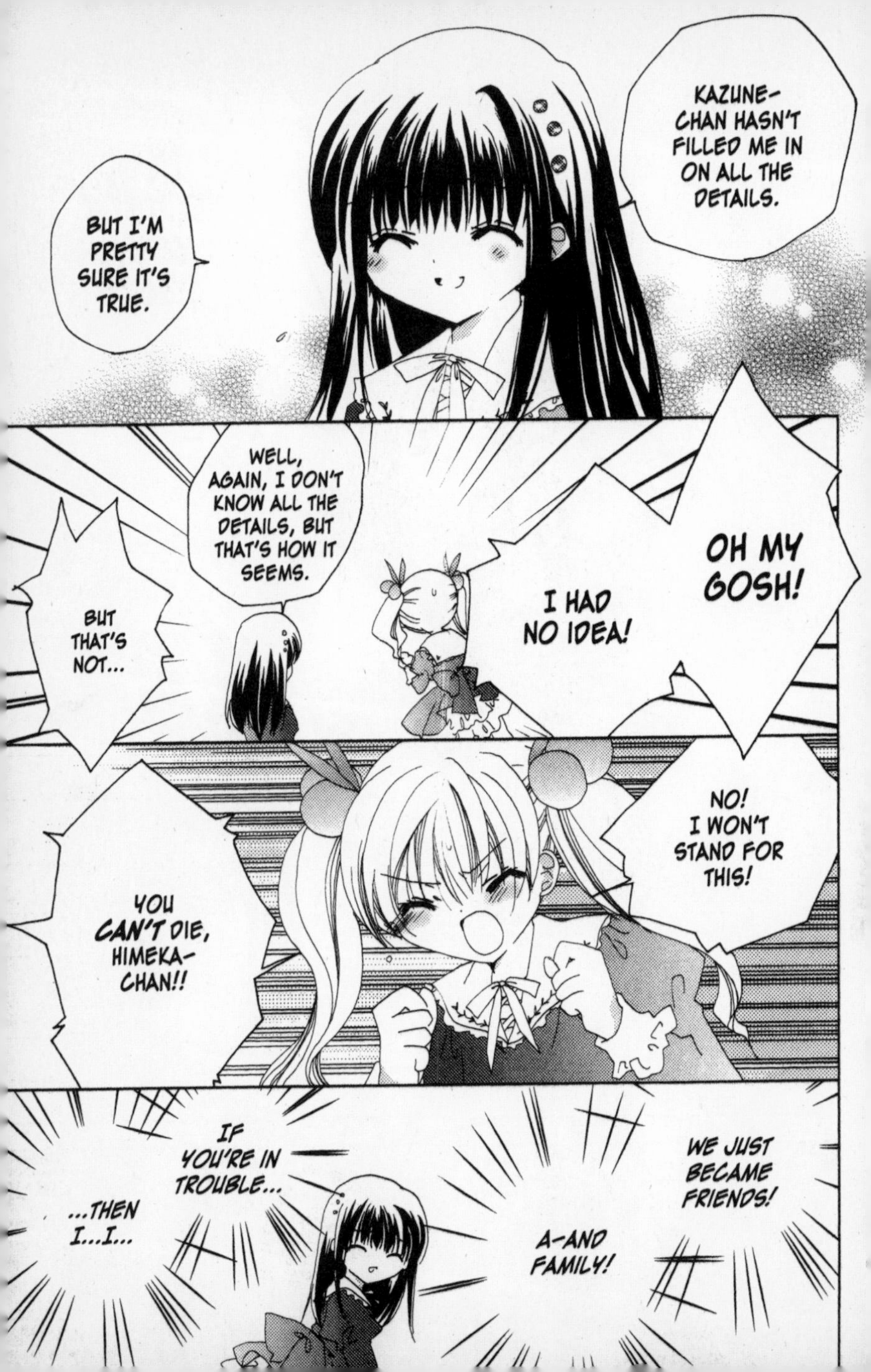
KAZUNE-CHAN HASN'T FILLED ME IN ON ALL THE DETAILS.
BUT I'M PRETTY SURE IT'S TRUE.
OH MY GOSH!
I HAD NO IDEA!
WELL, AGAIN, I DON'T KNOW ALL THE DETAILS, BUT THAT'S HOW IT SEEMS.
BUT THAT'S NOT...
NO! I WON'T STAND FOR THIS!
YOU *CAN'T* DIE, HIMEKA-CHAN!!
WE JUST BECAME FRIENDS!
A-AND FAMILY!
IF YOU'RE IN TROUBLE...
...THEN I...I...

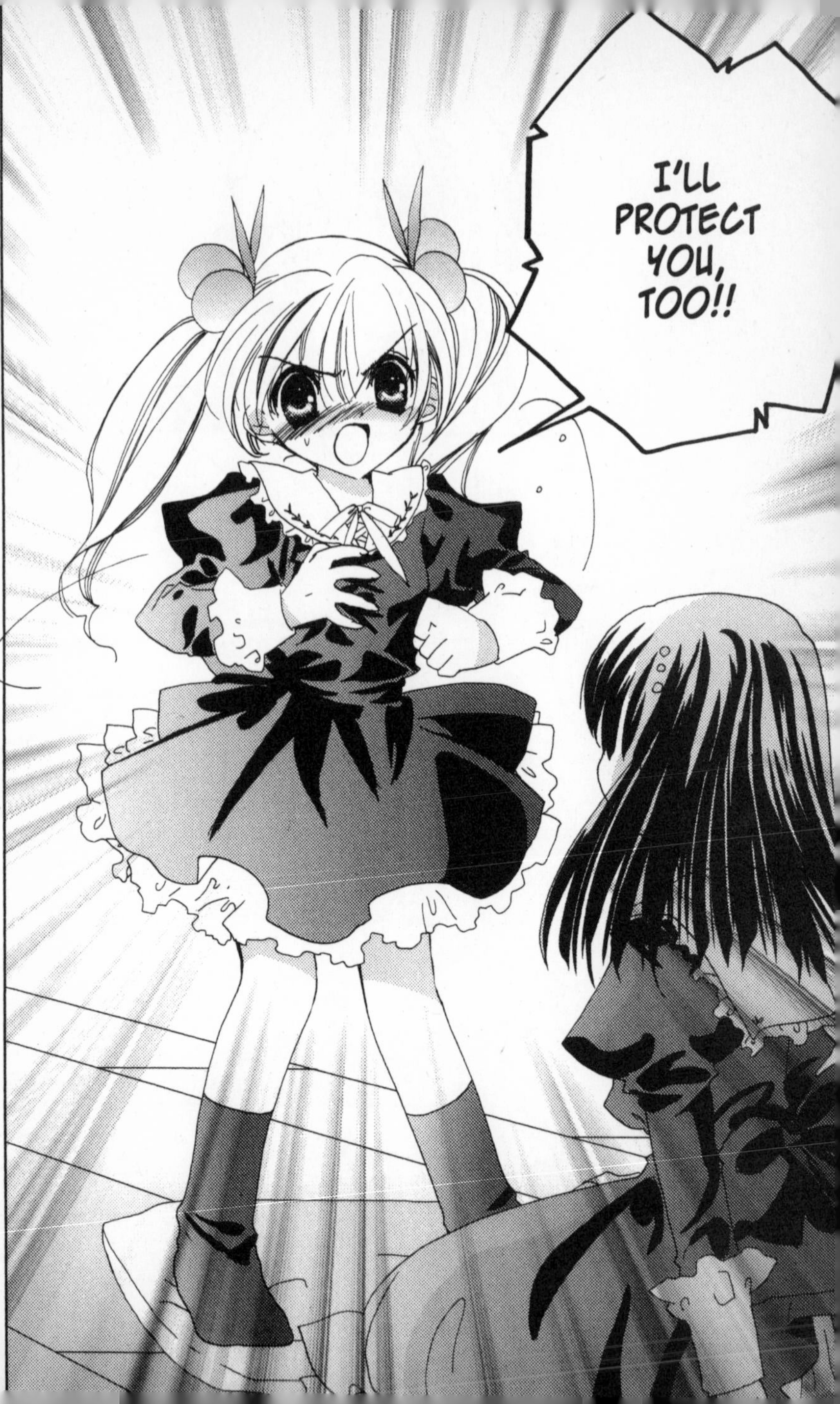
I'LL PROTECT YOU, TOO!!

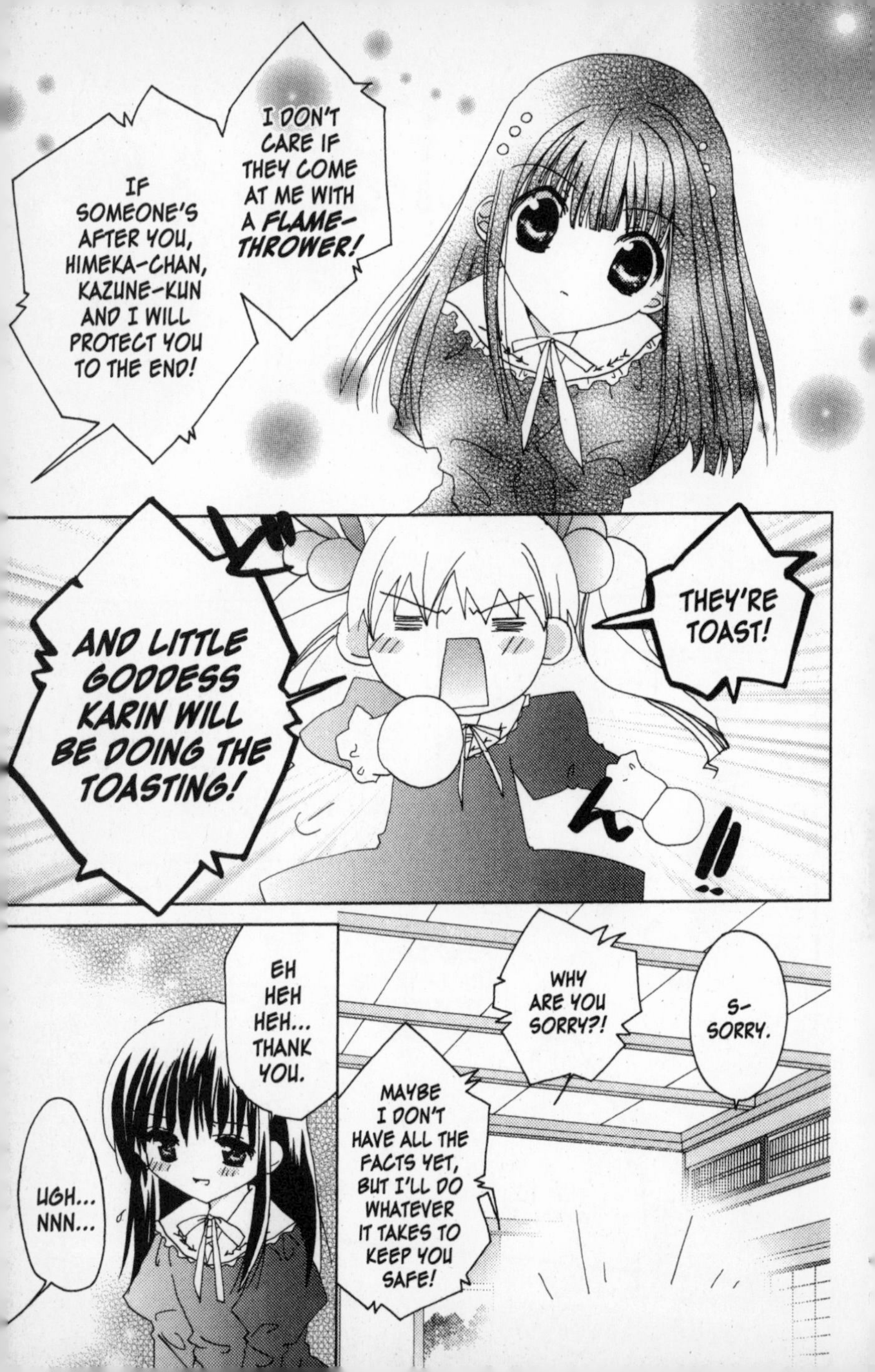
I DON'T CARE IF THEY COME AT ME WITH A FLAME-THROWER!
IF SOMEONE'S AFTER YOU, HIMEKA-CHAN, KAZUNE-KUN AND I WILL PROTECT YOU TO THE END!
THEY'RE TOAST!
AND LITTLE GODDESS KARIN WILL BE DOING THE TOASTING!
S-SORRY.
WHY ARE YOU SORRY?!
MAYBE I DON'T HAVE ALL THE FACTS YET, BUT I'LL DO WHATEVER IT TAKES TO KEEP YOU SAFE!
EH HEH HEH... THANK YOU.
UGH... NNN...

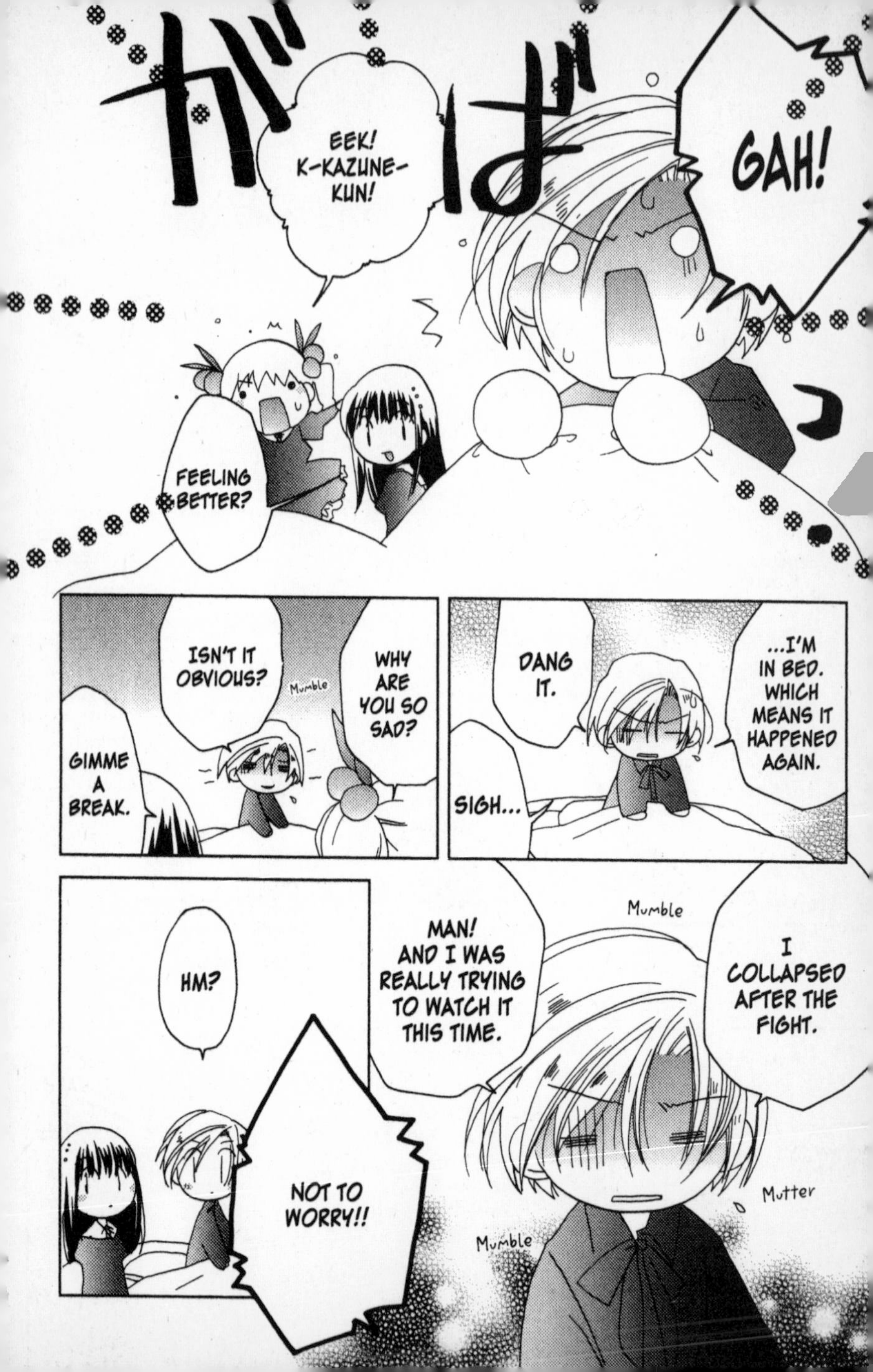
GAH!
がば
EEK! K-KAZUNE-KUN!
FEELING BETTER?
...I'M IN BED. WHICH MEANS IT HAPPENED AGAIN.
DANG IT.
SIGH...
WHY ARE YOU SO SAD?
Mumble
ISN'T IT OBVIOUS?
GIMME A BREAK.
I COLLAPSED AFTER THE FIGHT.
Mumble
MAN! AND I WAS REALLY TRYING TO WATCH IT THIS TIME.
Mutter
Mumble
HM?
NOT TO WORRY!!

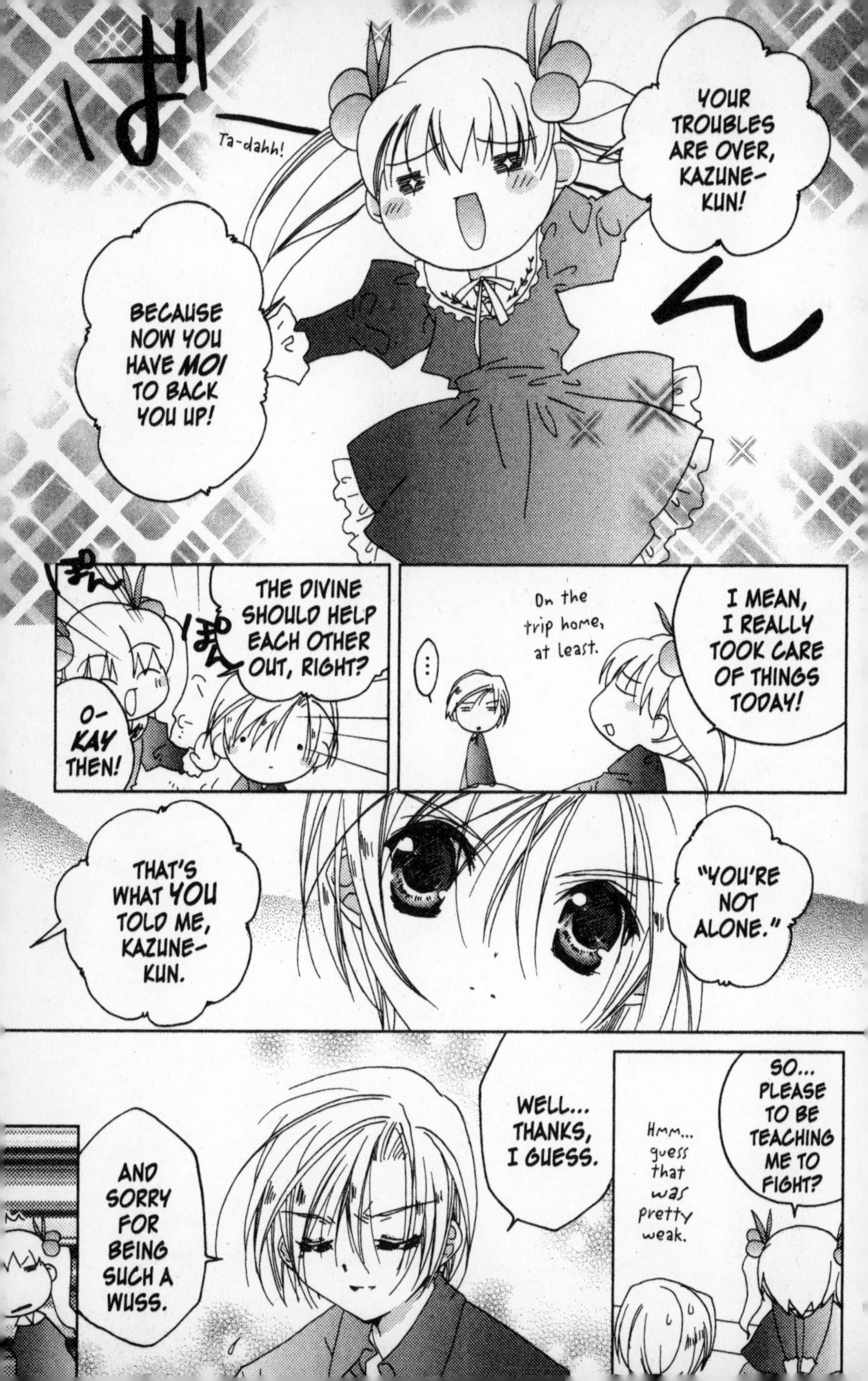
ぱーん
Ta-dahh!
YOUR TROUBLES ARE OVER, KAZUNE-KUN!
BECAUSE NOW YOU HAVE MOI TO BACK YOU UP!
I MEAN, I REALLY TOOK CARE OF THINGS TODAY!
On the trip home, at least.
...
THE DIVINE SHOULD HELP EACH OTHER OUT, RIGHT?
ぽん
ぽん
O-KAY THEN!
"YOU'RE NOT ALONE."
THAT'S WHAT YOU TOLD ME, KAZUNE-KUN.
SO... PLEASE TO BE TEACHING ME TO FIGHT?
Hmm... guess that was pretty weak.
WELL... THANKS, I GUESS.
AND SORRY FOR BEING SUCH A WUSS.

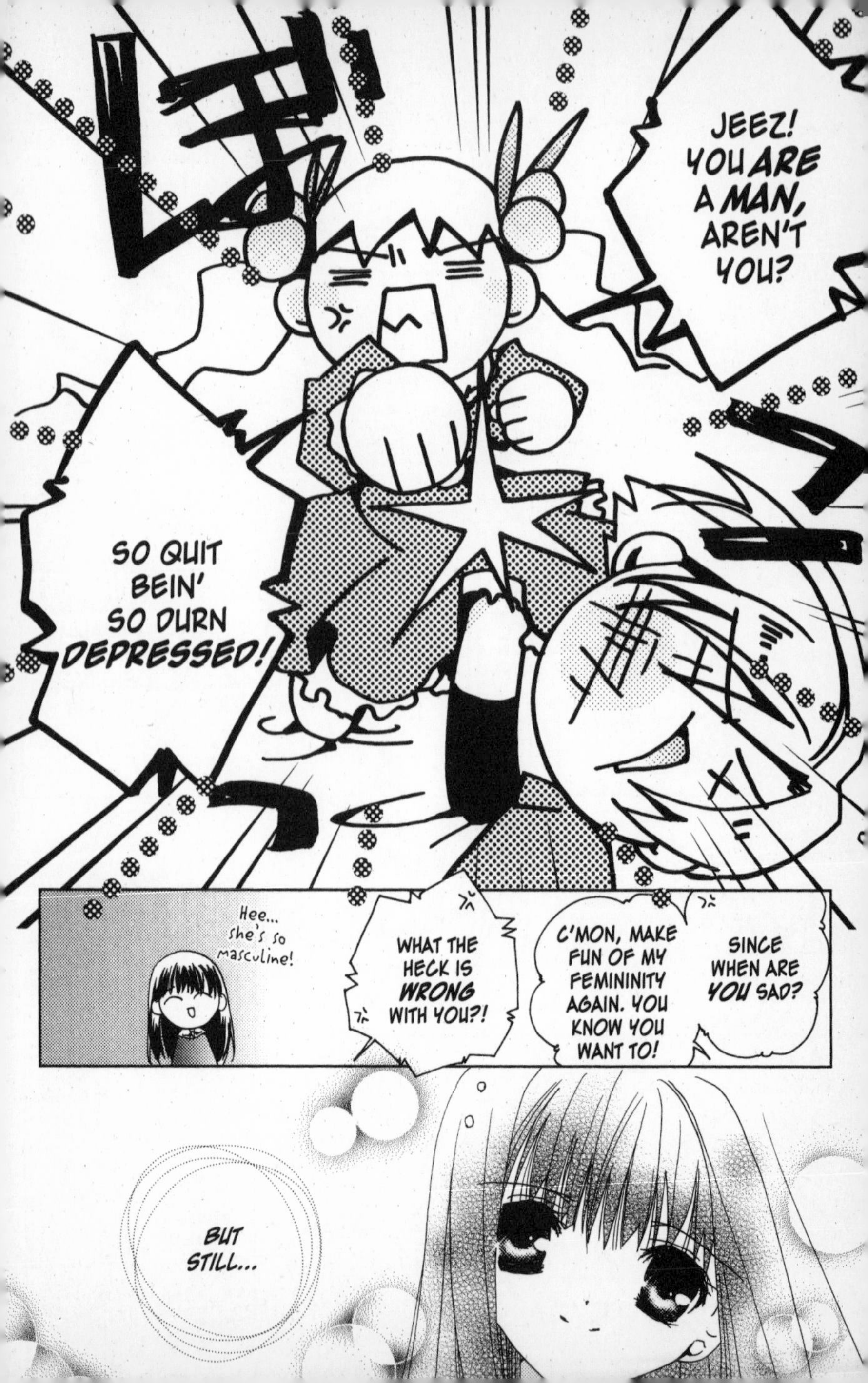
JEEZ! YOU ARE A MAN, AREN'T YOU?
SO QUIT BEIN' SO DURN DEPRESSED!
SINCE WHEN ARE YOU SAD?
C'MON, MAKE FUN OF MY FEMININITY AGAIN. YOU KNOW YOU WANT TO!
WHAT THE HECK IS WRONG WITH YOU?!
Hee... she's so masculine!
BUT STILL...

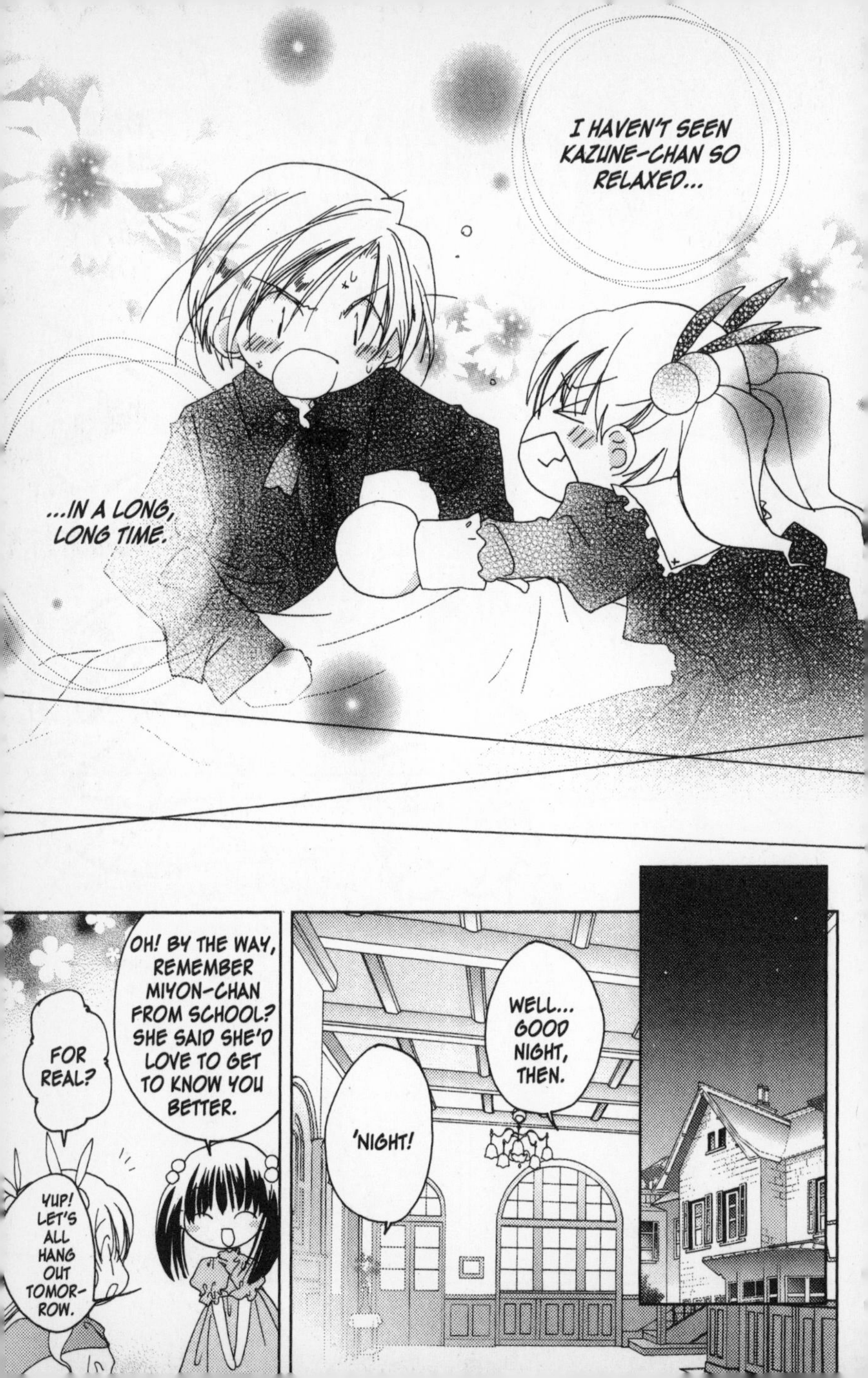
I HAVEN'T SEEN KAZUNE-CHAN SO RELAXED...
...IN A LONG, LONG TIME.
WELL... GOOD NIGHT, THEN.
'NIGHT!
OH! BY THE WAY, REMEMBER MIYON-CHAN FROM SCHOOL? SHE SAID SHE'D LOVE TO GET TO KNOW YOU BETTER.
FOR REAL?
YUP! LET'S ALL HANG OUT TOMORROW.

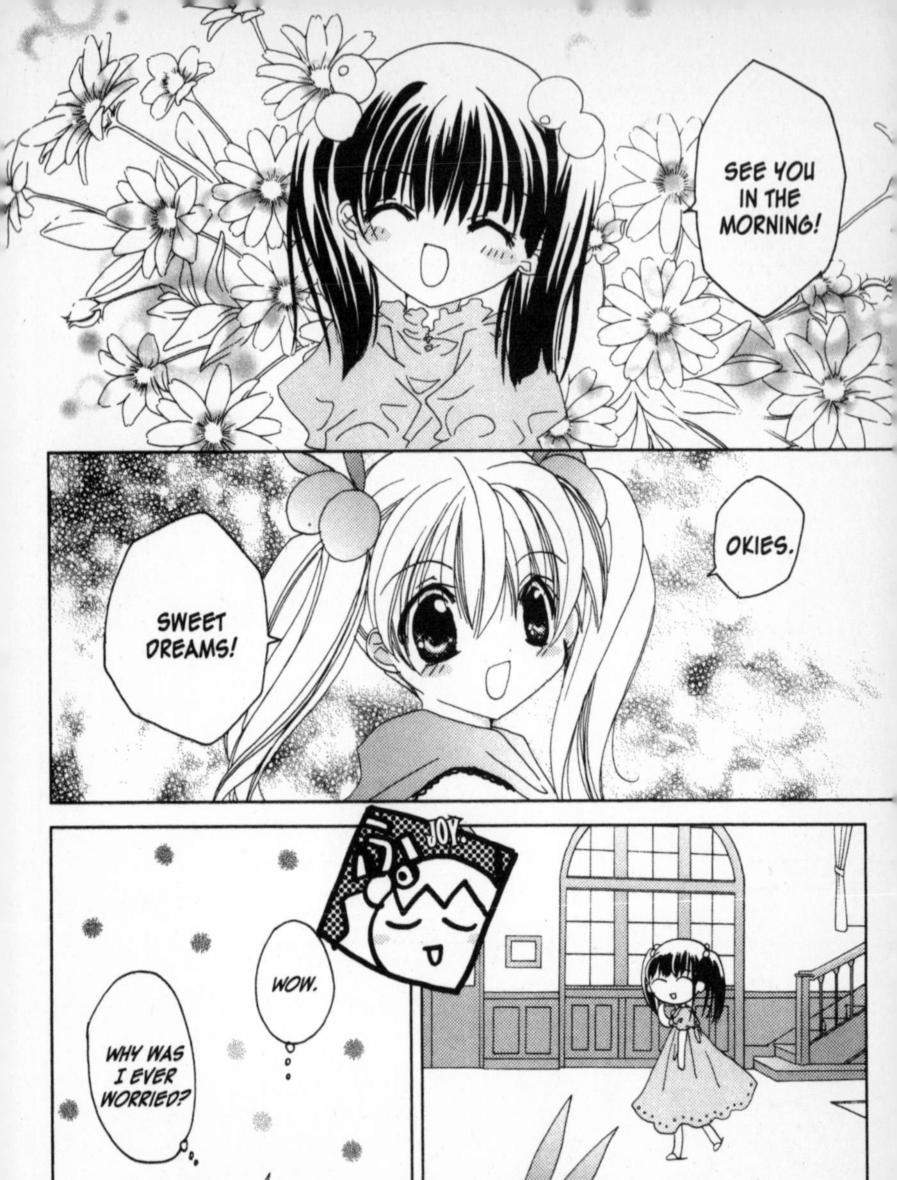
SEE YOU IN THE MORNING!
OKIES.
SWEET DREAMS!
JOY.
WOW.
WHY WAS I EVER WORRIED?

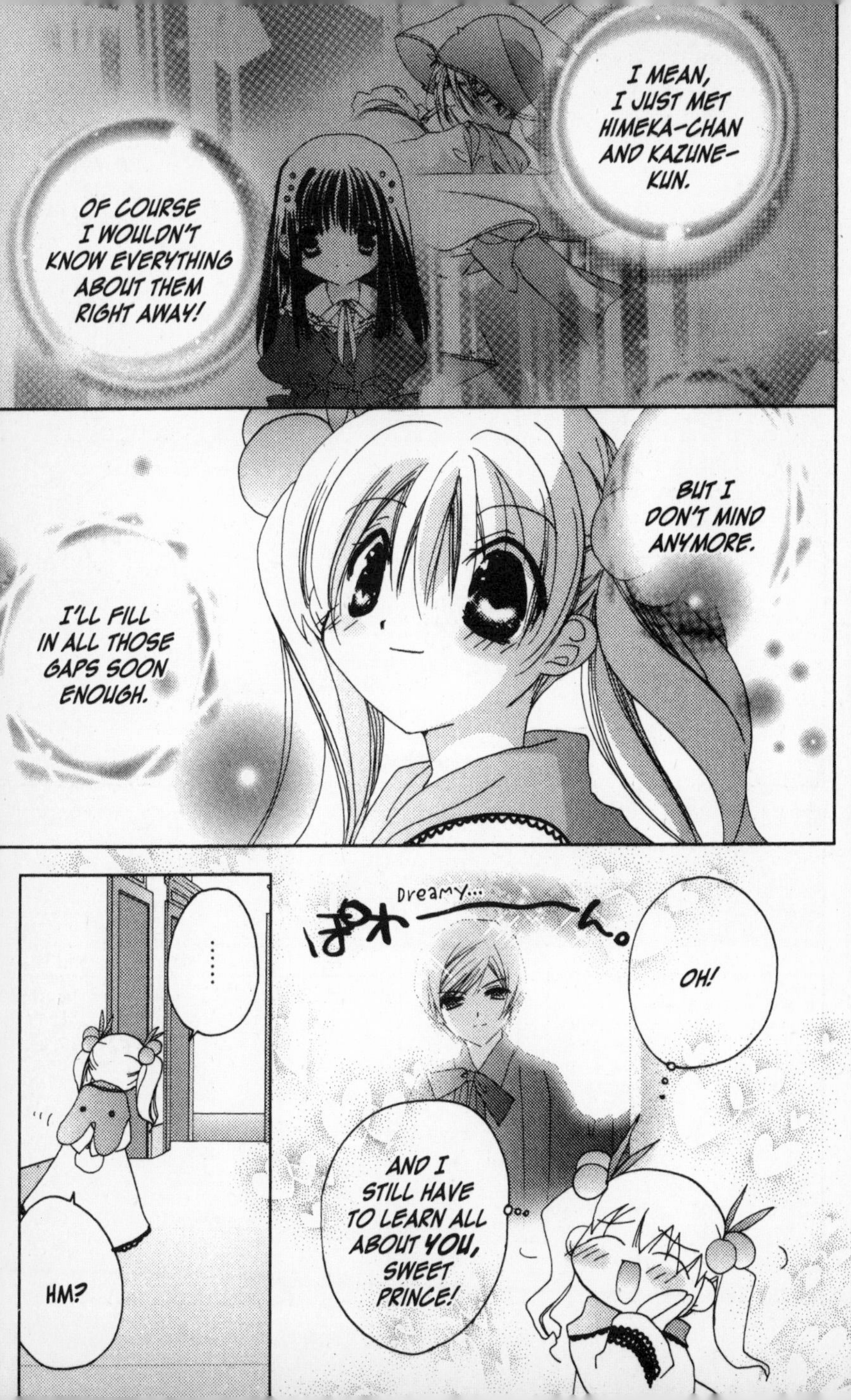
I MEAN, I JUST MET HIMEKA-CHAN AND KAZUNE-KUN.
OF COURSE I WOULDN'T KNOW EVERYTHING ABOUT THEM RIGHT AWAY!
BUT I DON'T MIND ANYMORE.
I'LL FILL IN ALL THOSE GAPS SOON ENOUGH.
OH!
ぽわーーーん。
Dreamy...
AND I STILL HAVE TO LEARN ALL ABOUT YOU, SWEET PRINCE!
......
HM?

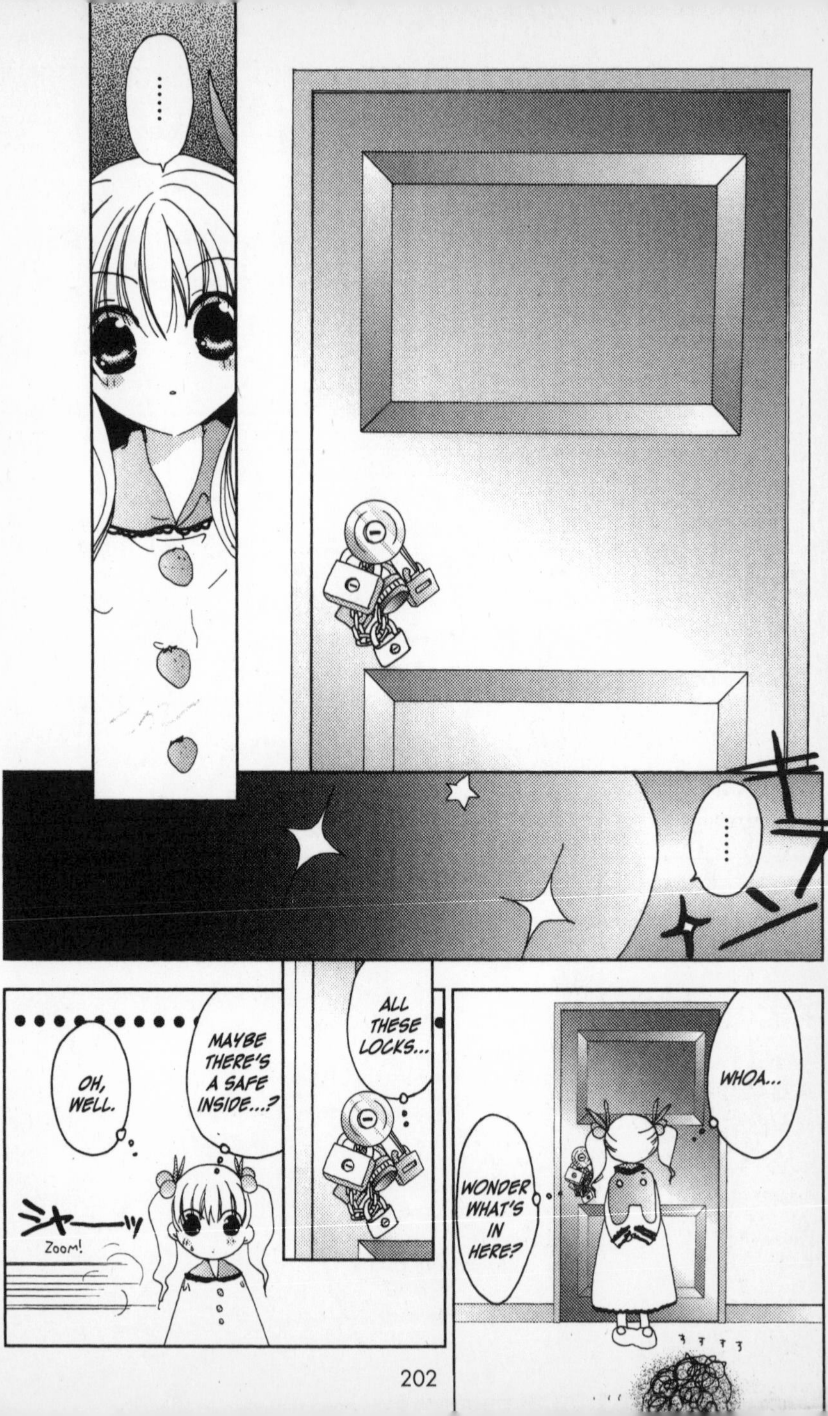
……
……
キラーン
WHOA...
WONDER WHAT'S IN HERE?
ALL THESE LOCKS...
MAYBE THERE'S A SAFE INSIDE...?
…………
OH, WELL.
シャーッ
Zoom!

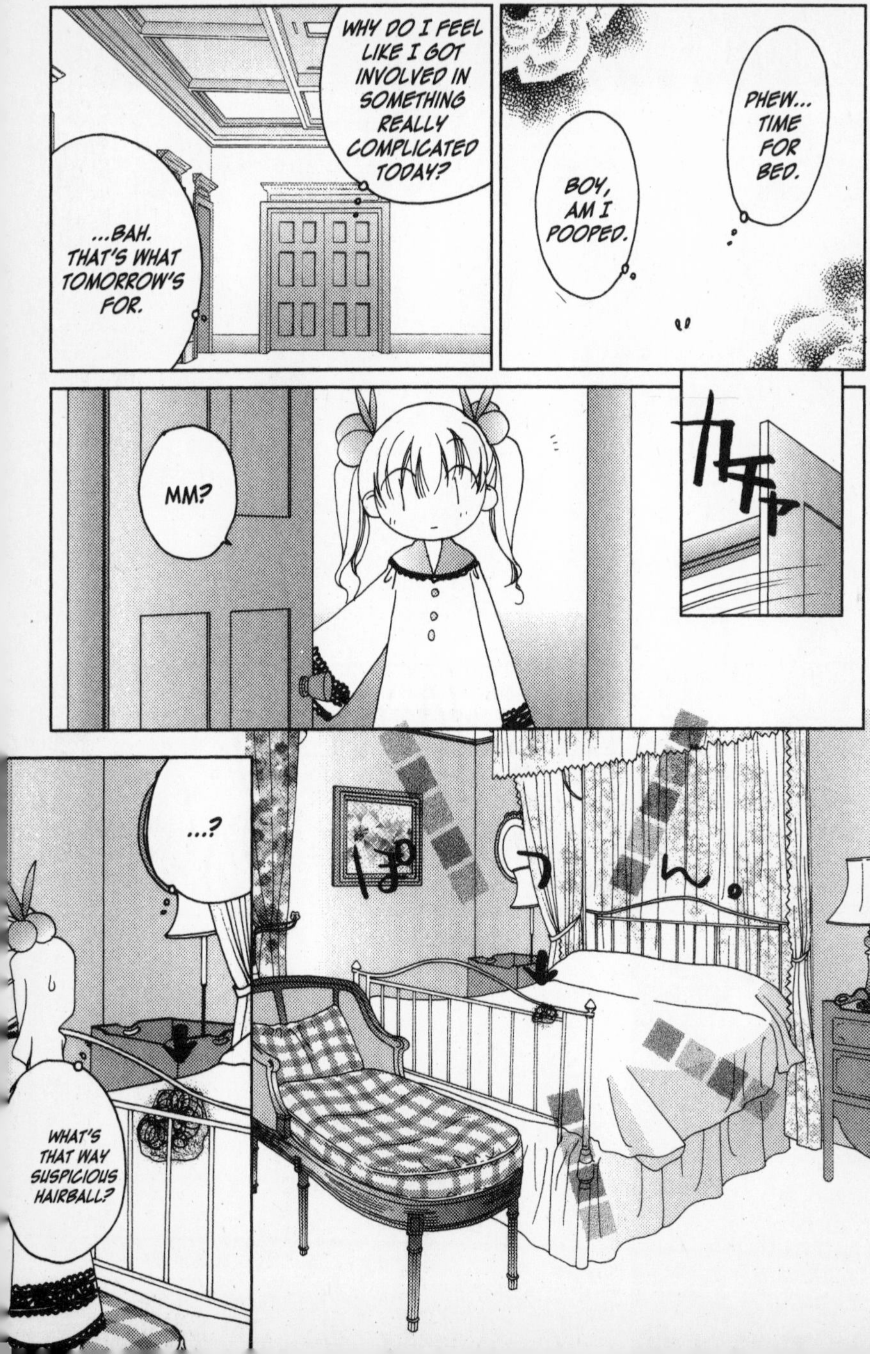
PHEW... TIME FOR BED.
BOY, AM I POOPED.
WHY DO I FEEL LIKE I GOT INVOLVED IN SOMETHING REALLY COMPLICATED TODAY?
...BAH. THAT'S WHAT TOMORROW'S FOR.
カチャ
MM?
ぽつん。
...?
WHAT'S THAT WAY SUSPICIOUS HAIRBALL?

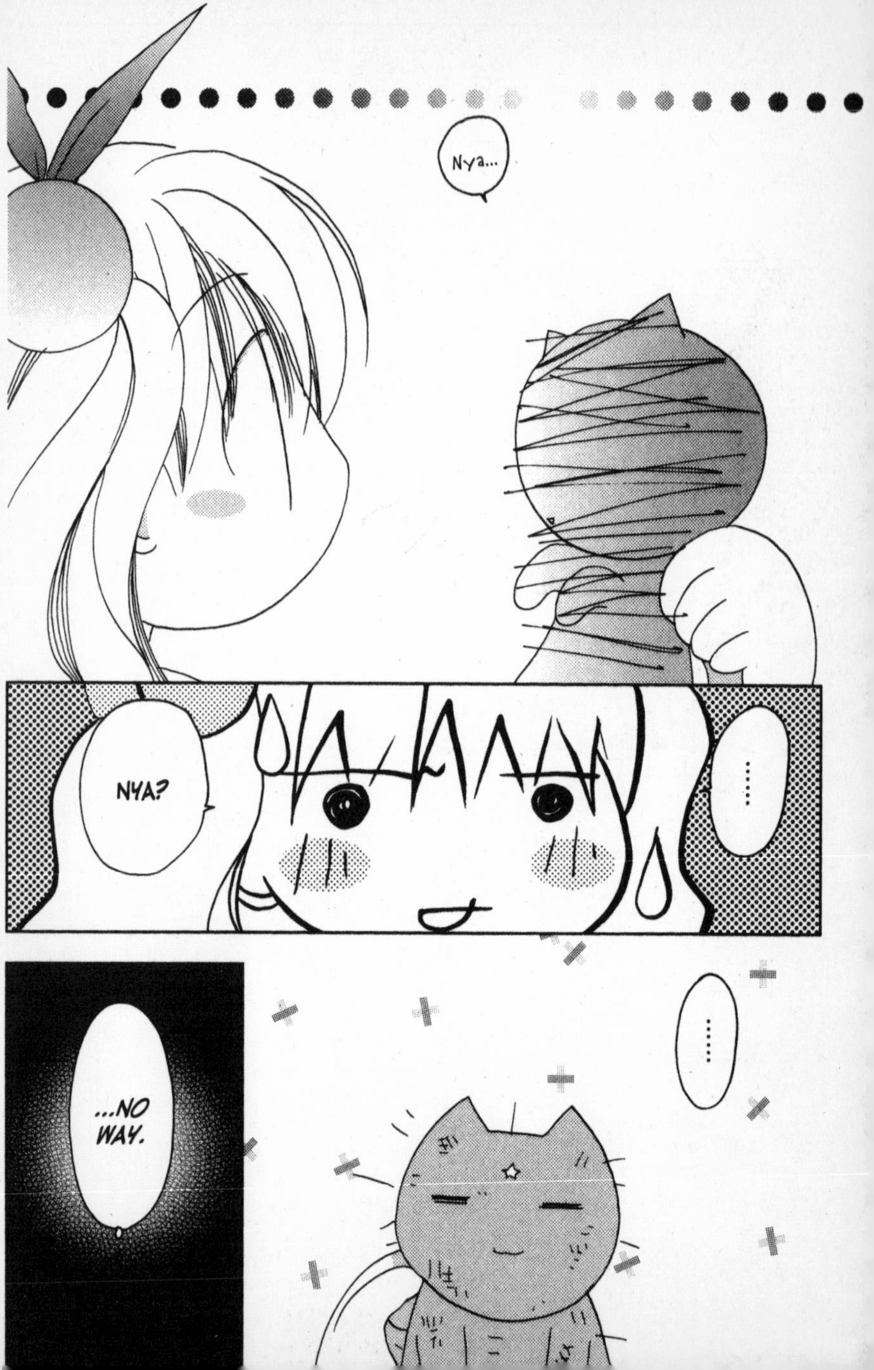
Nya...
......
NYA?
......
...NO WAY.

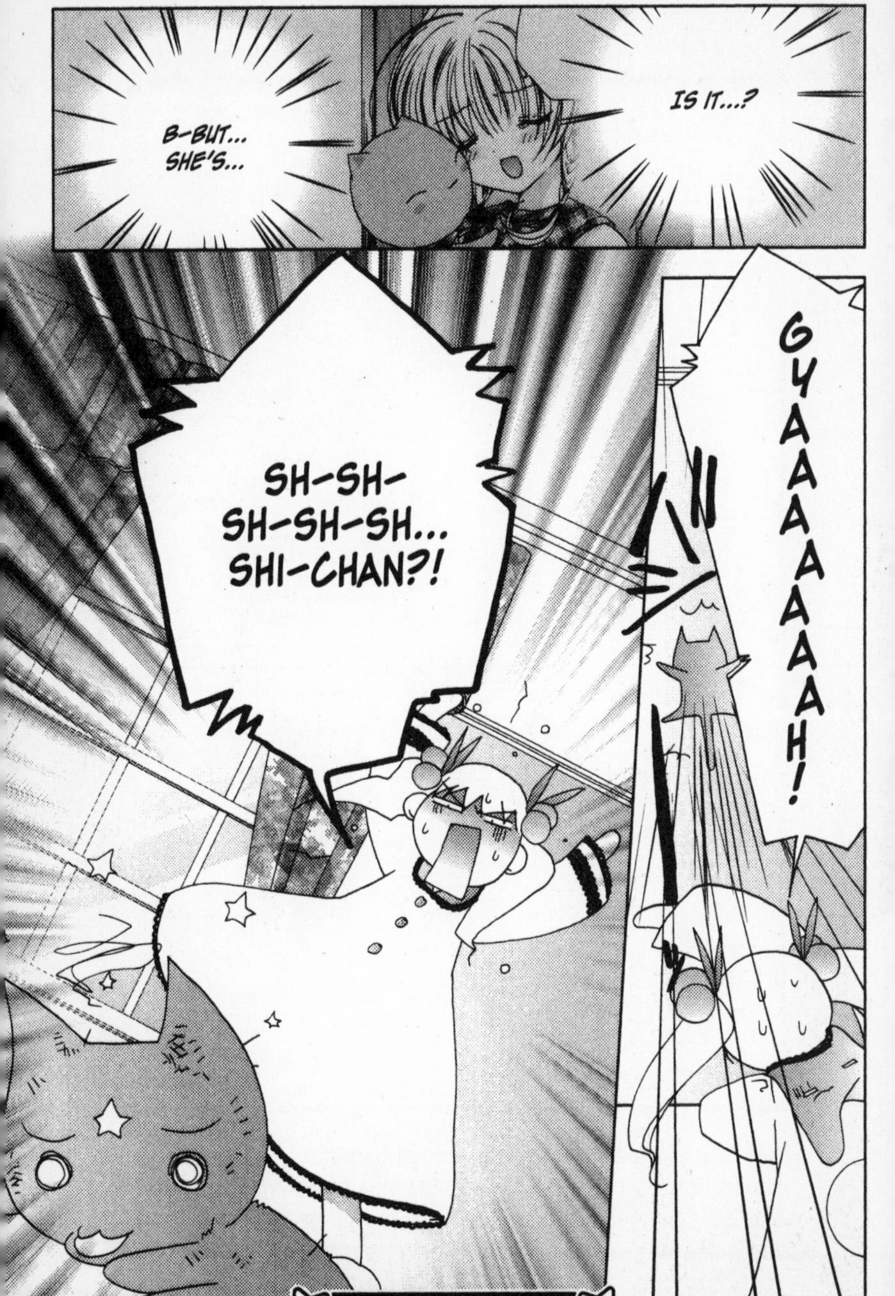
IS IT...?
B-BUT... SHE'S...
GUAAAAAAAH!
SH-SH-SH-SH-SH... SHI-CHAN?!

Continued in Book 2!

Next time in...

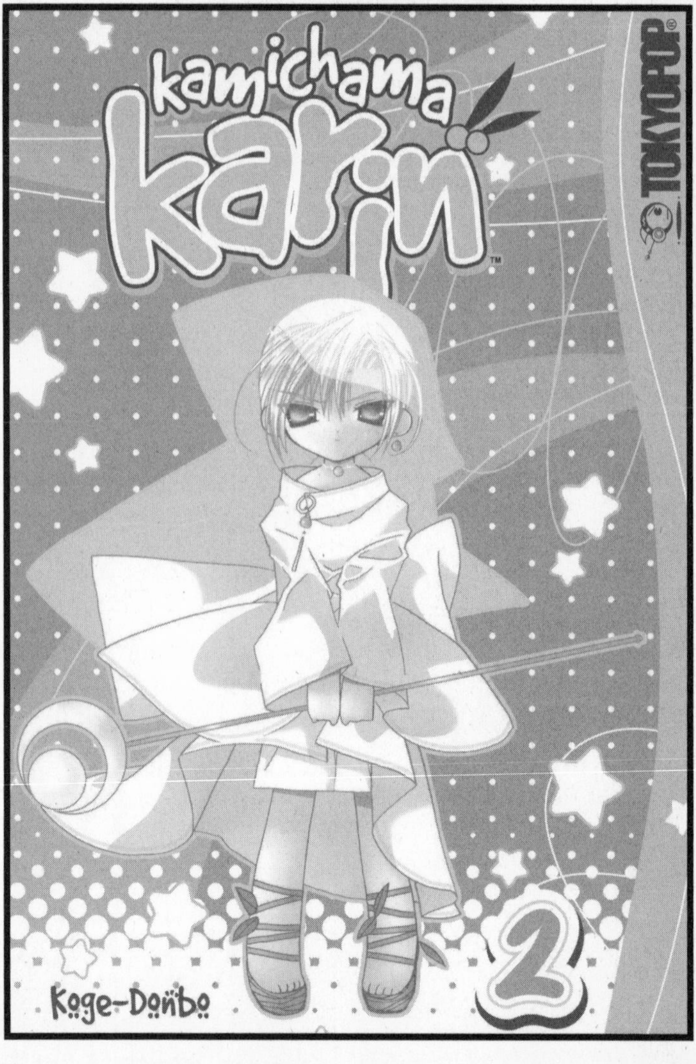
kamichama
karin
TM
TOKYOPOP
2
Koge-Donbo

As if the problems of being a little goddess weren't enough, Karin has to raise her grade on the next test or she'll be expelled! Luckily, she gets help from her crush, Kirika-senpai. Kazune seems jealous...but before he can complain much, he is attacked by Kirio! Will Karin be able to save him?

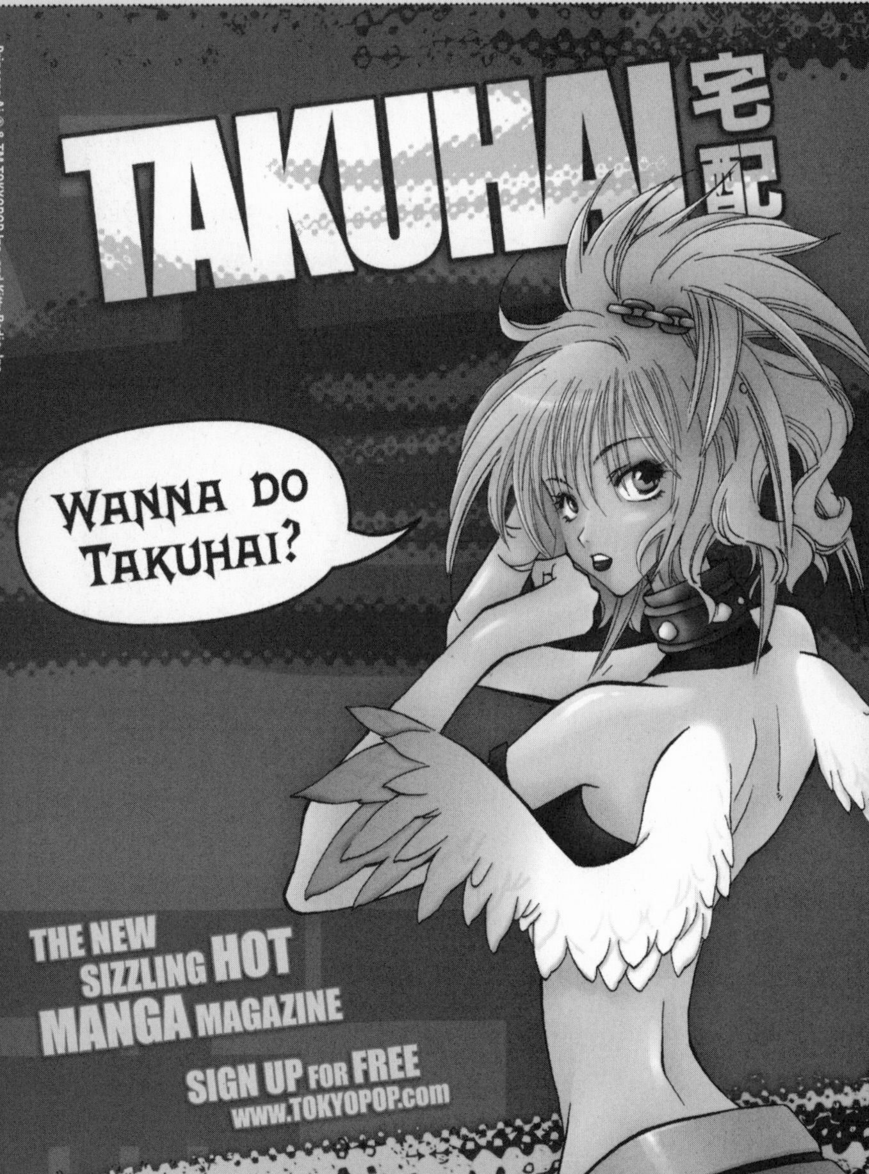

SIGN UP NOW FOR FREE AT: WWW.TOKYOPOP.COM

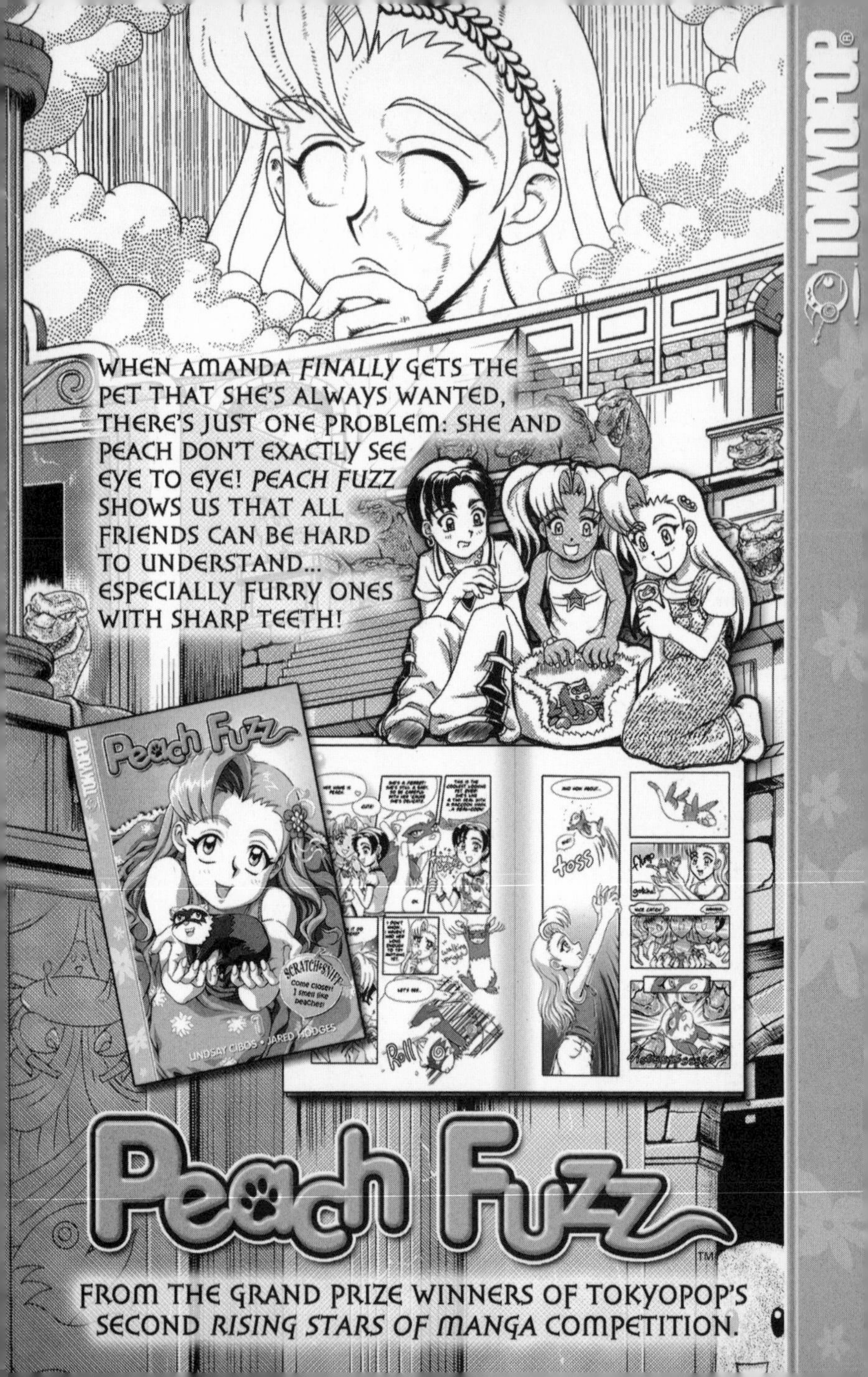
TOKYOPOP®
WHEN AMANDA *FINALLY* GETS THE PET THAT SHE'S ALWAYS WANTED, THERE'S JUST ONE PROBLEM: SHE AND PEACH DON'T EXACTLY SEE EYE TO EYE! *PEACH FUZZ* SHOWS US THAT ALL FRIENDS CAN BE HARD TO UNDERSTAND... ESPECIALLY FURRY ONES WITH SHARP TEETH!
Peach Fuzz
TOKYOPOP
SCRATCH&SNIFF
Come closer! I smell like peaches!
LINDSAY CIBOS • JARED HODGES
toss
Roll
Peach Fuzz™
FROM THE GRAND PRIZE WINNERS OF TOKYOPOP'S SECOND *RISING STARS OF MANGA* COMPETITION.

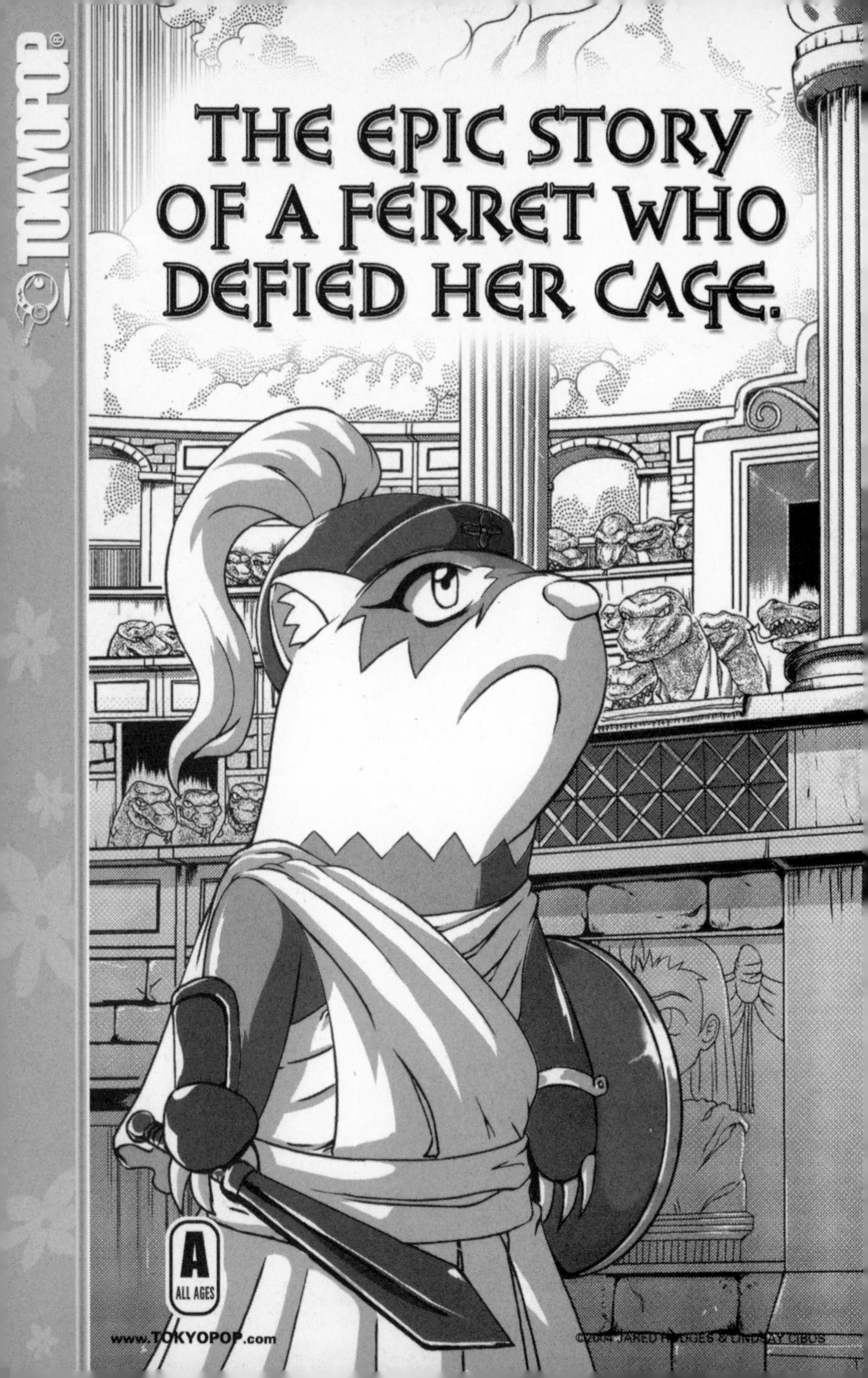
TOKYOPOP
THE EPIC STORY OF A FERRET WHO DEFIED HER CAGE.
A
ALL AGES
www.TOKYOPOP.com
©2004 JARED HODGES & LINDSAY CIBOS

When darkness is in your genes,
only love can steal it away.

D·N·ANGEL·

TOKYOPOP SHOP

WWW.TOKYOPOP.COM/SHOP

HOT NEWS!
Check out the
TOKYOPOP SHOP!
The world's best
collection of manga in
English is now available
online in one place!

SAKURA TAISEN

BECK: MONGOLIAN CHOP SQUAD

Princess Ai
and other hot
titles are
available at
the store that
never closes!

PRINCESS AI VOL. 2: LUMINATION

- LOOK FOR SPECIAL OFFERS
- PRE-ORDER UPCOMING RELEASES
- COMPLETE YOUR COLLECTIONS

STOP!

This is the back of the book.
You wouldn't want to spoil a great ending!

This book is printed "manga-style," in the authentic Japanese right-to-left format. Since none of the artwork has been flipped or altered, readers get to experience the story just as the creator intended. You've been asking for it, so TOKYOPOP® delivered: authentic, hot-off-the-press, and far more fun!

DIRECTIONS

If this is your first time reading manga-style, here's a quick guide to help you understand how it works.

It's easy... just start in the top right panel and follow the numbers. Have fun, and look for more 100% authentic manga from TOKYOPOP®!